A CONCISE HISTORY OF THE ARAB-ISRAELI CONFLICT

IAN J. BICKERTON
University of New South Wales, Australia

CARLA L. KLAUSNER
University of Missouri-Kansas City

PRENTICE HALL, Englewood Cliffs, N.J. 07632

Library of Congress Cataloging-in-Publication Data

Bickerton, Ian J.
     A concise history of the Arab-Israeli conflict / by Ian J.
Bickerton, Carla L. Klausner.
        p.   cm.
     Includes bibliographical references and index.
     ISBN 0-13-173634-5
     1. Jewish-Arab relations--1917- 2. Israel-Arab conflicts.
3. Palestine--History--1917-1949. 4. Israel--History.
I. Klausner, Carla L.   II. Title.
DS119.7.B49 1991
956--dc20   90-44294
                                                      CIP

Editorial/production supervision
  and interior design: Bayani Mendoza de Leon
Cover design: Ben Santora
Manufacturing buyers: Debbie Kesar/Mary Ann Gloriande
Map preparation: Bill Clipson, for Maps 1.1, 2.2, 4.1, 4.2, 6.1, 8.2, 9.1, 9.2, 9.3,
  9.4, and Rhonda Roosa, for Maps Intro, 3.1, 3.2
Cover photo: Raffi Safieh Garabedian

Subject coverage of this edition has been adapted in part from *The Arab-Israeli Conflict: A History* by Ian J. Bickerton and M. W. Pearson (Longman Cheshire, Melbourne, Australia, 1986) by permission of the publisher.

 © 1991 by Prentice-Hall, Inc.
A Division of Simon & Schuster
Englewood Cliffs, New Jersey 07632

Printed in the United States of America

10 9 8 7 6 5 4 3 2 1

ISBN 0-13-173634-5

Prentice-Hall International (UK) Limited, *London*
Prentice-Hall of Australia Pty. Limited, *Sydney*
Prentice-Hall Canada Inc., *Toronto*
Prentice-Hall Hispanoamericana, S.A., *Mexico*
Prentice-Hall of India Private Limited, *New Delhi*
Prentice-Hall of Japan, Inc., *Tokyo*
Simon & Schuster Asia Pte. Ltd., *Singapore*
Editora Prentice-Hall do Brasil, Ltda., *Rio de Janeiro*

CONTENTS

2

PALESTINE DURING THE MANDATE   35

3

WORLD WAR II, JEWISH DISPLACED PERSONS, AND PALESTINE   66

4

THE U.N., ISRAEL ESTABLISHED, THE FIRST
ARAB-ISRAELI WAR   87

5

THE CONFLICT WIDENS: SUEZ, 1956   114

6

THE TURNING POINT: JUNE 1967   138

7

HOLY DAYS AND HOLY WAR: OCTOBER 1973   162

DOCUMENTS

PREFACE

The Middle East is a puzzle to most people, and the continuing Arab-Israeli conflict is perhaps the most confusing dimension of the modern history of the area. Team-teaching a history colloquium on the Arab-Israeli conflict at the University of Missouri-Kansas City, we discovered that, like the general public, our students had lots of opinions but only fragmentary knowledge. We found that before we could discuss the topic, we needed to spend time providing background information and tackling preconceptions and emotional biases. Moreover, our students required more than a knowledge of the events in order to understand the conflict. They needed ready access to the documents most relevant to the issues, they needed maps, and they needed guidance as to their further reading. We found no single book that met these requirements.

The present book is intended to fulfill that need. The text is basically a chronological narrative; however, within that framework, we have tried to highlight certain themes that we regard as central to the conflict. We have brought the book as up to date as possible in an area that is constantly changing.

We believe that this book will also be of interest to a wider audience, since the Middle East is an area of significance and importance not only to students but also to an educated public.

We hope that it will be accepted as an attempt to achieve some balance and objectivity about a subject upon which most people feel it necessary to adopt a partisan point of view. Throughout the book, we have tried to present both sides of the issues, although we realize that even the selection of material to be included reveals some subjective judgment on our part. If the book succeeds in provoking thoughtful discussion of the Arab-Israeli conflict, we will have achieved our goal.

We would like to acknowledge the assistance of the University of New South Wales and the University of Missouri-Kansas City, from which we received faculty research grants. We are also appreciative of the detailed and constructive comments and criticisms of Professor Arthur Goldschmidt, Jr., who read the manuscript for the publisher. Thanks are also due Rhonda Roosa and Bill Clipson who helped with maps, our history department office staffs, and the editorial and production staff at Prentice Hall, especially Bayani Mendoza de Leon. Finally, we thank our families, friends, and colleagues for their patience and support.

Ian J. Bickerton
Carla L. Klausner

A CONCISE HISTORY OF THE ARAB-ISRAELI CONFLICT

And thus is the way of the world.
No, rather, thus is the way we have made the world.
                                                    —Anonymous

INTRODUCTION

In this book we shall examine one of the most widely known and complex conflicts of the modern period. Scarcely a week goes by without some reference in our daily press or television news to the conflict between Israel and its Arab neighbors. In some ways this is curious. The Arab–Israeli conflict is only one of the forty or so separate wars fought since the end of World War II; the loss of life of both soldiers and civilians has been small compared to Korea or Vietnam, for example; and the area being fought over is tiny in world terms.

Yet many reasons lie behind why this conflict attracts so much attention, and why we should seek to understand the causes and course of events taking place. It has been a particularly tragic conflict in that there is scarcely a family on either side in the immediate region of the conflict in which a relative has not suffered injury or loss of life. In addition to being the modern expression of an historic territorial battle between two traditional ethnic rivals, the Arab–Israeli conflict directly involves two great world religions; it is caught up in the great-power rivalries of the Cold War, and the outcome is of major concern to Jewish, Islamic, and Christian communities around the world. Furthermore, the establishment of Israel is the pivotal event of the last 2,000 years of Jewish history, and the attitude toward Israel is central to Islam's response to the modern world.

Finally, given the seeming absolutes at stake, the threat of the activities of either party to the conflict escalating into a nuclear holocaust cannot be ignored. And to date, despite the peace treaty between Israel and Egypt, and movement on the question of the Palestinians, there seems little sign of a resolution of the fundamental issues.

The primary object of this study is to make the Arab–Israeli conflict more intelligible without the distortions that result from oversimplification. This involves tracing the broad sweep of the history of the region and the perceptions both parties have of each other. Both the Arabs and the Israelis are locked into the histories they have created for themselves—into the dreams of their pasts. Both also seek to set in our minds favorable cultural images and symbols of themselves and unfavorable ones of their opponents. Remember that legitimizing one's position is an essential element in any international conflict—that is one reason why the Arab–Israeli conflict is so passionately argued over, by participants and observers alike. The distinction between the past and the present is an artificial one; there is only the present. But constructing and controlling "the truth" about the past to justify one's actions in the present is an important function of all political activity, and one of your tasks as a student is to separate the rhetoric designed by both sides to create a usable, legitimizing, and heroic past from the reality of past events. The primary sources included in this text will provide you with the opportunity to reach your own conclusions as to the issues involved and the way they are portrayed by both sides.

It is also important to recognize that neither side is a monolith; there are divisions and tensions within both sides along ethnic, class, and religious lines that lead to many different political attitudes. One aim of this book is to assist you in sorting out the various groups and their opinions, assessing which ones are more likely to lead to peaceful rather than violent solutions. As David K. Shipler points out in *Arab and Jew: Wounded Spirits in a Promised Land:* "The time has passed when Jews and Arabs could face each other in simple conflict. They live together now in rich variety. There is no single Arab–Jewish relationship; there are many, and they require an elusive tolerance that must somehow run against the forces of war, nationalism, terrorism and religious certainty."

DEFINING THE QUESTION

How, then, can the Arab–Israeli conflict be explained? Is it a religious war between the followers of Islam and Judaism in which the protagonists are driven by deep-seated suspicions and hostilities concerning the Divine instructions to each other? Is it an ethnic war between traditionally rival groups, reflecting changing demographic patterns? Is it a war of territorial expansion in which one state is attempting to expand its borders at the expense of its neighbors? Is it a war of self-defense in which a newly established state is defending itself against the determination of its neighbors to destroy it? Is it a war of national liberation in which rival militant nationalisms are seeking to establish their "place in the sun?" Is it an imperial war reflecting the history of the rivalries and ambitions of the imperial states of Europe, and more lately the United States and the Soviet Union in the Middle East? Is it the inevitable consequence of the disruptive process of transition from traditional society to modern state taking place in the Middle East? Or is it simply a series of random, unconnected events that have had tragic and unforeseen consequences for the people involved?

All these elements are present in the Arab–Israeli conflict, but to single out any one of them as *the* explanation for the events that make up the conflict is to oversimplify a situation that has developed over the past century. As we shall see, the tragedy of the Arab–Israeli conflict is that it is the collision of two sets of historic and moral rights of groups who are both victims—victims of outsiders as well as each other's violence. The opposing claims differ, of course. In Shipler's words: "To draw the boldest outline of the past is to make Israel's basic case. To sketch the present is to see the Arab's plight."

WHO ARE THE ARABS AND JEWS?

We must begin with a definition of Arabs and Jews. Both terms have a historical and cultural meaning. Mythically, Arabs and Jews have a common origin. Thus, some regard Noah's eldest son, Shem, as the ancestor of the Hebrews and Arabs. Arabs as well as Jews see themselves as descendants of the patriarch Abraham, and therefore as inheritors of the Promised Land—Palestine. Arabs trace their lineage to Ishmael, Abraham's first son born of Hagar, Sarah's handmaiden, while Jews, or Israelites, trace themselves to Isaac, son of Abraham and his wife, Sarah. In the Hebrew Bible, known to Christians as the Old Testament, the term Arab referred to the nomadic inhabitants of the central and northern Arabian Peninsula. Over the centuries, these nomadic tribes, headed by a sheikh who acted as a first among equals, developed a structure shaped by the harsh deserts and dependent on the camel. Survival depended upon the strength and solidarity of the tribe, and on obedience to custom and an unwritten code of honor called *muruwwa*. We can learn more about Arab values and the Arab experience during the period just before Muhammad through the heroic poetry they spoke and sang in the sixth and early seventh centuries. The greatest of these poems are the "Seven Odes" or "Mu'allaqat" (qasidahs of Imru al-Qays, ruler of an ephemeral desert kingdom between the fourth and sixth centuries). When the Arab conquest of the Middle East occurred in the seventh and eighth centuries of the common era (C.E.),* following the founding of Islam, Arabic became the language and Islam the religion of the region. The term Arab acquired a new cultural definition that lasted during the period of Arab hegemony until the Mongol sack of Baghdad in 1258. Not all the inhabitants adopted the new language and religion, however. Some remnants of early Christianity remained: Nestorians in Persia and Iraq, the Christians of Syria, the Maronite Christians of Mount Lebanon (who use Syriac in their liturgy but recognize Rome as the head of the Christian Church), and some Greek Orthodox. And, of course, Jews resisted the new conquerors.

Arabs today do not form one nation-state although, like Jews, they consider themselves a people and national group. They constitute a majority in many modern nation-states (Egypt, Saudi Arabia, Jordan, Lebanon, Iraq, Syria, Yemen, South Yemen, the United Arab Emirates, Kuwait, Bahrain, Qatar, Oman, Sudan, Libya, Morocco, Tunisia, Algeria). Today there are more than 100 million in the region from Morocco to Iraq who consider themselves Arab. Nor are Arabs a race in the commonly understood sense. Neither are they a religion, for many Arabs—about 5 million—are Christian. And only about one-fifth of the world's Muslims are Arab. Indeed, the largest concentration of Muslims in the world is in Indonesia. In the final analysis, Arab can be applied to those who use Arabic as their language and identify with Arab culture and Arab causes.

*The term C.E. is preferred by Muslims and Jews to the corresponding designation A.D. (the year of Our Lord).

The term Jew is as difficult to define as the term Arab. Jews trace their history to the Semitic tribe or groups of tribes who claimed descent from Abraham through his son Isaac who were known as Hebrews or Israelites. Although Jews consider themselves a people, as do the Arabs, Jews are not simply a nationality, not a race, and are more than a religion. They are at once an ethnic group, a religious group, and a cultural group. Even identifying as Jews those who use Hebrew as a language does not help us much as it is the native language of only about one-third of the inhabitants of Israel, and many who identify themselves as Jews have little or no familiarity with the language. The term Jew can be best applied to those who have a Jewish mother, or who call themselves Jews because of conversion to Judaism.

One problem for Europeans in discussing Arabs and Jews is to free themselves from the distorting lens of two destructive ideologies: anti-Semitism (in the sense of anti-Jewishness), and Orientalism (anti-Arabness). Irrational suspicion, fear, and hatred of Jews, as Jews, have characterized European history for centuries, leading to almost uninterrupted oppression and persecution of Jews throughout all the countries of Europe. Anti-Semitism—the term was first used by the German racist Wilhelm Marr in 1879—in its modern form defined and attacked Jews in terms of race rather than religion and relied on pseudo-scientific Social-Darwinist theories in attempting to prove the superiority of the "Aryan" race over the "inferior" Semitic Jews. These twisted ideas found their ultimate expression in the Holocaust, in Hitler's attempt to exterminate the Jews.

Westerners have also exhibited a contempt, disregard, and sense of arrogance toward Arabs and Muslims. Thus, as they have also done with Jews, Westerners have failed to recognize the intrinsic value and contributions of Arabs to history. These assumptions, or more correctly, limitations, have been defined by one scholar, Edward Said in his book *Orientalism,* as "Orientalism." Said describes Orientalism as the racist way we view the inhabitants of the Orient, including the Middle East, in relation to ourselves as Europeans. The West, Said argues, has tried to establish the idea that Europe, by defining the political, economic, and cultural characteristics of the people of the Orient as inferior to those of the West, has the right to hegemony or dominance over the Orient. Thus non-Middle-Easterners have come to regard the Middle East as politically despotic, economically backward, and culturally decadent. As a result, there is a tendency to overlook completely the contributions of the Middle East to the development of Western European civilization and, in restructuring the realities of Middle Eastern life and history, to distort them. The cultural or intellectual assumptions that Occidentals bring to their study of Jews and Arabs make an understanding of the Arab–Israeli conflict considerably more difficult.

More serious as far as solving the conflict is concerned, Jews and Arabs bring their own prejudices and negative stereotypes—exaggerated by past and recent history—to bear upon each other. For Jews, the most pervasive stereotype of the Arab according to Shipler is "the fearsome violent figure of immense strength and duplicity. . . . Capable of great cruelty, given to fanatical disregard for human life, he murders easily, either out of a crazed lust for blood or as an emotional animal easily incited and manipulated by murderous leaders." Arab stereotypes of Jews are remarkably similar to those of their Jewish counterparts. Jews are seen by Arabs as violent and cowardly. Ignoring the ancient ties of the Jews to Palestine, the Arabs regard them as aliens, as outsiders, as interlopers who do not belong. Jews and Arabs also share Western views of each other as backward and primitive. Needless to say, these prejudices add significantly to the passions of the participants in the conflict.

THE RELIGIOUS DIMENSION: ISLAM AND JUDAISM

Much of the Arab–Israeli conflict is secular, involving issues of territory, security, and ethnic and cultural differences. In many respects the sources of tensions are non-religious, resembling those of any conflict. But religion is an element of the conflict and adds an extra dimension and sense of inevitability to the unfolding events. Despite the fact that only a minority of Arabs and Jews are strictly observant religiously, religion has been, and continues to be, a focal point for the peoples involved in this conflict. And religion significantly shapes the attitudes of the protagonists toward each other, which is, no doubt, why the conflict is sometimes described as a religious war.

Judaism is the oldest monotheistic religion and is the forerunner of both Christianity and Islam. Judaism refers to the faith and ceremonies of Jews, and is a faith that is revealed by God and interpreted by religious teachers, namely rabbis. In its widest sense, Judaism is the entire Jewish tradition and Jewish way of life. Central to Judaism is the belief that God acted personally in history through a Chosen People, the Jews (the people called Israel), and that God entered into a Covenant with the Jews that if they obeyed God's teachings He would, through them, save all mankind. God's instructions to the Jews are contained in the *Torah* (literally teachings), or Pentateuch, which consists of the Five Books of Moses. The Torah contains the laws God revealed to the Jews, including the Ten Commandments. It also includes the message to establish an independent society based on Divine precepts, which are elaborated in great detail. One finds in the Torah, as well, God's promise to establish the Jews in the land of Israel—the Promised Land—the state in which people would live in truth, justice, and peace. Thus the Torah is more than just a "Bible"; it is a blueprint for existence, and in the minds of many religious Jews today it should be the constitution of any Jewish state.

Judaism has gone through several stages in its long history. The first stage could be said to be that described in the Hebrew Bible, consisting of the Torah, the books of the Prophets, and a collection of other writings such as Chronicles, Kings, Ruth, Esther, and the Song of Solomon. It tells of the Jews' search under Moses for the land promised them by God after their expulsion from Egypt (the Exodus), and describes the Kingdoms of David and Solomon.

The northern part of the kingdom, or Samaria, was conquered by the Assyrians in 721 B.C.E.* The Jews of the Southern Kingdom, or Judea, were exiled to Babylonia in 586 B.C.E. after the destruction of the First Temple built by Solomon in Jerusalem, which had become the center of Jewish worship until it was destroyed by the army of King Nebuchadnezzar. Restored to Palestine by the Persians, the Jews built a Second Temple in Jerusalem and lived autonomously under a succession of foreign rulers until 70 C.E. when the Romans destroyed the Second Temple and dispersed them (the Diaspora).

Following the destruction of the Temple and the disappearance of the priestly class, synagogues (places of worship, study, and community gathering) came into existence throughout the Jewish world, and teachers, or rabbis, interpreted the law. This oral law of the rabbis was later codified in a work known as the *Mishna*. The accumulated mass of law and lore based on the Torah and Mishna and known as the Talmud was then codified by about 500 C.E. In subsequent centuries, living under Muslim or Christian rulers, Jewish thinkers and teachers continued to study and in-

---

*The term B.C.E. (before the common era) is used throughout the text and corresponds to the designation B.C.

terpret their traditions. In the Middle Ages, Moses ben Maimon, or Maimonides (1135–1204), a Jew living in Islamic Spain, immigrated to Egypt, where he served as a physician at the court of the Muslim rulers. Recognized as the most learned and authoritative figure of his age, Maimonides codified Talmudic law up to his time in the *Mishneh Torah,* and dealt with fundamental theological and philosophical questions in the *Guide of the Perplexed.* Maimonides distilled thirteen articles of the faith, and enumerated 613 positive and negative commandments found in the Torah, which form the basis of Judaic law and faith.

Further changes took place in the eighteenth and nineteenth centuries as the Jews of Western Europe were emancipated and as many older customs and rituals were rejected to enable Judaism to accommodate the modern world. Thus Reform Judaism, Zionism, and secular Yiddish culture emerged. Today, the largest Jewish communities are in the United States, the Soviet Union, and Israel. Devout Jews maintain traditional Jewish observances in their individual and familial practices, including attendance at synagogue, observing special holy days, periods of fasting, and ceremonies. Although divided into Reform, Orthodox, and Conservative branches of Judaism, the vast majority of Jews in the United States support the existence of the Jewish state of Israel.

Islam asserts that God has revealed himself several times in history and accepts the validity of scriptural religions like Judaism and Christianity. Muslims believe that the transmitter of God's final revelations to mankind was Muhammad, a member of the Quraysh tribe of the trading city, Mecca. Muhammad was born about 570 C.E. and is regarded by Muslims as the last of God's prophets in a line that includes Abraham, Moses, and Jesus. Not much is known about Muhammad's life, except that he came from a poor family of the clan of Hashim, married Khadija, a wealthy widow fifteen years his senior, became a successful businessman, was ambitious, and was also deeply religious. According to tradition, the archangel Gabriel (the same archangel who appeared to Mary in Christian tradition) appeared to Muhammad and revealed the word of Allah (al-Illah, or The God), whom Muhammad accepted as the One True God—the same monotheistic deity of the Jews and Christians.

Around the year 610 C.E., Muhammad began to preach the word of God, and the passages of rhythmic prose that he uttered were copied down and later collected to form the *Quran* (or Koran), the holy book of Islam, considered by pious Muslims to be the divine word of God. Within a few years, and especially after his flight (*Hijra,* or Hegira) from Mecca to Medina in the year 622, the year 1 of the Islamic calendar, Muhammad was the acknowledged religious, political, and military leader of a new community of believers, or Ummah, as it was called.

In 630 C.E., after taking over Mecca and reconsecrating the Kaaba (a cubelike structure that had previously housed 360 idols) to Allah alone, delegations of tribes from all over Arabia accepted Muhammad's authority. The precepts of the Quran thus became, theoretically, the law of a new religious-political entity. Muhammad died in 632 C.E., however, and it was left to his successors, the caliphs (who inherited his manifold functions, but not his power of revelation), to put down revolts of recalcitrant tribes and then to lead Muslim Arab armies out of Arabia to conquer within a century an area extending from the Pyrenees in the west to the Punjab in the east and the borders of China in the North. Arabic soon became the language of the entire Middle East and Islam the dominant religion, and it remains so today.

Islam means *submission,* and for Muslims the purpose of existence is to submit to the will of God as revealed in the Quran. Muslims believe, like Jews, that the state should exist to do God's will; the Quran, covering all aspects of living, therefore, became the foundation of a legal system for a community in which religion and politics (or church and state) were one and the same thing. The Sharia, or "straight path," the corpus of Islamic law that developed over about three centuries, consists of the Quran, the traditions of the Prophet Muhammad himself (*Hadith*), and, for Sunni Muslims, legal points derived from analogous situations (*Qiyas*), and material accepted by the consensus (*Ijma*) of the community, or more accurately, by the learned men or jurists, often based on local traditions and customs. The entire Sharia, once compiled, was considered to be divine; it continues to form the basis of the legal system in many Middle East countries today.

Islam is no more unified than Christianity, and conflicts over the question of leadership in the early community led to a schism between the followers of tradition (Sunnis), who insisted on an elective element to the position of caliph, and the followers of Ali (the Shia or Shiites), the fourth caliph, Muhammad's son-in-law and the father of Muhammad's only two grandchildren to survive into maturity, Hassan and Hussein. Regarding the leadership of the Ummah, the Shiites insisted on the principle of designation in the house of the Prophet through Ali's family. They called their leaders *Imams*. This conflict, which continues into the present day, began as a political rather than as a theological one. The great majority of Muslims, however, are Sunnis; the Shiites constitute about 10 to 15 percent of Muslims (about 50 million to 60 million), although they are in a majority in Iran, Iraq, Bahrain, and Yemen.

Islam has no centralized authority, no overall clergy; a religious elite—*ulema* (learned theologians, jurists, and teachers)—wield authority. Islam is more than a religion as such. It is a sense of belonging to a cultural tradition; a kind of "secular" identity that, for many Muslims, is closely related to being an Arab. The major problem faced by Islam today is to bring about change within sanctified tradition, and not go counter to those traditions. As in Judaism, there is no division between the secular and sacred, or the temporal and spiritual realms, in Islam.

The expansion of Europe in the eighteenth century challenged the power of Islam. Because Islam had established and maintained various Islamic empires for centuries, accepting other political and religious structures on equal terms was a major problem; Muslims were especially confounded by the military and economic superiority of European colonialism. Thus, the Arab response to the establishment of Israel is, in part at least, a particularly acute example of the difficulties Muslims have in accepting the political sovereignty of a previously "tolerated minority." The sense of Islamic community that all Muslims share was weakened at first by the impact of Western colonialism, but later, and especially since World War II, Muslims believe Islam has helped them in their struggle to gain political freedom and independence. Most states with Muslim majorities have created modern political and economic infrastructures and are in the often slow and painful process of accommodating Islam to modern social patterns.

Because Christianity and Islam both emerged out of Judaism, it is not surprising that a number of striking similarities exist among these three Middle Eastern religions. They all believe in the existence of the same God. All three religions believe in a final Day of Judgment; all have prophets, in many cases the same ones; and all are intolerant of what they regard as deviation, or heresy. Where they differ is in their historical experience. Thus, Islam and Christianity became universal religions whereas Judaism remained the religion of a single group. This has led to the particularism or exceptionalism that characterizes Judaism, but there is little reason to think that had the Jews of Palestine had a different historical experience, had they taken an imperial path, for example, they would not have adopted the universalistic principles of Islam and Christianity that all mankind could—indeed should—belong to their religion.

The major departure of Islam and Judaism from Christianity stems from their different attitudes toward Jesus. Muslims and Jews do not believe the claim, accepted by Christians, that Jesus Christ was the Messiah, the Son of God sent to redeem mankind. Indeed, it has been Judaism's unwillingness to accept this claim, at times even hostility to it, together with the perceived role of Jews in the events leading to the death of Jesus, that has led to much of the Christian hostility toward Jews throughout history. Christianity takes the view that the failure of the Jews to recognize the divinity of Jesus means that they can no longer claim to be the Chosen People, and indeed many have used the term "Chosen People" in pejorative ways to reinforce hostility against the Jews. Judaism, on the other hand, retains the continuity of the Jews as God's Chosen People, and the religion teaches that the Messiah (the anointed Saviour) is yet to come.

Islam and Judaism differ from Christianity in other fundamental ways. First, neither religion has a hierarchical clergy as most Christian churches do. Because there are no sacraments, neither the ulema nor the rabbis perform sacerdotal functions as do the Christian clergy, and they do not act as mediators between the people and God. They are learned men who live in the community at large, marry, have families, and act as teachers and guides rather than as priests and bishops. Judaism differs from both Islam and Christianity in one important respect, however. Both Islam and Christianity were militarily and politically successful over the centuries, establishing empires or states in which their respective beliefs and principles were put into practice. Judaism had no such experience from the destruction of the Second Temple in 70 C.E. until the establishment of Israel in 1948.

Judaism is unique in that it is a religion limited to one people, and while not all Jews live by their Judaic traditions, religion is a central element of their history, binding them in a spiritual, as well a historical, unity. The emphasis of Judaism upon the Jews as the Chosen People links the salvation of the Jewish people and all of mankind through a restoration of the Jews to Palestine. In this book we will examine the two pivotal events in modern Judaism: the Holocaust and the establishment of the state of Israel. Both events have raised the fundamental question of Judaism in the most dramatic way for 2,000 years—namely, the nature of the presence and role of God in history in relation to God's chosen people.

Although in many respects Judaism and Islam are similar, important differences exist that lead to tension between the two religious groups. Bernard Lewis in *Semites and Anti-Semites* has observed:

> Jews have lived under Islamic rule for fourteen centuries, and in many lands, and it is therefore difficult to generalize about their experience. This much, however, may be said with reasonable certainty—that they were never free from discrimination, but only rarely subject to persecution; that their situation was never as bad as in Christendom at its worst, nor ever as good as in Christendom at its best. There is nothing in Islamic history to parallel the Spanish expulsion and Inquisition, the Russian pogroms, or the Nazi Holocaust; there is also nothing to compare with the progressive emancipation and acceptance accorded to Jews in the Democratic West during the last three centuries.

While Judaism is not a proselytizing religion, and does not seek converts, Islam, with its universalistic implications, divides the world into two groups: the first, where Islamic law and order prevail (*Dar-al-Islam*—the House of Submission); the second, which constitutes the areas that have not yet submitted to Allah (*Dar-al-Harb*—the Abode of War). One of the important duties of Muslims is to extend Islam through all means such as international diplomacy, economic pressure, and war if necessary. The

Jihad (Holy Struggle or Holy War) is increasingly interpreted by Muslims these days as the duty to fight a defensive rather than aggressive war, although the term is very flexible and capable of various interpretations—indeed, it has been used to justify initiating war across a wide range of situations. We should not infer, however, that Arabs oppose Israel simply because Jihad (often falsely construed as forced conversion) is a duty for Muslims, just as we should not infer that because it does not make converts, Judaism has a live-and-let-live attitude. Arabs and Israelis have other reasons besides religion to oppose each other, as we shall see in the following chapters. The establishment of Israel has not only raised central questions for Judaism but has also dramatically highlighted a major question facing Islam today. That issue is how to accommodate other political and economic structures on equal terms. The Arab and Muslim response to Israel is, in part at least, a particularly acute example of the difficulty this poses.

A key question in both religions as far as the Arab–Israeli conflict is concerned is: what is the attitude of the religion to the outsider? Both religions are ambiguous and contradictory in relation to this question. They make positive and negative references to others, and are both welcoming and exclusive. As in all religions, in both Islam and Judaism, justifications can be found to sanctify the basest as well as the noblest actions. Disturbingly, increasingly, fundamentalist (a term borrowed from Protestantism) religious leaders on both sides—imams and rabbis—responding, in part at least, to the perceived failure of secular nationalism to meet people's spiritual and material needs, are lending their voices to the cause of violence.

THE TASK OF THE HISTORIAN

At the outset, we must ask ourselves: just what is the task of the historian? Is the historian a participant in the events he or she describes, or simply an observer? Does the historian set out to make a political case for one position or another, or to "tell the truth"—letting the chips fall where they may? Determining what we mean by the truth is difficult enough as it is. Does the historian set out to re-create the past as fully as possible? What do we mean by this expression, and how would we set out to re-create the past? What kind of events should the historian look at: political, social, cultural, economic? Should we look at society from the top down; that is, at leaders, or from the bottom up; at those who were the actual hewers of stone and carriers of water?

There are, of course, no easy answers to these questions. It is difficult to tell where the boundaries between these categories begin and end. They are all intellectual constructs, and our perceptions and interpretations are in constant flux. In this book we have tried to relate what we regard as the most important events and to explain how both sides have interpreted the unfolding of these events.

One of the central questions historians investigate is the role of force and violence in history. Force and violence are certainly one of the major aspects of Arab–Jewish relations over the past century. How much could have been avoided? Need violence continue? These are crucial questions. It is essential, we believe, to keep in mind that history is not some sort of seamless web of necessity. There is no law of inevitability in history, however passionately politicians may argue that in such and such a case the use of force was "necessary." History is not a process determining events in which humans are powerless to act and to change things. Human agency is the key to understanding the past, as it is to an understanding of the present and future. Throughout history, there have always been alternatives to the resort to force, es-

Israel Superimposed
on Southern California
(to scale)

R. Roosa

pecially war, however unpalatable those options might have appeared to leaders at the time. Throughout this text we have tended to assess actions with this thought in mind.

All investigations must begin with an awareness of self and how we define ourselves in relation to others. The distinguishing element in the study of history is to explore how that definition relates to, and changes over, time. Central to how we define ourselves is an understanding of our relationship to the space around us. A knowledge of the environment, or at the very least the landscape, of the Middle East—especially that area embracing Palestine—is crucial to an understanding of the Arab-Israeli conflict. The most important aspect of landscape to the Jews and Arabs of Palestine is the concept of homeland and the meaning attached to this concept.

Almost all concepts of homeland have included the notion that such a place is the center of the world and that it is of supreme value. A homeland is usually tied to a specific location spiritually; it is a place to consort and speak with the gods, and continuity with the location takes on a special meaning, with dislocation causing chaos. This was especially true of the ancient religions. We must also keep in mind that the value peoples attach to such concepts are historically as well as culturally derived. A homeland provides nourishment, permanency, reassurance, and an identification with the soil, and it provides historical ties of identity. Looked at in this way, we can quickly see that Palestine takes on special significance to the two groups who have been in such bitter conflict for almost a century.

THE LANDSCAPE OF PALESTINE

Let us now turn to the landscape of Palestine itself. The area of the former Ottoman Empire today thought of as Palestine received its rather arbitrary boundaries between 1920 and 1922 as the result, as we shall see later, of discussion between the great powers following the end of World War I. Throughout this book, the area we refer to when we speak of Palestine is that which was administered by the British as a mandated territory between World War I and 1948. It does not include Transjordan, which was administered separately after 1921. It is impossible to understand the depth of feeling on both sides without an awareness of the ecological or environmental relationship that exists between the Jews and Arabs who inhabit the region, as well as the historical and cultural ties that link the two peoples to the land. These boundaries circumscribe a total land area of about 26,320 square kilometers, about the size of New Hampshire (see accompanying map in which Palestine/Israel is superimposed on a map of Southern California drawn to scale).

The center of the country consists of a central mass of hills running from northern Galilee to southern Judea. While these are often steep and rocky, their very highest peaks reach an altitude of only 2,400 to 3,000 feet. On either side of the hills lie lowlands—the Maritime plain to the West and the Jordan Valley to the East. On the South sprawls the desert district now commonly known as the Negev. Bisecting the hills on a northwest to southeast axis are the contiguous valleys of Esdraelon and Jezreel, which separate Samaria from Galilee.

The hills of Palestine cover approximately 2 million acres of which over a half million are largely uninhabited wilderness. That area of the hills that is inhabited consists of some scattered valleys of great fertility, but overall the steepness of the hillsides, the numerous rock outcroppings, and the very high limestone content, combined with an unpredictable rainfall, make the area generally very poor agriculturally. Much of it is simply uncultivable. The terracing of hillsides and the exploitation of

Jerusalem in late nineteenth century.

those springs and streams that do exist have enabled the limited cultivation of grains, olives, vines, and deciduous fruits.

The hills are surrounded by five principal plains. The largest and most important is the Maritime plain from Rafah to Mount Carmel, which includes, in its northern section, the Plain of Sharon. This plain occupies over 800,000 acres, of which two thirds or more are capable of being irrigated. The mild lowland winters and the light sandy soils make this excellent citrus-growing country. The Plain of Acre covers about 140,000 acres lying along the coast north of Haifa. Here there is plentiful water from springs and streams, and the heavy alluvial soils lead to intensive cultivation of a wide variety of vegetables, fodders, and deciduous fruits. The Plain of Esdraelon, which comprises about 100,000 acres, has traditionally been regarded as the most fertile and productive district in Palestine, and cereals and fruit are grown on its alluvial clays. The Huleh Plain is to be found in the extreme northeast corner of Palestine, and about one-fifth of this plain, the area to the south ending in Lake Huleh, was marshlands before it was reclaimed. Lastly, there is the valley of the Jordan River, which if the Jezreel Valley is included—and Jezreel is even richer than the Esdraelon—occupies about 250,000 acres. This region is extremely productive when irrigated with the waters from the Jordan river. Palestine also includes the mostly desert region south of Beersheba (the Negev), which extends over 3,140,000 acres or about 48 percent of the entire country. Irrigated parts of this district have proven fertile.

There has been, and still exists, a very close link between the landscape and the pattern of settlement in Palestine. These patterns, reinforced by historical, cultural, and religious experiences, reflect fundamental attitudes that the inhabitants, both Arabs and Jews, hold about the region and their identification with it as place and homeland. Both groups have sought once again to give practical expression to these attitudes and aspirations over the past century, and in so doing have revealed vastly different visions. How those visions have led to the bloodshed of the past century will be the subject of our inquiry.

SUGGESTIONS FOR FURTHER READING

CARR, EDWARD, H., *What Is History*, New York, Alfred A. Knopf, 1962.

ESPOSITO, JOHN L., *Islam: The Straight Path*, New York, Oxford University Press, 1988.

JACKSON, J. B., *The Interpretation of the Ordinary Landscape*, New York, Oxford University Press, 1979.

KHOURI, FRED J., *The Arab-Israeli Dilemma* (3rd ed.), Syracuse, N.Y., Syracuse University Press, 1985.

LEWIS, BERNARD, *The Arabs in History* (2nd ed.), New York, Harper & Row, 1962.

SACHAR, HOWARD, M., *A History of Israel*, Vol. 1 (2nd ed.), New York, Alfred A. Knopf, 1986, and Vol. 2, New York, Oxford University Press, 1987.

SAID, EDWARD, *Orientalism*, London, Routledge & Kegan Paul, 1978.

SHIPLER, DAVID, *Arab and Jew; Wounded Spirits in a Promised Land*, New York, Times books, 1986.

See also the *Encyclopedia of Islam* and the *Encyclopedia Judaica*.

CHAPTER 1

PALESTINE IN THE NINETEENTH CENTURY

CHRONOLOGY

1516–1918	Ottoman rule over Palestine	**1892**	Railroad between Jerusalem and Jaffa completed
1791	Pale of Settlement established in Russian Empire	**1894**	Trial of Alfred Dreyfus in France
		1896	Publication of Herzl's *Der Judenstaat*
1860–1904	Life of Theodor Herzl	**1897**	Formation of World Zionist Organization at the first Zionist Congress in Basel, Switzerland
1879	Establishment of Anti-Semitic League		
1876–1909	Rule of Sultan Abdul-Hamid II	**1901**	Establishment of Jewish National Fund
1881	Assassination of Czar Alexander II of Russia	**1904**	Second *aliyah* begins
		1905	Railroad between Haifa and Deraa completed
1882	Beginning of first *aliyah*		
1882	Landing of first group of Zionist *Hibbat Zion* at Jaffa	**1908**	Young Turk revolution
		1909	Abdul-Hamid II deposed
1882	Turkish legislation restricting Jewish immigration to Palestine	**1909**	Establishment of Tel Aviv

14

For us to understand nineteenth-century Palestine, we must view the topic from several sides. We need to look at the diplomatic history of the European powers who struggled for influence in the area—notably England, France, and Russia—and the impact these nations left on the local society. We must also examine the political, socioeconomic, and cultural-ideological developments among the local population. These developments include the rise of local leaders and notables, demographic changes and economic conditions, intercommunal relationships, the status of the Jewish population, and the emergence of the Zionist and Arab national movements. In this chapter we shall try to bring these aspects together to describe the situation in Palestine at the beginning of the new era, which began in 1914.

PALESTINE UNDER THE OTTOMAN EMPIRE

Under Ottoman rule, which lasted four centuries (1516–1918), Palestine never formed a political administrative unit of its own. It was divided into several districts, called *sanjaks* and these were part of larger provinces or administrative units, called *vilayets*. Most of Palestine was part of the vilayet of Syria governed by the pasha of Damascus, but after 1841, following a decade of occupation of the region by Egypt, except for an area east of the Jordan River, which remained part of the vilayet of Syria, it consisted of a northern portion placed in the vilayet of Beirut, and a southern portion, the sanjak of Jerusalem (see map 1–1). The Ottoman government in Constantinople did not attach much importance to the Palestine districts until the middle of the nineteenth century; the area raised very little revenue, it had little military or strategic importance, and its borders were not precisely defined. The Muslim Sultan did feel a political and religious obligation to protect the Holy Places of Islam, Christianity, and Judaism. His need to maintain cordial relations with the European powers meant that he also had to protect Christian and Jewish pilgrims to Palestine.

The attainment of virtual autonomy from the Ottoman Empire by Egypt in the mid-nineteenth century, and Anglo-French strategic rivalry to control the Suez isthmus, meant that the Palestine districts became more strategically and politically important to Constantinople. Accordingly, the Ottomans tightened their control of Syria and Palestine. The sanjak of Jerusalem was given higher status and made directly responsible to Constantinople in an attempt by the imperial government to regain central control over the region and to make the administration more efficient. Palestine had been a poor and neglected part of the Ottoman Empire. Over the previous two centuries, local governors had become independent of Ottoman control, had become corrupt and had neglected their duties, with the result that there was considerable disorder and insecurity; public works had not been carried out; agriculture and trade had declined; and the majority of the population were impoverished and oppressed.

Much of this oppression had come from local leaders like the rural sheikhs of Nablus, the Judean Hills, and Hebron; Druze emirs in southern Lebanon and northern Palestine; and Bedouin chiefs in other areas. Heads of prominent families, called *notables,* sought to gain political power in order to collect land taxes and security payments from pilgrims. During the second half of the nineteenth century, the Ottomans gradually reestablished central control, Bedouin attacks became less frequent, general security increased, oppression of the urban population diminished somewhat, and the European powers greatly expanded their involvement in Palestine, as in the rest of the Levant. As a result, the areas's economy and the conditions of the inhabitants significantly improved. Under Sultan Abdul-Hamid II, who ruled the Ottoman Empire

MAP 1–1

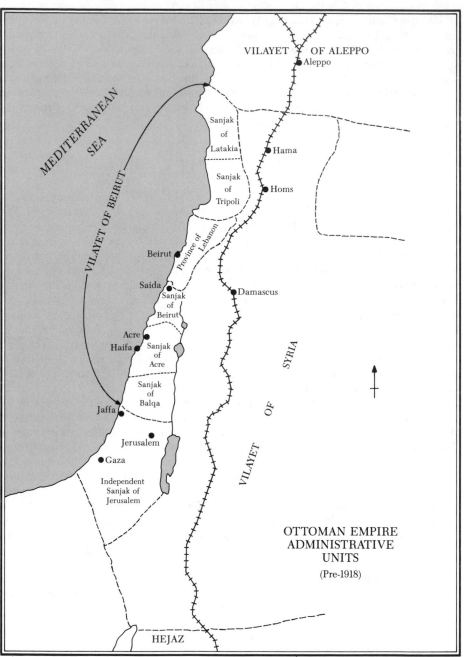

OTTOMAN EMPIRE
ADMINISTRATIVE
UNITS
(Pre-1918)

Source: William R. Polk, David M. Stamler and Edmund Asfour, *Backdrop To Tragedy,*
Boston, Beacon, 1957. p. 53.

from 1876 to 1909, important changes took place in Palestine. Abdul-Hamid encouraged modernization in communications, education, and the military in order to strengthen his control. When he began his rule, Palestine had no railroad, hardly any carriage roads, and no developed port. There were few medical services, and disease and illiteracy were widespread. Within a few years of Abdul-Hamid's accession, new roads were opened and European companies completed a railroad between Jerusalem and Jaffa in 1892, and another between Haifa and Deraa, Transjordan, in 1905. In reorganizing the Ottoman Empire and attempting to strengthen central control by using European engineers and investors, the Sultans, paradoxically, encouraged the very European penetration of Palestine they were seeking to prevent.

THE ARABS OF PALESTINE

The population of Palestine, which reached around 650,000 by 1914, was heterogeneous and divided, especially among the Arabs. In addition to the divisions among urban, rural, and nomadic populations, continual rivalries existed within the villages and among the nomads. There was a great gulf between the Palestine gentry and the peasants (*fellahin*). City dwellers had nothing but contempt for the peasants and had almost no contact with them. Much of the land in Palestine was state land (*miri*). Whether state or private, the land was cultivated by fellahin who exercised a kind of communal, as opposed to formal-legal, ownership over it. The fellahin were frequently in debt and did all they could to avoid paying taxes. Peasant reluctance to pay taxes or gain legal title to their land was stimulated in part by their fear of being subject to military recruitment.

The villages of Palestine were small, isolated, and poor. In northern Palestine, the vast majority of the fellahin were tenant farmers who lived in villages while working the land owned by absentee landowners, most of whom lived in Beirut or Damascus. By the time of Zionist immigration in the 1880s, the land had, legally at least, passed from the peasants to Palestinian notables, many of whom had gained wealth as tax collectors or as merchants living elsewhere. Consequently, some Arabs of Palestine regarded themselves not as Palestinians but identified themselves with Syrian or Lebanese centers. By the last quarter of the century, only 20 percent of the land in the Galilee and 50 percent of Judea remained in the hands of the fellahin. Nevertheless, the land they possessed represented two-thirds of the arable land, for much of the land purchased by the notables and absentee landowners was not being tilled. The primary identification and loyalty of the peasants was undoubtedly a kind of "village patriotism," which stemmed from their attachment to the land they worked, regardless of who had legal title to it, and to the village in which they and their families lived.

Villagers supported themselves by growing crops and raising a few sheep or goats. Methods of agriculture had changed very little over the centuries, although demand for Palestinian grain, cotton, and citrus fruits had increased in the last half of the century. Nevertheless, many villagers sought some relief from their poverty by moving into the towns. The social relations of the village were based on kinship; this was because the village was frequently made up of one or more extended families. Thus, what might seem to modern Europeans to be a lack of privacy, or overcrowding, in the village was to the Palestinian peasant a sense of security, continuity, and familial cohesiveness. In southern Palestine, most of the population were the nomadic Bedouin who made a meager living through raising and selling sheep, camels, and goats.

There were also religious divisions within the Arab population of Palestine.

Sunni Muslims, Shiites, and Druze were at odds, and there were constant rivalries between Muslims and Christian Arabs (approximately 16 percent of the population—mostly Greek Orthodox). The Muslims of Palestine were overwhelmingly Sunni, and the local Muslim elites to whom they gave their loyalty gained their political identity and position through loyalty to the Sultan. As a result of all the factors mentioned above, there was no strong impetus toward Palestinian nationalism among the Muslim Arabs during this period. Any sense of nationalism that did exist among the Arabs came mainly from the Christian Arabs who were influenced by their European Christian contacts, both in the Middle East and in Europe. They were in the forefront of a literary and cultural movement in the nineteenth century that led to the rediscovery of the glorious heritage of the Arabs and reawakened a sense of ethnic identity. Initially, these Arab nationalists were concerned about parity between Arabs and Turks, and between Arab Muslims and Arab Christians within the Ottoman Empire. (See Documents 1–1 and 1–2.)

Several significant events occurred in the first decade and a half of the twentieth century. The Young Turk revolution of 1908 brought to the forefront Turkish nationalists who intended to preserve the Ottoman Empire through ruthless policies of centralization and Islamization. As historian Zeine N. Zeine has noted, the seeds of Arab nationalism sprouted from the soil of Turkish nationalism. Groups now formed that were dedicated to achieving political independence as Arabs from the Ottoman Empire. Moreover, as the century progressed, nationalist sentiment among Arabs, including those in Palestine, also grew as a response to the strong nationalist feelings of Jews toward Palestine, or *Eretz Yisrael* (the land of Israel).

Like Arab nationalism, Jewish nationalism remained a religious and cultural phenomenon until the nineteenth century, when the idea of creating a Jewish state in Eretz Yisrael assumed the character of a political ideology. It was the product of the European environment, and was influenced by Western ideologies like rationalism and secular nationalism. The situation of the Jews in Europe had taken a different course from that of the Jews who lived under Islam. In the Islamic world, Jews had lived for hundreds of years as *Ahl-ad-Dhimma,* or people of a contract or covenant, with the Muslim rulers. As *dhimmis,* Jews, like Christians, were given the status of second-class citizens. They were subject to heavy land and poll taxes (*jizyah*) and discriminatory social regulations, and were forbidden from exercising control over Muslims, although these restrictions were sometimes ignored. Dhimmis were allowed to worship freely, to live under their own laws, and to enjoy a large measure of self-government. There were no restrictions on their travel or economic life. Although there were occasional massacres of Jews, attacks against them, and sometimes even forced conversions, no Islamic ruler ever instituted a policy of wholesale expulsion or extermination of the Jews. Arabized Jews tended to take on the characteristics of their surroundings. Defined in terms of their religion, they tended to think of themselves as a religious group. Moreover, like their Arab neighbors who lived under Ottoman imperial rule until the twentieth century, they were affected somewhat later than their European counterparts by Western developments and ideologies such as secularism and nationalism.

THE JEWS IN EUROPE

The history of Jews in Christian Europe was different from the Jewish experience under the Muslims. This is a story that reflects very little credit on European Christianity, as it is a story of almost uninterrupted oppression and persecution of Jews throughout all the countries of Europe. And, of course, it culminated in the horrific genocide of Hitler's "final solution," which Jews since that time have called the Holocaust. Historians have offered several reasons for the shocking ways Jews were treated in Europe, especially during and after the Middle Ages, and it is difficult to escape the conclusion that it was based largely on irrational and ill-informed religious prejudice. This has led most interpretations of Jewish history to concentrate on the religious and ideological aspects of anti-Semitism and Jewish responses to it, to the exclusion of social and economic factors present. We believe that this emphasis distorts our understanding of Jewish history. The traditional view tends to stress the image of Jews as victims and emphasizes the importance of Zionism as an ideology in recent Jewish history. Recent historians, however, while acknowledging the importance of religious identification as a factor in shaping both Christian and Muslim attitudes and behavior toward Jews, have drawn a more complete picture of Jewish history.

By placing more importance on the socioeconomic elements in the story, recent historical interpretations have restored dignity and pride to Jews. Throughout European history Jews made significant contributions in all walks of life; something quite inconsistent with the picture of a small religious, passive minority suffering unmitigated persecution and oppression. There is no doubt that Jews suffered persecution because of their religion at various times in European history, but that is far from the whole story. The Jewish people have maintained their ethnic, religious, and linguistic characteristics through the centuries primarily because they have been an ethnic minority that has fulfilled a distinct socioeconomic role in the societies in which they have lived. Most historians agree that Jews migrated from Palestine voluntarily long before the Christian epoch, forming merchant classes around the Mediterranean basin. The destruction of the Second Temple by the Romans in the year 70 C.E. led to a considerable increase in the number of the Jewish Diaspora, as those Jews who lived outside Palestine were called, and they were gradually transformed into a mercantile class.

In the Roman Empire, Jews played an important role in the economy as traders, financiers, goldsmiths, jewelers, and craftsmen, and, in doing so, they preserved their ethnic identity and separateness. After the Christianizing of the Roman Empire in the fourth century, during the Middle Ages, although Jews were permitted communal autonomy and self-government, religious antagonism against them led to Jews being gradually deprived of their rights as citizens and they were increasingly limited to certain professions.

In the High Middle Ages, Jews functioned primarily as moneylenders, and were dependent upon the rulers for protection. When Italian and other bankers began to take over their limited economic functions, the Jews were expelled, as from England in 1290, from France by the end of the next century, and from Spain in 1492. Where Jews remained in Europe, they were forced into prescribed residential areas that we know as *ghettos*. The first ghetto appeared in Italy in the sixteenth century. Many Jews left Western Europe for the Ottoman Empire and Eastern Europe—particularly Greater Lithuania (which included much of what is today western Russia and the Ukraine) and Poland—where they were initially welcomed because of their commercial skills. The Jewish community of greater Poland became the largest in the world, with impressive political and cultural institutions, but economic rivalry and religious antagonism eventually impoverished and threatened the community.

The growth of industrial capitalism more or less altered the economic function of Jews in Western Europe, and Jews gradually integrated into the capitalist and professional classes. The rationalism of the eighteenth century Enlightenment had also benefitted Jews and paved the way for their "emancipation" after the French Revolution. The ideals of the French Revolution nurtured the ideology of secular nationalism, so that by the end of the nineteenth century Jews had widely assimilated into the population of most Western European countries.

In Eastern Europe, however, the slow rate of industrialization and the hostile political and religious conditions led to the dislocation of Jews there, forcing them to seek new social and geographical horizons. As for the Russian Empire, ever since 1791 the Jews had been restricted to a region between the Black Sea and the Baltic known as the Pale of Settlement where they lived in poverty in small towns called *shtetls*. Much of the Pale was formerly Poland (in the late eighteenth century Poland was partitioned among Russia, Prussia, and Austria), and about three quarters of a million of the inhabitants of the Pale were former Polish Jews. Jews were excluded from the larger Russian cities and other parts of the country. In Czarist Russia, the ideas of the French Revolution were anathema, and Jews continued to be a scapegoat of the Russian people and Orthodox Church. Throughout the century Russian Jews were subjected to numerous restrictions and state-sponsored persecutions (pogroms). By 1850, there were about 2.3 million Jews in Russia, and despite massive emigration, forced conscription into the Russian Army, and deportations this figure was 5 million by the end of the century. In the 1880s, under the impact of successive savage pogroms in Russia and discriminatory legislation, many Eastern European Jews fled to the United States and, to a far lesser extent, to Palestine.

The Russian government sponsored massacres, restrictions, and persecutions of Jews following the assassination of Czar Alexander II of Russia in 1881 in which one of the plotters was found to be a young Jewess. The restrictions enforced within the Pale and in other Russian areas led to a mass migration in the next twenty years. Over a million people fled to the United States between 1880 and 1900; and this figure was to reach over 2.6 million by 1914. Others stayed and tried to revolutionize the system, but few chose this course. Those who did joined a radical socialist organization called the Bund, which, although it represented only a minority of the Jewish population, constituted a dynamic faction within the Russian revolutionary intelligentsia. Another solution was the reaffirmation of Jewish identity in a secular, socialist form through a movement whose goal was an autonomous Jewish nation-state. This was advocated by Leo Pinsker in his book, *Auto-Emancipation,* written in 1882, following the 1881 pogroms. However, the movement which would come to be known as Zionism received its greatest impetus from events that occurred in France in the 1890s.

THE BIRTH OF MODERN ZIONISM

The emancipation of the Jews in Western Europe aroused powerful anti-Semitic reflexes among the middle classes. Racial anti-Semitism—which defined and attacked Jews in terms of race rather than religion—emerged both in Germany and France from the 1840s on. Racial anti-Semitism relied on pseudo-scientific Social-Darwinian theories to "prove" the superiority of the Aryan race over the inferior Semitic race, and it was largely in response to this outbreak of anti-Semitism that modern Zionism emerged as presenting a viable alternative. It became clear to some that complete emancipation and equality of Jews was unobtainable even in advanced and enlightened Western Europe. Their solution was an autonomous Jewish nation-state.

This aspiration tapped another trend among the traditionalist Jews of Eastern Europe—that of preserving Judaism and the Jewish tradition through the reestablishment of a religious-based Jewish culture located in the traditional Jewish homeland Eretz Yisrael. The coming together of these two aspirations—one secular, the other religious—led to the birth of modern Zionism as a political ideology and organizational tool, and it contributed to the settlements that became the foundation of the economic, social, and cultural rebirth of the Jewish nation. Small groups of Jewish youths (mainly students) met in Russia and other parts of Eastern Europe and planned the kind of settlements they would set up in Eretz Yisrael.

The first small group of the new movement, known as *Hibbat*—or *Hovevei*— *Zion* (Lovers of Zion), numbering fourteen and including one woman, landed at Jaffa on July 7, 1882. This was the beginning of the first modern wave of Jewish immigrants to Palestine, which lasted from 1881 to 1903 and is known as the first *aliyah,* which means "going up" to the Land of Israel. By 1903 about twenty new agricultural villages had been founded, about 90,000 acres of land had been purchased, and some 10,000 Jews had settled in the country, about half of them on the soil. Hebrew was being spoken and taught in a few schools, but by and large the settlers were not accustomed to farm work; they had insufficient funds, and had it not been for the generous support of Baron Edmond de Rothschild, who assisted the newcomers, the entire venture could have failed. As it was, the scheme had come to a standstill by 1903.

The French philanthropist Baron Edmond de Rothschild was not a Zionist, but he was interested in sponsoring Jewish settlement in Palestine as an investment, and as an act of piety. He bought land from the Arab effendi (landowners), now and then using bribes to do so, and drove the fellahin off the land. They were then replaced by Jewish settlers. By 1900 he had subsidized over 350 families and 19 Jewish settlements and had established a Jewish agricultural school: altogether a population of around 5,000 and over 68,000 acres. Until he transferred the venture to the Jewish Colonization Association, led by Baron Maurice de Hirsch in 1900, Rothschild maintained strict control over his settlements, and several Jewish settlers soon took to employing Arabs as peasant farmers, in some cases treating them with hostility and cruelty, rather than working the land themselves.

By 1904, these early Jewish settlements were Jewish in name only, as almost all the labor was performed by Arab peasant workers. One observer noted that for every few dozen Jews, there appeared to be hundreds of Arabs. We should note that Rothschild was not the only wealthy Jew the Ottoman Sultan had allowed to purchase land for Jewish settlement in Palestine. Sir Moses Montefiore, a British Jew, was permitted to buy land as early as 1856, and the Belgian railroad magnate Baron Maurice de Hirsch, an associate of Rothschild, was another who poured millions of francs into Palestinian settlement schemes.

SOCIALISM AND ZIONISM

The second aliyah, which began in 1904, was made up of many young Russian pioneers who were committed to a return to the land. Dismayed at the course which Zionist colonization had been taking, they attempted to reintroduce the idea of Jewish labor. They differed from the earlier settlers also in that the land they worked was purchased by the Jewish National Fund (established in 1901) and was deemed to be inalienable Jewish national property and thus protected from property speculation and the kinds of contracts imposed on the settlers by Rothschild. The new pioneers were also strongly influenced by socialist ideas and many belonged to the *Poalei-Zion*—

Socialist or Labor Zionist—party that was formed between 1903 and 1906. Among the leaders of this group were David Ben-Gurion and Izhak Ben-Zvi, and they introduced a spirit of enterprise in the settlements and also in the towns. This aliyah, for example, established the garden suburb of Tel Aviv on the outskirts of Jaffa in 1909. By 1914, it had a population of 2,000. In 1909, the first collective settlement, or *kibbutz,* Deganiah—the birthplace of Moshe Dayan—was established, and, in 1921, the first *moshav,* or cooperative village—an outgrowth of the kibbutz—was established.

Of the approximately 40,000 new immigrants who arrived between 1904 and the outbreak of World War I, a very large number left the country because of the inhospitable climate and conditions. Some estimate the figure of emigrants as high as 90 percent. By 1914, there were about forty Jewish settlements in Palestine, owning about 100,000 acres, but only about 4 percent of this land was owned by the Jewish National Fund. The population of Palestine at that time was over half a million (estimated to be 650,000); 85,000 (13%) were Jews, of whom about 12,000 belonged to kibbutzim and moshavim. About 5,000 Arabs worked on Jewish land. Between 1882 and 1914 more than 100,000 Jews had emigrated to the Holy Land, but only about 50,000 remained.

Many Zionists have explained the increase in Jewish settlement in Palestine as a reflection of the growing appeal and strength of Zionism. The difficulty with this explanation is that, despite the deep feeling of attachment to the land of Israel, which is such a distinctive feature of Jewish self-identity, the simple reality is that Jews did not move to the land of Zion, a land they prayed to be delivered to three times a day. This is the paradox of Zionism. Only about 1 percent of the almost 3 million Jews who emigrated from Russia in the thirty-five years following 1880 went to Palestine, and very few emigrated from Western Europe. Zionism was not the answer to the "Jewish question" for the great majority of Jews. This is largely because Zionism was not seen as a solution to the traditional Jewish problems of economic, political, social, religious, and racial oppression in Europe. Indeed, the Jewish experience in the United States, where so many settled, has proven a viable alternative to resettlement in Palestine. And despite the exceptions, in the period between 1815 and 1914, Jews had moved from the periphery to the center of European society; they had been great beneficiaries of the Enlightenment, Emancipation, and Industrial Revolution. From any conceivable point of view, the nineteenth century was the best century Jews had ever experienced, collectively and individually. The European Jewish population increased from 2 million at the end of the eighteenth century, to 7.5 million in 1880 and 13 million by 1914. This was twice the rate of population increase of non-Jews. The Jewish problem by the end of the nineteenth century was a new one: how could Jews and Christians define themselves in an emancipated and liberal secular environment where none of the traditional religious barriers existed?

The nineteenth century saw the emergence of the modern, secular liberal state in Europe, and increasingly Christians began to identify themselves in these secular and ethnic terms. Zionism was the Jewish answer to establishing this secular identity—a national state for Jews. It is sometimes called "secular messianism." It was this nationalist dimension that transformed the passive, quietistic, and pious hope of the Return to Zion into an effective social force. Zionism, then, was not simply an assertion of the links of Jews to Palestine; nor was it just a reaction of a people to persecution. It was a quest for self-determination and liberation in a modern, secular, and liberal age. Zionism was also a recognition that it was futile, impossible, and pointless to try to fight anti-Semitism; Zionism was an escape from it. Looking back, especially at events in Nazi Germany, the fears of Zionists seem to have been reinforced beyond all measure. Understanding Zionism in this way enables us to explain the role of Theodor Herzl.

THEODOR HERZL AND THE EMERGENCE OF POLITICAL ZIONISM

Theodor Herzl, more than any other person, has become identified with the emergence of modern Zionism. His life (1860–1904) has acquired legendary proportions, his portrait one of the trademarks of Zionism, and the symbolism of charismatic leadership attached to his personality has become a powerful element in Zionism. In many ways this is strange, because few of Herzl's ideas were new or original. He had no financial backing and no political support; indeed, many Jewish leaders saw him as an eccentric, irresponsible egotist. He was not a political extremist; in fact, his politics were conservative and reflected his middle-class background. But Herzl was incredibly successful in bringing ideas that were known only in Jewish communities to the attention of the world and into the general consciousness of the age. He transformed one solution to the plight of Jews into a major issue in world politics.

Herzl was born in Budapest where his father was a well-to-do merchant. When he was young, his family moved to Vienna where he graduated in law and became one of the most popular journalists of the liberal Viennese newspaper, the *Neue Freie Presse*. Herzl was a typical product of the emancipation of European Jewry, and as a journalist in Vienna, and from 1891 in Paris, he worried about the increasing ambiguity of the position of Jews in Europe, and the anti-Semitism that was so dramatically illustrated by the notorious Dreyfus Affair.

Alfred Dreyfus was a Jewish officer of the French General Staff who in 1894 was convicted of treason and sentenced to a life term on Devil's Island. Herzl was one of many who believed that Dreyfus had been framed and the trial rigged. That this was the case emerged later with the confession in 1899 of one of the French officers involved, and the lifting of Dreyfus's sentence, following a second retrial, in 1906. But Herzl, who covered the trial and public disgrace of Dreyfus for the *Neue Freie Presse*, was

Theodor Herzl with his mother.

shocked by the anti-Semitism the trial unleashed in France, the land of Liberty, Equality, and Fraternity. The Dreyfus Affair became the symbol of Jewish inequality and anti-Semitism in Europe and confirmed in Herzl's mind the belief that anti-Semitism was an incurable Gentile pathology. The only solution was for Jews to have a nation state of their own. Herzl set out this proposition in his book *Der Judenstaat (The Jews' State)*, published in 1896. (See Document 1–3.)

An early theoretician of Zionism had been Moses Hess, a German Jew who in his youth was associated with Karl Marx and Friedrich Engels. Hess, unlike Marx, maintained his Judaism and kept up the Yiddish he learned as a child. Hess wrote two works outlining his ideas for Jewish return to Palestine: *Rome and Jerusalem* (published in 1862) and *Plan for the Colonization of the Holy Land* (1867). However, Hess's books, which advocated the colonization of Palestine as a solution to the Jewish problem, were not considered seriously, as Western Jews felt settled in the countries in which they had lived for hundreds of years, and Eastern Jews were yet to experience the pogroms of twenty years later. Herzl, as noted above, had also been foreshadowed by Leo Pinsker. The word "Zionism" itself was probably first used in an article published in 1886 by Nathan Birnbaum. The term has come to mean the movement to reestablish a Jewish nation in Palestine, although for many years the more vague phrase "national home" was used.

The turning point in the history of Zionism came with the first Zionist Congress, which met in Basel (Switzerland) on August 29, 1897, with 204 delegates from all over the world. The assembly defined the objective of Zionism: "to create for the Jewish people a home in Palestine secured by public law." To achieve this goal the assembly resolved to promote systematically the settlement of Palestine with Jewish agriculturalists, artisans, and craftsmen; to organize all Jews and strengthen the national consciousness of Jews; and to seek the approval of whatever governments were necessary to achieve the goals of Zionism. (See Document 1–4.)

What is important to recognize about these goals is their vagueness or open-endedness. We must keep this in mind when we consider the response of Herzl and later Zionist leaders to offers that were made to them by various governments in subsequent years. Herzl was quite prepared, for example, to consider the British offer of the el-Arish region in the Sinai Peninsula made in 1902, and the offer in the following year of a territory in Kenya (the so-called Uganda Plan), although Russian Jews were not happy with these schemes. Cyprus had also been considered briefly in 1899. Nevertheless, however vague Herzl's Zionist vision, dependence upon a European power was prophetic of what later happened.

Although Herzl left open the specific location of the Jewish homeland, he had a clear idea of how to implement the plan. A Jewish company would be formed to purchase land and to organize the settlers, rather like the Rhodesian experience. Following the Basel Congress, the newly formed World Zionist Organization set out to build the financial and economic instruments and political structure to achieve these aims. In 1901, the Jewish National Fund was established for the purchase of land, and in 1908 the Palestine Land Development Company, linked to the Jewish National Fund, was also created to assist in the colonization. Herzl continued his efforts to gain international support for the plan, but he was unsuccessful in his negotiations with the Sultan Abdul-Hamid, with the German Kaiser, and, in October 1902, with British Colonial Secretary Joseph Chamberlain. Although a persuasive speaker and a striking figure of a man, Herzl was unable to gain the support he needed from Europe's political leaders, or within the Zionist organization he had done so much to create.

Herzl's political goals, for example, were not supported by all Zionist leaders. Asher Ginsberg, a Russian intellectual better known by his pen-name Ahad Ha-Am ("One of the People"), one of the most influential voices in the Zionist movement, feared the consequences of a purely political entity. He saw Zionism as a spiritual-cultural phenomenon, and envisaged the gradual building up of Palestine by only those committed to the task. Moreover, unlike some Zionists leaders who viewed Palestine as a "land without people for a people without land," Ahad Ha-Am recognized the Arab presence in Palestine, and, in an 1891 essay again attacking the "mere" political Zionism of Herzl, he warned against neglecting the Arab question.

JEWS IN NINETEENTH CENTURY PALESTINE

The Jewish population of Palestine and Syria at the beginning of the nineteenth century totalled about 25,000. Most were *Sephardim;* that is, descendants of Spanish Jewry and ancient local families, and they were Ottoman subjects. The rest were *Ashkenazim;* that is, Jews of European origin who had come to the Holy Land throughout the centuries, and they retained their former citizenship. The Jews lived mostly in cities: about half of them in the four towns particularly holy to Jews—Jerusalem, Hebron, Safed, and Tiberias, and half in the Syrian cities of Aleppo, Damascus, Beirut, and Tripoli. The Muslim-Ottoman state was organized on a system of self-governing groups (*millets*), and the Jewish communities were given a considerable degree of autonomy and self-government in matters of religious worship, education, and other areas, but overall the position of Jews was precarious. The Ottoman state was based on the principle of Muslim superiority, and the Jews, along with the Christians, were regarded as unbelievers and second-class citizens (dhimmis), and had to pay a special poll tax (*jizyah*) for the protection of the state, and as a sign of their inferior status.

Jews were subject to a number of discriminatory regulations. For example, their testimony against Muslims in a court of law was not accepted; they were normally not

Tel Aviv in 1921 with the Arab city of Jaffa in the background (*Photo courtesy of the Israel Office of Information*).

The Jewish Population of Palestine

eligible for appointment to the highest administrative offices; they were forbidden to carry arms or to serve in the army; and they were often subjected to oppression, extortion, or violence by both the local authorities and the Muslim population. During the 1840s and 1850s the position of Jews in Palestine improved, however, This significant change in their religious, economic, and political conditions led to a considerable increase in the numbers of Palestinian Jews through immigration from Europe, and by the end of the century they had consolidated their position.

The improvement in the situation of Jews in Palestine coincided with the end of the decade of Egyptian rule of Palestine and Syria, which occurred between 1831 and 1840. The change was brought about partly because of reforms within the Ottoman Empire itself (the Tanzimat reform), which aimed at political and religious equality for all Ottoman subjects, and partly because of increasing indirect European involvement and intervention in the affairs of the Empire. Consular reports from the 1850s indicate, for example, that Jews obtained more redress from the local governors in Palestine and that the oppression of the Turkish governors almost completely ceased. Jews observed their religion without opposition, and they gradually obtained better treatment and more justice in the courts. Some European consulates, particularly the British, and to a lesser extent the Russian, Austrian, and Prussian, also intervened more actively on behalf of Jews of their nationalities.

BRITISH AND RUSSIAN POLICY

The British Government in particular began showing an interest in the Jews of Palestine. This interest was both humanitarian and political. Even at this early stage, Viscount Palmerston, the British Foreign Secretary, perceived the emerging Jewish national feeling for Palestine, and he hoped that he could gain the support of the Jewish community for British aims in the Middle East in return for British protection. During the 1850s, the Russian government also assisted Russian and Polish Jews in Palestine and even allowed Jewish emigrants to travel cheaply in Russian ships that were sailing from Odessa to Palestine. Not surprisingly, the number of Jews emigrating from Europe, especially from Russia, dramatically increased during these decades. Thus, the Jewish population of Jerusalem increased from around 5,000 in 1839 to about 10,000 by the late 1850s. Of course, European protection of Jews was not comprehensive because most Jews in Palestine were Ottoman subjects, and sometimes foreign protection was a liability rather than an asset, because such Jews were regarded as collaborating with foreign powers.

In the final analysis, the welfare of local Jews was dependent upon the attitudes of the local Ottoman authorities and the Muslim population, and during the second half of the nineteenth century the attitudes of both these groups toward Jews underwent a gradual improvement because of the new generation of more liberal pashas. The Jews of Palestine also made an effort to live independently of assistance from Europe, making their living as artisans, craftsmen, and agricultural workers. At the same time, Western European Jews were becoming increasingly aware of the depressed condition of their brethren in Eastern Europe and they increased the level of their aid. The improved Muslim-Jewish relations provided the Jews of Palestine the opportunity to consolidate their position, to advance socially and economically, and, perhaps even more importantly, to increase considerably in number through immigration from Europe, and to become an important element in the country.

PALESTINE ON THE EVE OF WORLD WAR I

By the outbreak of World War I the Jewish community (*Yishuv*) numbered about 90,000 people, or about 12 to 14 percent of the total population of Palestine. This represented a higher proportion of Jews than in any other country, and in some sanjaks, like that of Jerusalem, they represented about 25 percent of the population. Jewish population figures in the major centers were as follows: 45,000 out of 80,000 in Jerusalem; 5,000 out of 8,000 in Tiberias; 7,000 out of 15,000 in Safed; 12,000 out of 50,000 in Jaffa; and 3,000 out of 20,000 in Haifa. The Jewish community presented a strange paradox, however. It constituted the center of traditional Judaism and of the Jewish national movement; but at the same time it was the most divided Jewish community in the world. Not only did it fail to establish an organization uniting the Jewish population of the country as a whole, but it also had great difficulty in unifying individual local communities.

Internal divisions before 1914 were so deeply entrenched in the social character of the Yishuv that even "practical" Zionists, those determined to establish a modern title to Palestine through Jewish economic enterprise and colonization, were unable to achieve much success. Events in the Ottoman Empire after 1908 set in motion a process that did lead to the overall organization and unification of the Yishuv but, by 1914, this process had not been achieved. Even the millet framework of the Ottoman Empire, which, following the millet law of 1865, granted fairly wide judicial powers to the rabbinical authorities, did not unite the Jews of Palestine—again because it applied only to Ottoman subjects. The great majority of Jews who migrated to Palestine up until the 1880s retained their previous nationalities, and the division between the Sephardic (non-European) Jews and the Ashkenazic (European) Jews kept them apart organizationally, ethnically, liturgically, and linguistically. Attachment to a particular ethnic or national community was stronger for most Jews than attachment to the Yishuv as a whole.

The new settlements of the early 1880s—the "new" Yishuv—carried with them the idea of national unity, but they lacked cohesion from the very beginning. They were not the result of a comprehensive organization or program, but were founded by various associations and individuals who lacked a practical economic plan. Nor did they consider the relationships that should exist among the new settlements and the existing Jewish communities, the local population, or the government. Indeed, the early groups did little beyond purchasing land and setting up newly formed settlements. They did not seek Ottoman citizenship, but, as in the case of one of the first such settlements, Rosh Pina, instead sought to establish separate Jewish settlements adjacent to existing Arab communities under the protection of the European consuls.

While there was contact between the existing Jewish community and the new settlers, there was little sign of communal unity before 1908, although some young intellectuals, merchants, and professionals did form groups such as *Bnei Israel* and *Bnei Yehuda* to overcome communal divisions. The *Hibbat Zion* movement attempted without much success to unite the various national communities. The conflict was based on ideological and practical differences between the old and new Yishuv. The new settlers regarded the existing Jewish community as nonproductive, living off *halukkah* (donations from Jews abroad). The older community, which comprised a large number of artisans, unskilled laborers, small shopkeepers, and Talmudic scholars, did live a rather precarious life. Nevertheless, they resisted attempts to change their traditional ways. Some of the new Yishuv also moved into the cities, but where they did so, in towns like Jaffa and Haifa, they took up trades and commerce so as to be independent of overseas support. The Young Turk revolution in 1908 highlighted the divisions between the old and new Yishuvim. The older Sephardic intelligentsia and leadership saw the revolution as leading to Jewish development within the Ottoman Empire. The new Yishuv and "practical" Zionists, on the other hand, believed that little could be achieved through negotiations with Constantinople and stressed the importance of strengthening the Yishuv in Palestine, independently of Constantinople.

There was little unified Arab opposition to Jewish immigration and land purchases in the late nineteenth and early twentieth centuries. Ottoman officials and large landowners in the north seemed willing to ignore regulations restricting Jewish immigration and land sales. Local authorities frequently allowed Jewish land purchases in return for financial favors. Initial Arab peasant opposition subsided when the peasants realized that Jewish landowners would maintain the tradition of permitting them to work the land and keep their income. Interestingly, public opposition to Zionist settlement was led by the Greek Orthodox Christians of Palestine. The editors of the two newspapers most vociferous in their hostility to Jewish settlement and exclusiveness, *al-Karmal* (established in 1908) and *Filastin* (1911), were both Greek Orthodox.

Jewish settlement in early twentieth century, Palestine (*Photo courtesy of The Library of Congress*).

We can see then that at the outbreak of World War I Palestine was at a critical juncture as far as relations between Palestinian Arabs and Jews were concerned. There was, on the one hand, a rapidly increasing Jewish population with very different attitudes and aspirations from the traditional Jewish population both with regard to the future of the land itself and the existing Arab population. And, on the other hand, there was an Arab population experiencing dramatic changes as the result of the actions of their own leaders, as well as those of the Jewish arrivals and their supporters overseas. Not only was some of the Arab land they worked on being sold to Jewish settlers, but Palestine was being slowly but surely integrated into the European world economy. This was bringing with it changes in the traditional methods of agriculture, and in the government and administration of their lives. The region was also being drawn into the diplomatic vortex of the world powers; all this was to change Palestine in ways no one could have foreseen in 1914.

SUGGESTIONS FOR FURTHER READING

ANTONIUS, GEORGE, *The Arab Awakening: The Story of The Arab National Movement,* New York, Capricorn Books, 1946.

HAIM, SYLVIA, ed., *Arab Nationalism: An Anthology,* Berkeley, University of California Press, 1964.

LAQUEUR, WALTER, *A History of Zionism,* New York, Weidenfeld & Nicholson, 1974.

MANDEL, NEVILLE, *The Arabs and Zionism before World War I,* Berkeley, University of California Press, 1976.

MA-OZ, MOSHE, ed., *Studies on Palestine During the Ottoman Period,* Jerusalem, Magnes Press, 1975.

PAWEL, ERNST, *The Labyrinth of Exile: A Life of Theodor Herzl,* New York. Farrar, Straus & Giroux, 1989.

**Program of the
League of the Arab Fatherland
Negib Azoury**

THERE IS NOTHING MORE liberal than the league's program.

The league wants, before anything else, to separate the civil and the religious power, in the interest of Islam and the Arab nation, and to form an Arab empire stretching from the Tigris and the Euphrates to the Suez Isthmus, and from the Mediterranean to the Arabian Sea.

The mode of government will be a constitutional sultanate based on the freedom of all the religions and the equality of all the citizens before the law. It will respect the interests of Europe, all the concessions and all the privileges which had been granted to her up to now by the Turks. It will also respect the autonomy of the Lebanon, and the independence of the principalities of Yemen, Nejd, and Iraq.

The league offers the throne of the Arab Empire to that prince of the Khedivial family of Egypt who will openly declare himself in its favor and who will devote his energy and his resources to this end.

It rejects the idea of unifying Egypt and the Arab Empire under the same monarchy, because the Egyptians do not belong to the Arab race; they are of the African Berber family and the language which they spoke before Islam bears no similarity to Arabic. There exists, moreover, between Egypt and the Arab Empire a natural frontier which must be respected in order to avoid the introduction, in the new state, of the germs of discord and destruction. Never, as a matter of fact, have the ancient Arab caliphs succeeded for any length of time in controlling the two countries at the same time.

The Arab fatherland also offers the universal religious caliphate over the whole of Islam to that sherif (descendant of the Prophet) who will sincerely embrace its cause and devote himself to this work. The religious caliph will have as a completely independent political state the whole of the actual vilayet of Hijaz, with the town and the territory of Medina, as far as Aqaba. He will enjoy the honors of a sovereign and will hold a real moral authority over all the Muslims of the world.

Le Réveil de la Nation Arabe dans l'Asie Turque en Présence des Intéréts et des Rivalités des Puissances Étrangères, de la Curie Romaine et du Patriarcat Oecuménique (Paris, 1905), pp. 245–247, 248. (S. G. H.)

Source: Sylvia Haim, *Arab Nationalism: An Anthology* (Berkeley: University of California Press, 1964), pp. 81–82.

Announcement to the Arabs, Sons of Qahtan

*See how on the day of battle we fill
the universe with flame and fire*

O SONS OF QAHTAN! O Descendants of Adnan! Are you asleep? And how long will you remain asleep? How can you remain deep in your slumber when the voices of the nations around you have deafened everyone? Do you not hear the commotion all around you? Do you not know that you live in a period when he who sleeps dies, and he who dies is gone forever? When will you open your eyes and see the glitter of the bayonets which are directed at you, and the lightning of the swords which are drawn over your heads? When will you realize the truth? When will you know that your country has been sold to the foreigner? See how your natural resources have been alienated from you and have come into the possession of England, France, and Germany. Have you no right to these resources? You have become humiliated slaves in the hands of the usurping tyrant; the foreigner unjustly disposseses you of the fruit of your work and labor and leaves you to suffer the pangs of hunger. How long will it be before you understand that you have become a plaything in the hand of him who has no religion but to kill the Arabs and forcibly to seize their possessions? The Country is yours, and they say that rule belongs to the people, but those who exercise rule over you in the name of the Constitution do not consider you part of the people, for they inflict on you all kinds of suffering, tyranny, and persecution. How, then, can they concede to you any political rights? In their eyes you are but a flock of sheep whose wool is to be clipped, whose milk is to be drunk, and whose meat is to be eaten. Your country they consider a plantation which they inherited from their fathers, a country the inhabitants of which are their humble slaves. Where is your Qahtanic honor? Where your Adnanian pride?

Manifesto of Arab Nationalists disseminated from Cairo at beginning of World War I, printed by Ahmed Izzat al-A'zami, *The Arab Question,* vol. IV (Baghdad, 1932), pp. 108–117.

Arise, O ye Arabs! Unsheathe the sword from the scabbard, ye sons of Qahtan! Do not allow an oppressive tyrant who has only disdain for you to remain in your country; cleanse your country from those who show their enmity to you, to your race and to your language.

O ye Arabs! Warn the people of the Yemen, of Asir, of Nejd, and of Iraq against the intrigues of your enemies. Be united, in the Syrian and Iraqi provinces, with the members of your race and fatherland. Let the Muslims, the Christians, and the Jews be as one in working for the interest of the nation and of the country. You all dwell in one land, you speak one language, so be also one nation and one hand. Do not become divided against yourselves according to the designs and purposes of the troublemakers who feign Islam, while Islam is really innocent of their misdeeds. . . .

Unite then and help one another, and do not say, O ye Muslims: This is a Christian, and this is a Jew, for you are all God's dependents, and religion is for God alone. God has commanded us, in his precious Arabic Book and at the hand of his Arab Adnanian Prophet, to follow justice and equality, to deal faithfully with him who does not fight us, even though his religion is different, and to fight him who uses us tyrannously. . . .

Know, all ye Arabs, that a *fada'i* society has been formed which will kill all those who fight the Arabs and oppose the reform of Arab lands. The reform of which we speak is not on the principle of decentralization coupled with allegiance to the minions of Constantinople, but on the principle of complete independence and the formation of a decentralized Arab state which will revive our ancient glories and rule the country on autonomous lines, according to the needs of each province. This state will begin by liquidating some flattering foxes among the Arabs who are, and have always been, the means whereby these murderous minions have trampled on our rights, as the world will see when they proceed to bring about the disasters they have in store for us.

Source: Haim, *Arab Nationalism: An Anthology,* pp. 83–84.

Excerpts from Theodor Herzl, *Der Judenstaat* (*The Jews' State*), published in 1896.

. . . The Jewish question still exists. It would be foolish to deny it. It is a remnant of the Middle Ages, which civilized nations do not even yet seem able to shake off, try as they will. They certainly showed a generous desire to do so when they emancipated us. The Jewish question exists wherever Jews live in perceptible numbers. Where it does not exist, it is carried by Jews in the course of their migrations. We naturally move to those places where we are not persecuted, and there our presence produces persecution. This is the case in every country, and will remain so, even in those highly civilized—for instance, France—until the Jewish question finds a solution on a political basis. The unfortunate Jews are now carrying the seeds of Anti-Semitism into England; they have already introduced it into America.

I believe that I understand Anti-Semitism, which is really a highly complex movement. I consider it from a Jewish standpoint, yet without fear or hatred. I believe that I can see what elements there are in it of vulgar sport, of common trade jealousy, of inherited prejudice, of religious intolerance, and also of pretended self-defence. I think the Jewish question is no more a social than a religious one, notwithstanding that it sometimes takes these and other forms. It is a national question, which can only be solved by making it a political world-question to be discussed and settled by the civilized nations of the world in council.

We are a people—one people.

.   .   .

Oppression and persecution cannot exterminate us. No nation on earth has survived such struggles and sufferings as we have gone through. . . .

No one can deny the gravity of the situation of the Jews. Wherever they live in perceptible numbers they are more or less persecuted. Their equality before the law, granted by statute, has become practically a dead letter. They are debarred from filling even moderately high positions, either in the army, or in any public or private capacity. And attempts are made to thrust them out of business also: "Don't buy from Jews!" . . . .

Everything tends, in fact, to one and the same conclusion, which is clearly enunciated in that classic Berlin phrase: *Juden Raus!"* (Out with the Jews!)

I shall now put the Question in the briefest possible form: Are we to "get out" now and where to?

Or, may we yet remain? And, how long?

Let us first settle the point of staying where we are. Can we hope for better days, can we possess our souls in patience, can we wait in pious resignation till the princes and peoples of this earth are more mercifully disposed towards us? I say that we cannot hope for a change in the current of feeling. And why not? Even if we were as near to the hearts of princes as are their other subjects, they could not protect us. They would only feel popular hatred by showing us too much favor. By "too much," I really mean less than is claimed as a right by every ordinary citizen, or by every race. The nations in whose midst Jews live are all either covertly or openly Anti-Semitic.

The common people have not, and indeed cannot have, any historic comprehension. They do not know that the sins of the Middle Ages are now being visited on the nations of Europe. We are what the Ghetto made us. We have attained pre-eminence in finance, because mediaeval conditions drove us to it. The same process is now being repeated. We are again being forced into finance, now it is the stock exchange, by being kept out of other branches of economic activity. Being on the stock exchange, we are consequently exposed afresh to contempt. At the same time we continue to produce an abundance of mediocre intellects who find no outlet, and this endangers our social position as much as does our increasing wealth. Educated Jews without means are now rapidly becoming Socialists. Hence we are certain to suffer very severely in the struggle between classes, because we stand in the most exposed position in the camps of both Socialists and capitalists. . . .

The Plan

The whole plan is in its essence perfectly simple, as it must necessarily be if it is to come within the comprehension of all.

Let the sovereignty be granted us over a portion of the globe large enough to satisfy the rightful requirements of a nation; the rest we shall manage for ourselves.

The creation of a new State is neither ridiculous nor impossible. We have in our day witnessed the process in connection with nations which were not largely members of the middle class, but poorer, less educated, and consequently weaker than ourselves. The Governments of all countries scourged by Anti-Semitism will be keenly interested in assisting us to obtain the sovereignty we want.

The plan, simple in design, but complicated in execution, will be carried out by two agencies: The Society of Jews and the Jewish Company.

The Society of Jews will do the preparatory work in the domains of science and politics, which the Jewish Company will afterwards apply practically.

The Jewish Company will be the liquidating agent of the business interests of departing Jews, and will organize commerce and trade in the new country.

We must not imagine the departure of the Jews to be a sudden one. It will be gradual, continuous, and will cover many decades. The poorest will go first to cultivate the soil. In accordance with a preconceived plan, they will construct roads, bridges, railways and telegraph installations; regulate rivers; and build their own dwellings; their labor will create trade, trade will create markets and markets will attract new settlers, for every man will go voluntarily, at his own expense and his own risk. The labor expended on the land will enhance its value, and the Jews will soon perceive that a new and permanent sphere of operation is opening here for that spirit of enterprise which has heretofore met only with hatred and obloquy.

This pamphlet will open a general discussion on the Jewish Question, but that does not mean that there will be any voting on it. Such a result would ruin the cause from the outset, and dissidents must remember that allegiance or opposition is entirely voluntary. He who will not come with us should remain behind.

Source: Walter Laqueur and Barry Rubin, eds., *The Israel–Arab Reader: A Documentary History of the Middle East Conflict,* 4th ed. (New York: Penguin Books, 1984), pp. 6–11.

DOCUMENT 1–4

The Basel Declaration

This official statement of Zionist purpose was adopted by the first Zionist Congress in Basel in August 1897.

The aim of Zionism is to create for the Jewish people a home in Palestine secured by public law.

The Congress contemplates the following means to the attainment of this end:

1. The promotion, on suitable lines, of the colonization of Palestine by Jewish agricultural and industrial workers.

2. The organization and binding together of the whole of Jewry by means of appropriate institutions, local and international, in accordance with the laws of each country.

3. The strengthening and fostering of Jewish national sentiment and consciousness.

4. Preparatory steps toward obtaining government consent, where necessary, to the attainment of the aim of Zionism.

Source: Laqueur and Rubin, *Israel–Arab Reader,* pp. 11–12.

CHAPTER 2 | PALESTINE DURING THE MANDATE

CHRONOLOGY

Aug. 1914	World War I begins	**Spring 1921**	Haycraft investigation
Nov. 1914	Ottoman Empire enters war on side of Germany	**June 1922**	British White Paper reaffirms Balfour Declaration; limits Jewish immigration to economic absorptive capacity of country
May 1915	The Damascus Protocol		
July 1915– March 1916	Hussein–McMahon Correspondence	**July 1922**	Palestine Mandate ratified by League of Nations. Includes Balfour Declaration but provides for possible separate development of Transjordan
May 1916	Sykes–Picot Agreement		
June 1916	Arab Revolt begins		
Nov. 1917	Balfour Declaration		
Dec. 1917	Allenby captures Jerusalem	**Sept. 1922**	Transjordan exempted from provisions of Balfour Declaration
June 1918	Declaration to the Seven		
1918– 1919	Meetings between Feisal and Weizmann	**June 1925**	Hebrew University opens
Aug. 1919	King–Crane Commission report	**Aug. 1929**	Riots at Western (Wailing) Wall and massacre of Jews in Jerusalem, Safed, and Hebron
March 1920	Arab Nationalist Congress proclaims Feisal King of Greater Syria		
		March 1930	Shaw Commission Report
April 1920	San Remo Conference assigns mandate for Palestine to Great Britain	**Oct. 1930**	Hope–Simpson Report and Passfield White Paper halting Jewish immigration and land sales
July 1920	Feisal expelled from Syria by French; established as King of Iraq by British		
		Feb. 1931	MacDonald letter negates White Paper provisions
1920 1921	Arab attacks on Jewish areas of Jerusalem and Jaffa	**April 1936**	Arab Higher Committee formed
March 1921	Haganah formed	**1936– 1939**	Arab Rebellion in Palestine
March 1921	Transjordan becomes separate entity within Palestine Mandate; Abdullah established as emir, or prince	**July 1937**	Peel Commission Report
		July 1938	Evian-les-Bains Refugee Conference
		May 1939	White Paper restricts Jewish land purchases and immigration
April 1921	Haj Amin al-Husseini appointed Grand Mufti and head of the Supreme Moslem Council by British High Commissioner, Sir Herbert Samuel	**Sept. 1939**	World War II begins
		May 1942	Biltmore Declaration calls for Jewish state in all of Palestine
		Nov. 1942	Allied victory at el-Alamein

At the outbreak of war in 1914, Palestine was the southern part of what was known as geographical Syria. This area, situated between the Suez Canal to the west and the Persian Gulf and India to the east, was of strategic importance especially for the British and was considered vital to their geopolitical and economic interests. When the Ottoman Empire, the "sick man of Europe," joined Germany against the Allied powers of England, France, and Russia, the opportunity arose for Britain to secure allies and influence in the region by appealing to the aspirations of the Empire's subject peoples. Many of these groups were eager to achieve self-determination should the Ottoman Empire go down to defeat. The British, quick to see the advantages of the situation, held discussions with both Arabs and Jews about support for Allied war aims in return for pledges to support the goals of both communities in the region after the war. The tragedy of the Arab–Israeli conflict is that both Arabs and Jews have equally persuasive claims to the same piece of territory. In 1914, that territory was under the control of a third party, the Turks, about to be defeated by powers that manipulated the situation primarily in their own interests.

The British had to coordinate policy with their allies and planned the partition of the Ottoman Empire with France, Russia, and Italy even while the war was in progress. The welter of secret agreements and public declarations both during and immediately following the hostilities resulted in misunderstanding, confusion, and contradictions that have plagued the Middle East ever since. With regard to the Fertile Crescent area generally, and to Palestine in particular, there were three such sets of agreements and statements that enormously complicated the postwar settlement. These were the Hussein–McMahon Correspondence of 1915–1916; the Sykes–Picot Agreement of 1916; and the Balfour Declaration of 1917.

THE HUSSEIN–MCMAHON CORRESPONDENCE

Sherif Hussein of Mecca, ruler of the Hejaz, was perhaps the one Arab figure at that time with prestige and potential power. As a Hashemite, and therefore a member of the Prophet Muhammad's house, and as guardian of the Holy Places of Islam, he was the natural spokesman for the Arabs. Contacts between Hussein and the British High Commissioner in Egypt, Sir Henry McMahon, had begun as early as 1914. After the war broke out, they exchanged a series of letters that discussed the conditions for an Arab uprising against the Turks in return for the independence of the Arabs and perhaps the reestablishment of an Arab Caliphate under Hussein, a pressing concern of the Sherif. In the letters, the British expressed sympathy for Arab claims to the Arabic-speaking parts of the western Asian provinces of the Ottoman Empire, excluding Egypt and Aden, which Hussein recognized as areas of British hegemony. McMahon, moreover, also excluded from consideration in an Arab state or states the southern parts of Iraq from Baghdad to Basra, which he asked the Arabs to acknowledge as a region of British-established position and influence; the districts of Mersin (in the vilayet of Adana) and Alexandretta in northern Syria; and those parts of Syria to the west of the districts of Aleppo, Hama, Homs, and Damascus. (See Documents 2–1 through 2–3.) This area of the Levant had had a somewhat separate history since 1861, when the Ottoman government created a special administrative council consisting of representatives of the principal religious groups in Lebanon. In the following years, close religious, commercial and cultural ties developed between the French and the Maronite Christians in particular. In the Hussein–McMahon exchange, the British recognized the special interest of their ally France in the vilayets of Aleppo and Beirut.

For the purposes of this book, the central question is whether the Hussein–McMahon correspondence viewed Palestine as part of an Arab state or states. "Palestine" was a vague geographical expression, not an Ottoman province, in the nineteenth century, and its boundaries would not be precisely defined until after World War I. What we now think of as Palestine consisted of the sanjak of Jerusalem and part of the vilayet of Beirut. The correspondence between Hussein and McMahon, the full text of which was not published until 1939, was in Arabic. Subsequently, disagreement arose over the meaning of the word "vilayet" (Arabic: *wilayah*), which both Hussein and McMahon had used generally to mean *district* and specifically to refer to an Ottoman administrative unit. The British later claimed that in excluding certain parts of the Levant, they had meant the area west of the districts of the towns of Aleppo, Hama, and Homs and of the Ottoman administrative division, or vilayet, of Syria (of which Damascus was the capital), in which case Palestine would have been excluded. (See Map 1–1 in Chapter 1.) The Arabs later argued that they had understood British use of the word "vilayet" to mean the districts of the towns mentioned, and that Palestine, therefore, was to have been included in an Arab state.

Moreover, during their correspondence, Hussein wrote McMahon that the Arabs were prepared temporarily to await a definite decision until an Allied victory was assured, but that they considered all the territory of the eastern Mediterranean to be purely Arab and were opposed to its being surrendered to France or any other power. It should also be noted that while care was taken to name various Ottoman administrative divisions, including the vilayet of Beirut, which included part of northern Palestine, nowhere in the Hussein–McMahon letters did the British mention the sanjak of Jerusalem, in which lay most of the rest of Palestine. Therefore, the Arabs argued, Palestine was never specifically excluded from territory promised to the Arabs.

The Hussein–McMahon correspondence was not a formal agreement, but Hussein and those Arab notables who had been made privy to it assumed that the British would honor their wartime promises and would support Arab claims to independence after the war. In June 1916, therefore, the Arab Revolt began, led by Feisal, son of Sherif Hussein and eventually aided by the colorful British colonel T. E. Lawrence (Lawrence of Arabia), whose involvement was subsequently publicized by the American broadcaster Lowell Thomas and chronicled in Lawrence's own books, *Seven Pillars of Wisdom* and *Revolt in the Desert,* its popular abridgement.

The Arab Revolt, fueled by British gold, aided the Allied effort by diverting and harassing the Turkish forces, both in Arabia and later in Syria. It began in western Arabia and succeeded by September 1916 in capturing the principal towns of the Hejaz with the important exception of Medina. While one group of Arabs remained in Arabia to lay siege to Medina, another column under Feisal marched north to aid British General Allenby's main expeditionary force heading east and north out of Egypt. As Allenby pushed up the Mediterranean coast, capturing Gaza and then marching inland to take Jerusalem by December 1917, Feisal proceeded on a parallel course east of the Jordan River. Before launching the final offensive against the Turks by an attack on Damascus and northern Syria, Allenby planned to sever vital Turkish communications between Damascus and the south. The Arabs cooperated with the British by blowing up part of the Hejaz railroad linking Damascus and the holy places of Mecca and Medina, first between Deraa and Amman, and then at points to the north and west of Deraa. The way was clear for a sweep to Damascus, which the Arab armies reached just ahead of an Australian force at the beginning of October 1918. By the end of

October, Aleppo and the rest of Syria had been occupied, with the Arabs playing a considerable role in the advance from Damascus through Homs and Hama to Aleppo. On October 30, 1918, the Ottoman Empire signed the Mudros Armistice.

The Arab Revolt did not involve large numbers of men; the majority of the Arabs of the Ottoman Empire remained loyal subjects of the Ottoman Sultan, who had in the nineteenth century revived and appropriated the title of Caliph in order to appeal to his Muslim subjects. Furthermore, the sultan had co-opted many Arabs by appointing them to high positions. The British later claimed that Hussein and his sons were acting in their own behalf in their negotiations with the British. However, there was an Arab nationalist movement in Syria, with which Feisal had made contact even before the initiation of the Hussein–McMahon correspondence.

Al-Fatat and al-Ahd were two secret societies that had been formed before the war to work for Arab independence from the Ottomans. Founded in 1911 in Paris by seven young Arabs, al-Fatat was basically a civilian group. It shifted its activities to the Middle East in 1914, and its numbers grew to around 200. Al-Ahd was an association of army officers whose program at first called for a kind of dual monarchy. In early 1914, its leader was arrested and tried by the Turkish authorities on a number of unrelated and trumped-up charges, which infuriated his supporters and encouraged the members of al-Ahd to broaden their goals. In May 1915, al-Fatat and al-Ahd established contact and produced a document called the Damascus Protocol, which outlined their own conditions for cooperation with the British and an Arab revolt against the Turks. The provisions of the Damascus Protocol were remarkably similar to those presented by Hussein later that summer to the British and indicated an Arab nationalist sentiment that was quite real, even if limited in its constituency.

To buttress their arguments that the British intended to satisfy their aspirations, the Arabs also pointed to a later public statement issued in June 1918, when the British Foreign Office replied to seven Arab notables who had asked for a clarification of British policy. The "Declaration to the Seven" stated that with regard to the future government of territories liberated by the Allies, the principle of the consent of the governed should apply. In a Fourth of July speech that same year, president Woodrow Wilson of the United States enunciated his famous Fourteen Points, one of which was the principle that a postwar settlement must be acceptable to the people immediately concerned. The twelfth point explicitly mentioned the Ottoman Empire. These British and American statements may have helped allay Arab doubts and fears raised in the meantime by two other documents that had become known to them. These documents, containing provisions that appeared to contradict pledges made to the Arabs, were the Sykes-Picot Agreement and the Balfour Declaration.

THE SYKES–PICOT AGREEMENT

At the same time that Hussein and McMahon were exchanging letters, the British were also holding discussions with their allies about the future partition of the Ottoman Empire. With regard to Palestine, the relevant document is the Sykes–Picot Agreement, named after the chief negotiators, Sir Mark Sykes for the British, and Charles François George-Picot for the French. In this agreement, the two powers divided the Levant and Iraq areas into zones in which they would exercise either direct or indirect influence. (See Map 2–1.) In the areas of indirect British or French control, semi-independent Arab states or a state might be established. Regarding Palestine, the

MAP 2–1

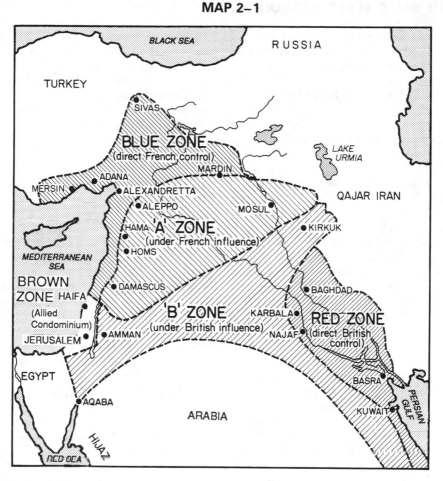

The Sykes–Picot Agreement, 1916

Source: Arthur Goldschmidt, Jr., *A Concise History of the Middle East* (Boulder, Colo., Westview Press, 1979).

territory west of the Jordan River and including Jerusalem but excluding the Negev would be placed under international administration. Interestingly, British and French discussions referred obliquely to the Hussein–McMahon correspondence, with the British indicating that in return for cooperating with the Allies, the Arabs would obtain the towns of Homs, Hama, Damascus, and Aleppo, but under French supervision. Russia approved the Sykes–Picot Agreement in return for recognition by Britain and France of Russian rights to control parts of eastern Anatolia from Trebizond to the Caucasus. The Russians had previously gained Allied support of their claim on the Bosphorus and Dardanelles straits. Initialed in May 1916, the Sykes–Picot Agreement contained provisions that to some later interpreters contradicted the terms of the Hussein-McMahon correspondence that had preceded it.

THE BALFOUR DECLARATION

A third document dealing specifically with Palestine further complicated the situation and lends credence to the saying that Palestine was "the much promised land." The Balfour Declaration, issued on November 2, 1917, was a public statement of the British government in the form of a letter from the Foreign Secretary, Arthur J. Balfour, to Lord Rothschild, head of the British Zionist Organization. (See Document 2–4.) The declaration stated first that the British government "viewed with favor" the establishment *in* Palestine of *a* homeland for the Jewish people. It then declared that in facilitating this objective, nothing should be done that might prejudice the "civil and religious rights of existing non-Jewish communities" in Palestine, or the rights and political status enjoyed by Jews in other countries.

Several drafts were prepared, and the final version was attenuated and ambiguous. This was due primarily to opposition in the British cabinet of, ironically, its one Jewish member, Sir Edwin Montagu, who feared that an endorsement of Jewish nationality would lead to a charge of dual loyalty. (See Document 2–5.) The phrase *in* Palestine, and of *a* national home, left the proposed entity vague and without defined borders. Moreover, the section relating to the civil and religious rights of the existing non-Jewish communities, while accurately reflecting the profusion of religious groups and the predominantly religious and cultural basis of identity among the Arabs at that time, mentioned nothing about their economic, political, and national rights. The last part of the declaration clearly attempted to emphasize that Jews could be and were patriotic citizens of countries in which they already resided, and that their rights and political status should not be harmed by the enthusiasm of Zionist co-religionists.

The wartime situation pushed British policymakers to endorse Zionist goals. For one thing, supporting a Jewish national home in Palestine might enable the British to establish a protectorate or at least continue to exert influence in a strategic area on the eastern flank of the Suez Canal. Palestine was a vital link on the land routes to India. The growing importance of oil and of air transport also necessitated the continuance of British hegemony over the important communications lanes of the Middle East. Moreover, there was the chance that issuing such a declaration would persuade the new revolutionary leaders of Russia, many of whom were Jews, not to leave the war. It might also influence American Jews to press the U.S. government, which had just entered the war, to prosecute it with vigor. The intent may also have been to forestall a similar declaration by either the German or the Ottoman government, which might appeal to the Jews to help achieve its particular purposes.

It has also been suggested, in a more cynical vein, that a Jewish national home in Palestine would attract Jewish immigrants especially from Eastern Europe, who were not always welcomed with open arms in the West. Balfour, himself, as British Prime Minister in the early twentieth century, had introduced a bill to limit Jewish immigration into Britain. A Jewish homeland, as Herzl had proposed, could serve the needs of Jews and anti-Semites alike.

Jews generally supported the Allied war effort. In Palestine, a Jewish spy ring known as NILI (*Netzach Yisrael Lo Y'shaker*—The Strength of Israel Will Not Deceive) operated between 1916 and September 1917 when it was uncovered by the Turks. It supplied the British with vital information that greatly aided the Allied effort and facilitated Allenby's successful march to Jerusalem.

Also important to the British war effort was the contribution of Chaim Weizmann, a Russian-born chemist at the University of Manchester who was called to London to devise a process for synthesizing acetone, a chemical needed to produce the explosive cordite. An avid Zionist, and then president of the World Zionist Organization, Weizmann took the opportunity to make contact with many British leaders whom he swayed to the Zionist cause. Some, influenced already by a romantic, back-to-the-Bible, strain in English literature of the previous century, or by the idea that the Second Coming of Christ would be hastened by the restoration of the Jews in the land of Israel, needed little urging to support the idea of a Jewish national home. Others were compelled by Weizmann's brilliant mind, dignified bearing, and personal charm and charisma. Thus, David Lloyd George, who would become British Prime Minister in 1916; Winston Churchill, who would become Colonial Secretary; Henry Wickham Steed, editor of the London *Times;* C. P. Scott, editor of the *Manchester Guardian;* Mark Sykes, Chief Secretary of the War Cabinet; Colonel Richard Meinertzhagen, member of a distinguished family, who had served to the Near East; Balfour himself and many others were willing to lend a sympathetic ear to those ideas that resulted in issuance of the Balfour Declaration.

POSTWAR SETTLEMENT

Once the war ended and the Peace Conference got underway in Paris, problems regarding the postwar settlement rapidly surfaced. The Arabs in particular were confused about British policy, especially since the new government in Russia had published the wartime secret arrangements, including the Sykes–Picot Agreement. Regarding Palestine, contradictions were apparent between British commitments to the Jews in the Balfour Declaration and the Arab interpretation of British pledges in the Hussein–McMahon correspondence, as well as in public statements like the "Declaration to the Seven." Meanwhile, France was laying claim to most of the Levant coast, which would surely restrict Arab independence elsewhere in the area. Hussein and Feisal, inexperienced in dealing with the European powers, seemed to be even more wary of French ambitions in the Levant than of the British and the Zionists. Because

Chaim Weizmann and Emir Feisal near Aqaba, June 4, 1918 (*Photo courtesy of The Weizmann Archives, Rehovot*).

the British and the French distrusted each other, they encouraged these Arab concerns. Although the British seemed to be firm in their support of the Balfour Declaration, they also indicated their readiness, albeit vaguely, to honor Arab aspirations. Therefore, at the suggestion of the British, Feisal and Weizmann met, first at Aqaba in the spring of 1918 and later in the year in London, to discuss matters of mutual concern.

In January 1919, Feisal made a provisional agreement with Weizmann in which they alluded to the common ancestry of the two groups and the hope that they could work together in the Near East. (See Document 2–6.) It stated that, provided the rights of the Arab peasant and tenant farmers were protected and that there were no restrictions on religious freedom, the Arabs would work with the Jews to implement the Balfour Declaration. The document clearly envisaged a Jewish state in Palestine alongside an Arab state and spoke about Jewish help in surveying the economic possibilities of the Arab state and assisting in its development. However, in 1919, the fate of both Arab and Jewish nationalists was in the hands of the victorious Allies. Feisal therefore appended a proviso that he would not honor the agreement with Weizmann in any way unless the Arabs received their independence. A few months later, however, Feisal wrote Felix Frankfurter, the American Zionist leader, that it was a "happy coincidence" that Arabs and Jews who are "cousins in race" were taking the first steps toward the attainment of their national ideals together, and that there was room in "Syria" for both national movements. (See Document 2–7.)

Both the British and the Zionists ignored or failed to appreciate the views of the indigenous Arab population. This was due not only to the fact that they were concerned primarily with their own interests, but also to the fact that there were few Arabs except Feisal in a position to speak authoritatively on behalf of the Arab people, and that there were internal divisions and rivalries among the Arabs themselves. However, Feisal was not as much a free agent as he had believed, nor were the Arabs altogether mute. Feisal's right to represent "the Arab people" was open to question, and an Arab congress at Damascus repudiated his dealings with the Zionists. This action reflected growing local opposition to the Balfour Declaration and fear of unlimited Jewish immigration, with its probable economic, cultural, and political consequences. This negative attitude was observed by the King–Crane Commission, dispatched to Syria and Palestine by President Wilson during the peace conference to gauge the sentiment of the local population regarding the future of the region. (See Document 2–8.) The commission confirmed the Arab rejection of Zionist goals, as well as Arab opposition to the possible imposition of French rule. If independence were unattainable, and if they had to accept a form of temporary outside control, then the Arabs preferred American or, secondarily, British supervision. Nobody, however, took any notice of the King–Crane report. In any event, it found no evidence that the Arabs in 1918 would have been able to govern themselves, or that the British and French were willing to let them try. The United States under the ailing President Wilson withdrew from the peace negotiations, and the postwar settlement regarding the Middle East was left in the hands of the British and French.

It is not surprising, therefore, that the actual postwar settlement in the Levant area came close to the provisions of the Sykes–Picot Agreement. The arrangements were agreed upon at San Remo in April 1920. They were incorporated into the Treaty of Sèvres of August 1920, and were ratified by the League of Nations in 1922. Instead of zones of British or French direct or indirect influence and internationalized areas, however, the territory was divided into new entities, called *mandates*. The mandates would be administered like trusts by the British and French, under supervision of the League of Nations, until such time as the inhabitants were ready for independence and self-government. The mandate idea was a kind of compromise between the principle of self-determination stressed in Wilson's Fourteen Points, and the desire of the colonial powers to maintain control in the region at the same time that they attempted to neutralize each other's potential power. Wartime pledges and promises to Arabs and Jews alike were postponed, if not altogether negated, by these arrangements.

THE MANDATES

The mandate territories were Syria and Lebanon, which emerged from those portions of the Levant awarded to France; Iraq, awarded to Britain; and a new entity called Palestine, which was also placed under British control. Palestine, as defined for the first time in modern history at San Remo, included the land on both sides of the Jordan River and encompassed the present-day countries of Israel and Jordan. However, boundary changes were soon made. As the British and French moved in to assume their new responsibilities, Arab nationalists rebelled in Iraq and Syria. Feisal, who, in March 1920, had been proclaimed King of Greater Syria by a nationalist congress in Damascus, was summarily expelled from Syria by the French. Abdullah, brother of Feisal, appeared east of the Jordan at Ma'an and was said to be recruiting a force to reclaim Syria for his brother. In order to defuse the situation, Winston Churchill, then British Colonial Secretary, convened a conference of British officials and soldiers in Cairo in March 1921. There, the British decided to install Feisal as constitutional monarch in Iraq, and to carve out of the Palestine mandate a new entity east of the Jordan River. This would be administered as a separate emirate ruled over by Abdullah as Emir, or prince. Transjordan, as the new territory came to be known, consisted in 1921 of about 300,000 inhabitants, mostly Bedouin, and was heavily fractionated by tribe and clan loyalties.

In July 1922, the League of Nations ratified the mandate arrangements, including the changes that had been made since 1920. (See Map 2–2.) The preamble of the Palestine mandate reaffirmed the obligation of Britain to put the Balfour Declaration into effect. It recognized "the historical connection of the Jewish people with Palestine" and referred to their justification for "reconstituting their national home in that country." Article Four suggested that the British recognize the Zionist Organization as a Jewish agency to cooperate with the mandatory government in establishing the national home and to represent the interests of the Jewish population. Article Six instructed the British to "facilitate Jewish immigration under suitable conditions" and to encourage "close settlement by the Jews on the land" while ensuring "that the rights and position of other sections of the population are not prejudiced." Presumably, the latter statement referred to the Arabs, then 85 to 90 percent of the population. The mandate instrument never mentioned the Arabs by name, however, and members of the League of Nations were evidently thinking of the various religious communities that then existed in Palestine rather than a national group as such other than the Jews.

Only in Article 25, which referred to "the territories lying between the Jordan and the eastern boundary of Palestine as ultimately determined" (that is, Transjordan), were there statements about the possibility of postponing or withholding implementation of the provisions of the mandate should they be "inapplicable to the existing local conditions." In September 1922, because of disturbances caused by continuing Arab nationalist frustration and growing hostility to Jewish immigration into Palestine, the British officially stated that the Balfour Declaration would not apply to Transjordan, which would be closed to Jewish immigration. With regard to Jewish hopes, it was

MAP 2-2

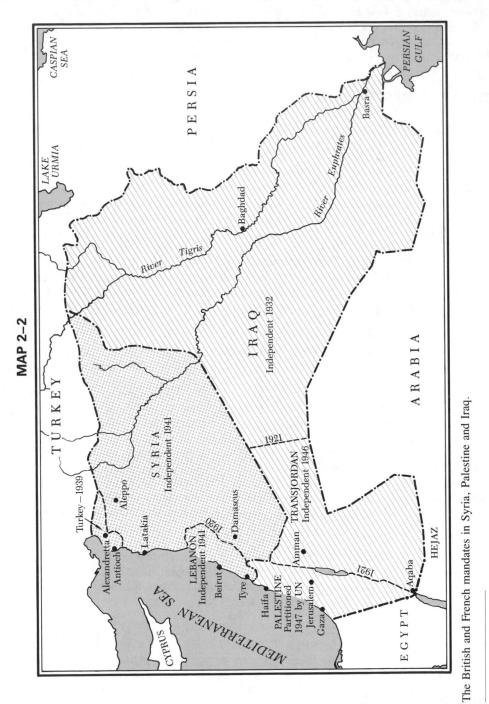

The British and French mandates in Syria, Palestine and Iraq.

Source: Reprinted by permission of the Putnam Publishing Group from *The Arab Awakening* by George Antonius. Copyright © 1939 by G. P. Putnam's Sons.

therefore clear that if there were to be a Jewish homeland in Palestine, it would emerge somewhere west of the Jordan River. This book will now call only the land west of the river (Cisjordan) "Palestine," keeping in mind that Transjordan, the area east of the Jordan River, was still technically part of Britain's mandatory obligations.

But what kind of state would emerge if and when the mandate ended? Did a national home for the Jews imply eventual political sovereignty? Would Palestine, even if restricted to land west of the Jordan River, become a Jewish state? And how were the provisions of the Balfour Declaration consistent with the rights of the existing non-Jewish communities, that is, the majority Arab population? What would the relationship be between Arabs and Jews in Palestine during the mandate? Both communities realized, of course, that the eventual outcome would be determined by numbers and ownership of land. Therefore, the issues of immigration and land purchase became crucial in the mandate period, with the Jews attempting to increase both, and the Arabs to slow down or halt Jewish immigration and land purchases. Very often these issues spawned violence, and the British were forced to respond, a lesson not lost on either community. When we examine the mandate period in Palestine, therefore, it must be from three different perspectives: the Jewish, the Arab, and the British.

The Jews and the Mandate

At the beginning of the mandate period, the Jews of Palestine thought it served their best interests to work closely with the British. This was facilitated greatly by that provision of the mandate instrument suggesting that a Jewish agency be established to take care of the needs of the population and to cooperate with the mandatory administration. The World Zionist Organization (WZO) was recognized as the Jewish Agency, but its president, Chaim Weizmann, remained in London to be close to British centers of power. David Ben-Gurion headed the standing executive committee of the WZO in Palestine. Being on the spot, the executive, for all intents and purposes, became the Jewish Agency and, for the most part, it accommodated itself to the mandate arrangements and to cooperation with the British.

The Jewish community in Palestine, or Yishuv, elected its own assembly, the Vaad Leumi, which contained political parties representing all viewpoints on the Zionist spectrum. The Histadrut, an originally apolitical federation of labor and trade union organizations, established a system of universal medical coverage, set up an extensive network of schools, and controlled several industries. Because of Arab attacks on Jewish settlements, the Jews also formed a defense organization called the Haganah. As for education, the Haifa Technion had been operating since 1912, and in 1925 the Hebrew University opened on Mount Scopus, capping a Jewish school system that produced high literacy rates among the Jewish population. The Yishuv had its own courts and tax collection. And the kibbutzim and moshavim, as well as growing urban and industrial enterprises, provided an economic base. There was a high degree of organization and cooperation within the Jewish community, which was creating the institutions of national life.

This does not mean, however, that the Jewish community was united internally. Serious differences existed among the myriad groups over ideology, relations with the Arabs, and the degree of cooperation with the authorities. The majority of the Labor Zionists who controlled the Jewish Agency were socialists who ardently desired good relations with the Arabs and myopically believed that Zionism was good for the Arabs as well as the Jews. Although all the activities of the Jewish Agency were geared to the development of an eventual state, this political goal remained unarticulated throughout most of the mandate period.

On the other hand, the Revisionist Zionists, founded in 1925 and led by Vladimir Jabotinsky, never accepted what they called the first partition of Palestine in 1921 and explicitly demanded a Jewish state, not merely a homeland, on both sides of the Jordan River. They sought a political entity with an army and all the other trappings of national life, and they viewed the leaders of the Jewish Agency as accommodationist, weak-willed, and cowardly. The Revisionists fully realized that their goals were inconsistent with those of the Arabs, but for Jabotinsky (and especially later, when the situation of the Jews in Europe became desperate) the moral claim of the Jews to Palestine outweighed that of the Arabs. In 1937, in testimony before the Palestine Royal Commission, Jabotinsky stated that given the fact the Arabs already had several states and the Jews had such great need for just one safe refuge, Arab claims on Palestine were like the claims of appetite versus the claims of starvation. Although the Revisionists were a minority representing particularly urban, non-socialist, property-owning Jews, they were a vocal and ideologically consistent group throughout the mandate period. In 1931, they formed their own military arm, called at first Haganah Bet, later renamed the Irgun Zvai Leumi (ETZEL), or national military group, which actively retaliated against Arab marauders. During World War II and with the death of Jabotinsky in 1940, the Irgun ceased its activities. In 1942, however, the Irgun was revitalized when a deserter from General Anders' refugee-recruited Polish army-in-exile arrived in Palestine. This was Menachem Begin, who later led the maximalist Herut party and became Prime Minister of Israel between 1977 and 1983.

At the other end of the Zionist spectrum were individuals and groups who perceived the incompatibility of Jewish and Arab goals and who cared about the relationship between Jews and Arabs in Palestine. Brit Shalom was one such group that advocated a binational state in Palestine. Judah Magnes, an American-born Reform rabbi who became chancellor of Hebrew University in 1925, as well as important intellectuals like Martin Buber, advocated this kind of solution. A more politically active group was HaShomer HaZair, or "Young Guard," a left-wing party that advocated equality between the Jewish and Arab working classes in a binational state.

The Yishuv, despite its internal differences, however, was creating the institutions of statehood while building up the national home. Moreover, ideological discussions became academic as World War II broke out, and as details of the Holocaust in Europe became known. In 1942, at the Biltmore Hotel in New York, the World Zionist Organization for the first time unequivocally called for a Jewish state in all of Palestine that was under mandate.

The Arabs and the Mandate

For the most part the Arab community within Palestine remained opposed to the mandate and to Zionism. They saw the Balfour Declaration as encouraging the Jews to establish a politically sovereign state in Palestine, which they were determined to resist. They were hampered throughout the mandate period, however, by their lack of organization and by the maximalist position that many of their leaders adopted. This often prevented them from reacting in ways that could have achieved their aims and thwarted those of the Zionists.

There was no Arab agency like the Jewish one, although the British proposed such a body in 1923. The Arabs believed that since the mandate instrument specifically mentioned a Jewish agency to cooperate with the British in facilitating Zionist objectives, it would signal their acquiescence to the Balfour Declaration and to Zionism were they to cooperate in any way with the British. Therefore, the Arab community failed to form a representative body.

Moreover, the British retained the previous Ottoman millet system, which recognized the division of the population into fairly self-governing autonomous confessional units. This tended to reinforce religious, cultural, and economic differences between Muslims and Christians. Educationally, too, although the mandate did provide some funds for public education, for the most part the various religious groups ran their own schools. Thus, while literacy among the Arabs (especially Christians) rose overall during the mandate period, public schools did not suffice to serve the Arab population, and their literacy lagged behind that of the Jews. A certain, if declining, proportion of the Arab population also remained nomadic.

Politically, the Arabs were also divided. Disagreements were particularly acute between the two most influential Arab Muslim families, the Husseinis and the Nashashibis. In 1921, the British High Commissioner, Sir Herbert Samuel, appointed Haj Muhammed Amin al-Husseini as Grand Mufti of Jerusalem and head of the Supreme Muslim Council, which controlled the Muslim courts and schools and much of the revenue generated by religious charitable endowments. The Mufti was supposed to be chosen from three candidates who received the greatest number of votes from a convocation of Islamic scholars and notables. Samuel appointed Haj Amin despite the fact that he had received fewer votes than the top three candidates. Although a lower-ranking British civil servant evidently pushed the idea of co-opting a strong Arab nationalist, it is sometimes argued that Samuel, a Jew himself, bent over backwards to illustrate his impartiality by choosing the violently anti-Zionist Haj Amin as Mufti. Because the High Commissioner was committed to facilitating Jewish immigration in accordance with British mandatory obligations, it is possible that he appointed Haj Amin to placate the Arabs. Unfortunately, the Mufti and the Husseinis remained implacably opposed to the mandate, the British, and the Jews. The Nashashibis were

Haj Amin al-Husseini, Grand Mufti of Jerusalem (*Photo courtesy of Wide World Photos, Inc.*).

The Mandates

also opposed to Zionism but were somewhat more inclined to cooperate with the British to achieve Arab aims. The two groups fought against and sometimes murdered each other in their jockeying for power and influence.

The Arabs were constrained not only by their maximalist position but also by lack of organization. An Arab executive existed between 1920 and 1934. Headed by Musa Kazem al-Husseini, a relative of the Mufti, it presented Arab views to the High Commissioner, called political strikes, and convened Palestine Arab congresses. When it dissolved after the death of Musa Kazem in 1934, several political "parties" appeared, usually organized around a powerful personality and representing family or parochial interests. In 1936, leaders of five of the six parties (that of the Nashashibi family remained aloof) formed a body called the Arab Higher Committee, with Haj Amin al-Husseini as its president. This move had been catalyzed largely by independently organized "national committees," which had begun a general strike. (This will be discussed later.) Escalating violence and political murders led the British to ban the Arab Higher Committee and to issue a warrant for the arrest of Haj Amin. He escaped, however, and orchestrated Arab resistance to the British and the Jews from various capitals, including Berlin, during World War II.

Economically, there were many advances in the Arab sector during the mandate, especially in construction, agriculture, and citriculture. However, in terms of services, industrial growth, and the development of agricultural land, there was never enough capital to support the Arab population, which doubled during the mandate period. The death rate declined, infant mortality decreased, and thousands of Arabs immigrated into Palestine. These newcomers, it seems, were attracted by the generally higher living standard than in the surrounding areas, and by opportunities opened up by developments in the Jewish sector. Nevertheless, the Arabs remained hostile to Zionism, and their hostility manifested itself over issues of land purchase and immigration, as we shall see. It was abundantly clear that the more land the Jews purchased and the more Jews who arrived, the more chance the Arabs would one day find themselves in the minority.

The British During the Mandate

British colonial rule was in general conscientious, efficient, and responsible. In India and Iraq, for example, the British attracted capable people who did a creditable job in training lower-echelon administrators and providing some opportunities for local populations to gain experience in self-government. The British had a good record in Palestine, too, in terms of developing administrative institutions, municipal services, public works, and communications. The mandate government laid water pipelines, extended railroad lines, and completed port facilities at Haifa. An electric power grid was begun by a Russian Jewish engineer, Pinchas Rutenberg, who obtained a concession from the mandate government. But Palestine was a special case, and the British were caught in a web of their own making by the contraditions inherent in the mandate instrument and the conflicting claims of Arabs and Jews. Policy was shaped by a series of "white papers" issued usually in response to outbreaks of violence over land or immigration issues. As many observers have noted, the British seemed to be muddling through, while trying to keep the peace.

The aims and aspirations of the three protagonists appeared incompatible. The Arabs feared, and especially after the rise of Nazism in Germany, that continuing Jewish immigration would result in a Jewish majority that would claim all of Palestine. The Jews sought to build a viable base both in numbers and in land that would make feasible a national home. The British wished to retain their influence and keep the peace, while, in accordance with the obligations imposed upon them by the mandate, they tried simultaneously to implement the Balfour Declaration, safeguard the civil and religious rights of all the inhabitants, and develop self-governing institutions. Lacking a clear policy on how to proceed, the British responded to the sporadic violence by dispatching commissions of inquiry and then issuing a white paper based on the findings of the commission.

LAND, IMMIGRATION, AND THE WHITE PAPER OF 1922

In 1920, the British reopened the Land Registry, which had been closed since 1918 because of the war and the dissolution of the Ottoman Empire. Jews immediately began to buy land, some from the British, who had taken over the former state lands of the Ottoman Empire, but mostly from Arab landowners. Zionist purchases from Arabs were facilitated by the fact that the Ottoman system of land registration had been fairly chaotic, and that most land had not been registered by the peasants working it, but by wealthy city merchants or absentee landowners willing to sell it at vastly inflated prices. Zionist agencies like the Jewish National Fund (JNF) utilized contributions of Jews all over the world to purchase land on behalf of the Jewish people and to coordinate its development. In 1917, the JNF possessed only about 160,000 dunams (1 dunam equals approximately ¼ acre) in Palestine. The first major purchase after the war was of about 80,000 dunams, containing some twenty-two Galilee villages, in the Vale of Esdraelon, or Jezreel Valley. The land was purchased in 1921 from the Sursuk family of Lebanon for £726,000. (Sursuk himself had purchased the land from the Ottoman government in 1872 for about £20,000.)

Because of the predominantly socialist ideology of the Yishuv, and the preponderance of Labor Zionists in important leadership positions both in Palestine and in the World Zionist Organization, land acquired during the mandate was usually made into kibbutzim or moshavim. The Jews hoped to avoid the creation of a Jewish landlord class exploiting a landless Arab peasantry, but land purchases often led to the eviction of Arab peasants. This occurred in the Jezreel Valley, where about twenty collective settlements were founded on the principle of Jews performing their own labor. It is important to remember that all the land purchased in the mandate period was legally purchased, and much of its was swamp or marshland or was otherwise uninhabited. Nevertheless, some Arabs lost land that they had worked and that had been in the hands of their families for centuries. Moreover, socialist idealism notwithstanding, the almost total lack of contact and exchange between Jews and Arabs engaged in agriculture resulted in lost opportunities for Jewish and Arab cooperation on the land.

While land purchases continued in the 1920s, there were also spurts of Jewish immigration, although the number of Jews leaving Palestine exceeded the number entering for many years of the decade. Not surprisingly, Jewish immigration was viewed with great suspicion by the Arabs. As the mandate arrangements were being worked out in 1920 and 1921, Arab sentiment became inflamed against the British and the incoming Jews.

The White Paper of 1922

In 1920, the Arabs attacked Tel Chai and other Jewish settlements in the Galilee, and anti-Jewish riots broke out in Jerusalem. In 1921, Jaffa was subjected to violence,

British authorities quelling Arab riot at Jaffa Gate, Jerusalem in October, 1927
(*Photo courtesy of The Library of Congress*).

which spread to Petach Tikvah, Hadera, and other Jewish communities. Forty-seven Jews were killed and 140 wounded. Forty-eight Arabs were killed and scores were wounded, mostly by British troops trying to keep the peace.

The Chief Justice of Palestine, Sir Thomas Haycraft, headed a commission of inquiry into the disturbances. He concluded that, whereas the Arabs had been responsible for the violence, Arab resentment had a legitimate basis in the Arab fear of economic danger posed by Jewish immigrants and the perceived political influence of the Jews on the mandatory government. In a pattern that repeated itself throughout the mandate period, immigration was temporarily suspended and then resumed, as the Colonial Secretary, Winston Churchill, attempted to clarify his government's policy. The Churchill White Paper reaffirmed Britain's commitment to the Balfour Declaration and stated that the Jews were in Palestine "by right and not on sufferance," but that all citizens of Palestine were Palestinians. (See Document 2–9.) It went on to say that the document meant what it said—there would be a Jewish home *in* Palestine, and that Jewish immigration should not exceed the economic absorptive capacity of the country, a principle extrapolated from the mandate instrument and enunciated at the time of the first immigration ordinance in 1920. The explicit reference to economic absorptive capacity in the 1922 White Paper, however, highlighted this consideration and raised new questions and doubts about its meaning.

What, in fact, did "economic absorptive capacity" mean? The 1922 White Paper provided no definition, but the Jews interpreted the phrase as an incentive for further economic development. In their view, economic growth and opportunities would justify continued Jewish immigration. Indeed, there was general economic growth in Palestine, in both the Arab and the Jewish sectors, most notably in agriculture and citriculture. The mandatory authorities were responsible for great strides in basic administration, public works, and expansion of infrastructure. Compared to the surrounding Arab areas, the economic situation of Palestine was sufficiently favorable, and the living standard notably enough higher, to attract Arabs from outside Palestine, particularly to the cities and urban areas.

Historians have debated whether changes in the Arab economy and increases in the Arab population were due to developments in the Jewish sector. The third wave of Jewish immigration, or *aliyah,* between 1919 and 1923 brought into Palestine about 35,000 young Jews primarily from Russia and Eastern Europe who had already attended agricultural training programs and were enthusiastic and experienced "pioneers" on the land. The fourth aliyah (1924–1928) consisted mainly of middle-class shopkeepers and artisans fleeing from economic depression and anti-Semitic outbreaks in Poland. These arrivals tended to settle in the towns and cities. The fifth aliyah of the early 1930s brought many well-educated German immigrants who also settled mainly in urban areas and who arrived with capital that contributed greatly to growth in construction and industry as well as agriculture. Zionist proponents stress that development in the Jewish sector created new and attractive work opportunities for Arabs as well as Jews, and that the rapid growth of the Arab population owing to natural increase resulted from the introduction by the Jews of improved health and sanitary conditions. Arab population changes within the country caused a relative decrease of the rural population and an increase of Arabs in cities and areas where there were large numbers of Jews. This urbanization of the Arabs, some observers claim, resulted from increased opportunities caused by Jewish development.

Others point out, however, that the economy grew not only because of Jewish development, but also because of efforts by the mandatory government and changes in the Arab sector. The British established a framework through administrative institutions and infrastructure. The awareness of the Arab population of Palestine was stimulated not only by developments within Palestine but also by strides being made by Arabs in the surrounding countries. These historians point out, too, that while there may have been mutual influence and interchange between Jews and Arabs in the urban centers, the effect, positively or negatively, was still limited because the two groups seldom interacted. Rural populations, especially peasants and farmers, almost never had contact with each other. The resources of Palestine were limited, and although there was general economic growth, Jews and Arabs were basically in conflict in the economic sphere.

The Political Situation

Politically, Palestine took a very different course from the other mandate areas. In Iraq, Syria, and Lebanon, even after delays and false starts, constituent assemblies, parliaments, constitutions, and other institutions of self-government that were supposed to be modeled on those of the Western democracies, eventually emerged. In Palestine, the Jewish and Arab communities rarely cooperated, except at the local and sometimes municipal level. In order to encourage the development of self-governing institutions at a "national" level, in 1922, and again in 1923, the High Commissioner attempted to establish a legislative council, which would have reflected the Arab majority. The Arabs rejected the idea of a council, however, partly because they suspected British manipulation, but largely because to join such a council would mean to acquiesce in the imposition of the Mandate and the Balfour Declaration. The Arabs did not wish to legitimize a situation that they rejected in principle.

The White Paper of 1930

Personal relationships between Jews and Arabs could be friendly at times, even if they competed economically and politically at the national level. This was especially true in the 1920s as Jewish immigration leveled off and indeed fell below emigration in some years. In 1929, however, as a result of the worldwide economic depression and anti-Semitic outbreaks in Europe, Jewish immigration to Palestine began to rise once again, engendering fear and anger among the Arabs. An incident around the Western (or Wailing) Wall in August 1929 inflamed Arab mobs and set off riots that resulted in the death of Jews in Jerusalem, Safed, and Hebron. The killings in Hebron, where more than sixty Jews were murdered, were especially traumatic; Hebron was the burial place of the Patriarchs, and Jews had lived there from the time of Abraham.

The British responded by sending an investigative commission, headed by Sir Walter Shaw, which conducted hearings and issued a report on March 31, 1930. While blaming the Arabs for the violence, it went on to say that the disappointment of Arab political and national aspirations and fear for their economic future were the fundamental causes of the disturbances. It further recommended that a study be made of land and immigration issues. Sir John Hope-Simpson was dispatched to conduct this inquiry, and Jewish immigration was temporarily suspended. On the basis of Hope-Simpson's report in 1930, the British issued another statement, the Passfield White Paper, which called for a halt to Jewish immigration. It recommended that government land be sold only to landless Arabs, and that determination of "economic absorptive capacity" be based on levels of Arab as well as Jewish unemployment. The outcry from Palestine Jews and Zionists in London and throughout the world caused Prime Minister Ramsey MacDonald to issue an explanatory letter the following year that in effect nullified the provisions of the Passfield White Paper. The Arabs referred to MacDonald's statement as the Black Letter, and various Arab groups began to boycott government activities and to subvert its functioning whenever possible.

By this time, the early 1930s, events in Europe once again began to influence the situation in Palestine. Government-sponsored anti-Semitism led to Jewish emigration from Poland, Hungary, and Romania. The rise to power in Germany of Adolf Hitler, the Nuremberg racial laws, and subsequent legislation directed against the Jews, and the deliberate encouragement of Jews to leave the country, led to new waves of Jewish immigration into Palestine. Between 1933 and 1936 approximately 165,000 Jews entered Palestine, and by 1936 the Jewish population of Palestine stood at almost 400,000 or 30 percent of the total. For the first time, there seemed a real possibility that the Jews might eventually outnumber the Arabs. There were serious outbreaks of violence against Jews in 1933 and again in 1935 in reaction to these new waves of immigration.

At the end of 1935, the British broached the idea of a Palestinian constitution and a legislative council, but both the Arabs and the Jews rejected the proposal. The Arabs would have had a majority on the council, but the British would have maintained control through their selection of nonelected representatives and a provision that no legislation could abrogate or supersede the authority of the mandatory government. The Mufti and his followers rejected the proposal anyway, because the Jews would have been represented. The Jews rejected it because they were still a minority, and because the British proposed restrictions on land purchases. In Britain the program was attacked for one reason or another by both Houses of Parliament. It was in this situation of tension that the great Arab rebellion began, reflecting an Arab nationalist sentiment that had grown along with, and partly in response to, Jewish nationalism. This rebellion persisted for three years until 1939 and the outbreak of World War II.

Arab Rebellion

The Arab rebellion began with rather spontaneous acts of violence by a religiously and nationalistically motivated group inspired by Sheikh Izz ad-Din al-Qassam, who was killed by the British in 1935. Qassamite groups had already achieved some notoriety in the previous few years, but the robbery and murder of three Jews in April 1936, followed by retaliation against two Arabs, sparked a general strike initiated by groups in Jaffa and Nablus. This was taken up by "national committees" in other towns. It was at this point that five of the Arab political parties put aside their differences to form the Arab Higher Committee, under the leadership of the Mufti. The Arab Higher Committee loosely coordinated various Arab organizations, sports clubs, Boy Scouts, women's committees, a labor organization, the Jaffa Boatmen's Association, and others participating in the strike. The committee held a congress that called for civil disobedience, nonpayment of taxes, and shutting down the municipal governments. Arabs reluctant to participate were intimidated and sometimes even murdered by the Mufti's followers. Even though the government adopted punitive measures, violence continued against the British and in some instances the Jews. Arabs inside Palestine were aided by those outside. Fawzi al-Qawuqji, a guerrilla leader in Syria, for example, entered Palestine, and with Syrians, Iraqis, and Palestinian Arabs attacked British installations in the northern part of the country.

One result of this activity was a kind of temporary cooperation between the British and Jews. The British recognized the Haganah for the first time as a legitimate Jewish defense force and agreed to its receiving arms and training legally. The principle of *Havlagah,* or restraint—that is, defending the Jewish community without retaliation, which the Haganah had adopted largely in order to maintain the goodwill of the British—now gave way to the "active defense" concept of Yitzhak Sadeh, the Haganah field commander. Haganah members were trained as uniformed auxiliary guards authorized by the British. An important figure in their training was Orde Wingate, another colorful British personality like T. E. Lawrence. Wingate, a fundamentalist Christian, believed the Jews must be in Palestine in order for the biblical prophecies to be fulfilled, and he became a passionate Zionist. Placing an emphasis on night patrols and mobile units to counter the Arab guerrilla tactics, Wingate developed Jewish special night squads and provided invaluable training for a whole generation of later leaders of Israel's army, including Moshe Dayan and Yigal Allon.

Peel Commission Report

The situation in Palestine remained volatile, and another Royal Commission, headed by Lord Robert Peel, was sent to investigate. The Peel Commission Report, issued in 1937, was significant in that it recommended for the first time that the territory be partitioned into separate Jewish and Arab states. (See Document 2–10.) Meanwhile, arson, bombings, and assassinations continued. In 1937, the murder of the British district commissioner for the Galilee led to the dissolution of the Arab Higher Committee and the Supreme Muslim Council, which was put under British control. The British arrested most of the members of the Higher Committee and deported them to the Seychelles, thus depriving the Arabs of their leadership. Haj Amin, however, escaped to Lebanon and eventually made his way, via Iraq, Iran, and Turkey, to Rome, and eventually to Berlin.

Far from defusing the Arab national movement, however, the British acts seemed only to inflame it. At the same time, all the parties were debating partition. Arabs continued to insist that Palestine was indissolubly Arab. Jews, however, tended to regard the idea more favorably. An international conference on refugees at Evian-les-Bains, France, in 1938 made dramatically clear the increasingly perilous position of the Jews in Europe. Only one of the thirty-one countries represented at Evian, the Dominican Republic, was prepared to lift or alter immigration quotas. Jews who could still leave Germany in 1938, to say nothing of those who managed to escape the Nazi net once the war started, were severely restricted in the number of places they could go. To the Jewish Agency, therefore, a partitioned Palestine became increasingly acceptable as a possible asylum for their beleaguered co-religionists.

In 1938, the British established yet another commission of inquiry under the chairmanship of Sir John Woodhead to determine whether or not partition was practical, and, if so, what the boundaries of the two states should be. Woodhead's report concluded that the Peel partition plan was not feasible and suggested boundaries that enraged the Jewish leaders, since many Jewish settlements and developed areas were excluded from the proposed Jewish entity. The arrangement was absolutely unacceptable to the Arabs; they rejected all attempts to give any part of Palestine over to Jewish sovereignty.

As it happened, the British themselves were not prepared to implement the scheme. Shortly after Woodhead's report was issued, the British government rejected any partition of Palestine as impractical. To dampen the conflict, the British resumed the curtailing of Jewish immigration and land purchases, even rejecting a request in 1938 for the admission of 10,000 Jewish children from Central Europe, although the government eventually admitted the children into Great Britain.

Still attempting to find a solution acceptable to both parties, the British government announced it would convene a meeting in London of representatives of the Zionists, Palestinian Arabs, and Arabs from the surrounding countries to try to work out an agreement. If this attempt failed, the British government stated it would make a policy decision itself. Significantly, the British accepted the request of the Mufti, at this time still in Lebanon, that members of the Arab Higher Committee interned in the Seychelles be released and allowed to represent the Palestine Arabs. Other Arab delegates included Emir Abdullah of Transjordan, Nuri al-Said of Iraq, Prince Feisal of Saudi Arabia, and representatives from Egypt and Yemen. The Jewish delegation included Chaim Weizmann, David Ben-Gurion, the American Zionist Rabbi Stephen Wise, and others. Except for one session, the talks, which began in February 1939, were conducted by the British with the Jews and the Arabs separately, since the Arabs would not sit in the same room with the Jews. It was obviously not going to be possible to achieve an agreement acceptable to both groups at the "Roundtable Conference"; therefore, the Colonial Secretary, Malcolm MacDonald, proposed a new formula, which was embodied in an official White Paper on Palestine in May 1939. (See Document 2–11.)

1939 White Paper

The 1939 White Paper declared that Palestine would become an independent state allied to the British Empire within ten years. This would obviously be an Arab state, since Jewish immigration was limited to 75,000 over the next five years, with Arab consent being necessary thereafter. Land sales to Jews were severely reduced by being prohibited or restricted to certain parts of the territory at the discretion of the High Commissioner. This new white paper in essence repudiated the Balfour Declaration and reversed British policy in Palestine of the previous twenty years. By 1939, however, as a global conflict again appeared imminent, the British were concerned about having reliable bases in the Middle East and could not afford to risk alienating the Arabs or their Muslim co-religionists in India.

The 1939 White Paper on Palestine, coming at a desperate time for European Jewry, shocked and enraged the Yishuv, and the Jewish community refused to cooperate further with the mandate authorities. Ben-Gurion later declared: "We shall fight the war as if there were no White Paper; we shall fight the White Paper as if there were no war!" Both Jews and Arabs for the most part supported the British war effort against the Germans. Once the immediate threat to the British receded after the Allied success at el-Alamein in 1942, however, both communities resumed the war in Palestine, and the British position became increasingly untenable, as we shall see in the next chapter.

SUGGESTIONS FOR FURTHER READING

ABU-LUGHOD, IBRAHIM, ed., *The Transformation of Palestine: Essays on the Origin and Development of the Arab-Israeli Conflict*, Evanston, Ill., Northwestern University Press, 1971.

ANTONIUS, GEORGE, *The Arab Awakening*, London, Hamish Hamilton, 1938; New York, Capricorn Books, 1965.

BETHELL, NICHOLAS, *The Palestine Triangle, 1935–1946*, London, Andre Deutsch, 1979.

ESCO Foundation for Palestine, Inc., *Palestine: A Study of Jewish, Arab and British Policies*, 2 vols., New Haven, Conn., 1947; Kraus Reprint.

FROMKIN, DAVID, *A Peace to End All Peace: Creating the Modern Middle East, 1914–1922*, New York, Henry Holt & Company, 1989.

HUREWITZ, J. C., *The Struggle for Palestine*, New York, W. W. Norton & Co., Inc., 1950. 1968 Reprint, Greenwood Press, Westport, Ct.

KEDOURIE, ELIE, *In the Anglo-Arab Labyrinth: The McMahon–Hussein Correspondence and Its Interpretations, 1914–1939*, Cambridge, Cambridge University Press, 1976.

KHALIDI, WALID, ed., *From Haven to Conquest: Readings in Zionism and the Palestine Problem until 1948*, 2nd ed., Washington, D.C., Institute for Palestine Studies, 1987.

LESCH, ANN M., *Arab Politics in Palestine 1917–1939: The Frustration of a Nationalist Movement*, Ithaca, N.Y., Cornell University Press, 1979.

MATTAR, PHILLIP, *Mufti of Jerusalem: Muhammad Amin al-Husayni and the Palestinian Question*, New York, Columbia University Press, 1988.

POLK, W. R., STAMLER, D., and ASFOUR, E., *Backdrop to Tragedy: The Struggle for Palestine*, Boston, Little Brown, 1957.

SANDERS, RONALD, *The High Walls of Jerusalem: A History of the Balfour Declaration and the Birth of the British Mandate for Palestine*, New York, Holt, Rinehart & Winston, 1983.

STEIN, KENNETH, *The Land Question in Palestine, 1917–1939*, Chapel Hill and London, University of North Carolina Press, 1984.

SYKES, CHRISTOPHER, *Crossroads to Israel: Palestine from Balfour to Bevin*, London, New English Library, 1969, or Cleveland and New York, World Publishing Company, 1965.

WEIZMANN, CHAIM, *Trial and Error*, Westport, Conn., Greenwood Press, 1971.

DOCUMENT 2-1

Correspondence of Sherif Hussein and Sir Henry McMahon [Excerpts]

Sir Henry McMahon's Second Note to the Sharif Husain

Cairo, October 24, 1915.

Complimentary titles.

I have, with gratification and pleasure, received your note of the 29th Shawwal, 1333, and its tokens of sincere friendship have filled me with satisfaction and contentment.

I regret to find that you inferred from my last note that my attitude towards the question of frontiers and boundaries was one of hesitancy and lukewarmth. Such was in no wise the intention of my note. All I meant was that I considered that the time had not yet come in which that question could be discussed in a conclusive manner.

But, having realised from your last note that you considered the question important, vital and urgent, I hastened to communicate to the Government of Great Britain the purport of your note. It gives me the greatest pleasure to convey to you, on their behalf, the following declarations which, I have no doubt, you will receive with satisfaction and acceptance.

The districts of Mersin and Alexandretta, and portions of Syria lying to the west of the districts of Damascus, Homs, Hama and Aleppo, cannot be said to be purely Arab, and must on that account be excepted from the proposed delimitation.

Subject to that modification, and without prejudice to the treaties concluded between us and certain Arab Chiefs, we accept that delimitation.

As for the regions lying within the proposed frontiers, in which Great Britain is free to act without detriment to the interests of her ally France, I am authorised to give you the following pledges on behalf of the Government of Great Britain, and to reply as follows to your note:

(1) That, subject to the modifications stated above, Great Britain is prepared to recognise and uphold the independence of the Arabs in all the regions lying within the frontiers proposed by the Sharif of Mecca;

(2) That Great Britain will guarantee the Holy Places against all external aggression, and will recognise the obligation of preserving them from aggression;

(3) That, when circumstances permit, Great Britain will help the Arabs with her advice and assist them in the establishment of governments to suit those diverse regions;

(4) That it is understood that the Arabs have already decided to seek the counsels and advice of Great Britain exclusively; and that such European advisers and officials as may be needed to establish a sound system of administration shall be British;

(5) That, as regards the two vilayets of Baghdad and of Basra, the Arabs recognise that the fact of Great Britain's established position and interests there will call for the setting up of special administrative arrangements to protect those regions from foreign aggression, to promote the welfare of their inhabitants, and to safeguard our mutual economic interests.

I am confident that this declaration will convince you, beyond all doubt, of Great Britain's sympathy with the aspirations of her friends the Arabs; and that it will result in a lasting and solid alliance with them, of which one of the immediate consequences will be the expulsion of the Turks from the Arab countries and the liberation of the Arab peoples from the Turkish yoke which has weighed on them all these long years. . . .

Compliments.

Source: George Antonius, *The Arab Awakening* (New York: Capricorn Books, 1965), pp. 419–420. Reprinted by permission of The Putnam Publishing Group. Copyright © 1939 by G. P. Putnam's Sons.

DOCUMENT 2-2

The Sharif Husain's Third Note to Sir Henry McMahon

Mecca, Zul-Hejja 27, 1333.
[November 5, 1915.]

Complimentary titles.

With great gratification have we received your note of the 15th Zul-Hejja [October 24] to which we would reply as follows.

First, in order to facilitate agreement and serve the cause of Islam by the removal of possible sources of hardship and tribulation, and in earnest of the particular esteem in which we hold Great Britain, we no longer insist on the inclusion of the districts of Mersin and Adana in the Arab Kingdom. As for the vilayets of Aleppo and Bairut and their western maritime coasts, these are purely Arab provinces in which the Moslem is indistinguishable from the Christian, for they are both the descendants of one forefather. And we Moslems intend, in those provinces, to follow the precepts laid down by the Commander of the Faithful, 'Umar ibn al-Khattab (God have mercy upon him!), and the caliphs who came after him, when he enjoined upon the Moslems to treat the Christians on a footing with themselves, saying: they are to enjoy the same rights and bear the same obligations as ourselves. They will have, moreover, their denominational privileges, as far as the public interest allows. . . .

The Arabs firmly believe that, after the War, the German-ridden Turks will try to give them constant provocation, in religious as well as temporal matters, and to wreak the utmost vengeance upon them. On their side, the Arabs have resolved and vowed to fight the Turks and continue fighting them until not one of them (save for women and children) remains in any of the Arab countries. Our present deliberation is on account of the considerations stated above. . . .

Source: Antonius, *Arab Awakening,* pp. 421–422.

DOCUMENT 2-3

Sir Henry McMahon's Third Note to the Sharif Husain

Cairo, December 13, 1915.

Complimentary titles.

Your note of the 27th Zul-Hejja, 1333, has reached me, and I was glad to find that you consent to the exclusion of the vilayets of Mersin and Adana from the boundaries of the Arab countries. . . .

As for the vilayets of Aleppo and Bairut, the Government of Great Britain have fully understood your statement in that respect and noted it with the greatest care. But as the interests of their ally France are involved in those two provinces, the question calls for careful consideration. We shall communicate again with you on this subject, at the appropriate time. . . .

In token of our good faith, and as a contribution to your endeavours in our joint cause, I am sending the sum of £20,000 with your trusted messenger.

Compliments.

Source: Antonius, *Arab Awakening,* pp. 423–424.

DOCUMENT 2–4

Letter by Arthur James Balfour to Lord Rothschild (The Balfour Declaration)

Foreign Office
November 2nd, 1917.

Dear Lord Rothschild,

I have much pleasure in conveying to you, on behalf of His Majesty's Government, the following declaration of sympathy with Jewish Zionist aspirations which has been submitted to, and approved by, the Cabinet.

"His Majesty's Government view with favour the establishment in Palestine of a national home for the Jewish people, and will use their best endeavours to facilitate the achievement of this object, it being clearly understood that nothing shall be done which may prejudice the civil and religious rights of existing non-Jewish communities in Palestine, or the rights and political status enjoyed by Jews in any other country."

I should be grateful if you would bring this declaration to the knowledge of the Zionist Federation.

Yours sincerely,
ARTHUR JAMES BALFOUR.

Source: Walter Z. Laqueur and Barry Rubin, eds., *The Israel-Arab Reader: A Documentary History of The Middle East Conflict,* 4th ed. (New York: Penguin Books, 1984), p. 18.

DOCUMENT 2–5

**British Cabinet Discussion on Support for Zionism,
4 October 1917–　(Excerpt.)**

Mr. Montagu urged strong objections to any declaration in which it was stated that Palestine was the 'national home' of the Jewish people. He regarded the Jews as a religious community and himself as a Jewish Englishman. He based his argument on the prejudicial effect on the status of Jewish Britons of a statement that His Majesty's Government regarded Palestine as the national home of Jewish people. Whatever safeguarding words might be used in the formula, the civil rights of Jews as nations in the country in which they were born might be endangered. How could he negotiate with the peoples of India on behalf of His Majesty's Government if the world had just been told that His Majesty's Government regarded his national home as being in Turkish territory? He specially urged that the only trial of strength between Zionists and anti-Zionists in England had resulted in a very narrow majority for the Zionists, namely, 56 to 51, of the representatives of Anglo-Jewry on the Conjoint Committee. He also pointed out that most English-born Jews were opposed to Zionism, while it was supported by foreign-born Jews, such as Dr Caster and Dr Herz, the two Grand Rabbis, who had been born in Roumania and Austria respectively, and Dr Weizmann, President of the English Zionist Federation, who was born in Russia. He submitted that the Cabinet's first duty was to English Jews, and that Colonel House had declared that President Wilson is opposed to a declaration now.

Lord Curzon urged strong objections upon practical grounds. He stated, from his recollection of Palestine, that the country was, for the most part, barren and desolate; there being but sparse cultivation on the terraced slopes, the valleys and streams being few, and large centres of population scarce, a less propitious seat for the future Jewish race could not be imagined. How was it proposed to get rid of the existing majority of Mussulman inhabitants and to introduce the Jews in their place? How many would be willing to return and on what pursuits would they engage?

To secure for the Jews already in Palestine equal civil and religious rights seemed to him a better policy than to aim at repatriation on a large scale. He regarded the latter as sentimental idealism, which would never be realized, and that His Majesty's Government should have nothing to do with it.

Source: T. G. Fraser, *The Middle East, 1914–1979* (New York: St. Martin's Press, 1980), pp. 15–16.

DOCUMENT 2–6

Text of the Faisal-Weizmann Agreement

His Royal Highness the Amir FAISAL, representing and acting on behalf of the Arab Kingdom of HEJAZ, and Dr. CHAIM WEIZMANN, representing and acting on behalf of the Zionist Organisation, mindful of the racial kinship and ancient bonds existing between the Arabs and the Jewish people, and realising that the surest means of working out the consummation of their national aspirations, is through the closest possible collaboration in the development of the Arab State and Palestine, and being desirous further of confirming the good understanding which exists between them, have agreed upon the following Articles:

ARTICLE I

The Arab State and Palestine in all their relations and undertakings shall be controlled by the most cordial goodwill and understanding and to this end Arab and Jewish duly accredited agents shall be established and maintained in their respective territories.

ARTICLE II

Immediately following the completion of the deliberations of the Peace Conference, the definite boundaries between the Arab State and Palestine shall be determined by a Commission to be agreed upon by the parties hereto.

ARTICLE III

In the establishment of the Constitution and Administration of Palestine all such measures shall be adopted as will afford the fullest guarantees for carrying into effect the British Government's Declaration of the 2nd of November, 1917.

ARTICLE IV

All necessary measures shall be taken to encourage and stimulate immigration of Jews into Palestine on a large scale, and as quickly as possible to settle Jewish immigrants upon the land through closer settlement and intensive cultivation of the soil. In taking such measures the Arab peasant and tenant farmers shall be protected in their rights, and shall be assisted in forwarding their economic development.

ARTICLE V

No regulation nor law shall be made prohibiting or interfering in any way with the free exercise of religion; and further the free exercise and enjoyment of religious profession and worship without discrimination or preference shall for ever be allowed. No religious test shall ever be required for the exercise of civil or political rights.

Article VI

The Mohammedan Holy Places shall be under Mohammedan control.

Article VII

The Zionist Organisation proposes to send to Palestine a Commission of experts to make a survey of the economic possibilities of the country, and to report upon the best means for its development. The Zionist Organisation will place the aforementioned Commission at the disposal of the Arab State for the purpose of a survey of the economic possibilities of the Arab State and to report upon the best means for its development. The Zionist Organisation will use its best efforts to assist the Arab State in providing the means for developing the natural resources and economic possibilities thereof.

Article VIII

The parties hereto agree to act in complete accord and harmony in all matters embraced herein before the Peace Congress.

Article IX

Any matters of dispute which may arise between the contracting parties shall be referred to the British Government for arbitration.

Given under our hand at LONDON, ENGLAND, the THIRD day of JANUARY, ONE THOUSAND NINE HUNDRED AND NINETEEN.

[*Translation*]

Provided the Arabs obtain their independence as demanded in my Memorandum dated the 4th of January, 1919, to the Foreign Office of the Government of Great Britain, I shall concur in the above articles. But if the slightest modification or departure were to be made [*sc.* in relation to the demands in the Memorandum] I shall not then be bound by a single word of the present Agreement which shall be deemed void and of no account or validity, and I shall not be answerable in any way whatsoever.

FAISAL IBN HUSAIN (*in Arabic*)
CHAIM WEIZMANN

Source: Antonius, *Arab Awakening*, pp. 437–439.

DOCUMENT 2–7

Feisal-Frankfurter Correspondence

DELEGATION HEDJAZIENNE, *Paris, March 3, 1919.*

DEAR MR. FRANKFURTER: I want to take this opportunity of my first contact with American Zionists to tell you what I have often been able to say to Dr. Weizmann in Arabia and Europe.

We feel that the Arabs and Jews are cousins in race, having suffered similar oppressions at the hands of powers stronger than themselves, and by a happy coincidence have been able to take the first step towards the attainment of their national ideals together.

We Arabs, especially the educated among us, look with the deepest sympathy on the

Zionist movement. Our deputation here in Paris is fully acquainted with the proposals submitted yesterday by the Zionist Organization to the Peace Conference, and we regard them as moderate and proper. We will do our best, in so far as we are concerned, to help them through: we will wish the Jews a most hearty welcome home.

With the chiefs of your movement, especially with Dr. Weizmann, we have had and continue to have the closest relations. He has been a great helper of our cause, and I hope the Arabs may soon be in a position to make the Jews some return for their kindness. We are working together for a reformed and revived Near East, and our two movements complete one another. The Jewish movement is national and not imperialist. Our movement is national and not imperialist, and there is room in Syria for us both. Indeed I think that neither can be a real success without the other.

People less informed and less responsible than our leaders and yours, ignoring the need for cooperation of the Arabs and Zionists have been trying to exploit the local difficulties that must necessarily arise in Palestine in the early stages of our movements. Some of them have, I am afraid, misrepresented your aims to the Arab peasantry, and our aims to the Jewish peasantry, with the result that interested parties have been able to make capital out of what they call our differences.

I wish to give you my firm conviction that these differences are not on questions of principle, but on matters of detail such as must inevitably occur in every contact of neighbouring peoples, and as are easily adjusted by mutual goodwill. Indeed nearly all of them will disappear with fuller knowledge.

I look forward, and my people with me look forward, to a future in which we will help you and you will help us, so that the countries in which we are mutually interested may once again take their places in the community of civilised peoples of the world.

Believe me,

Yours sincerely,

(*Sgd.*) FEISAL.
5TH MARCH, 1919.

Source: Laqueur and Rubin, *Israel-Arab Reader,* pp. 21–22.

DOCUMENT 2–8

Recommendations of the King-Crane Commission, August 28, 1919

5. We recommend, in the fifth place, serious modification of the extreme Zionist program for Palestine of unlimited immigration of Jews, looking finally to making Palestine distinctly a Jewish State.

(1) The Commissioners began their study of Zionism with minds predisposed in its favor, but the actual facts in Palestine, coupled with the force of the general principles proclaimed by the Allies and accepted by the Syrians have driven them to the recommendation here made.

(2) The Commission was abundantly supplied with literature on the Zionist program by the Zionist Commission to Palestine; heard in conferences much concerning the Zionist colonies and their claims and personally saw something of what had been accomplished. They found much to approve in the aspirations and plans of the Zionists, and had warm appreciation for the devotion of many of the colonists, and for their success, by modern methods, in overcoming great natural obstacles.

(3) The Commission recognized also that definite encouragement had been given to the Zionists by the Allies in Mr. Balfour's often quoted statement in its approval by other representatives of the Allies. If, however, the strict terms of the Balfour Statement are adhered to—favoring "the establishment in Palestine of a national home for the Jewish people," "it being clearly understood that nothing shall be done which may prejudice the

civil and religious rights of existing non-Jewish communities in Palestine"—it can hardly be doubted that the extreme Zionist Program must be greatly modified. For "a national home for the Jewish people" is not equivalent to making Palestine into a Jewish State; nor can the erection of such a Jewish State be accomplished without the gravest trespass upon the "civil and religious rights of existing non-Jewish communities in Palestine". The fact came out repeatedly in the Commission's conference with Jewish representatives, that the Zionists looked forward to a practically complete dispossession of the present non-Jewish inhabitants of Palestine, by various forms of purchase.

In his address of July 4, 1918, President Wilson laid down the following principle as one of the four great "ends for which the associated peoples of the world were fighting": "The settlement of every question, whether of territory, of sovereignty, of economic arrangement, or of political relationship upon the basis of the free acceptance of that settlement by the people immediately concerned, and not upon the basis of the material interest or advantage of any other nation or people which may desire a different settlement for the sake of its own exterior influence or mastery". If that principle is to rule, and so the wishes of Palestine's population are to be decisive as to what is to be done with Palestine, then it is to be remembered that the non-Jewish population of Palestine—nearly nine-tenths of the whole—are emphatically against the entire Zionist program. The tables show that there was no one thing upon which the population of Palestine were more agreed than upon this. To subject a people so minded to unlimited Jewish immigration, and to steady financial and social pressure to surrender the land, would be a gross violation of the principle just quoted, and of the peoples' rights, though it kept within the forms of law.

It is to be noted also that the feeling against the Zionist program is not confined to Palestine, but shared very generally by the people throughout Syria, as our conferences clearly showed. More than 72 per cent—1350 in all—of all the petitions in the whole of Syria were directed against the Zionist program. Only two requests—those for a united Syria and for independence—had a larger support. This general feeling was only voiced by the "General Syrian Congress," in the seventh, eighth and tenth resolutions of their statement.

The Peace Conference should not shut its eyes to the fact that the anti-Zionist feeling in Palestine and Syria is intense and not lightly to be flouted.

Source: Laqueur and Rubin, *Israel-Arab Reader,* pp. 28–29.

DOCUMENT 2–9

The Churchill White Paper—1922

The tension which has prevailed from time to time in Palestine is mainly due to apprehensions, which are entertained both by sections of the Arab and by sections of the Jewish population. These apprehensions, so far as the Arabs are concerned, are partly based upon exaggerated interpretations of the meaning of the Declaration favouring the establishment of a Jewish National Home in Palestine, made on behalf of His Majesty's Government on 2nd November, 1917. Unauthorized statements have been made to the effect that the purpose in view is to create a wholly Jewish Palestine. Phrases have been used such as that Palestine is to become "as Jewish as England is English." His Majesty's Government regard any such expectation as impracticable and have no such aim in view. Nor have they at any time contemplated, as appears to be feared by the Arab Delegation, the disappearance or the subordination of the Arabic population, language, or culture in Palestine. They would draw attention to the fact that the terms of the Declaration referred to do not contemplate that Palestine as a whole should be converted into a Jewish National Home, but that such a Home should be founded *in Palestine.* . . .

So far as the Jewish population of Palestine are concerned it appears that some among them are apprehensive that His Majesty's Government may depart from the policy embodied in the Declaration of 1917. It is necessary, therefore, once more to affirm that these fears are unfounded, and that that Declaration, re-affirmed by the Conference of the Principal Allied Powers at San Remo and again in the Treaty of Sèvres, is not susceptible of change. . . .

When it is asked what is meant by the development of the Jewish National Home in Palestine, it may be answered that it is not the imposition of a Jewish nationality upon the inhabitants of Palestine as a whole, but the further development of the existing Jewish community, with the assistance of Jews in other parts of the world, in order that it may become a centre in which the Jewish people as a whole may take, on grounds of religion and race, an interest and a pride. But in order that this community should have the best prospect of free development and provide a full opportunity for the Jewish people to display its capacities, it is essential that it should know that it is in Palestine as of right and not on sufferance. That is the reason why it is necessary that the existence of a Jewish National Home in Palestine should be internationally guaranteed, and that it should be formally recognized to rest upon ancient historic connection.

This, then, is the interpretation which His Majesty's Government place upon the Declaration of 1917, and, so understood, the Secretary of State is of opinion that it does not contain or imply anything which need cause either alarm to the Arab population of Palestine or disappointment to the Jews.

For the fulfilment of this policy it is necessary that the Jewish community in Palestine should be able to increase its numbers by immigration. This immigration cannot be so great in volume as to exceed whatever may be the economic capacity of the country at the time to absorb new arrivals. It is essential to ensure that the immigrants should not be a burden upon the people of Palestine as a whole, and that they should not deprive any section of the present population of their employment.

Source: Laqueur and Rubin, *Israel-Arab Reader,* pp. 45–48.

DOCUMENT 2–10

The Peel Commission's Justification for Proposing Partition for Palestine, 1937

An irrepressible conflict has arisen between two national communities within the narrow bounds of one small country. About 1,000,000 Arabs are in strife, open or latent, with some 400,000 Jews. There is no common ground between them. The Arab community is predominantly Asiatic in character, the Jewish community predominantly European. They differ in religion and in language. Their cultural and social life, their ways of thought and conduct, are as incompatible as their national aspirations. These last are the greatest bar to peace. Arabs and Jews might possibly learn to live and work together in Palestine if they would make a genuine effort to reconcile and combine their national ideals and so build up in time a joint or dual nationality. But this they cannot do. The War and its sequel have inspired all Arabs with the hope of reviving in a free and united Arab world the traditions of the Arab golden age. The Jews similarly are inspired by their historic past. They mean to show what the Jewish nation can achieve when restored to the land of its birth. National assimilation between Arabs and Jews is thus ruled out. In the Arab picture the Jews could only occupy the place they occupied in Arab Egypt or Arab Spain. The Arabs would be as much outside the Jewish picture as the Canaanites in the old land of Israel. The National Home, as we have said before, cannot be half-national. In these circumstances to maintain that Palestinian citizenship has any moral meaning is a mischievous pretence. Neither Arab nor Jew has any sense of service to a single State.

Palestine Royal Commission Report,
(Cmd. 5479, 1937)

Source: Fraser, *The Middle East,* pp. 22–23.

DOCUMENT 2–11

The 1939 White Paper on Palestine (Excerpt)

In the light of these considerations His Majesty's Government make the following declaration of their intentions regarding the future government of Palestine:

(1) The objective of His Majesty's Government is the establishment within ten years of an independent Palestine State in such treaty relations with the United Kingdom as will provide satisfactorily for the commercial and strategic requirements of both countries in the future. The proposal for the establishment of the independent State would involve consultation with the Council of the League of Nations with a view to the termination of the Mandate.

(2) The independent State should be one in which Arabs and Jews share in government in such a way as to ensure that the essential interests of each community are safeguarded.

. . .

14   It has been urged that all further Jewish immigration into Palestine should be stopped forthwith. His Majesty's Government cannot accept such a proposal. It would damage the whole of the financial and economic system of Palestine and thus affect adversely the interests of Arabs and Jews alike. Moreover, in the view of His Majesty's Government, abruptly to stop further immigration would be unjust to the Jewish National Home. But, above all, His Majesty's Government are conscious of the present unhappy plight of large numbers of Jews who seek a refuge from certain European countries, and they believe that Palestine can and should make a further contribution to the solution of this pressing world problem. In all these circumstances, they believe that they will be acting consistently with their Mandatory obligations to both Arabs and Jews, and in the manner best calculated to serve the interests of the whole people of Palestine, by adopting the following proposals regarding immigration:

(1) Jewish immigration during the next five years will be at a rate which, if economic absorptive capacity permits, will bring the Jewish population up to approximately one-third of the total population of the country. Taking into account the expected natural increase of the Arab and Jewish populations, and the number of illegal Jewish immigrants now in the country, this would allow of the admission, as from the beginning of April this year, of some 75,000 immigrants over the next five years. These immigrants would, subject to the criterion of economic absorptive capacity, be admitted as follows:

(*a*) For each of the next five years a quota of 10,000 Jewish immigrants will be allowed on the understanding that a shortage in any one year may be added to the quotas for subsequent years, within the five-year period, if economic absorptive capacity permits.

(*b*) In addition, as a contribution towards the solution of the Jewish refugee problem, 25,000 refugees will be admitted as soon as the High Commissioner is satisfied that adequate provision for their maintenance is ensured, special consideration being given to refugee children and dependants.

(2) The existing machinery for ascertaining economic absorptive capacity will be retained, and the High Commissioner will have the ultimate responsibility for deciding the limits of economic capacity. Before each periodic decision is taken, Jewish and Arab representatives will be consulted.

(3) After the period of five years no further Jewish immigration will be permitted unless the Arabs of Palestine are prepared to acquiesce in it.

(4) His Majesty's Government are determined to check illegal immigration, and further preventive measures are being adopted. The numbers of any Jewish illegal immigrants who, despite these measures, may succeed in coming into the country and cannot be deported will be deducted from the yearly quotas.

15 His Majesty's Government are satisfied that, when the immigration over five years which is now contemplated has taken place, they will not be justified in facilitating, nor will they be under any obligation to facilitate, the further development of the Jewish National Home by immigration regardless of the wishes of the Arab population.

Palestine: Statement of Policy, (Cmd. 6019, 1939)

Source: Fraser, *The Middle East,* pp. 23–24.

CHAPTER 3

WORLD WAR II, JEWISH DISPLACED PERSONS, AND PALESTINE

CHRONOLOGY

Jan. 30, 1933	Adolf Hitler assumes power in Germany	**April 12, 1945**	Death of FDR. Harry S. Truman becomes U.S. President
Sept.–Nov. 1935	Nuremberg Laws against Jews passed	**May 25, 1945**	Germany surrenders
April 1936	Formation of Arab Higher Committee	**Nov. 13, 1945**	Anglo-American Committee of Inquiry into Jewish refugee question announced
July 1937	Report of Peel Commission		
July 1938	Evian Refugee Conference	**May 1, 1946**	Anglo-American Committee report issued
May 1939	MacDonald White Paper		
Dec. 1941	Death camps put into operation	**July 22, 1946**	British H.Q. in King David Hotel, Jerusalem, bombed
May 1942	Zionist Conference at Biltmore Hotel, New York City	**Oct. 4, 1946**	Truman announces support for partition of Palestine into Jewish and Arab states
Nov. 4, 1944	Churchill makes promise to Weizmann		
Nov. 6, 1944	Lord Moyne assassinated in Cairo	**Jan. 1947**	British Cabinet decide to refer Palestine question to the United Nations
Feb. 1945	President Roosevelt meets with Ibn Saud, King of Saudi Arabia	**April 28, 1947**	Opening of special session of U.N. General Assembly on Palestine
March 22, 1945	Arab League founded in Cairo		

World War II was a major event in twentieth-century Palestine history as well as the central event of twentieth-century Europe. Historians disagree on how greatly the war and the Holocaust affected Palestine. The majority of Zionist historians stress the importance of the Holocaust, the Allied victory, and the centrality of the survivors in shaping the events leading to the vital United Nations' decision to partition Palestine into a Jewish state and an Arab state, and the solution most Zionists reluctantly supported. Pro-Palestinian historians, on the other hand, while not entirely ignoring the destruction of European Jewry and efforts to find a safe homeland for the "remnants" following the war, emphasize the "gun-Zionism" of segments of the Yishuv in Palestine itself, and their effective use of terror and guerilla tactics in ousting the British from Palestine and later defeating the Palestinian Arabs and their supporters. Interestingly, both groups of historians stress the role of the United States government and of American Jewry in influencing American policy toward support for the partition of Palestine.

In this chapter we shall trace the events leading to the decision of the United Nations General Assembly on November 29, 1947, recommending the partition of Palestine into a Jewish state and an Arab state with economic union, and we will weigh the arguments of both sides about the significance of World War II and the Holocaust on the history of Palestine.

What is noteworthy about British policy during and immediately after World War II, especially in the light of the Holocaust, is just how closely it preserved the intent of the White Paper of 1939, issued before Hitler embarked upon the "final solution." Considering what Britain and its allies later learned about the fate of European Jewry in all its horrific detail, and the continued tragedy of the survivors following Germany's defeat, the British government's adherence to its stated 1939 policy concerning the admission of Jewish refugees into Palestine is quite extraordinary. It does, however, add weight to the argument that if World War II was important in the establishment of Israel, it was not because the Christian nations felt an obligation to the Jews of Europe to provide them with a homeland. British policy, at least in this respect, tends rather to support the view that the war was important because it forced the Yishuv to realize that if Jews wanted a state, they would have to win it with deeds as well as words.

In fact, during the war the British government did reconsider its postwar policy toward Palestine. Recognizing that the end of the mandate was inevitable, in December 1943, a cabinet committee on Palestine backed by Churchill recommended British support for the partition of Palestine—the plan first proposed by the 1937 Peel Commission. Chaim Weizmann and the Jewish Agency knew of this decision. The assassination in Cairo of Lord Moyne, deputy minister of state for Middle East Affairs and a close personal friend of Churchill's, by the Jewish terrorist group LEHI (the Stern Gang) on November 6, 1944, prevented this recommendation from becoming official British policy.

Had there been no war in Europe, the Jews of Palestine in their resort to arms would, presumably, have met the same fate at the hands of the British army as had the Arabs of Palestine in the 1936–1939 uprising. In this context it is perhaps also worth considering what would have happened to the Jews of Palestine had the German General Erwin Rommel won his North African campaign. Clearly the history of Palestine and the Middle East would have been entirely different; under an agreement signed by the Mufti of Jerusalem, Haj Amin el-Husseini, and the Italian dictator Benito Mussolini in October 1941, the Jews of Palestine would have been exterminated by the Germans, with the help of the Arabs.

Both Arabs and Jews objected to British policy in 1939. The Arabs felt cheated;

their hoped-for independence had once again been deferred, and Jewish immigration was going to continue for five more years. Zionists had to face the unacceptable idea that the British felt that the existing Jewish population and their institutions were such that they had fulfilled their promise of establishing a Jewish national home in Palestine. Although most people see the two statements of British policy as mutually contradictory, the 1939 White Paper may be compared with the previous major document of British policy toward Palestine—the Balfour Declaration. Both documents appear to make contradictory promises; both appear to be the result of compromises that failed to satisfy fully either Jews or Arabs; and while Jews accepted the Balfour Declaration, both Jews and Arabs rejected the 1939 White Paper.

THE HOLOCAUST

During World War II, Zionists supported the Allies against Germany. They had no alternative. Haj Amin al-Husseini, the most influential leader of Palestinian Arabs, supported Germany, and many Arab leaders, including Anwar Sadat, for example, joined German-front organizations. But far more important was the Nazi policy of extermination of the Jews both in Europe and, if they had been victorious, in Palestine. At the beginning of World War II, there were approximately 18.5 million Jews in the world; by the end of the war, 6 million had been murdered. Only a million of Europe's 7 million Jews survived the Holocaust. Beginning in 1942, extermination of Jews ranked high in priority among the Nazis' activities. The Holocaust differed quantitatively and qualitatively from previous European anti-Semitism. Hitler's 'final solution' was the logical conclusion of neo-Darwinian views: Aryans were superior to Jews (Gypsies and Slavs as well), who were polluters of civilization and culture. The Jews should, therefore, be eliminated. In addition, Hitler believed that Jews were part of a Jewish, Communist conspiracy that, in his mind, was responsible for Germany's defeat in World War I.

What do we mean when we speak of the Holocaust? It was not simply a larger version of previous Jewish persecutions, or an extended pogrom. Nor does the Holocaust mean that Jews just suffered more death and destruction than other groups in Europe, such as the Russians or Poles, or others, such as the Cambodians, who have been massacred by the millions since that time. There are many examples in history of mass murder, for example, the Armenians by the Turks during World War I, and we should remember that 29 million non-Jews perished in World War II in addition to the approximately six million Jews. But the Holocaust differs from these events in one basic way: the Holocaust was the attempt to annihilate—indeed, totally exterminate—all the Jews of Europe. None of the other massacres, however horrifying, had as their basic aim the total elimination of a people.

Although the Holocaust may be viewed as the catalyst in the establishment of Israel after World War II, the internal forces of Jewish history striving toward independent statehood had been set in motion long before the extermination of European Jewry. Zionist leaders did not learn the facts of the Holocaust until the summer of 1942, following the Biltmore Conference held in New York City. Even then they did not grasp its scale and extent. It was deeply shocking that such events could happen in the twentieth century. While for world Jewry—and doubtless also for the majority of Christians in Britain and the United States—the Holocaust created an irresistible sense that something should be done in Palestine to atone for the Holocaust and to compensate the remnants of European Jewry, this attitude did not prevail over all other concerns among British and American policymakers. The Holocaust clearly did not influence Ernest Bevin, the British Foreign Secretary in the new Labor government, who resisted efforts to admit Jewish displaced persons into Palestine between 1946 and 1948. Nor did it figure in the minds of American State Department officials, including Secretary of State George Marshall, whose prime concern was European security and the future interests of American oil firms in the Middle East. Harry Truman, the grandson of Southerners forced to become refugees after the Civil War, was an exception, but even he had many other reasons for his attempt to persuade the British to admit 100,000 Jewish displaced persons into Palestine. And the Holocaust certainly did not figure in the minds of Palestinian Arabs. They took the understandable view that they did not perpetrate the Holocaust, and if Europeans felt, rightly, that they should make amends, they should not do so at the expense of the Arabs.

The German government had not embarked on mass murder of Jews at the outset; the 'final solution' was reached by stages. The first step was to define Jews in terms of race. The Nuremberg Laws of 1935 prohibited marriage and sexual relations between Aryans (the designations "Aryan" and "non-Aryan" were introduced in 1933) and Jews in an attempt to isolate and identify Jews. Nazi regulations became more and more repressive; Jews were required to register with the state and to wear the Jewish badge—a large yellow six pointed star worn on the back and on the chest.

With the events of *Kristallnacht* in November 1938, when roving Nazi gangs destroyed Jewish homes, property, and synagogues throughout Germany, Nazi policy approached that of inciting a pogrom. Jews were "encouraged" by threats of internment in concentration camps to leave Germany and to abandon their possessions. The majority did not leave, of course, because they either felt assimilated, believed that the danger would pass, or had nowhere else to go. Remember, most European nations had their own problems at that time—it was still the period of world depression—and non-European Western countries like the United States, Australia, South Africa, and nations in South America had restrictions (usually economic and/or racial) upon the number and type of immigrants they would admit. These restrictions barred most of Europe's Jews. The depressed economic conditions most nations were experiencing during the late 1930s probably made it easier for most statesmen to believe Hitler would not carry out his stated policies toward Jews, even though it was becoming clearer day by day that he would indeed exterminate them.

Some belated steps were taken, however, although it was pretty much a case of too little too late. In July 1938, President Franklin Delano Roosevelt had convened an international Conference at Evian, on the French shore of Lake Geneva, to discuss ways of rescuing Jewish refugees from Germany. It was a failure. Most countries would take very few if any Jews. Moreover, leaders of world Zionism did not really want the Jews to go to lands other than Palestine. The British, as we noted earlier, would not allow increased Jewish entry into Palestine, but they did try to find alternative locations for some Jewish refugees, such as Guyana and, later, Australia.

After the Germans marched into Poland in 1939, Jews were rounded up and concentrated in ghettos. Nazi leaders decided on mass murder as the 'final solution' to the "problem" of European Jewry after the invasion of the Soviet Union in 1941. Several methods were used. At first, the *Einsatzgruppen*, killing squads of the S.S. (*Schutzstaffel*) who were especially selected and trained, followed front-line troops, and, after rounding up suspected Jews, shot them en masse and buried them in huge graves that they had forced their victims to dig. The S.S., formed in 1925, became the elite organization of the Nazi party and carried out the central tasks in the 'final solution.' Hitler placed Adolf Eichmann in charge of ridding Germany and German-occupied Europe of all Jews, and gave him practically unlimited powers. Heinrich Himmler, head of the S.S., became the chief executor of the 'final solution.' Gassing in sealed trucks became the preferred method of killing as early as December 1941, and eventually special camps, or extermination centers, were created for the purpose of mass murder. It is impossible to convey the brutal, sadistic, and terrifying nature of these camps by merely describing them. All we can say is that the use of death camps by the Nazis was a debasement of humanity. (See Document 3–1.)

JEWISH RESISTANCE TO THE HOLOCAUST

Prompted by the stupefying immensity of the Holocaust, people continue to ask questions about the Jewish response to these events. How much Jewish resistance was there? What did the Allies do? What could they have done? A popular notion was that the Jews somehow contributed to the magnitude of their own destruction because they went without resistance "like lambs to the slaughter." In a sense, the murdered victims have become the defendants. The absurdity of this view can be seen when we recall that the German Army swept through most of Europe in less than a year. France surrendered in the *Blitzkrieg* without a major battle, and the Baltic and Balkan states, many of whose people were deported for slave labor and never returned, capitulated with little defense or defiance. In addition, the Nazi policy of persecuting Jews, if not actively supported, certainly was not opposed by large sections of the non-Jewish populations of Germany and Eastern Europe, especially in Poland. Some Gentiles, to be sure, did attempt to help individual Jews, but the number was small. The best-known "Righteous Gentile" was Raoul Wallenberg, a Swedish diplomat who was instrumental in saving the lives of thousands of Hungarian Jews before his capture and imprisonment by the Russians in 1945. Even the Roman Catholic Church was ambivalent in its response to Jewish persecution at the hands of the Nazis. Finally, the entire operation of the death camps was shrouded in secrecy.

What is surprising about Jewish resistance when we consider these facts is not that there was so little resistance, but that there was so much. Despite the lack of arms, or the means to buy them, there are countless stories of active Jewish resistance to the Nazis both inside and outside the death camps. The Warsaw Ghetto uprising in April 1943 is the most dramatic example. The Allied war planners contented themselves with the belief that the most effective method of assisting Jews was victory over Germany.

Jewish resistance to the Holocaust also included Jewish Agency efforts to rescue Jews from Europe and transport them to Palestine, and offers to form Jewish fighting units with the British against the Germans in North Africa. Both these activities formed part of the broader Zionist goal of circumventing the Malcolm MacDonald White Paper and securing ultimate Jewish statehood. And both were opposed by the British, who were anxious not to anger the Arabs whose support they would need for their own postwar interests. The conflict between Jewish efforts to spirit Jewish refugees to Palestine and British determination to stop them from reaching their destination was dramatically highlighted with the sinking of two ships, the *Patria* and the *Struma*, filled with refugees. In November 1940, the *Patria*, with over 1,700 "illegal" refugees whom British authorities were deporting to Mauritius, was sabotaged by the Haganah and sank in Haifa bay with the loss of more than 100 lives. In February 1942, 770 refugees were lost when the *Struma* sank in the Black Sea after being delayed by British pressure on Turkey to prevent its passage to Palestine.

Meanwhile, Chaim Weizmann, the Jewish Agency, and the Haganah sought to gain British approval for the formation of a Jewish unit, either a brigade or division, to fight under the Zionist flag alongside British troops. There were several reasons for this proposal. One was for the Haganah to gain greater military training, experience, and access to arms; another was to strengthen Jewish claims on British gratitude in the negotiations over Palestine that would take place after the war. Finally, of course, was the desire to defeat the Nazis. Winston Churchill supported the idea, but it was not until late 1944 that a Jewish infantry brigade was formed that fought as a separate unit in Europe (in Italy), although many Jews fought in regular British units. Altogether, some 26,000 Palestinian Jews had joined British forces by the end of the war. Some Zionist goals were realized. A considerable number of arms were stored by the Haganah. Several underground paramilitary groups had been formed; the Irgun, led by a young Polish soldier, Menachem Begin, and LEHI (the Stern Gang), organized along militaristic lines. The function of the Irgun and LEHI was to strengthen the armed capabilities of the Yishuv for what they regarded as the inevitable war with the Arabs, as well as with the British. This was done by building up the supply of weapons (mainly stolen from the British), conducting guerrilla—or terrorist—attacks on the local British forces and police, and by arranging the illegal entry of refugees from Europe on ships secretly purchased or leased for this purpose by the Jewish Agency. Communication networks were established for the movement of refugees from Europe to Palestine. These networks later became especially useful to the B'richa, the organized underground network of Jewish fighters and Zionist leaders from Palestine who helped many thousands of Holocaust survivors break the British blockade to reach Palestine between 1945 and 1948. The function of B'richa was essentially that of getting the refugees to the point of embarkation in Europe.

THE UNITED STATES, AMERICAN JEWS, AND PALESTINE TO 1945

As the dimensions of the Holocaust became clearer, Jewish communities everywhere became increasingly anxious and united, and support for Zionist aspirations dramatically grew in strength. This was particularly true of the 4.5 million Jews in the United States. Many claims have been made about the persuasiveness of Zionist pressure groups in influencing American policy; indeed, it has been argued by some that Jewish control of the mass media meant that Zionists were able to manipulate American public opinion at large. These claims are mostly exaggerations, based either on ignorance of the situation of Jews in America, or on hostility to Zionism, which stems often from opposition to policies pursued by Israel in its relations with its Arab neighbors and with the Palestinian refugees who resulted from the establishment of the Jewish state. However, it should also be said that these claims are also made by pro-Zionists attempting to emphasize the importance of Zionism in the United States. Thus, this view that Jews are far more significant in American politics than their numbers suggest is very widespread. There is some truth in this, as in all such exaggerations, but as we shall see when we look at the events between 1942 and 1948, there were also many other factors at work in shaping American policy toward the Middle East. Only where there was a coincidence of Jewish (or Zionist) and non-Jewish aspirations did the Zionists achieve their goals.

Given the importance that historians have attached to American Jewry in influencing U.S. policy toward supporting a Jewish state in Palestine, we should say something about the political activities of American Jews during and after the war. The

Jews of the United States, some 1.5 million of whom had migrated from Russia and Eastern Europe in the first decade of the twentieth century, were a highly assimilated group by the 1930s, although they were hardly as well-off or as educated as Jews are today. There were still visible signs of anti-Semitism in those years, and Jews were excluded from joining certain organizations and clubs. In particular, America's restrictive immigration laws were based on a quota system, which discriminated against people of Eastern European origin, thereby limiting the number of Jews admitted. If Jewish immigrants—refugees—were to be admitted, it would be at the expense of nationals of predominantly Catholic, or possibly even Protestant, countries. Neither Catholics nor Protestants, inside or outside of Congress, desired this. Nor, it must be said, did some Zionist leaders. They believed that if refugees could be resettled anywhere, including the United States, it would weaken their claim on Palestine as the only homeland for Jews. In addition, many feared that additional Jewish immigrants would inflame anti-Semitism and cost money to absorb.

The Jewish population of the United States was heavily concentrated in the urban states of New York, New Jersey, Pennsylvania, Illinois, and California. For a number of reasons, mostly to do with the policies of the Democratic administration of Franklin Delano Roosevelt during the Great Depression, the role of many Jews in the New Deal, and FDR's opposition to Nazi Germany even before the outbreak of the war, Jews identified with the Democratic party and supported it with their votes and campaign funds. Before the war, the Zionist movement in the United States was opposed by most of the religious establishments and Jewish organizations. Orthodox rabbis objected to Zionism for upsetting the messianic idea, and Reform rabbis objected to its parochial nationalist emphasis rather than the universal sense they attached to it. Some Jewish organizations rejected the notion that Jews everywhere constituted one nation and were unassimilable as casting doubt on their loyalty to the United States. They feared such views would only fuel anti-Semitism throughout the country.

Zionist leaders, on the other hand, believed that the war in Europe and the Holocaust made it essential that they enlist American Jewry in an attempt to get U.S. government support for a Jewish state. To Zionists, the Holocaust proved beyond all doubt that security was a vain dream. They argued that neither emancipation nor assimilation had stayed the hands that throughout history had been raised against the Jews. The survivors would find security and peace only in a national home in Palestine.

Prior to World War II, the American government had regarded Palestine as a British responsibility. The oil resources of the Middle East, and the strategic importance of Palestine in relation to containing Soviet expansion into the region, did not emerge as major considerations until the postwar years. The United States had officially endorsed the Balfour Declaration in 1922, but beyond sending an American delegation—which included Senator Warren Austin (later to be the U.S. Ambassador to the United Nations at the time of the partition resolution)—to Palestine in 1936 at the time of the Arab Rebellion, the United States had not shown much interest. The war was to change that situation. By March 1943, the U.S. State Department was concerned about American production of oil for the war and the supply of oil for postwar Europe. In May 1943, alarmed over the security of the Middle East and its oil supplies, the State Department advised President Roosevelt that he should reassure the Arab world of American friendship. In early 1945, returning from the Yalta conference shortly before his death, Roosevelt met with the king of Saudi Arabia, Abdul-Aziz Ibn Saud, and promised him that no decision would be made concerning the future of Palestine without full consultation with both Arabs and Jews.

Meanwhile, in May 1942, an Extraordinary Conference was called by the Emergency Committee for Zionist Affairs in the United States and held at the Biltmore Hotel in New York City. At this conference, Zionist leaders finally called unequivocally for the establishment of Palestine (defined as the original British Mandate including Transjordan) as a Jewish Commonwealth (that is, a Jewish state). (See Document 3–2.) From this point on, this extended goal became the policy of the World Zionist Organization. Shortly after the Biltmore conference, Chaim Weizmann was replaced as Zionist leader by David Ben-Gurion. Weizmann, longtime president of the World Zionist Organization, had advocated a policy of gradualism, which meant using diplomacy and working with the political leaders of Britain and the United States. Ben-Gurion, at the time leader of the Mapai party (Labor Party) in Palestine and chairman of the Jewish Agency Executive in Palestine, was an activist. He advocated achieving immediate statehood by the use of force if necessary, and he backed a policy of pressuring the United States into supporting a revolutionary change in Palestine to which the British would then have to agree. The conflict over the role of diplomacy, or the role of force, as a means of achieving their goals has remained a major source of division among Zionists.

By the end of 1943, to Jews throughout the world, the situation seemed hopeless. Groups sympathetic to Zionism such as the Christian American Palestine Committee, formed in 1941 and chaired by New York Senator Robert Wagner, a Roman Catholic, joined with the newly formed American Zionist Emergency Council, jointly chaired by two rabbis, Stephen S. Wise and Abba Hillel Silver, in lobbying Congress and the White House to support a Jewish state in Palestine and unrestricted immigration of Jews into Palestine. Early in 1944, the American Palestine Committee was able to have resolutions introduced into the Congress calling on the United States to urge Britain to permit unrestricted Jewish immigration into Palestine. Both Secretary of State Cordell Hull and Chief of Staff George C. Marshall strongly opposed any resolutions on the grounds that they might very well involve American troops in maintaining oil supplies to the Allies were the Arabs to carry out their threats. Thus the resolutions were dropped. At this stage, as throughout, national interest defined in military and strategic terms by the State Department won out over moral and humanitarian considerations. The only significant step taken in this direction by the U.S. Government was the establishment, in January 1944, of the War Refugee Board to bring help to the persecuted Jews and other minorities in Europe, but by then it was too late to save most of the victims.

In October 1944, President Roosevelt promised that if reelected he would help bring about "the establishment of Palestine as a free and democratic Jewish Commonwealth." Nevertheless, there was little President Roosevelt could or would do in relation to Palestine. He was advised by the State Department that a pro-Zionist stance could prompt the Arabs to turn to the Soviet Union for support and trade, and generally hurt U.S. interests in the Arab world. The British had not changed their mind about limiting the number of Jews to be admitted to Palestine, and they already suspected that the United States was trying to replace them as the major Western power in the Middle East.

Moreover, both the British and U.S. governments opposed these Zionist policies because they realized that the Arabs would not support the Allies if it meant that Palestine would then be handed over to the Jews. Prime Minister Churchill was sympathetic to the Zionist cause, and on November 4, 1944, he promised Chaim Weizmann unreservedly to find an acceptable solution. He told Weizmann of his government's plans for the immediate immigration of 100,000 Jewish orphans, settlement of 1.5 million refugees over a ten-year period, and the partition of Palestine. On the other hand, the Foreign Office under Anthony Eden was unsympathetic. As with the U.S. State Department, the British Foreign Office did not wish to antagonize Arab leaders. Britain's oil interests and its pre-eminent influence in the Middle East would be endangered, it was argued, by the establishment of a Jewish state. Furthermore, there was increasing violence from the Jewish extremists in Palestine. On November 6, 1944, just two days after Churchill's promises to Weizmann, the British Resident Ambassador in the Middle East, Lord Moyne—who had in fact supported the partition of Palestine—was murdered in Cairo by the Stern Gang. The Jewish Agency attempted to curb terrorist activity, but the damage had been done; the British were not prepared to consider a change in their Palestine policy in these circumstances.

PALESTINE AFTER WORLD WAR II

At the end of the war in Europe no one knew what would happen in Palestine. The British government wanted an end to the mounting violence perpertrated by the Yishuv, and it wanted to retain its predominance in the Middle East; particularly, the British wished to keep control of the strategic oil port of Haifa. The U.S. government wanted to increase its share of the oil resources in the Middle East. It did not, however, want to send in troops in the event of a Soviet intrusion or a possible conflict between Arabs and Jews over the future of Palestine. The U.S. government was prepared to let the British have that responsibility. The Palestinian Arabs wanted an end to Jewish immigration and an independent Arab state, while Palestinian Jews wanted a Jewish state, probably achieved by partition of the mandated area, although the Revisionists always envisaged having a Jewish state on both sides of the Jordan River. The other factor pervading all the discussions on the future of Palestine was the question of the fate of the survivors of the Holocaust. Between May 1946 and November 1947, events moved in the direction of partition and the establishment of a Jewish state.

The most important factors leading to the formation of Israel in this postwar period were, first, the success of the Yishuv in creating a situation that forced the British to take the issue to the United Nations, and second, activities related to Europe's Jewish displaced persons. During the war, the Jewish Agency and its military arm, the Haganah, had greatly strengthened the position of the Yishuv in Palestine. The Yishuv, fired by shame, agony, and hatred caused by the Holocaust, merged into a cohesive and determined national community. They were, in reality, far stronger than Cairo, Damascus, London, or Washington believed. The Haganah had operated on several fronts, in line with Ben-Gurion's motto to fight the British as if there were no war and to fight the war as if there were no White Paper.

THE DISPLACED PERSONS AND PALESTINE

After Germany's surrender in May 1945, the Allied forces faced the staggering problems of repatriating about 7 million dislocated and displaced persons (DPs). By September 1945, 1.5 million refused to, or could not, return to their former homes. Of these, 50,000 to 100,000 DPs were Jews who had been liberated by the Allied armies. By 1946, this number had swelled to 250,000 with the arrival of refugees from Eastern Europe. The story of the Jews in the DP camps, and the emigration of the survivors over the next three years, is the last chapter in the Nazi persecution of the Jews. We should note several aspects of this story.

First, various Jewish and non-Jewish philanthropic organizations such as the American-based Joint Distribution Committee and the United Nations Relief and Rehabilitation Agency (established in November 1943), together with the Allied armies, provided for the immediate physical and material needs of the DPs. Second, Zionist groups worked in Europe to assist Jews to get to Palestine or to DP camps in the American Zone of Germany and Austria. Third, the Jewish Agency and Zionist organizations in Britain and especially the United States tried to influence their respective governments to solve the problem of admitting the Jewish DPs to Palestine. Fourth, the British and American governments moved slowly in deciding the fate of the DPs and accepting the viability of a Jewish state in Palestine. And finally, the Yishuv and the Haganah used all the means at their disposal to win a Jewish state. All these factors can be seen in the web of events leading to the United Nations General Assembly Resolution to partition Palestine into a Jewish and an Arab state.

The Allied forces, especially Supreme Commander General Dwight D. Eisenhower, were shocked by the discovery of the concentration camps and the condition of the prisoners. Nothing had prepared the officers or troops for what they found, and they worked feverishly to restore some level of health, nutrition, decency, and self-esteem to the survivors. Despite their best efforts, however, conditions remained far from desirable. The United States had trouble feeding and clothing the DPs, and many remained billeted in the camps where they had been prisoners, wearing the same striped uniforms the Nazis had required them to wear. And after the initial shock, many American GIs began to regard the Jewish DPs as a nuisance. Officers complained that the Jews wanted special consideration and did not seem very grateful to their liberators. Nor were Jewish philanthropic organizations much able to alleviate the situation.

April 12, 1945, Gotha, Germany. General Eisenhower and other Allied generals tour a concentration camp (*Photo courtesy of U.S. Army Dwight D. Eisenhower Library*).

The Displaced Persons and Palestine

In fact, Jewish survivors from Germany and Austria could not return because their homes were either destroyed or occupied, and there was no legal mechanism for recovery or compensation from the governments of those countries. The Jewish communities, synagogues, and schools were virtually nonexistent, and survivors could not bear to return to such devastated places. In other countries like Poland, the anti-Semitism was still so strong that returning Jews risked their lives. In July 1946, in Kielce, Poland, over 130 returning refugees were killed by the local inhabitants. Not surprisingly, thousands of Eastern European Jews made their way to the American Zone in Germany for protection. The B'richa set up an underground railroad to get their fellow Jews to safety. The Jewish Agency encouraged this process in the hope that if enough Jews congregated in the American Zone, the U.S. government would pressure the British government to allow 100,000 Jews into Palestine.

The Allied nations had not planned much beyond the immediate locating of Jewish DPs into camps at the end of the fighting, as they hoped that most would return to their former homelands. When it became apparent, as it had by June–July 1945, that 50,000 to 100,000 Jews were either stateless or homeless, the Allies did not know what to do. The British government wanted the survivors to stay and rebuild their lives in Europe, and it was unwilling to allow further immigration into Palestine. Its opposition was strengthened by the increase in Jewish terrorist activity against the British in Palestine, and by attempts to embarrass London by the highly publicized voyages of ships packed with refugees trying to run the British blockade that was enforcing the restrictions.

Perhaps the best-publicized venture was that of the ship *Exodus,* which in 1947 arrived in Haifa with 4,500 refugees but which was forced to return to Europe. Another dramatic humiliation for the British was the bombing of the King David Hotel in Jerusalem in July 1946. The hotel was the main British military and civilian headquarters in Palestine and was heavily fortified. Irgun leader Menachem Begin planned the bombing, and on July 22 the wing of the hotel housing the military headquarters was blown up, killing approximately ninety people, many of them Arabs and Jews. Begin and others claimed that the British had been warned of the impending explosion in time to evacuate the hotel, but the evidence is conflicting, and not everyone has accepted Begin's version.

The United States government wanted to resolve the situation of the DPs for several reasons. The DP camps could not remain in existence indefinitely—conditions there were not acceptable, and the United States felt an obligation to care for the survivors. Also, the camps were expensive to maintain. The new American President, Harry Truman (FDR, exhausted by the war, had died on April 22, 1945), prompted by Jewish complaints, sent Earl G. Harrison, who was experienced in assisting refugees, to report on the condition of the camps in July 1945. Among his many observations, Harrison noted that the majority of the DPs wanted to go to Palestine, and he recommended that 100,000 be allowed to do so as soon as possible.

Truman was appalled by the conditions Harrison described. He immediately ordered General Eisenhower to place the Jews in separate camps and to move them into towns and villages, and he wrote to British Prime Minister Clement Attlee (the Labor party had defeated Churchill and the Conservatives in the British elections in July), urging him to admit 100,000 Jews into Palestine without delay. Americans might have felt an obligation to rehabilitate the survivors of the German death camps, but they were not, it seems, willing to admit them to the United States—although it must be said that Truman did try to get Congress to enact legislation that would allow for this. Despite the fact that some estimates suggested that almost half the DPs would have preferred to come to the United States or some other European nation, Congress allowed only 20,000 Jewish survivors into the country.

POSTWAR BRITISH AND AMERICAN POLICY

The new Labor government once again assessed Britain's situation in the Middle East. The new Foreign Secretary, Ernest Bevin, worried about Britain's ability to defend the Middle East oil fields and pipelines from the designs of the Soviet Union. And the Soviet Union seemed to the British and the United States very interested indeed in establishing itself in the Middle East and was causing great anxiety by its presence in Iran, and by an unstable Greece and Turkey. It seemed to Bevin more urgent than ever to foster Arab goodwill. Accordingly, he pursued two policies.

First, he opposed large-scale Jewish immigration to Palestine. Second, he tried to involve the United States not only in solving the refugee crisis but also in securing the Middle East for the West. These policies antagonized Zionists everywhere, and Bevin was bitterly attacked as anti-Semitic. This was not altogether fair since Bevin had supported the Zionists in the early 1930s, and he was not opposed to a Jewish state in Palestine as such. He was, however, very blunt in his manner, and he may have shared many of the vulgar anti-Jewish prejudices of his working-class background, a background he had not forgotten. Furthermore, he was undoubtedly the strongman of the British Labor party. He could not be threatened or intimidated, and he resented what he regarded as undue Zionist pressure. In addition, he was to some extent in the hands of his Foreign Office officials. Nevertheless, Bevin also believed in conciliation, and he did not want to get involved in a major conflict over Palestine; thus, he tried to get the United States to share the responsibility.

Both the U.S. State Department and President Truman shared Bevin's reluctance to get involved in a shooting war in the Middle East. The Joint Chiefs of Staff told Truman that it would take 100,000 troops to keep the peace in the event of hostilities in Palestine, and while Truman was ready to do what he could to help get Jewish DPs to Palestine, he was not prepared to send American soldiers. We must keep in mind that everyone, except the Jewish Agency and the Haganah, believed at that time that if hostilities did break out in Palestine, the Yishuv, which at that time numbered only 560,000 while the Arab population of Palestine was 1.2 million, would be convincingly defeated, even massacred, by the Arab armies opposing them. (For population and land ownership, see maps 3–1 and 3–2.)

THE ANGLO-AMERICAN COMMITTEE OF ENQUIRY

On November 4, 1945, Bevin proposed an Anglo-American Committee of Enquiry into the refugee problem. Truman agreed. The committee, consisting of six Britons and six Americans, held hearings and heard proposals from spokespersons for both Jews and Arabs in Washington, London, Palestine, and Europe where the committee visited the DP camps. (See Documents 3–3 and 3–4.) In its report, issued on May 1, 1946, the committee unanimously recommended that 100,000 Jews be immediately admitted into Palestine, but on the future of the area they could not reach agreement. As a result, the report rejected either a Jewish or an Arab state, and recommended a vague kind of unitary state to which Jews could be allowed to immigrate, but in which they would not constitute a majority. Until this was established, the mandate should continue. Despite

MAP 3–1

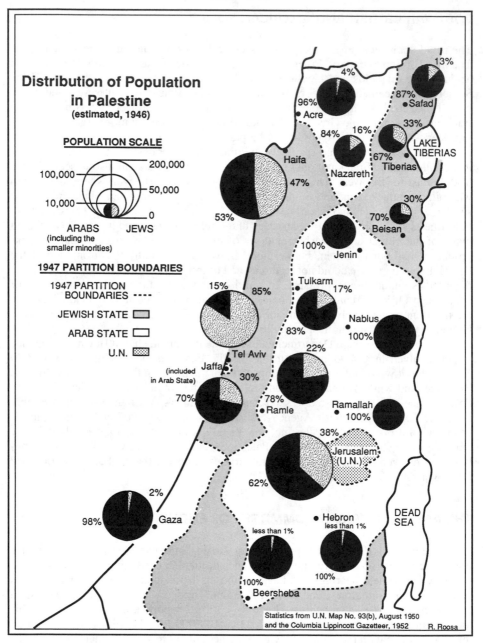

Distribution of Population
in Palestine
(estimated, 1946)

POPULATION SCALE

100,000
10,000
200,000
50,000
0

ARABS   JEWS
(including the
smaller minorities)

1947 PARTITION BOUNDARIES

1947 PARTITION
  BOUNDARIES ----
JEWISH STATE ▢
ARAB STATE ▢
U.N. ▨

Acre 96% 4%
Safad 87% 13%
Haifa 53% 47%
Nazareth 84% 16%
Tiberias 67% 33% LAKE TIBERIAS
Beisan 70% 30%
Jenin 100%
Tulkarm 83% 17%
Tel Aviv 15% 85%
Nablus 100%
Jaffa (included in Arab State) 70% 30%
Ramle 78% 22%
Ramallah 100%
Jerusalem (U.N.) 62% 38%
Gaza 98% 2%
Hebron less than 1% 100%
Beersheba less than 1% 100%
DEAD SEA

Statistics from U.N. Map No. 93(b), August 1950
and the Columbia Lippincott Gazetteer, 1952
R. Roosa

MAP 3–2

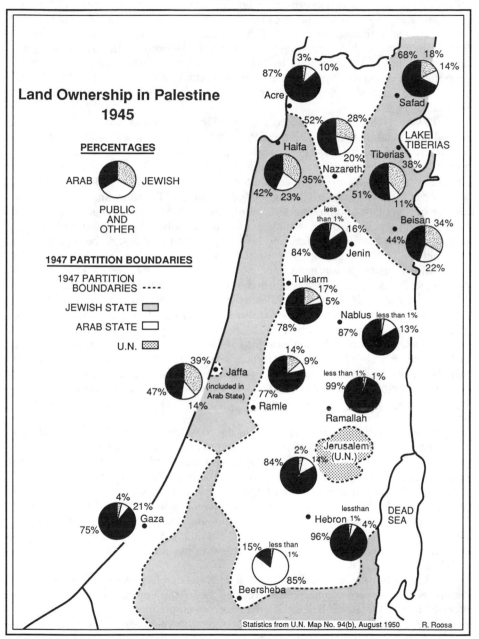

Land Ownership in Palestine
1945

PERCENTAGES

ARAB   JEWISH

PUBLIC
AND
OTHER

1947 PARTITION BOUNDARIES

1947 PARTITION
   BOUNDARIES ----

JEWISH STATE

ARAB STATE

U.N.

Acre

3%
87%   10%

68%   18%
14%
Safad

52%   28%

LAKE
TIBERIAS

Haifa
20%   Tiberias
Nazareth   38%
35%
42%   23%   51%
11%

less
than 1%
16%
84%   Jenin

Beisan   34%
44%
22%

Tulkarm
17%
5%
78%

Nablus   less than 1%
87%   13%

39%   Jaffa
(included in
Arab State)
47%
14%   Ramle
77%

14%
9%
77%

less than 1%   1%
99%
Ramallah

2%   1%
84%   Jerusalem
(U.N.)

4%   21%
Gaza
75%

lessthan
Hebron 1%   4%
96%

DEAD
SEA

15%   less than
1%
85%
Beersheba

Statistics from U.N. Map No. 94(b), August 1950   R. Roosa

The Anglo-American Committee of Enquiry   **79**

his assurance that he would support a unanimous report, Bevin flatly rejected the proposal to admit 100,000 refugees into Palestine.

Looking back, we can say that Bevin's refusal to admit the suggested number of DPs at this point was a serious error of judgment. It would have taken much of the force out of the Zionist arguments and would probably have avoided much of the subsequent bloodshed. Nevertheless, he followed the advice of his military planners, who informed him that such a step would require eight divisions of troops and over £40 million, neither of which Britain in 1946 could afford. Truman, on the other hand, supported the proposal. Prime Minister Clement Attlee cabled Truman on May 26 that if the United States helped with costs and troops he would go ahead. Further talks were scheduled.

These developments produced considerable friction and hostility between the United States and Britain. The future of Palestine, coupled as it was with the fate of the Jewish DPs and the many other strategic and economic considerations already mentioned, was a highly emotional issue. All those involved—Jews, Arabs, British, and American leaders—were deeply committed to finding a solution. The only problem was they all believed they had the right or only solution. Truman wanted the British to resolve the problem by allowing DPs into Palestine, a stand that angered Attlee and Bevin. Bevin accused Truman of bowing to domestic political pressure from Jews, and he accused the Americans of favoring Jewish migration to Palestine because they did not want the Jews admitted into the United States.

British frustration was understandable. Between May 1945 and September 1946, the United States had admitted fewer than 6,000 Jewish refugees. The British, on the other hand, had 80,000 troops in Palestine by the end of 1945, and Jewish terrorist activity was increasing. Between November 1945 and July 1946, approximately twenty British army personnel had been killed and over 100 wounded, and the police had about the same number of casualties at the hands of the Irgun or Stern groups. Railway installations and airfields were also targets of sabotage, which caused damage estimated at around £4 million British. In return, the British, already laden with heavy military commitments elsewhere, sought out arms caches and carried out raids on the Jewish Agency and Haganah headquarters, arresting suspected ringleaders. Attitudes on both sides hardened.

Several solutions were considered in the next few months. At the end of June 1946, the United States War Department agreed to provide the transportation necessary to move 100,000 Jews to Palestine. In July, Bevin suggested that an Arab province that included part of Transjordan and Lebanon could be formed, and an independent Jewish state created. Truman indicated that he would ask Congress to admit 50,000 Jewish refugees into the U.S. A second Anglo-American Committee (the Morrison–Grady Committee) recommended another plan involving the immediate immigration of 100,000 refugees into Palestine and thereafter unlimited immigration. But this plan specified that Palestine should be neither a Jewish nor an Arab state, a solution that satisfied no one.

The failure to reach a satisfactory solution was due largely to the fact that many Zionist activities were counterproductive, and that Arab opposition to the establishment of a Jewish state in Palestine remained, not surprisingly, inflexible. American Zionists and the Jewish Agency in Palestine were frustrated and angry by the turn of events. It was about this time that Polish and Eastern European Jews were learning how much anti-Semitism remained in their homelands. Between July and September 1946, 90,000 of them fled to the safety of the American zones in Germany and Austria. By the end of the year, more than 25,000 Jews crowded the DP camps of West Germany.

This situation alarmed the Americans. Many in the State Department and the military in Europe thought that it was a deliberately organized mass movement planned by Zionists to force a decision in favor of their migration to Palestine. It should be said that many of Ben-Gurion's remarks as head of the Jewish Agency, and the creation of the underground railroad moving Jews around Europe, lent credence to this point of view. Ben-Gurion had told the Anglo-American Committee of Enquiry in relation to the DPs, for example: "We are not going to renounce our independence, even if we have to pay the supreme price, and there are hundreds of thousands of Jews . . . both in the country and abroad who will give up their lives, if necessary, for Jewish independence—for Zion." From this time on, as noted earlier, Haganah harassment of the British and illegal Jewish immigration increased. The violence between the British and the Jewish military organizations in Palestine not only increased in terms of the number of clashes but also in cruelty and vindictiveness. Bevin, in particular, resented the fact that Jews were killing English soldiers who, in his view, had fought the battles of the Jews against the Nazis. Let us cite one example of the process of brutalization that was taking place. A sixteen-year-old convicted Zionist terrorist, too young to be hanged, was sentenced in December 1946, to eighteen years' imprisonment and given eighteen lashes with a cane. This humiliation outraged Menachem Begin, and his Irgun kidnapped four British officers and flogged them, giving each eighteen cuts with rawhide whips. The act and the reprisal did not reflect well on either side.

The Arabs told the British in October 1946 that they wanted a unitary Arab state in which they would be the permanent majority. They feared that a Jewish state would transform the region economically as well as demographically. By now, Bevin had begun to think seriously about handing the entire problem over to the United Nations. In this, he was helped by events in the United States.

The Zionist leader, Nahum Goldman, had indicated in August 1946 that the Jewish Agency in Palestine would accept partition, and Truman believed that if this could be achieved peacefully, it was a solution that would not involve the United States directly. American oil interests in the Middle East would, therefore, not be threatened. At the same time, it would enable the American President to satisfy Jewish voters in the forthcoming congressional elections, thereby retaining their support for the Democratic party. Thus, on October 4, on the eve of the Jewish Day of Atonement, Truman announced that he believed partition would "command the support of public opinion in the United States."

Truman's Day of Atonement statement accomplished few, if any, of the things he had hoped for. The Saudi king, Ibn Saud, not to mention the Arab League, was angry that Truman favored admitting 100,000 Jewish refugees to Palestine. At home, the Republicans won a majority in both Houses of Congress in the 1946 congressional elections despite Truman's words. Furthermore, Truman was becoming very annoyed with the threats of political retaliation by American Zionist leaders if he did not pursue a pro-Zionist line. Truman indicated to Britain that the United States would take responsibility for the protection of Greece and Turkey from Russian aggression but hinted that this might depend on the British finding a peaceful settlement to the Palestine question. This was a half-hearted threat, for, as with the emergence of the Cold War, the security of Greece, Turkey, and Iran was far too important to the United States to be jeopardized by the situation in Palestine.

In January 1947, the British government decided that if no settlement could be reached the matter would have to go to the United Nations, and, on February 14, the British took that course without recommending any preferred solution. We shall look at what happened in the next chapter.

SUGGESTIONS FOR FURTHER READING

BAUER, YEHUDA, *A History of the Holocaust,* New York, Franklin Watts, 1973.

COHEN, MICHAEL J., *Palestine and the Great Powers,* Princeton, N.J., Princeton University.

HILBERG, RAUL, *The Destruction of the European Jews,* New York, Franklin Watts, 1973.

LOUIS, W. ROGER, & STOOKEY, ROBERT, *The End of the Palestine Mandate,* Austin, University of Texas Press, 1986.

WYMAN, DAVID, *The Abandonment of the Jews,* New York, Pantheon, 1985.

DOCUMENT 3-1

Rudolf Hoess on the Methods of the 'Final Solution'

The 'final solution' of the Jewish question meant the complete extermination of all Jews in Europe. I was ordered to establish extermination facilities at Auschwitz in June 1941. At that time there were already in the general government three other extermination camps: Belzek, Treblinka and Wolzek. These camps were under the Einsatzkommando of the Security Police and SD. I visited Treblinka to find out how they carried out their extermination. The Camp Commandant at Treblinka told me he had liquidated 80,000 in the course of one-half year. He was principally concerned with liquidating all the Jews from the Warsaw ghetto. He used monoxide gas and I did not think that his methods were very efficient. So when I set up the extermination building at Auschwitz, I used Cyclon B, which was a crystallized prussic acid which we dropped into the death chamber from a small opening. It took from 3 to 15 minutes to kill the people in the death chamber depending upon climatic conditions. We knew when the people were dead because their screaming stopped. We usually waited about one-half hour before we opened the doors and removed the bodies. After the bodies were removed our special commandos took off the rings and extracted the gold from the teeth of the corpses.

Nazi Conspiracy and Aggression, vol. VI, document 3868-PS.

Source: T. G. Fraser, *The Middle East, 1914–1979* (New York: St. Martin's Press, 1980), pp. 25–26.

DOCUMENT 3-2

Declaration Adopted by the Extraordinary Zionist Conference, Biltmore Hotel, New York City, May 11, 1942

1. American Zionists assembled in this Extraordinary Conference reaffirm their unequivocal devotion to the cause of democratic freedom and international justice to which the people of the United States, allied with the other United Nations, have dedicated themselves,

and give expression to their faith in the ultimate victory of humanity and justice over lawlessness and brute force.

2. This Conference offers a message of hope and encouragement to their fellow Jews in the Ghettos and concentration camps of Hitler-dominated Europe and prays that their hour of liberation may not be far distant.

3. The Conference sends its warmest greetings to the Jewish Agency Executive in Jerusalem, to the Va'ad Leumi, and to the whole Yishuv in Palestine, and expresses its profound admiration for their steadfastness and achievements in the face of peril and great difficulties. The Jewish men and women in field and factory, and the thousands of Jewish soldiers of Palestine in the Near East who have acquitted themselves with honor and distinction in Greece, Ethiopia, Syria, Libya and on other battlefields, have shown themselves worthy of their people and ready to assume the rights and responsibilities of nationhood.

4. In our generation, and in particular in the course of the past twenty years, the Jewish people have awakened and transformed their ancient homeland; from 50,000 at the end of the last war their numbers have increased to more than 500,000. They have made the waste places to bear fruit and the desert to blossom. Their pioneering achievements in agriculture and in industry, embodying new patterns of cooperative endeavor, have written a notable page in the history of colonization.

5. In the new values thus created, their Arab neighbors in Palestine have shared. The Jewish people in its own work of national redemption welcomes the economic, agricultural and national development of the Arab peoples and states. The Conference reaffirms the stand previously adopted at Congresses of the World Zionist Organization, expressing the readiness and the desire of the Jewish people for full cooperation with their Arab neighbors.

6. The Conference calls for the fulfilment of the original purpose of the Balfour Declaration and the Mandate which *"recognizing the historical connection of the Jewish people with Palestine"* was to afford them the opportunity, as stated by President Wilson, to found there a Jewish Commonwealth.

The Conference affirms its unalterable rejection of the White Paper of May 1939 and denies its moral or legal validity. The White Paper seeks to limit, and in fact to nullify Jewish rights to immigration and settlement in Palestine, and, as stated by Mr. Winston Churchill in the House of Commons in May 1939, constitutes "a breach and repudiation of the Balfour Declaration." The policy of the White Paper is cruel and indefensible in its denial of sanctuary to Jews fleeing from Nazi persecution; and at a time when Palestine has become a focal point in the war front of the United Nations, and Palestine Jewry must provide all available manpower for farm and factory and camp, it is in direct conflict with the interests of the allied war effort.

7. In the struggle against the forces of aggression and tyranny, of which Jews were the earliest victims, and which now menace the Jewish National Home, recognition must be given to the right of the Jews of Palestine to play their full part in the war effort and in the defense of their country, through a Jewish military force fighting under its own flag and under the high command of the United Nations.

8. The Conference declares that the new world order that will follow victory cannot be established on foundations of peace, justice and equality, unless the problem of Jewish homelessness is finally solved.

The Conference urges that the gates of Palestine be opened; that the Jewish Agency be vested with control of immigration into Palestine and with the necessary authority for up-building the country, including the development of its unoccupied and uncultivated lands; and that Palestine be established as a Jewish Commonwealth integrated in the structure of the new democratic world.

Then and only then will the age-old wrong to the Jewish people be righted.

Source: Walter Laqueur and Barry Rubin, eds. *The Israel-Arab Reader: A Documentary History of the Middle East Conflict,* 4th ed. (New York: Penguin Books, 1984), pp. 77–79.

The Zionist Case: Golda Meir, Testimony before the Anglo-American Committee of Enquiry, Jerusalem, March 25, 1946.

This generation decided that the senseless living and senseless dying of Jews must end. It was they who understood the essence of Zionism—its protest against such a debased existence. The pioneers chose to come to Palestine. Other countries in the world were open to Jews, but they came to Palestine because they believed then, as they believe now, as millions of Jews believe, that the only solution for the senselessness of Jewish life and Jewish death lay in the creation of an independent Jewish life in the Jewish homeland.

The pioneer generation had still another purpose in coming here. They had two goals which inevitably shaped themselves into one. Their second aim was the creation of a new society built on the bases of equality, justice, and cooperation. When they arrived here, they were faced with tough realities. Their mission was to conquer not their fellowmen, but a harsh natural environment, marshes, deserts, the malaria-bearing mosquito. They had also to conquer themselves for these young people were not accustomed to physical labor. They had no experience of a society based on principles of cooperation. They had to overcome much within themselves in order to devote themselves to physical labor, to agriculture, and to the making of a cooperative society.

From the outset they sought to achieve these goals in complete friendship and cooperation with the Arab population and with Arab laborers. It is significant that the first organization of Arab labor in this country was founded by the Jewish workers who came at that time.

As I have said, we came to Palestine to do away with the helplessness of the Jewish people through our own endeavors. Therefore, you will realize what it meant for us to watch from here millions of Jews being slaughtered during these years of war. You have seen Hitler's slaughterhouses, and I will say nothing about them. But you can imagine what it meant to us to sit here with the curse of helplessness again upon us; we could not save them. We were prepared to do so. There was nothing that we were not ready to share with Hitler's victims.

I don't know, gentlemen, whether you who have the good fortune to belong to the two great democratic nations, the British and the American, can, with the best of will to understand our problems, realize what it means to be the member of a people whose very right to exist is constantly being questioned: our right to be Jews such as we are, no better, but no worse than others in this world, with our own language, our culture, with the right of self-determination and with a readiness to dwell in friendship and cooperation with those near us and those far away. Together with the young and the old survivors in the DP camps, the Jewish workers in this country have decided to do away with this helplessness and dependence upon others within our generation. We Jews only want that which is given naturally to all peoples of the world to be masters of our own fate—only of our fate, not of the destiny of others; to live as of right and not on sufferance, to have the chance to bring the surviving Jewish children, of whom not so many are now left in the world, to this country so that they may grow up like our youngsters who were born here, free of fear, with heads high. Our children here don't understand why the very existence of the Jewish people as such is questioned. For them, at last, it is natural to be a Jew.

We are certain that given an opportunity of bringing in large masses of Jews into this country, of opening the doors of Palestine to all Jews who wish to come here, we can go on building upon the foundation laid by the labor movement and create a free Jewish society built on the basis of cooperation, equality, and mutual aid. We wish to build such a society not only within the Jewish community, but especially together with those living with us in this country and with all our neighbors. We claim to be no better but surely no worse than other peoples. We hope that with the efforts we have already made in Palestine and will continue to

make we, too, will contribute to the welfare of the world and to the creation of that better
social order which we all undoubtedly seek.

Source: Golda Meir, *A Land of Our Own: An Oral Autobiography* (New York: G. P. Putnam's Sons,
1973), pp. 53–55.

DOCUMENT 3–4

The Palestine Arab Case: Jamal Bey Husseini, Arab Higher Committee, before the *Ad Hoc* Committee on the Palestinian Question on Palestinian Arab reactions to the UNSCOP proposals, 29 September 1947

The case of the Arabs of Palestine was based on the principles of international justice;
it was that of a people which desired to live in undisturbed possession of the country where
Providence and history had placed it. The Arabs of Palestine could not understand why their
right to live in freedom and peace, and to develop their country in accordance with their
traditions, should be questioned and constantly submitted to investigation.

One thing was clear; it was the sacred duty of the Arabs of Palestine to defend their
country against all aggression. The Zionists were conducting an aggressive campaign with
the object of securing by force a country which was not theirs by birthright. Thus there was
self-defence on one side and, on the other, aggression. The *raison d'être* of the United
Nations was to assist self-defence against aggression.

The rights and patrimony of the Arabs in Palestine had been the subject of no less than
eighteen investigations within twenty-five years, and all to no purpose. Such commissions of
inquiry had made recommendations that had either reduced the national and legal rights of the
Palestine Arabs or glossed them over. The few recommendations favourable to the Arabs had
been ignored by the Mandatory Power. It was hardly strange, therefore, that they should have
been unwilling to take part in a nineteenth investigation. It was for that, and for other reasons
already communicated to the United Nations, that they had refused to appear before the
United Nations Special Committee on Palestine. Mr Husseini assured the Committee, however, of the respect felt by the Arab Higher Committee for the United Nations and emphasized
that his Committee looked to it for justice and equity.

The struggle of the Arabs in Palestine had nothing in common with anti-Semitism. The
Arab world had been one of the rare havens of refuge for the Jews until the atmosphere of
neighbourliness had been poisoned by the Balfour Declaration and the aggressive spirit the
latter had engendered in the Jewish community.

The claims of the Zionists had no legal or moral basis. The case was based on the
association of the Jews with Palestine over two thousand years before. On that basis, the
Arabs would have better claims to those territories in other parts of the world such as Spain or
parts of France, Turkey, Russia or Afghanistan, which they had inhabited in the past.

Mr Husseini disputed three claims of world Jewry. The claim to Palestine based on
historical association was a movement on the part of the Ashkenazim, whose forefathers had
no connexion with Palestine. The Sephardim, the main descendants of Israel, had mostly
denounced Zionism. Secondly, the religious connexion of the Zionists with Palestine, which
he noted was shared by Moslems and Christians, gave them no secular claim to the country.
Freedom of access to the Holy Places was universally accepted. Thirdly, the Zionists claimed
the establishment of a Jewish National Home by virtue of the Balfour Declaration. But the
British Government had had no right to dispose of Palestine which it had occupied in the
name of the Allies as a liberator and not as a conqueror. The Balfour Declaration was in
contradiction with the Covenant of the League of Nations and was an immoral, unjust and
illegal promise.

The solution lay in the Charter of the United Nations, in accordance with which the Arabs of Palestine, who constituted the majority, were entitled to a free and independent State. Mr Husseini welcomed the recent declaration of the representative of the United Kingdom that the Mandate should be terminated and its termination followed by independence and expressed the hope that the British Government would not on that occasion, as in the past, reverse its decision under Zionist pressure.

Regarding the manner and form of independence for Palestine, it was the view of the Arab Higher Committee that that was a matter for the rightful owners of Palestine to decide. Once Palestine was found to be entitled to independence, the United Nations was not legally competent to decide or to impose the constitutional organization of Palestine, since such action would amount to interference with an internal matter of an independent nation.

The future constitutional organization of Palestine should be based on the following principles: first, establishment on democratic lines of an Arab State comprising all Palestine; secondly, observance of the said Arab State of Palestine of human rights, fundamental freedoms and equality of all persons before the law; thirdly, protection by the Arab State of the legitimate rights and interests of all the minorities; fourthly, guarantee to all of freedom of worship and access to the Holy Places.

In conclusion, Mr Husseini said that he had not commented on the Special Committee's report because the Arab Higher Committee considered that it could not be a basis for discussion. Both schemes proposed in the report were inconsistent with the United Nations Charter and with the Covenant (sic) League of Nations. The Arabs of Palestine were solidly determined to oppose with all the means at their command any scheme which provided for the dissection, segregation or partition of their country or which gave to a minority special and preferential rights or status. Although they fully realized that big Powers could crush such opposition by brute force, the Arabs nevertheless would not be deterred, but would lawfully defend with their life-blood every inch of the soil of their beloved country.

UNO *Ad Hoc* Committee on the
Palestinian Question, Third Meeting

Source: Fraser, *The Middle East,* pp. 49–51.

THE U.N., ISRAEL ESTABLISHED, THE FIRST ARAB-ISRAELI WAR

CHAPTER **4**

CHRONOLOGY

May 13, 1947	UN General Assembly establishes a Special Committee on Palestine (UNSCOP)
Aug. 31, 1947	UNSCOP report presented to General Assembly
Nov. 29, 1947	UN General Assembly votes for partition
Jan. 1948	Arab Liberation Army enters Palestine
March 18, 1948	Weizmann sees Truman
March 19, 1948	U.S. proposes UN trusteeship in Palestine
April 9, 1948	Jewish attack on Deir Yassin
April 13, 1948	Arab attack on bus convoy to Mt. Scopus
April 22, 1948	Haganah captures Haifa
May 14, 1948	Ben-Gurion proclaims state of Israel; British depart Palestine and Mandate ends.
May 14, 1948	U.S. extends de facto recognition to Israel
May 15, 1948	Arab armies invade Israel

May 17, 1948	U.S.S.R. extends full recognition to Israel
Sept. 17, 1948	Count Bernadotte assassinated
Dec. 1, 1949	Abdullah annexes that part of Palestine occupied by Arab League and East Jerusalem
Jan. 6, 1949	Israel and Egypt announce cease-fire
Jan. 25, 1949	First Israeli elections; Ben-Gurion (Mapai party) elected Prime Minister
Jan. 29, 1949	Great Britain extends de facto recognition to Israel
Jan. 31, 1949	U.S. extends full recognition to Israel and Transjordan
Feb. 24, 1949	Egypt and Israel sign armistice agreements at Rhodes
March 11, 1949	Israel and Transjordan sign cease-fire
April 26, 1949	Transjordan to be called Jordan
May 11, 1949	Israel admitted to the United Nations
July 27, 1949	UN mediator Ralph Bunche reports end of military conflict in Palestine

PALESTINE BEFORE THE UNITED NATIONS

The future of Palestine was among the first questions addressed by the new United Nations Organization. To meet the hopes of its founders, especially the United States, the world organization would have to settle this issue, set in a most strategic region. In place of war, public debate and private bargaining were to resolve international conflicts. The United States also hoped to use the United Nations as a tool to contain Communist influence and Soviet expansion. The Palestine question was, for the new world body, a crucial test case.

As it happened, there was no real issue between the United States and the Soviet Union over partition and the founding of a Jewish state in Palestine. The Soviets welcomed the idea of a Jewish state as a way of extending their influence into the Middle East; they believed that the predominantly Socialist ideology of the Israeli leaders would gain them an ally in the region. It would also mean the departure of Britain from at least one area of the region. In fact, one of the worries that the American intelligence community (the OSS, now the CIA) had about the establishment of Israel was the number of Communists from Soviet satellites who might take up residence in the new nation. In February 1947, Britain turned the Palestine question over to the United Nations. The British government, at first, had hoped that the General Assembly might not be able to find an acceptable formula, and would turn the matter back to it. Britain did not want to give up this strategically valuable area. However, the British had gone through a cold winter in 1946/47, with fuel shortages, exhausted credit reserves, and growing Communist pressure in Greece and Turkey, all of which made the maintenance of a garrison in Palestine unpalatable. Moreover, the British were finding it increasingly difficult to keep the peace.

The UN General Assembly met in April 1947 and agreed to a British request for a Special Session to consider the problem. This Special Session, the first such, immediately set up a Special Committee on Palestine (UNSCOP) of eleven "neutral" nations to investigate and draw up recommendations. The nations comprising UNSCOP were Australia, Canada, Czechoslovakia, Guatemala, India, Iran, the Netherlands, Peru, Sweden, Uruguay, and Yugoslavia. It was a reasonably balanced group, and it was given the task of investigating all aspects of the Palestine question, including the plight of the displaced persons. The committee's hearings included five weeks in the Middle East gathering evidence from the Jewish Agency and nations of the recently formed Arab League. The Arab League had been established in Cairo in 1945, and was endorsed by Great Britain as a possible way of continuing to exert influence and provide a sounding board and outlet for ideas of Arab nationalism. Despite the tension and disorder in Palestine created in part by the Haganah's hostility to the British, the Jewish Agency cooperated fully with the committee. The Palestine Arab Higher Committee, on the other hand, boycotted the proceedings and treated the committee with defiance, asserting that Arab rights were self-evident, and that the committee's membership was weighted in favor of the Zionists. Delegates from some states of the Arab League did meet with UNSCOP in Lebanon, however, to present the Arab case. On August 31, 1947, UNSCOP presented its report to the General Assembly at its second regular session. (See Document 4–1.)

The members unanimously recommended termination of the mandate, the granting of independence to Palestine, provision of a transitional period before independence, and they agreed on a number of other related issues. On the vital question of the future shape of Palestine, a majority of seven (Canada, Czechoslovakia, Guatemala, the Netherlands, Peru, Sweden, Uruguay) recommended partition into an Arab state, a

Jewish state, the internationalization of Jerusalem, and economic union between the two states. Britain was to administer the mandate during a two-year interim period under UN auspices and admit 150,000 refugees into the proposed Jewish state. The minority (India, Iran, and Yugoslavia) proposed an independent federal state. Australia abstained.

UNSCOP MAJORITY REPORT

In the majority proposal, of the 10,000 square miles comprising Palestine, the Arabs were to retain 4,300 square miles. The Jews, who at that time made up one-third of the population (the population of Palestine at the end of 1946 was estimated at 1,269,000 Arabs and 650,000 Jews), were allotted 5,700 square miles. At this time Jews owned 6 to 8 percent of the total land area representing approximately 20 percent of the arable land. The Arab territory was to be the less fertile hill country of central Palestine and northern Galilee. The Jewish territory was to be the more fertile coastal plain from a line south of Acre to a line south of Jaffa. Jaffa, almost totally Arab, was included in the Jewish state. The Jewish state also would include most of the Negev Desert. Strangely, the Jews were denied those places such as Jerusalem and Hebron to which they were most sentimentally attached. Demographically, the Jewish state would face the problem of a built-in hostile fifth column. As envisaged, it was to contain almost as many Arabs (approximately 497,000) as Jews (approximately 498,000) at least until the immigrants arrived. And the boundaries of the Jewish state seemed to make it virtually indefensible in the event of hostilities with the Arabs. The Arab state would have 725,000 Arabs and 10,000 Jews.

Despite its shortcomings from their point of view, the Jewish Agency welcomed the majority report of UNSCOP. It was preferable to the minority report, and it did offer two essential requirements: sovereignty and uninterrupted immigration. The Arabs rejected both reports outright. The reports, by legitimizing the Balfour Declaration and the mandate, in essence stated that the claims of the Jews, the majority of whom had been in Palestine less than thirty years, were equal to those of the Arabs, many of whose ancestors had lived there for hundreds of years. The Arabs were so angered by the UNSCOP reports that the Arab League threatened war if the United Nations approved either report. There was no room for negotiation between the two positions. The British stated that they would accept the recommendation to end the mandate, but would remain neutral on the outcome for Palestine; the General Assembly would have to decide the future of the region. The British did not want to be seen in the eyes of the Arabs—especially the Egyptians with whom they were negotiating the future of their Suez Canal bases—as participating in something as objectionable to the Arabs as a Jewish state.

The British, too, were determined to get out of Palestine as soon as possible; they had had enough and were bitter toward the Zionists. During the months of the UNSCOP investigations, the attacks on British soldiers and police, especially by the Irgun, reached new levels of ferocity and barbarism. One particularly horrifying incident had occurred in July 1947. Two British Army sergeants were hanged in retaliation for the execution of Zionist terrorists. British and American outrage was triggered not so much by the hanging of two innocent men as by the fact that their bodies had been left booby-trapped. Menachem Begin boasted: "We repaid our enemy in kind," but many Americans as well as British wondered about the sanity of the terrorist mentality that lurked behind such outrages. It was this event, as much as any other, that led

British Foreign Secretary Ernest Bevin to refuse to allow the 4,500 illegal DPs aboard the *Exodus* to land in Palestine. Britain could no longer support the financial and human drain of maintaining troops in Palestine. In 1947, about 80,000 troops and 16,000 British and local police tried to preserve the peace in Palestine, and the British had spent £50 million since the Labor party had come to power. In September 1947 the British government decided to end the mandate by May 1948, and Bevin made this public the following month. By announcing in advance of the United Nations General Assembly's (UNGA) decision that it would surrender the mandate, and that it would not participate in enforcing any UNGA decision, it could be argued that Britain was sabotaging the United Nation's solution. Britain's stance—together with the pro-Zionist positions taken by the United States and the Soviet Union—strengthened the views of both Arabs and Zionists that they could achieve their objectives without compromise.

THE UNITED STATES AND THE PARTITION PROPOSAL

The United States supported the UNSCOP majority plan. President Truman had indicated in November 1946 that he favored partition. Many historians have explained the President's support for a Jewish state as the result of domestic political considerations. They argue that Truman and the Democratic party needed the strategically important Jewish vote for electoral success, and consequently American policy was shaped in ways demanded by Zionist pressure groups. They further argue that the President's policy was not in the nation's interest and was opposed by the State Department. Truman, in his memoirs, adds credence to this point of view. He expressed his displeasure at "the striped-pants boys" in the State Department, and he resented the patronizing attitude of pro-Arab foreign service officers.

Referring to Zionist pressure, Truman wrote that he had never had so much pressure on him as he had on the question of Palestine. And he certainly did have pressure placed on him. The Zionist Organization of America under the aggressive and dynamic leadership of Rabbi Abba Hillel Silver, and other organizations like the American Christian Palestine Committee, constantly sent letters of advice, comment, and threats of political retaliation to the White House, and many meetings were held between the President and Jewish leaders. But Truman was not a man who gave way to threats; his record as President suggests a strong, independent, even stubborn Missourian. All chief executives are subject to domestic political pressure in reaching their decisions. The mere existence or even the amount of that pressure does not mean that it is effective.

Zionist pressure was often counterproductive since it made Truman angry. He wrote a friend in October 1946, for example, that the Jews themselves were making it impossible to do anything for them. And, in May 1947, the President told one of his White House advisors that Rabbi Silver was a cause of some if not all the troubles they were facing in getting partition accepted. In reality, Truman felt strongly that something had to be done for the Jewish refugees, and largely because of his fundamentalist Protestant background he believed that the Jews should be allowed to return to their ancient homeland. If he was influenced by domestic political considerations, it was not because of the letters and pressure from Zionist groups, but because of the advice of his White House political consultants, David Niles, himself a Jew and a Zionist, and Clark Clifford—who was later to become Secretary of Defense in the Johnson administration. Certainly, Truman did not go nearly as far in his support for partition as American

Zionist leaders wanted. Indeed, in the 1948 Presidential election—despite Truman's apparent giving way to Zionist pressure—the President did not carry the heavily Jewish State of New York.

There were many factors influencing Truman in addition to domestic political considerations. Truman shared the concern of the State Department over the postwar spread of Soviet influence especially in the increasingly important and unstable Middle East. The degree of conflict between the President and Foggy Bottom has been over-stated; Truman and Secretary Marshall had an unusually close working relationship. In addition to its own oil interests in Saudi Arabia, the United States was concerned about Europe's access to the region's oil for postwar reconstruction. By 1947, American oil companies owned about 42 percent of Middle Eastern supplies. The Middle Eastern desk of the State Department argued, wrongly as it turned out, that American support for partition would drive the Arabs into the waiting arms of the Soviet Union. Some even believed that the new Jewish state would be a Communist regime.

As we noted in the previous chapter, the Joint Chiefs of Staff believed that in the event of Soviet penetration of the Middle East the United States would have to fight a war without the oil resources of the region. There was also the possibility that the United States might have to send troops to the area once the British had withdrawn. Truman was more convinced by the Zionist's argument that the new Jewish state would be a bastion of democracy in the Middle East, and that supporting Israel would be a clear indication of the world leadership role America was to assume. These arguments, whether used by Zionists as propaganda pressure on the White House or not, influenced Truman much more than those suggesting the political expediency of gaining Jewish votes.

UNGA APPROVES THE PARTITION OF PALESTINE

Two days after receiving the UNSCOP report, in September 1947, the General Assembly designated itself an Ad Hoc Committee to consider the two UNSCOP proposals. All members of the United Nations were represented on this Ad Hoc Committee. Between September 25 and November 25, the committee held thirty-four meetings. Both the Jewish Agency and the Arab Higher Committee—who had by now grasped their error of not cooperating with UNSCOP—made presentations. On November 25, 1947, the Ad Hoc Committee passed what was essentially an amended version of the UNSCOP majority partition proposal for consideration by the General Assembly. The amendments slightly altered the boundaries and the populations of the two proposed states. Jaffa was to be an Arab enclave in the Jewish state, and the Arab population of the Jewish state was to be reduced. The final outcome was as follows: The Arab state was to occupy 4,500 square miles and contain 800,000 Arabs and 10,000 Jews. The Jewish state was to be an area of 5,500 square miles and contain 498,000 Jews and 468,000 Arabs. (See map 4–1.)

On November 29, 1947, the General Assembly voted in favor of the partition of Palestine by a vote of 33 to 13 with 10 abstentions. The Muslim countries (together with India, Yugoslavia, and Greece) voted against partition. The United States and the Soviet bloc, together with several other nations, including France and Australia, sup-ported partition. Considerable controversy abounds over the role of the United States in securing a favorable outcome. In the few days prior to the vote, American Zionists exerted unprecedented pressure on the White House to influence the delegates of other nations to vote for partition. President Truman, however, refused, but in some cases

MAP 4–1

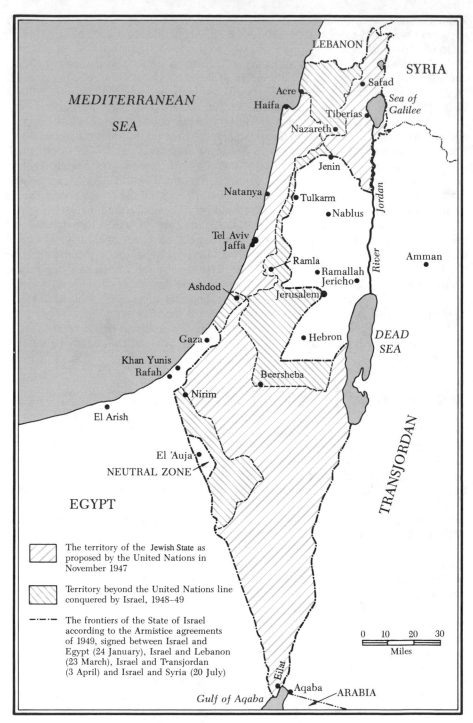

Israel's boundaries, April 1949–1967.

private American citizens did make strenuous efforts to secure votes. The pressure that was exerted on delegates who appeared hesitant—for example, those from Haiti, the Philippines, Liberia, Greece, and China—was primarily exerted by Jewish Agency representatives.

Not all of this pressure was effective; Greece and Turkey, for example, who were so dependent upon American aid, did not vote for partition. At the same time, Arab spokesmen, in their attempts to influence the outcome, warned that a bloodbath would erupt and retaliation would ensue against Western oil interests if partition were approved. In any event, partition was construed by most as an American plan. In the final analysis, partition was successful probably because the Jews were perceived as Western as opposed to the Eastern Arabs. And to a United Nations that consisted mostly of Western nations at the time, the Jewish argument was strengthened by the West's sense of guilt for its inaction, which was partly responsible for the Jews' present plight. This time the West would do something. In addition, a major push for adoption of the partition resolution came from Latin American and European nations, in part because Catholics liked the special international status planned for Jerusalem, a plan that the United Nations found it could not enforce.

Passage of the partition resolution in November 1947 virtually assured a Jewish state in Palestine. The resolution liquidated the mandate, defined a legal framework in which the Yishuv could establish a state, and gave to the Haganah a definite goal around which it could rally its forces. Passage of the resolution was, however, merely the acceptance of a principle; it was not a specific blueprint. This must be kept in mind when considering the events of the next six months, especially when reflecting on American policy. (See Document 4–2.)

PARTITION IN DOUBT

The Yishuv and the Arabs realized that the success or failure of the resolution depended upon them as much as the UN decision. In view of the lack of any UN military strength to support the partition plan, the Arabs began to carry out their threats, and some Arab irregulars moved in ostensibly to prevent the establishment of a Jewish state. The Haganah also moved to try to secure areas allotted to the Jewish state. Disorder, violence, and bloodshed erupted, with the British once more vainly attempting to establish some rule of law. By mid-January 1948, Palestine was in chaos. The UNSCOP reported the worsening state of affairs to the UN Security Council on February 16. It advised that an international police force would be required to put partition into effect. The following week, America's representative to the United Nations, Warren Austin, told the Security Council of American doubts as to the ability of the United Nations to carry out partition. Ambassador Austin did not formally present any specific American alternatives for consideration, but his comments, made on February 25, reflected President Truman's dilemma. The United States, Austin said, was not prepared to impose partition by force, but it would join any UN effort to safeguard international peace and security. Truman made another final appeal to the Arabs for peace, but it was summarily rejected. As March of 1948 drew to a close, there were signs that the Arabs were planning massive military action.

Faced with this prospect, President Truman agreed to Secretary of State Marshall's suggestion that Palestine be placed under a temporary United Nations trusteeship. He had little choice. If he stood by and did nothing, it seemed certain that the Jews would be driven into the sea. It was essential to the success of the Yishuv, however, with the British withdrawal now set for May 15, that the United Nations not abandon partition. Partition was, in fact, already crystallizing in Palestine. Both Jews and Arabs were, to a large degree, obedient to their own institutions. The central British administration was in a state of virtual collapse. The Jewish Agency intended to proclaim the state of Israel on May 15. But without continued American support for partition this seemed almost impossible.

Early in March of 1948, as American policy appeared to waver, Chaim Weizmann had sailed from Palestine to put the Zionist case before President Truman, but by this time Truman was refusing to see any one. Jewish leaders realized that this might be the turning point. At this juncture, the president of the B'nai B'rith, Frank Goldman, turned to the President's old friend and former partner in a Kansas City haberdashery, Eddie Jacobson, who agreed to intercede for Weizmann. Jacobson decided to visit the White House personally, and was given an appointment with Truman. According to Jacobson, Truman angrily refused to see Weizmann. Jacobson then appealed to Truman by using an analogy to Truman's hero, Andrew Jackson. Weizmann, Jacobson said, was *his* hero just as Jackson was Truman's hero. Jacobson voiced surprise that the President refused to see Weizmann simply because of the treatment the President had received at the hands of some of America's Jewish leaders. Truman relented, and a meeting was arranged.

Truman saw Weizmann on March 18, 1948. The Zionist leader stressed that abandonment of partition at a time when Palestine was threatened by outside Arab aggression and internal warfare would be disastrous. He also argued that there was no reason to think that the Arabs would accept, or assist in setting up, trusteeship any more than they would partition. Truman was convinced, and he told Weizmann that the United States would not abandon partition. However, on the following day, March 19, in the Security Council, Ambassador Austin called for a suspension of all efforts aimed at partition and asked for a special meeting of the General Assembly to approve United Nations' trusteeship.

Austin's announcement, coming as it did the day after the President's assurance to Weizmann, considerably embarrassed Truman, who was bitterly condemned by all sections of Jewish opinion for "betraying" the Jews, and was criticized in non-Jewish quarters for "brutally reversing" American policy. If the President was seeking political advantage in his Palestine policy, he was very inept in going about it. In fact, Truman had approved Ambassador Austin's statement prior to his meeting with the Zionist leader, but he had not known when it was to be made.

The U.S. Trusteeship proposal was not, in fact, an abandonment, reversal, or substitute for the partition plan. Truman was concerned that there would be no public authority in Palestine capable of preserving law and order when the mandate terminated. Trusteeship was the only solution. Secretary of State Marshall explained American thinking to the Senate Foreign Relations Committee a few days later. If partition had to be implemented by the use of United Nations' forces, this would involve Soviet troops. They, Marshall said, had shown a tendency to remain in the areas they occupied. The Soviets would again press down on Greece, Turkey, and the Arabian oil fields, which were vital for the entire European recovery program. The fact that the Soviets were looking for a warm-water port also added to the danger of Soviet troops in the area. The only solution, Marshall argued, was to turn the matter over to the UN Trusteeship Council. The Soviet Union was not represented on the council, so the danger of Soviet military intervention could be avoided.

The second Special Session of the General Assembly met briefly to discuss Palestine on April 1 and resumed on April 16 to discuss the American proposal. It soon became clear that discussion would be drawn out, and that trusteeship, like partition, could not be enforced without an adequately armed neutral force. Britain was determined not to remain longer than May 15, 1948, a fact only then being fully realized by the United States and both protagonists in Palestine.

ARAB AND JEWISH RESPONSE TO THE UN PARTITION RESOLUTION

These months were full of uncertainty and confusion as to the future of Palestine. Efforts by moderate Palestinian leaders to prevent bloodshed failed. Arab leadership was divided. World War II had led to the dispersion of the Husseini family; the Mufti, Haj Amin, had been exiled following his escape late in 1937, and his nephew, Jamal, was interned in Rhodesia during the war. This provided an opportunity for their rivals, the Nashashibis, to seek leadership of Palestinian politics. Two other groups also sought successfully to extend their power: the Palestine Arab party under the leadership of a Greek Orthodox, Emile al-Ghuri, and the popular and widely supported party *Istiqlal* (meaning Independence). At the end of the war, the Palestine Arab party was the most powerful Arab voice opposing a Jewish state and calling for an Arab government to control the entire mandate area. Nevertheless, by 1947–1948, using their local kin leaders and village heads, the urban-based notable family of the Husseinis had again reasserted their traditional leadership among the Palestinian Arabs.

In January 1948, the "Arab Liberation Army," formed in December 1947 and organized, trained, and armed by Syria for the Arab League states, began entering Palestine. By the end of March, 5,000 men, mainly Arab irregulars from Iraq, Syria, and Lebanon, had infiltrated the territory. Surprisingly few Palestinian Arabs joined the Arab Liberation Army (ALA). Many Palestinian Arabs were suspicious of the other Arab states. They feared, for one thing, that their neighbors had designs of their own for the future of Palestine, which did not include an independent Palestinian state. For that reason, many Palestinians favored partition and indicated a willingness to live in peace alongside a Jewish state. The strategy of the Arab armies was to dominate the roads, thus controlling the lines of communication. They hoped in this way to isolate the outlying villages from the main centers of Jewish population in Jerusalem, Haifa, and Tel Aviv. The ALA was also billeted in various Arab villages and in the major Arab towns where their presence was often a source of local resentment. At first, the ALA had considerable success; the Haganah was forced on the defensive, and the Yishuv was completely demoralized by Arab successes by the end of January 1948. At the time that President Truman was defending temporary trusteeship in Palestine as the only way to secure peace and stability, Jerusalem was virtually in the hands of the Arabs. Jewish hopes appeared slight without outside assistance. It was with the knowledge of these circumstances that Truman stated that he was prepared to send troops to Palestine to assist in enforcing U.N. trusteeship.

During April, the balance swung in favor of the Haganah. Armed with a shipment of arms that arrived from Communist-controlled Czechoslovakia at the end of March 1948, the Haganah took the offensive. Its most significant victory was the capture of Haifa on April 22, 1948. By early May, the Haganah also had control of Jaffa and most of eastern Galilee. But eastern Jerusalem remained in Arab hands. The most surprising aspect of the Haganah offensive was the complete evacuation of the Arabs from their towns and villages as the Jews advanced. Both sides resorted to terrorist atrocities against each other, especially in the major cities, with little regard for noncombatants, or women and children. In one series of attacks and retaliation, Jewish terrorists (Irgun or LEHI members) threw bombs at a group of Arab oil-refinery workers in Haifa, killing six and wounding forty-two. The Arabs then rioted and killed forty-one Jews and wounded forty-eight more before being quieted by British troops.

Two days later, Haganah members disguised as Arabs entered a village close to Haifa and killed approximately sixty people, including a number of women and children, to avenge the Jewish deaths in Haifa. Later we will discuss the well-known incidents at Deir Yasin and Mt. Scopus, which occurred at this time. British forces, who were withdrawing, found it increasingly difficult to be even-handed. They assisted Jewish settlers against a Syrian terrorist attack, and they arranged a truce for the withdrawal of about 10,000 Arabs from Haifa. Both sides accused the British of favoring the other. By May 2, the Haganah had carved out for itself a state roughly equivalent to that approved by the United Nations earlier in November 1947. The Jews went ahead with plans to announce an independent state on May 14. The United Nations let events take their course.

ESTABLISHMENT OF ISRAEL AND THE FIRST ARAB-ISRAEL WAR

On the morning of May 14, 1948, the Union Jack was hauled down from Government House in Jerusalem for the last time, and as the British High Commissioner, Sir Alan Gordon Cunningham, sailed out of Haifa at 11:30 that night, the British mandate came to an end. Already at 4 o'clock that afternoon, standing under a portrait of Theodor Herzl in a museum in Tel Aviv, David Ben-Gurion had proclaimed the state of Israel. (See Document 4–3.) The United States and the Soviet Union recognized the new nation immediately. On May 14, the General Assembly had passed a resolution providing for a UN mediator in Palestine. The mediator, Count Folke Bernadotte, was to work with the Truce Commission established by the Security Council to promote a peaceful settlement. On May 15, various Arab armies entered Palestine: the Arab Legion went into the area allocated to the Arabs in Judea and Samaria; the Egyptian army moved through Gaza and Beersheba; the Lebanese went into Arab Galilee; the Iraqis moved alongside the Arab Legion; the Syrians remained at the border. The first Arab–Israel war—the Israeli War of Independence—was under way.

Count Bernadotte arranged a month-long truce in mid-June. The Israelis used the truce to build up their supply of arms from Czechoslovakia and other countries, and when fighting resumed they embarked on a series of offensives that succeeded in stalling the Arabs and securing Tel Aviv. The most critical location for both sides was Jerusalem. On September 16, Bernadotte recommended to the United Nations that Jerusalem become an international city under UN control as envisaged in the Partition resolution; that the Negev be allocated to the Arabs and Galilee to Israel; and that Arab refugees be allowed to return home. The following day, Count Bernadotte was assassinated by members of the Stern Gang. Although Ben-Gurion then ordered the dissolution of the Irgun and Stern groups, and even though over 200 people were arrested as part of the investigation of Bernadotte's murder, no one was ever brought to trial, and Ben-Gurion never denounced terrorism as a weapon. While Stern Gang extremists doubtless regarded the UN mediator's recommendations as hostile to the Jewish state, it should be noted that Bernadotte had played a central role in rescuing over 5,000 Jews from concentration camps in March and April of 1945. In any event, following Ber-

General Alan Cunningham, British High Commissioner, saluting the colors as he leaves Government House Jerusalem, May 14, 1948 (*Photo courtesy of Illustrated London News*).

nadotte's death, fighting broke out again. On December 1, King Abdullah of Transjordan agreed to a cease-fire with Israel.

By January 1949, Egypt, its army in the Gaza and Negev in disarray, had had enough; on February 24, Egypt and Israel signed an armistice agreement at Rhodes. Ralph Bunche, an American who had been appointed by the United Nations as mediator to take Bernadotte's place, skillfully handled the difficult truce negotiations. As the result of these and later armistice agreements with Lebanon, Syria, and Transjordan, the land area of Israel increased by about 20 percent (some 2,500 square miles). In fact, Israel covered almost 80 percent of the area of western Palestine we have been regarding as the Palestine mandate. Transjordan continued to occupy the thickly populated hill country of Judea and Samaria (later called the "West Bank" after its annexation by Jordan) and also East Jerusalem, which was annexed by the Hashemite Kingdom of Jordan. Egypt retained and administered the Gaza Strip. The armistice agreements were not regarded as permanent border arrangements, but, despite constant violations, they did remain the boundaries between Israel and her neighbors until the Six-Day War of 1967.

Establishment of Israel and the First Arab-Israel War

There is disagreement among historians on almost every aspect of the first Arab–Israeli war. Claims and counterclaims have been made by both sides, so that it is virtually impossible to reach conclusions that are not disputed. Of the many questions raised by the first Arab–Israeli war, there are two that merit our attention. The first is: How did 600,000 Jews manage to defeat the 40 million Arabs ranged against them? The second is: How did the war result in 720,000 or more Palestinian Arab refugees? The short answer to the first question is, of course, that the Jews of Palestine did not defeat millions of Arabs. The number engaged in the fighting is hard to calculate exactly, but according to some estimates, in April 1948, the Zionists had about 30,000 armed men and women (about 15,000 were "on line" troops), with 10,000 for local defense and another 25,000 as a kind of home guard. There were, in addition, about 2,000 Irgun terrorists, and about 800 in the Stern Gang. However, they had few heavy weapons, and no artillery, armored vehicles, or planes. The combined Arab forces amounted to 40,000, of whom 10,000 (about 4,500 were battle ready) were in the British-trained Arab Legion. Many in the Arab armies were irregulars. The main strength of the Arab armies was their possession of armor, although they did not use it as effectively as they might have had they known the full extent of Jewish weakness.

The Arabs' major difficulties were logistical and organizational. The distance from Baghdad to Haifa is 700 miles; the Egyptians had a 250-mile line of supply across the desert; and the Arab Legion, the closest army, had to travel more than eighty miles to the front. Perhaps more importantly, the Arab armies had no unified command, nor did they have agreed-upon goals. On May 14, King Abdullah of Transjordan declared himself commander-in-chief, but it was a meaningless gesture; he had no control of the other Arab armies or their specific objectives. The Arabs remained divided along traditional rivalries. King Farouk of Egypt would rather not have fought at all, but his fear of domestic unrest and the increase in influence his rivals in the Arab world—the Hashemite kings of Transjordan and Iraq—would gain if they fought and he did not drove him to enter the conflict. In addition, Arab League Secretary General Abd al-Rahman, and others, played upon the king's vanity, and this was crucial in his decision to enter the war. Syria wanted the Arab areas of Palestine, and neither Syria nor Egypt wanted them to fall into the hands of Transjordan.

King Abdullah did not like the idea of an Arab Palestine under the control of either the Mufti (Haj Amin al-Husseini) or Syria. He entered the war to gain control of the Arab area of Palestine, especially Jerusalem, for Transjordan, and he too would have preferred not to fight. The Mufti envisaged an Arab Palestine ruled by himself. Haj Amin's forces were led by his nephew, Abd al-Qadir al-Husseini, son of a former mayor of Jerusalem, and the Mufti wanted control of all Arab funding to ensure his control over future Palestinian Arab affairs. The Arab League, however, refused to recognize Husseini as leader of a Palestinian government-in-exile and funded his rival, Fawzi al-Qawuqji, who led a group of non-Palestinian Arab volunteers. Egypt supported the Mufti as a way of preventing Abdullah—who was supported by the Nashashibi faction within the Palestinians—from gaining control of central Palestine and Jerusalem. These divisions among the Arab leadership meant that the war was fought with no unity of command or goals. It was largely localized as far as each Arab group was concerned, and this greatly assisted the centralized and unified Haganah. Nevertheless, the 650,000 Jews of Israel suffered the loss of 6,000 killed in the war—roughly 1 percent of their population. The Arab armies were far from untrained, undisciplined mobs; the majority were efficient and effective soldiers.

For the Yishuv, the first Arab–Israeli war was, in some ways, an extension of the military operation the Haganah had conducted against the British; this time it was directed against the Arab enemy. Many factors contributed to the Israeli victory. The Jewish forces had a unified command, and they fought with fierce determination, using weapons obtained from Czechoslovakia during the truce period. The war also set a pattern for terrorism, a tactic that had long been a part of Palestine's history, and one which both Jews and Arabs often employed in their future dealings with each other.

One of the most dramatic examples of this tactic took place on April 9, 1948, at Deir Yassin, a small village on the outskirts of Jerusalem eighteen miles outside the boundaries of the Jewish state outlined in the partition plan. On the morning of April 9, a group of 132 of Begin's Irgun and the Stern Gang attacked the sleeping village, which had, until then, avoided being involved in the fighting. The village was captured and two-thirds of the villagers, over 240 men, women, and children, were murdered. Many, including young girls and old women, were raped, and in some cases the dead were mutilated and their bodies thrown down a well. Although the Haganah high command condemned the massacre, the officers in charge of the attack were not punished.

The Arabs believed that Deir Yassin was part of a campaign of terrorism by the Haganah and the Jewish Agency to "encourage" the Arab population to leave their villages and homes. Begin, in *The Revolt* defends the "heroic" actions of his men (four were killed in overcoming the "fierce resistance" put up by the villagers), and asserts, as he did in relation to the King David Hotel bombing, that warnings were given for women and children to leave the village before the attack began. It is hard to describe Deir Yassin as a retaliation or reprisal raid. It took place outside the area assigned to the Jewish state in the partition plan, and, of course, it occurred before the Jewish state came into existence. Furthermore, the village had apparently entered into an "nonaggression" pact with the Haganah. It was, in fact, an integral part of Plan Dalet, a plan to acquire at least those areas of Palestine allocated to Israel in the Partition Resolution. This scheme—which involved the collaboration of the Irgun, the Haganah, and the elite commando force, the Palmach—was to undermine the morale of the Arab population through the use of terror, and to "cleanse" the area of the Arab inhabitants. It also required the establishing of a corridor connecting Tel Aviv with Jerusalem. Twenty villages had to be destroyed and evacuated. Deir Yassin was one of them.

In their own defense, Zionist historians point out that Iraqi troops and Palestinian irregulars had been using Deir Yassin as a base for snipers against Jewish occupants of Jerusalem, and that the attackers had allowed over 200 residents to leave the village unharmed. They call attention to a number of premeditated Arab atrocities prior to Deir Yassin; in mid-January 1948, for example, thirty-five members of the Palmach had been ambushed and their bodies mutilated by Arab soldiers. Deir Yassin was an unduly bloody incident, and while it cannot be condoned it should be borne in mind that the incident took place in the context of the general violence that occurred in April and May of 1948.

Some Zionists have argued that guerrilla reprisal tactics and the use of terror against Arab civilians was the only way Israelis could win the war—any war—against the overwhelming number of Arabs opposing them. And terrorism was certainly not confined to the Israelis; the British and the Arabs had utilized terror in their campaigns against the Zionists. Needless to say, the Arabs retaliated for Deir Yassin. On April 13, they besieged a convoy of mainly Jewish doctors and nurses on the road to the Hadassah hospital just outside Jerusalem on Mount Scopus, and they killed seventy-seven of them.

MAP 4–2

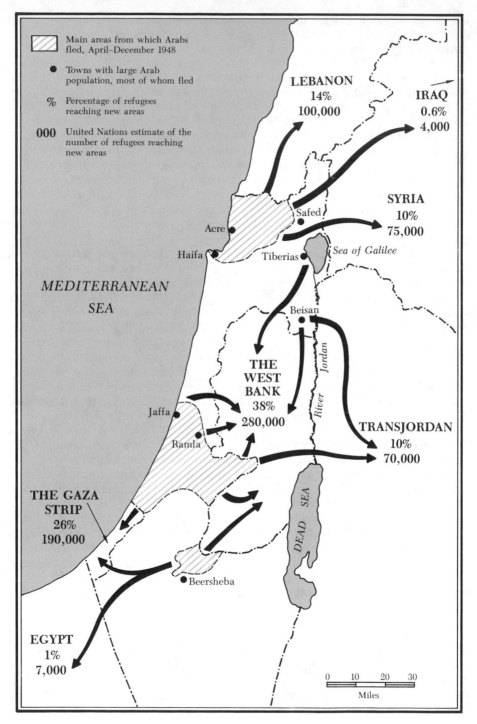

Main areas from which Arabs
fled, April–December 1948

● Towns with large Arab
population, most of whom fled

% Percentage of refugees
reaching new areas

000 United Nations estimate of the
number of refugees reaching
new areas

LEBANON
14%
100,000

IRAQ
0.6%
4,000

SYRIA
10%
75,000

Safed

Acre

Haifa

Tiberias

Sea of Galilee

*MEDITERRANEAN
SEA*

Beisan

THE
WEST
BANK
38%
280,000

River Jordan

Jaffa

Ramla

TRANSJORDAN
10%
70,000

THE GAZA
STRIP
26%
190,000

DEAD SEA

Beersheba

EGYPT
1%
7,000

0   10   20   30
Miles

The Palestinian Arab refugees, 1948.

Source: Martin Gilbert, *Atlas of the Arab-Israeli Conflict* (New York: Macmillan, 1974),
p. 49.

THE PALESTINIAN REFUGEES

The first Arab–Israeli war, in addition to securing the state of Israel, created about three quarters of a million homeless Palestinian Arabs. As noted earlier in this chapter, hundreds of thousands of Palestinian Arabs fled from their homes, or were expelled, during the Jewish War for Independence. At the end of hostilities early in 1949, the United Nations estimated that there were 726,000 Arab refugees from Israeli-controlled territories; about 70 percent of the Arab population of Palestine. The exact number is difficult to determine because it is impossible to know the true number of Arab illegals living in Palestine when the war broke out and the number of bedouin who had become refugees. A figure of about 600,000 to 760,000 is probably more accurate. (See map 4–2.)

Where did the refugees go? According to Benny Morris, in his analysis of the Palestinian refugee problem, the British estimated in February 1949 that about 320,000 Palestinians moved into, or already resided in, the eastern section of Palestine, which was controlled by the Arab Legion, and Transjordan. Approximately 210,000 were in camps in the Gaza region, 100,000 went into Lebanon, and 75,000 to Syria. Some refugees went to Egypt and others to Iraq. Some 150,000 remained within the Jewish state. The Israeli government was not prepared to allow the refugees to return; indeed, Ben-Gurion had told the Israeli cabinet on June 16, 1948, that Israel should "prevent their return." The future of the Palestinians has remained a major issue between Israel and the Arab states. No one in 1948 viewed the refugee problem in long-range terms. Neither Israel nor the Arabs, at least for many years, did very much toward finding a solution. In the years after the establishment of Israel it suited both Israel and the Arab states to do little. Nor was there a great deal that either the United States or the United Nations, working through its relief agency—the United Nations Relief and Works Agency (UNRWA)—could do other than try to alleviate the refugees' immediate situation.

Central to Israel's position is the argument that during the Israeli War of Independence the Palestinian Arabs abandoned their homes and villages of their own free will. Not only that, they did so at the urging of the Arab leadership, who, the argument goes, told the Palestinians to leave until the Jewish state was destroyed and then they could return. The evidence, however, is inconclusive. According to some sources, the Arab League, and the Mufti, ordered the Palestinians to remain where they were. Nevertheless, Israel insisted it had no moral responsibility or legal obligation to restore the Arab refugees to their property, or even compensate them for their losses. There was some flexibility on all this, at least until the summer of 1949. The Israelis then took the stand that all these matters were negotiable only within the framework of direct peace negotiations, which, by that time, the Arabs refused.

There were several reasons for the Arab exodus. Among the more important was the complete collapse of the Palestinian political and economic infrastructure. Just at the time when they were needed most, many of the local mayors, judges, communal and religious officials fled. Palestinian society, as noted in earlier chapters, was semifeudal in character, and once the landlords and other leaders had made good their own escape—as they did from Haifa, Jaffa, Safed, and elsewhere—the Arab townspeople, villagers, and peasants were left helpless. The Palestinians themselves refer to this episode in their history as *al-Nakba*, "the catastrophe." Their sense of helplessness and fear was greatly intensified by some of the savage attacks carried out by the victorious Jewish forces.

Benny Morris suggests that, as part of the campaign to evacuate Arabs from the

Beach Camp for Palestine refugees, Gaza Strip (*Photo courtesy of United Nations Relief and Works Agency for Palestine Refugees* [UNRWA]).

Jewish state, the Haganah deliberately destroyed Arab houses and villages, broadcast false stories in Arabic of the spread of cholera and typhus epidemics, and urged the population to escape the bloodbath while there was still time. Some efforts were made to reassure the Arabs, and in some instances Arabs were encouraged by the Jews to stay put, but by the first truce in mid-June 1948, over 250,000 Palestinians had fled, and this exodus had reached 300,000 by July. Arab Palestinians fled in some cases of their own free will or through terror; in other cases they were expelled. In any event, the truth was far from Chaim Weizmann's description of events as the "miraculous clearing of the land: the miraculous simplification of Israel's task." The Zionists had come a long way in the thirty years since Weizmann, who became the first president of Israel, had assured the Arabs of Jaffa that it was not the Zionists' intention "to turn anyone out of his property." It should be remembered, however, that Zionist leaders had stated

Beach Camp today (*Photo courtesy of UNRWA*).

President Chaim Weizmann presents a torah to President Harry S. Truman (*Photo courtesy of Israel Office of Information*).

they were prepared to accept the proposed Arab state in Palestine and the internationalization of Jerusalem although, evidently, the other Arab governments were not.

ISRAEL: A JEWISH STATE

One of the first tasks for the new nation of Israel was the formation of a system of government. Israel was ruled by a Provisional Council of State from May 1948 until the first constitutional government was installed on March 10, 1949, following elections held in January 1949. The Israeli form of government is a modified British system. The parliament—called the *Knesset*—consists of a unicameral (one chamber) legislature of 120 members elected by a system of proportional representation. All Israeli citizens above the age of eighteen are eligible to vote without distinction of race, creed, or sex. Twenty-one political parties put up candidates in the first election of January 25, 1949. Electors vote for the party list, decided by party caucus, rather than individuals standing as endorsed candidates. Parties must receive 1 percent of the vote before they are entitled to seat representatives. In the first election the Labor parties were awarded fifty-seven seats, the Center-Right parties thirty-one, and the Religious parties sixteen. Following the election, David Ben-Gurion (leader of the Mapai party) was asked by Chaim Weizmann, who had been elected Israel's first president by the provisional government, to form the state's first regular government.

The Knesset elects its own Speaker, draft bills go through three readings before becoming law, and much of the work of the Knesset is done through permanent standing committees. One of the results of the system of proportional representation is that throughout Israel's political history there have always been a large number of parties, many with very few representatives, and most governments have been coali-

On May 14, 1948 in Tel Aviv Museum, David Ben-Gurion, the country's first Prime Minister, declared the independence of Israel. The following day, the new state was invaded by five neighboring Arab nations (*Photo courtesy of Israel Office of Information*).

tion governments. Consequently, government in Israel has been largely conducted by the cabinet and the prime minister rather than by the legislature. Despite early factional divisions, which reflected differences within the Zionist movement, continuity was maintained until 1977; the predominant party was Ben-Gurion's moderate left Labor party (Mapai). It should, perhaps, be mentioned that Israel has no written constitution like that of the United States. The Israelis intended to draft a constitution but could not achieve consensus between secular and religious Jews; thus, Israel has fundamental or basic laws that govern the conduct of the country.

The establishment of Israel had ramifications beyond Palestine and its borders, of course. In the first place, it cleared the way for Jewish DPs to migrate to Palestine. Between September 1948 and August 1949, fifty-two European DP centers were closed. By the end of 1948, 100,000 DPs had arrived in Israel, and they were followed by Jews from Czechoslovakia, Bulgaria, Yugoslavia, Poland, Romania, and Hungary. By 1950, the population of Israel was 1,174,000. There were also demographic changes in Africa and the Middle East. By 1957, over half a million Jews had left or been expelled from Muslim countries in North Africa and the Middle East and had settled in Israel. Within the first five or six years of Israel's existence, approximately 47,000 immigrants came from Yemen, 113,000 from Iraq, 14,000 from Lebanon and Syria, and 39,000 from Iran. By the end of 1951, over 680,000 immigrants had arrived in Israel—one-third more than arrived in the sixty years prior to the establishment of the nation. They were divided almost equally between European Jews (Ashkenazim) on the one hand and non-European Jews (Sephardim and Oriental Jews) on the other. Before 1948, almost 90 percent had arrived from Europe. This coming together in Israel of the Ashkenazim from Eastern and Central Europe, who had played such a central role in building up the national home, with the non-European Jews, who were so different in language, customs, and culture, created great problems for Israel. In 1948, the Jews of Europe made up 75 percent of Israel's Jews; by 1961 they represented only 70 percent, and today Oriental and Sephardic Jews are in the majority. There was a danger that two Israels would be created—one consisting mainly of

Ashkenazi leaders who hold power and understood the state because they helped create it, and the other mostly of underemployed, undereducated, and underprivileged Sephardic and Oriental Jews.

Life was not easy for the new arrivals. There was no housing and rather chaotic government administration and bureaucracy. Many had to live in temporary reception centers, later called transit camps (by the end of 1951 about 250,000 were still in transit camps) while new self-supporting autonomous village settlements were established. Between 1948 and 1951, 345 villages were established; many were built on the sites of "abandoned" Arab villages and tracts of land. Some were kibbutzim but the majority were moshavim, a cooperative system in which each family was responsible for its own holding. The villages were located mainly in the Coastal Plain, but also in areas where only isolated settlements had existed previously: Upper Galilee, the Judean Hills, and the arid Negev. One of the first tasks was land improvement and forestation. In 1948, the land cultivated by Jews totaled 1.6 million dunams; by 1958, it was 3.9 million dunams (a dunam = ¼ acre). Fifty percent of the immigrants were unskilled. Despite the fact that, by 1958, about one-third of the newcomers who had settled in collective settlements had moved into the cities of Tel Aviv, Haifa, and Jerusalem, by the end of its first decade of existence, Israel was feeding itself in the key staples of dairy products, poultry, vegetables, and fruit.

Mass immigration, while essential to provide military manpower and to preempt vulnerable empty spaces, also created economic difficulties for Israel. Productivity was low, and capital costs for housing, health, and development were high; thus, taxes were high and rationing was introduced. In the years following the destructive War of Independence, Israel had no exports to speak of; trade with the Arab states ceased because of an Arab economic boycott; the Haifa Oil refinery closed; and citrus production was down. Israel depended upon outside assistance. That assistance came in the form of a $100 million loan from the Export-Import Bank in January 1949, and a series of Grants-in-Aid from the U.S. government. Diaspora Jews, especially those in the United States, also provided funds through various fund-raising campaigns such as the United Jewish Appeal. Private aid from the United States amounted to between $60 million and $100 million annually. Further assistance was provided by the Federal Republic of Germany (West Germany). Following an emotional and heated national controversy in Israel, an agreement was signed (in 1953) whereby West Germany was to pay Israel DM 3 billion ($715 million), most of it in machinery and goods over the next twelve years as partial reparations for material losses incurred by the Jews during the Nazi regime. In addition to the German reparations were restitution payments to individual Israeli Jews.

Slowly the state began to take shape. Compulsory education acts and labor laws (including equal rights for women in the work force in 1951) were passed. El Al, the Israel national airline, and a merchant marine were established; roads, hospitals, and schools were built and compulsory military service introduced. Nevertheless, despite the progress, the economic hardship the new state was experiencing led to a drastic reduction in immigration; 24,000 immigrants arrived in 1952 and only 11,000 in 1953.

To see Israel strictly as just another nation-state, or even to see it in the immediate terms of the triumph of modern Zionism, is, as one observer, Melvin Urofsky, has noted, "to miss the deeper meaning of Israel in the collective consciousness of the Jewish people." Zionism has been the only modern successful national movement based on the idea of a people's return, an expression that has been part of Jewish experience for nearly 2,000 years. Some black Americans tried to return to Africa, especially Liberia and Sierra Leone, but Zionism is clearly the greater success thus far.

Eretz Yisrael (the Land of Israel) was not only an ideal earthly dwelling place but it also reflected and supported the ideals and customs of Judaism. Now Jews were once again in their own land. But for Jews of the Diaspora, especially in Europe and the United States, the creation of Israel was not just the fulfillment of a long-cherished dream; it was a time of reckoning. David Ben-Gurion and the government of Israel made sure of that.

The Hebrew prophets had assumed that all Jews would live together. Dispersal, or exile, had been a temporary condition. The question for Jews around the world now became: How do I remain a Jew and not live in Israel? It remains a central question for Jews to this day. Ultra-orthodox Jews rejected Israel as an abomination; only God, not man, could cause the coming of the Messiah and thus redeem the Jewish people. Ultra-assimilationist Jews feared that a Jewish state would accentuate anti-Semitic hostility by questioning the loyalty of Jews to the countries in which they lived. They wanted to be regarded as, for example, Americans of the Jewish faith. The issue of emigration to Israel was, naturally, an important one. It had been widely assumed, in Europe at least, that given a choice between a homeland of their own and anti-Semitism in Exile, Jews would naturally emigrate. This attitude was not shared by Jews in the United States. Most Diaspora Jews resolved the issue, if not simply, by staying where they were.

If the vast majority of Diaspora Jews did not migrate to the Jewish nation, Israel nevertheless had a profound impact on Jews throughout the world. In the first place it made the memory of the Holocaust bearable. It was a kind of partial compensation for the memories of disaster that haunted the Jewish subconscious. Second, it provided dignity and pride; a model for the new, free, victorious Jew whose motto is "Never Again!" And it reinforced the idea of the continuity and vitality of the Jewish people. Israel and the Diaspora both exist as part of the larger *Klal Yisrael* (the Jewish people). For most of the world's Jews, then, Israel does not exist for itself alone; it exists, as Melvin Urofsky has observed, for the Jewish people everywhere; it is "the lamp of Jewish life and culture in the world today." This is why the issue of Israel's apparent indifference to the suffering of the Palestinian refugees is so important to the new generation of Jews.

David Ben-Gurion was determined that if the answer of Diaspora Jews was to stay where they were, they would make a substantial contribution, if not spiritually, then financially to assist the new state establish itself economically. in 1951, Ben-Gurion led a campaign for the "ingathering of the exiles." The Israeli position clearly and simply divided the Jewish world into *Moledet* and *Galut* (Homeland and Exile). All Jews, especially Zionists, should make aliyah (or immigrate) as soon as possible. Israelis found it hard to accept the permanence of the Jewish Diaspora, once the state was established. To Israelis, it was incomprehensible that all Jews would not wish to live in the security and normalcy of a reborn Jewish nation. To facilitate the process of aliyah, one of the first acts of the Israeli Knesset was The Law of Return, which stated that Jews immigrating to Israel were entitled to citizenship automatically—that is, without undergoing a naturalization process.

THE ARABS OF PALESTINE: 1948

For the Palestinian Arabs, May 1948 meant that Palestine no longer existed. Three-quarters of the land of western Palestine was taken over by Zionists, and the rest was absorbed by the Kingdom of Transjordan. Jerusalem became a divided city. More than half of the Arabs of the Mandate of Palestine, including Transjordan, became refugees;

the community was destroyed. More than 60 percent of Israel's total land area, excluding the Negev, was land formerly occupied by Palestinians. Furthermore, entire cities and towns were taken over by Israel. Jaffa, Acre, Lydda, Ramle, Beit Shean, and Majdal were among these 388 towns and villages. Large parts of ninety-four other towns were also seized by the new state. In all, a quarter of all buildings in Israel (100,000 dwellings, and 10,000 shops, businesses, and stores) were formerly Palestinian.

Those Palestinians with skills—intellectuals, businessmen, and professionals—went to cities such as Beirut, Damascus, and Amman, but the vast majority—about four-fifths—were fellahin, the unskilled workers and dispossessed peasants, and they went to refugee camps where they remained. The refugee camps were set up with the help of the United Nations Relief and Works Agency for Palestine Refugees in the Middle East (UNRWA) in the vicinity of the neighboring Arab capital cities, or on old unused British or French army camp-sites. Conditions were appalling; there was little sanitation, no sewage, and only basic medical facilities. Gradually tents were replaced with small huts, and electricity and communal running water were supplied in the 1950s. The camps were organized according to where the refugees came from, so that adjoining villages in Palestine found themselves neighbors to the camps. Nevertheless, the camps were places of desperation, degradation, and insecurity, and they remain so today. The situation was not helped by the refusal of the refugees to cooperate in making the camps more attractive places, or to consider UNRWA resettlement schemes, as they wanted to emphasize the temporary nature of the camps and their hope of someday returning home. The Palestinians did take advantage of the education and training programs provided by UNRWA. In the meantime, little work was available for the refugees and this demoralized them even more.

Opportunities differed depending upon where the refugees were. Palestinians in Jordan were allowed to become citizens of the Hashemite Kingdom—the only Arab country to extend them citizenship. Many joined the army and civil service; others entered business and the professions. In Syria, Palestinians could join the army and civil service, but Lebanon was the country where they fared best. Palestinians were successful in banking and business in Beirut, and the freedom of speech they enjoyed made that city the intellectual capital of the region. Some Palestinians (about 60,000) also moved to the Persian Gulf countries and the United Arab Emirates. It is possible to trace the dynamics of the Palestinian diaspora. Over a period of forty years, the sons and daughters of illiterate subsistence peasants who were turned into refugees obtained training or education, worked hard, saved money, and moved into the middle class and intelligentsia of other Arab countries.

And, at the time of the 1949 armistice agreements, there were around 150,000 Arabs residing in Israel, most of them in the north in Galilee. Once again, Israeli and Palestinian spokespersons differ in their interpretation of the condition of the Arab population of Israel. Israeli supporters point to a number of areas in which Arabs were treated well. They note that the Nationality Law of 1951, for example, was extended to all inhabitants of the state. Arabs were allowed to vote, run for office, and, on paper, enjoy equal rights with Jews, the notable exception being army duty. Arab women in Israel were the first Arab women anywhere to have the right to vote.

Palestinian advocates, on the other hand, describe the measures often employed by Israel as oppressive. The Palestinian Arabs in Israel were placed under military rule and forbidden to move outside their areas without permits. They were forbidden to form their own political parties. Under the Defense (Emergency) Regulations imposed, which were not lifted until 1966, military governors had extensive powers over the

Palestinians. Arabs could be exiled or arrested and detained without reason; villages and land could be expropriated by declaring an area a "security zone."

The Arabs of Israel also believe they were discriminated against in terms of educational and employment opportunities. They cite the history of Nazareth to illustrate the situation of the Palestinians. Nazareth has become the largest Arab town in Israel, and it has been neglected by the Israeli government; factories were closed and very little was spent on housing despite the dramatically increasing population. At the same time, during the 1950s, Arab land was expropriated to build an exclusively Jewish town on the hill overlooking Nazareth. Although Upper Nazareth was only one-third the population of Nazareth, it received more assistance from the state than did the Arab town, and it also had several factories. Despite the fact that accommodations are available in Upper Nazareth, Arabs are discouraged from buying or renting property there.

Arabs see the story of the Arab population in the Negev and Galilee as a similar case of denial of civil rights. The 10,000 bedouin remaining in the Negev lost nearly all their cultivable land and pasture and were transferred to an area northeast of Beersheba from which they were prevented from moving. In the "triangle" in the Galilee, originally under the partition plan to be located in the Arab state, some villagers were separated from their land, which was then expropriated as "absentee" property. In these ways, Arabs claim their agricultural economy was disrupted in the decade following Israel's establishment.

The situation of the Israeli Arabs was made even more difficult by their being a minority in a state that is at war with the neighboring Arab countries. They are bound to be regarded with suspicion and fear; they recognize this. Many have accepted the Jewish state and have cooperated with it; others have totally rejected it. And the majority, perhaps, remain ambivalent. The response of Israeli Arabs to Israel varied and depended largely upon their personal circumstances. The reason most frequently given for what was seen as the harsh and discriminatory treatment of the Arabs in Israel was Prime Minister Ben-Gurion's hostile or reactionary attitude to Arabs. Ben-Gurion's view was shared by many Israeli leaders, including Golda Meir. Israelis were also obsessed by the idea of national vulnerability, and their hostility and prejudice toward the Arabs stemmed from their largely unjustified fear that Israeli Arabs would act as a fifth column against them.

CONCLUSION

The armistices of early 1949 did not finalize any of the issues surrounding the existence of the new state. Arab neighbors still implacably opposed its existence. The future of the Palestinian refugees was still to be resolved. The United States and the United Nations tried unsuccessfully to get cooperation between Israel and the Arab states on such development schemes as the sharing of the Jordan River for irrigation. The United States, Britain, and France also attempted to limit further warfare in the region by a tripartite agreement in 1950 that restricted the sale of arms to either side. The allies worried about their future influence and strategic interests. Gradually, these issues got out of control just as they did in the events leading to the formation of Israel. The history of the first decade of Israel's existence, in addition to being the story of how the new Jewish state consolidated its internal structure, is also very much the story of just how the Western powers lost control of events in the region.

SUGGESTIONS FOR FURTHER READING

ABDULLAH, KING, *My Memoirs Completed,* Washington, 1954.

BEN GURION, DAVID, *Israel: Years of Challenge,* Holt, Rinehart & Winston, New York, 1963.

COLLINS, LARRY & LAPIERRE, DOMINIQUE, *O Jerusalem,* Simon & Schuster, New York, 1972.

GLUBB, SIR J. B., *A Soldier With The Arabs,* Harper & Row, New York, 1957.

HERZOG, CHAIM, *The Arab-Israeli Wars, War and Peace in the Middle East,* Random House, New York, 1982.

LOUIS, W. ROGER, *The British Empire in the Middle East, 1945–1951,* Oxford University Press, Oxford, 1984.

MEIR, GOLDA, *My Life,* Putnam, New York, 1975.

MORRIS, BENNY, *The Birth of the Palestinian Refugee Problem, 1947–1949,* Cambridge University Press, Cambridge, 1987.

SAYIGH, ROSEMARY, *Palestinians: From Peasants to Revolutionaries,* Zed Press, London, 1979.

TURKI, FAWAZ, *The Disenherited: Journal of a Palestinian Exile,* Monthly Review Press, New York, 1972.

UNSCOP's Plan of Partition with Economic Union

1   The basic premise underlying the partition proposal is that the claims to Palestine of the Arabs and Jews, both possessing validity, are irreconcilable, and that among all the solutions advanced, partition will provide the most realistic and practicable settlement, and is the most likely to afford a workable basis for meeting in part the claims and national aspirations of both parties.

2   It is a fact that both of these peoples have their historic roots in Palestine, and that both make vital contributions to the economic and cultural life of the country. The partition solution takes these considerations fully into account.

3   The basic conflict in Palestine is a clash of two intense nationalisms. Regardless of the historical origins of the conflict, the rights and wrongs of the promises and counter-promises, and the international intervention incident to the Mandate, there are now in Palestine some 650,000 Jews and 1,200,000 Arabs who are dissimilar in their ways of living and, for the time being, separated by political interests which render difficult full and effective political cooperation.

4   Only by means of partition can these conflicting national aspirations find substantial expression and qualify both peoples to take their places as independent nations in the international community and in the United Nations.

5   The partition solution provides that finality which is a most urgent need in the solution. Every other proposed solution would tend to induce the two parties to seek modification in their favour by means of persistent pressure. The grant of independence to both States, however, would remove the basis for such efforts.

6   Partition is based on a realistic appraisal of the actual Arab-Jewish relations in Palestine. Full political cooperation would be indispensable to the effective functioning of any single-State scheme, such as the federal State proposal, except in those cases which frankly envisage either an Arab or a Jewish-dominated State.

7   Partition is the only means available by which political and economic responsibility can be placed equally on both Arabs and Jews, with the prospective result that, confronted with responsibility for bearing fully the consequences of their own actions, a new and important element of political amelioration would be introduced. In the proposed federal-State solution, this factor would be lacking.

8   Jewish immigration is the central issue in Palestine today and is the one factor, above all others, that rules out the necessary cooperation between the Arab and Jewish communities in a single State. The creation of a Jewish State under a partition scheme is the only hope of removing this issue from the arena of conflict.

9   It is recognized that partition has been strongly opposed by Arabs, but it is felt that opposition would be lessened by a solution which definitively fixes the extent of territory to be allotted to the Jews with its implicit limitation on immigration. The fact that the solution carries the sanction of the United Nations involves a finality which should allay Arab fears of further expansion of the Jewish State.

10   In view of the limited area and resources of Palestine, it is essential that, to the extent feasible, and consistent with the creation of two independent States, the economic unity of the country should be preserved. The partition proposal, therefore, is a qualified partition, subject to such measures and limitations as are considered essential to the further economic and social well-being of both States. Since the economic self-interest of each State would be vitally involved, it is believed that the minimum measure of economic unity is possible, where that of political unity is not.

11   Such economic unity requires the creation of an economic association by means of a treaty between the two States. The essential objectives of this association would be a common customs system, a common currency and the maintenance of a country-wide system of transport and communications.

12   The maintenance of existing standards of social services in all parts of Palestine depends

partly upon the preservation of economic unity, and this is a main consideration underlying the provisions for an economic union as part of the partition scheme. Partition, however, necessarily changes to some extent the fiscal situation in such a manner that, at any rate during the early years of its existence, a partitioned Arab State in Palestine would have some difficulty in raising sufficient revenue to keep up its present standards of public services.

One of the aims of the economic union, therefore, is to distribute surplus revenue to support such standards. It is recommended that the division of the surplus revenue, after certain charges and percentage of surplus to be paid to the City of Jerusalem are met, should be in equal proportion to the two States. This is an arbitrary proportion but it is considered that it would be acceptable, that it has the merit of simplicity and that, being fixed in this manner, it would be less likely to become a matter of immediate controversy. Provisions are suggested whereby this formula is to be reviewed.

13   This division of customs revenue is justified on three grounds:

(1) The Jews will have the more economically developed part of the country embracing practically the whole of the citrus-producing area which includes a large number of Arab producers: (2) the Jewish State would, through the customs union, be guaranteed a larger free-trade area for the sale of the products of its industry: (3) it would be to the disadvantage of the Jewish State if the Arab State should be in a financially precarious and poor economic condition.

14   As the Arab State will not be in a position to undertake considerable development expenditure, sympathetic consideration should be given to its claims for assistance from international institutions in the way of loans for expansion of education, public health and other vital social services of a non-self-supporting nature.

15   International financial assistance would also be required for any comprehensive immigration schemes in the interest of both States, and it is to be hoped that constructive work by the Joint Economic Board will be made possible by means of international loans on favourable terms.

RECOMMENDATIONS.

A PARTITION AND INDEPENDENCE.

1   Palestine within its present borders, following a transitional period of two years from 1 September 1947, shall be constituted into an independent Arab State, an independent Jewish State, and the City of Jerusalem, the boundaries of which are respectively described in Parts II and III below.

UNSCOP *Report*, vol. 1, chapter VI, part I, Plan of partition with economic union.

Source: T. G. Fraser, *The Middle East, 1914–1979* (New York: St. Martin's Press, 1980), pp. 45–47.

DOCUMENT 4–2

United States Department of State Memorandum on American Policy at the United Nations, 30 September 1947

Basic Considerations

The position taken by the United States Delegation in the General Assembly on the Palestine question should take full account of the following principal factors:

1   The Near Eastern area is of high strategic significance in over-all American policy. Consequently the maintenance of good will toward the United States on the part of the Moslem world is one of the primary goals of American foreign policy.

2   The policy of the United States toward Palestine over the span of the years since the First World War shows a consistent interest in the establishment of a Jewish National Home. The United States has frequently stated its support of large-scale Jewish immigration into Palestine and has indicated that it might look with favor upon some arrangement providing for a partition of Palestine, provided that such an arrangement gave promise of being workable.

3   The position taken by the United States with regard to the report of the Special Committee on Palestine must indicate the confidence of this Government in the United Nations and United States support of the procedures for which, in this case, it assumed a large initiative.

4   The plan for Palestine ultimately recommended by the GeneralAssembly should be a *United Nations* solution and not a *United States* solution. It is essential that the basic position to be taken by the United States Delegation to the General Assembly with regard to the Palestine report and the specific tactics followed by the Delegation be such that the final recommendation of the General Assembly cannot be labeled 'the American plan'.

5   It is a matter of urgency that the General Assembly should agree at this session upon a definitive solution of the Palestine problem. The only immediate hope of restoring order in Palestine and thus promoting stability in the whole Near East lies in agreement by the United Nations upon a solution which the interested parties cannot expect by agitation and violence to alter.

6   It is essential that any plan for Palestine adopted by the General Assembly be able to command the maximum cooperation of all elements in Palestine.

FRUS 1947, vol. V, pp. 1166–70, 501.
BB Palestine/9-3047

Source: Fraser, *The Middle East*, pp. 48–49.

DOCUMENT 4–3

State of Israel Proclamation of Independence

The Proclamation of Independence was published by the Provisional State Council in Tel Aviv on May 14, 1948. The Provisional State Council was the forerunner of the Knesset, the Israeli parliament. The British Mandate was terminated the following day.

The Land of Israel was the birthplace of the Jewish people. Here their spiritual, religious and national identity was formed. Here they achieved independence and created a culture of national and universal significance. Here they wrote and gave the Bible to the world.

Exiled from the Land of Israel the Jewish people remained faithful to it in all the countries of their dispersion, never ceasing to pray and hope for their return and the restoration of their national freedom.

Impelled by this historic association, Jews strove throughout the centuries to go back to the land of their fathers and regain their statehood. In recent decades they returned in their masses. They reclaimed the wilderness, revived their language, built cities and villages, and established a vigorous and ever-growing community, with its own economic and cultural life. They sought peace, yet were prepared to defend themselves. They brought the blessings of progress to all inhabitants of the country and looked forward to sovereign independence.

In the year 1897 the First Zionist Congress, inspired by Theodor Herzl's vision of the Jewish State, proclaimed the right of the Jewish people to national revival in their own country.

This right was acknowledged by the Balfour Declaration of November 2, 1917, and reaffirmed by the Mandate of the League of Nations, which gave explicit international recognition to the historic connection of the Jewish people with Palestine and their right to reconstitute their National Home.

The recent holocaust, which engulfed millions of Jews in Europe, proved anew the need to solve the problem of the homelessness and lack of independence of the Jewish people by means of the re-establishment of the Jewish State, which would open the gates to all Jews and endow the Jewish people with equality of status among the family of nations.

The survivors of the disastrous slaughter in Europe, and also Jews from other lands, have not desisted from their efforts to reach Eretz-Yisrael, in face of difficulties, obstacles and perils; and have not ceased to urge their right to a life of dignity, freedom and honest toil in their ancestral land.

In the second World War the Jewish people in Palestine made their full contribution to the struggle of the freedom-loving nations against the Nazi evil. The sacrifices of their soldiers and their war effort gained them the right to rank with the nations which founded the United Nations.

On November 29, 1947, the General Assembly of the United Nations adopted a Resolution requiring the establishment of a Jewish State in Palestine. The General Assembly called upon the inhabitants of the country to take all the necessary steps on their part to put the plan into effect. This recognition by the United Nations of the right of the Jewish people to establish their independent State is unassailable.

It is the natural right of the Jewish people to lead, as do all other nations, an independent existence in its sovereign State.

ACCORDINGLY WE, the members of the National Council, representing the Jewish people in Palestine and the World Zionist Movement, are met together in solemn assembly today, the day of termination of the British Mandate for Palestine; and by virtue of the natural and historic right of the Jewish people and of the Resolution of the General Assembly of the United Nations.

WE HEREBY PROCLAIM the establishment of the Jewish State in Palestine, to be called Medinath Yisrael (The State of Israel).

WE HEREBY DECLARE that, as from the termination of the Mandate at midnight, the 14th–15th May, 1948, and pending the setting up of the duly elected bodies of the State in accordance with a Constitution, to be drawn up by the Constituent Assembly not later than the 1st October, 1948, the National Council shall act as the Provisional State Council, and that the National Administration shall constitute the Provisional Government of the Jewish State, which shall be known as Israel.

THE STATE OF ISRAEL will be open to the immigration of Jews from all countries of their dispersion; will promote the development of the country for the benefit of all its inhabitants; will be based on the principles of liberty, justice and peace as conceived by the Prophets of Israel; will uphold the full social and political equality of all its citizens, without distinction of religion, race, or sex; will guarantee freedom of religion, conscience, education and culture; will safeguard the Holy Places of all religions; and will loyally uphold the principles of the United Nations Charter.

THE STATE OF ISRAEL will be ready to co-operate with the organs and representatives of the United Nations in the implementation of the Resolution of the Assembly of November 29, 1947, and will take steps to bring about the Economic Union over the whole of Palestine.

We appeal to the United Nations to assist the Jewish people in the building of its State and to admit Israel into the family of nations.

In the midst of wanton aggression, we yet call upon the Arab inhabitants of the State of Israel to preserve the ways of peace and play their part in the development of the State, on the basis of full and equal citizenship and due representation in all its bodies and institutions—provisional and permanent.

We extend our hand in peace and neighbourliness to all the neighbouring states and their peoples, and invite them to co-operate with the independent Jewish nation for the common good of all. The State of Israel is prepared to make its contribution to the progress of the Middle East as a whole.

Our call goes out to the Jewish people all over the world to rally to our side in the task of immigration and development, and to stand by us in the great struggle for the fulfillment of the dream of generations for the redemption of Israel.

With trust in the Rock of Israel, we set our hand to this Declaration, at this Session of the Provisional State Council, on the soil of the Homeland, in the city of Tel-Aviv, on this Sabbath eve, the fifth of Iyar, 5708, the fourteenth of May, 1948.

Source: Walter Laqueur and Barry Rubin, eds., *The Israel-Arab Reader: A Documentary History of the Middle East Conflict,* 4th ed. (New York: Penguin Books, 1984), pp. 125–128.

CHAPTER 5 | THE CONFLICT WIDENS: SUEZ, 1956

CHRONOLOGY

1869	Suez Canal opens	May 2, 1953	Hussein becomes King of Jordan
1875	Britain becomes largest single shareholder in Suez Canal Company	June 18, 1953	Republic of Egypt declared
1876	Anglo-French debt commission arrives in Egypt	April 18, 1954	Gamal Abdul Nasser replaces Naguib as premier; emerges as real leader of revolution
1881	Colonel Arabi leads nationalist uprising in Egypt	July 1954	Lavon affair
1882	Britain occupies Egypt	July 27, 1954	Anglo-Egyptian agreement initialed to complete withdrawal of all British forces from Egypt; ratified in October
1888	Constantinople Treaty provides for international transit of Suez Canal		
1914	Egypt declared a British Protectorate	Feb. 28, 1955	Israel attacks Gaza
1922	Britain gives Egypt internal independence	April 1955	Nasser attends Bandung conference
1936	Farouk becomes King of Egypt	Fall 1955	Baghdad Pact in place
1936	Anglo-Egyptian Treaty provides for end to British occupation of Egypt and limiting of troops to Canal Zone and Sinai	Sept. 27, 1955	Nasser announces Soviet-bloc arms deal
		March 1, 1956	King Hussein of Jordan dismisses British General Glubb
Sept. 1, 1939	Outbreak of World War II	May 1956	Nasser recognizes Communist China
Feb. 4, 1942	Britain forces Farouk to accept Wafd cabinet	July 19, 1956	John Foster Dulles withdraws American offer to help finance High Dam at Aswan
Feb. 1949	Egypt signs armistice with Israel		
1949	Army coups in Syria	July 26, 1956	Nasser nationalizes Suez Canal Company
April 24, 1950	Jordanian parliament ratifies annexation of "West Bank" and East Jerusalem	Oct. 1956	Hungarian revolt begins
		Oct. 29, 1956	Israel invades Sinai
April 27, 1950	Great Britain recognizes annexation of "West Bank" and East Jerusalem. [Pakistan the only other country to do so.]	Oct. 31, 1956	British and French bomb Egyptian airfields
		Nov. 5, 1956	Britain and France invade Egypt
May 25, 1950	Tripartite Agreement among United States, France, and Britain	Nov. 6/7, 1956	Britain, France, and Israel agree to cease-fire
July 20, 1951	Assassination of King Abdullah	Jan. 9, 1957	Anthony Eden resigns as British Prime Minister
Oct. 27, 1951	Wafd parliament unilaterally abrogates 1936 Treaty	March 1, 1957	Israel agrees to withdraw from Sinai; Egypt agrees to deployment of UN Emergency Force on border between Gaza Strip and Israel and at Sharm al-Sheikh
July 23, 1952	Free Officers' coup; Muhammad Naguib emerges as leader; Farouk abdicates on July 26, 1952		
Feb. 12, 1953	Agreement with Britain on the Sudan issue		

ISRAEL AND THE ARABS, 1949–1956

The United Nations General Assembly had established a Palestine Conciliation Commission (PCC) in December 1948 to work toward a peace settlement between Israel and the Arab states, to facilitate the repatriation, resettlement and economic and social well-being of the Palestine refugees, and to consider establishing Jerusalem as an international city. The PCC, consisting of representatives of the United States, France, and Turkey, failed to achieve any of its goals. Both parties rejected the UN position that Jerusalem should become an international city. The Jordanians and the Israelis came to a working arrangement by dividing the city between them, essentially disregarding the views of other nations. Israel later proclaimed Jerusalem its capital and gradually transferred government departments to the city.

Recommendations by the United Nations regarding the refugees were also unacceptable to both sides. Israel insisted that any repatriation of refugees was dependent upon a directly negotiated peace treaty with the Arab governments. The Arabs were unwilling to accept resettlement schemes without acknowledgment of the refugees' right to return. Meanwhile, the Arab states also used the pitiful conditions of the Palestinian refugees as a political weapon. They argued that the camps were visible evidence to the world of the harmful results of Zionist success. They hoped in this way to call upon world opinion to force Israel to make concessions. Some observers have suggested that the Arab governments' cynical manipulation of the Palestinian refugees was a lesson learned only too well from Zionist exploitation of the Jewish refugee issue after World War II. The Arab states also encouraged the Palestinians in Jordan, the Gaza Strip, and the demilitarized zones to cross the borders to reclaim possessions and to harass the Israelis.

The 1949 Rhodes armistice agreements established four such demilitarized zones (DMZs). One of these was in the north along the former Palestine–Syrian border; another surrounded the Hebrew University and Hadassah Hospital on Mount Scopus outside Jerusalem; a third consisted of the High Commissioner's former palace; and a fourth was around al-Auja on the Egyptian border. The armistice talks also resulted in the drawing of temporary boundaries between Israel and its neighbors. They did not, however, lead to peace treaties between the new state of Israel and the Arabs. Iraq, in fact, refused to conclude even an armistice agreement.

Much of the explanation of Israel's relations with the Arab states can be understood by looking again at map 4–1 of the area after the conclusion of the armistice agreements, paying particular attention to the borders. Israel had over 600 miles of land borders, and 75 percent of her population lived in the coastal plain from Haifa to Tel Aviv and the corridor to Jerusalem. Many of Israel's cities were within eighteen miles of an Arab border, and at its "waist," Israel was less then ten miles wide from Jordan to the Mediterranean Sea. Not only was the population of the Arab states forty times that of Israel, but the Arab standing armies also outnumbered Israel eight to one. This situation, and the conviction that the Arabs were committed to the destruction of Israel as an independent state, had a profound effect on the thinking of Israeli leaders.

In fact, however, the Arab states were wracked by internal upheaval. The Arabs could do little except to utilize economic weapons against Israel. They imposed an economic boycott in January 1950, which was strengthened by the closure of the Suez Canal to Israeli shipping, and the removal to Tripoli of the Haifa refinery by the Iraq Petroleum Company. Having been defeated by Israel confirmed the view of the younger generation of Arab nationalists that the old leadership must be overthrown and the Arab states modernized. Thus, upheavals occurred throughout the Arab world in the next decade. The army led the first of many coups in Syria in March 1949. In Jordan, a Palestinian refugee assassinated King Abdullah in July 1951, and in 1953, his grandson, the eighteen-year-old Hussein, assumed power. In July 1952, a group of young army officers deposed King Farouk in Egypt, and in October 1954 the charismatic Gamal Abdul Nasser took over as president of Egypt. One of Nasser's primary goals was the removal of Western influence from the Middle East. He also became a symbol of pan-Arabism and its determination to eradicate Israel. The continuing Arab–Israeli conflict, however, provided another arena for the rivalries of outside powers, especially the United States and the Soviet Union, as the Cold War extended into the region. In the absence of peace, another war seemed all but inevitable, and in 1956 the Suez-Sinai war broke out. The background to this war begins with a discussion of Britain's influence in Egypt in the previous century.

BRITAIN AND EGYPT

Egypt had been a focus of European colonialism and imperialism ever since the beginning of the nineteenth century. The nineteenth-century rulers, or Khedives, whom the Ottomans recognized as semiautonomous rulers of the country, consciously embarked on modernization projects, utilizing foreign advisors and seeking foreign loans. In 1854, a preliminary concession was given to the Frenchman Ferdinand de Lesseps to cut a canal between the Red Sea and the Mediterranean, an idea advanced occasionally in the past, in order to provide an alternative route to the long sea voyage around the Cape of Good Hope. The Suez Canal, built by the unpaid labor of some 20,000 Egyptians and financed by various schemes that milked the Egyptian treasury, opened to great fanfare in 1869. It was operated by a commercial company, the Compagnie Universelle du Canal Maritime de Suez, and the company's concession was to run until 1968.

The Suez Canal would have revolutionary effects on Egypt, as that country, like others in Africa and Asia, became the focus of European imperialist interests. The canal would also have a dramatic impact on Europe's mercantile-based economies. In 1875, the British became the largest single shareholders when they bought the Khedive Ismail's 44 percent of the stock to help him defray interest payments on the many loans he had contracted.

Ismail could not avoid bankruptcy, however, and in 1876 a British and French debt commission arrived to supervise Egyptian finances. This engendered much xenophobia as well as resentment against the dynasty itself and against an upper class of Turks and Circassians who had seemed to work in concert with the foreigners to exploit the Egyptian masses. A nationalist uprising in 1881 led by an Egyptian colonel, Ahmad Arabi, resulted in the British occupying Egypt in 1882 to protect the European creditors and to preserve British interests in the region. The British were particularly concerned about the Suez Canal, which was assuming increasing importance militarily and strategically and which was their gateway to India. Other maritime nations were also concerned to protect their interests, and at an international conference in Constantinople in 1888, nine European countries signed an agreement providing for free passage to ships of all flags. The British signed with reservations and managed to circumvent this Constantinople Convention during both world wars.

At the outbreak of World War I, the British declared Egypt a protectorate and used the country as a base of operations. Egyptians were transported to Gallipoli to aid the Allies; the country's economy was geared to the war effort; and several hundred thousand English and Australian troops were stationed in Egypt, contributing to inflationary pressures on the economy. Nationalist sentiment ran high immediately after the war, and although the British would not give up their hold on Egypt, they did alter their relationship with the Egyptians by concluding a formal treaty in 1922. This treaty gave the Egyptians some internal independence under a constitutional monarch, while reserving important matters like foreign affairs and national defense to the British. The "reserved" areas also included the protection of foreign interests and minorities in Egypt, control over the Anglo-Egyptian Sudan, and the protection of the Suez Canal, considered by now to be the most vital link in the communications network of the British Empire.

In 1936, a revised treaty was initialed. Its provisions included the abolition of the High Commissioner's office, withdrawal of British troops except in the Canal Zone, greater Egyptian control over the judicial system, and membership of Egypt in the League of Nations. It gave the Egyptians a somewhat more visible role in the operation of the Suez Canal and a larger share of the profits. The treaty provided for the right of Britain to return to Egypt in case of emergency, however, an eventuality that the impending world war soon provided.

The conditions of World War I practically repeated themselves in Egypt during World War II, including the resentment of much of the population against the massive presence and obvious influence of the British. Just how much influence the British had in Egypt and over the young King Farouk, who had succeeded to the throne in 1936, was seen in 1942, when there was much pro-German sentiment in the country and a pro-German prime minister had been appointed. Egypt was too vital a base for Allied operations to be allowed to operate contrary to British interests. The British surrounded the Royal Palace and gave the young monarch the choice of abdicating or accepting a pro-British Wafd cabinet and prime minister. Farouk duly appointed Nahhas Pasha, but the incident was a turning point for the monarchy and the Wafd party, which were seen by Egyptian nationalists increasingly as British puppets. Egyptian army officers were humiliated by their inability to defend the throne and by their helplessness in the situation, but they remained loyal to the king. Later, however, stung by their defeat in the first Arab–Israeli war in 1948–1949, and by reports of corruption and a defective arms scandal involving even the palace, they turned against the monarchy, and indeed began to discuss ways of supplanting it.

In 1951, with the British still in Egypt and the Canal Zone, a defiant Egyptian parliament unilaterally (and ineffectually) nullified the 1936 treaty. Disturbances resulted, and confidence in the king, who had also lost respect because of his personal vulgarity and excesses, waned. Events were set in motion that led to the "free officers" coup the night of July 22/23, 1952. Although Muhammad Naguib emerged as the front man of the newly proclaimed Republic of Egypt, he was ousted in 1954 by the real leader of the revolution, Gamal Abdul Nasser. One of the primary goals of the revolution, and certainly of Nasser, was to remove the last vestiges of foreign control from Egyptian soil. In Nasser's book *The Philosophy of the Revolution,* it is clear that regaining Egypt for the Egyptians, and not challenging Israel, was the most important objective. Indeed, Nasser expressed admiration for the Jewish effort to eject the British from Palestine. At this point, Egypt under Nasser was Egypt-centered, and that meant removing the British from the Nile Valley and the Canal Zone.

NASSER AND BRITAIN

Great Britain had emerged after World War II as the only power of any importance in the Arab world, having influence and a large measure of control in Egypt, Iraq, and

Jordan, and important oil concessions in Iraq. The British were war-weary, however, financially exhausted, and inclined to come to terms with Nasser, as long as they retained control over the Suez Canal and the right of free passage for their ships. By the time of the 1952 coup in Egypt, Britain had already given up Palestine, granted independence to India and Pakistan, and was in the throes of a crisis in Iran, where Mohammed Mossadeq led a movement against the Anglo-Iranian Oil Company in an attempt to nationalize Iranian oil.

In 1953 and 1954, Britain negotiated with Egypt on the issues of the Sudan and on evacuation of British troops from the Canal Zone. Regarding the Sudan, it was agreed that the Anglo-Egyptian Condominium, a fiction of joint control that had been established in 1899, would end, and that after a transition period of three years, the Sudan would have the right of self-determination. Egypt believed that the Sudanese would opt for union with Egypt, but in 1956 the Sudan voted to become independent. As for the Canal Zone, the British agreed in October 1954 to abrogate the 1936 treaty and to evacuate their troops within twenty months. An important clause in the agreement, however, said that in case of attack on a member of the Arab League or on Turkey, Britain or its allies could reoccupy the Canal Zone. This pretext was used to justify the Anglo-French invasion in 1956. As the British presence in the postwar Middle East diminished, the United States became the most important Western player on the scene.

NASSER AND THE UNITED STATES

Except for Christian missions, educational efforts, and oil interests, the United States up to 1945 had not been very much involved in the Middle East. World War II brought with it various forms of economic and military involvement, and a growing concern about and dependence on Middle East oil, but the United States would probably have been satisfied to leave diplomacy and policy initiatives to the British. The perceived Soviet threat, however, coupled with the decline in British influence, led to a postwar policy of "containment" of communism. The first manifestation in the Middle East of American determination to check the spread of communism was the Truman Doctrine of 1947, which extended economic and military aid to Greece and Turkey. In the next year, Iran also received a small economic and military allocation.

As Communist pressures mounted in the postwar period, with the victory of the Chinese Communists in 1949, the Berlin blockade in 1948–1949, and the invasion of Korea in 1950, the policy of containment was extended to the Arab areas of the Middle East as well, now considered of vital geo-strategic importance to the free world, especially since the region contained two-thirds of the free world's oil reserves.

Additionally, and in order to maintain stability and the free flow of oil, the United States sought to neutralize the Arab–Israeli conflict and, if possible, to induce Arabs and Israelis to make common cause with the West against the threat of Soviet encroachment. In the Tripartite Declaration of May 1950, the United States, Britain, and France declared their commitment to establish and maintain peace and stability in the area and their opposition to the use or threat of force. They pledged to take action within and outside the United Nations to prevent violations of the frontiers or armistice lines. Further, they reiterated their opposition to the development of an arms race. The three powers recognized, however, that the Arab states and Israel needed to maintain a certain level of armed force for purposes of internal security and legitimate self-defense, and they declared that they would consider arms requests in light of these principles—including requests that would permit the countries to "play their part in the defense of the area as a whole." An important but somewhat unenforceable clause of the Tripartite agreement also stressed that the three powers would only sell arms with an assurance that the purchasing nations would not use them for acts of aggression against other nations.

On October 13, 1951, the United States, Britain, France, and Turkey proposed that Egypt, considered to be the strategic center of the Middle East, join in the formation of a Middle East Command (MECOM or MEC) against communism. At that time, MEC proposals provided for the withdrawal of British troops from Egypt except for those assigned to an Allied command. Not surprisingly, the Egyptian government, which just five days earlier had unilaterally abrogated the 1936 treaty, rejected the MEC idea, which it saw as a continuation of British and colonial interference in a new guise.

When the Egyptian revolution toppled King Farouk in 1952, American interests were in a state of flux. The change of regime in Egypt coincided roughly with the transition in the United States from the Truman to the Eisenhower administration. Relations between the two countries were cordial initially, as Egypt solicited American help in its negotiations with the British for evacuation of the Suez Canal Zone. The United States did intervene in Egypt's behalf, helping secure Britain's agreement to withdraw from the Sudan and to evacuate the Canal Zone bases. The United States, meanwhile, had been providing Egypt with technical aid through the Point IV program. This program, proposed by President Truman in January 1949, during his second Inaugural Address, was an attempt to help underdeveloped nations help themselves through technical assistance. Now, this aid was supplemented with further economic assistance, and the United States held open the promise of military aid as well.

America had its own agenda for the Middle East, of course, and still hoped for an alliance that would help secure reliable air bases in the region. To try to implement what the Eisenhower administration called its "New Look" foreign policy, Secretary of State John Foster Dulles made a trip to the Middle East in 1953. He concluded that it

U.S. Secretary of State John Foster Dulles in Cairo, May 1953, with Gamal Abdul Nasser (left) and Muhammad Naguib (right) (*Photo courtesy of Hero Books*).

was not at that time realistic to attempt to create a Middle East version of NATO. The United States was afraid of communism, but the Arabs were much more concerned about Israel. Moreover, having just gotten rid of Western entanglements in the previous few years, the Arabs had no desire to let the West in through a different door. The Arabs already had a collective security pact, signed in June 1950, which Egypt wanted Iraq to uphold, and Nasser believed that Israel was a greater military threat to the Arabs than was the Soviet Union. Nevertheless, although Egypt was cool to the idea of participating in Western defense arrangements, the United States hoped that eventually it might cooperate. American efforts, however, were beginning to focus on what Dulles called the "northern tier" nations bordering the Soviet Union, which he had found much more receptive to American proposals.

THE BAGHDAD PACT, 1955

As noted above, the United States had responded to the perceived Soviet threat against Greece, Turkey, and Iran by issuing the Truman Doctrine. The Eisenhower administration increased military aid to those countries and also invited Greece and Turkey in 1954 to become full members of NATO. In addition, a military assistance agreement with Pakistan planned in late 1953 came into effect in May 1954. In September, Pakistan joined the Southeast Asia Treaty Organization (SEATO) alliance. By 1954, therefore, the United States had what it believed to be a defense line from Europe to the Far East, and along the entire length of the southern border of the Soviet Union. It now sought to bring Iraq into this scheme, as another country that was on the southern flank of Russia and perhaps as a first step in encouraging other Arab countries to reconsider a collective security pact. The pro-British Hashemite monarchy, and especially the prime minister and strongman of the country, Nuri al-Said, were amenable. Nuri hated communism and feared the Soviet threat, and he was eager for the benefits that an alliance with the West would bring.

In April 1954, the United States extended Iraq military assistance, and in early 1955 Turkey and Iraq signed a mutual cooperation pact open to all members of the Arab League. Britain joined this alliance in April 1955. By the fall of 1955, Iran and Pakistan had also become members, and the Baghdad Pact was born. The United States did not become a full member, perhaps to avoid antagonizing Israel on the one hand, since Iraq was a member. On the other hand, American participation might have made the Iraqis think twice about joining, since the United States upheld the sovereignty of Israel, its avowed enemy. The Americans also wished to avoid offending the Arab anti-Hashemites like the Saudis, with whom the United States had mutual interests based on oil arrangements and fear of communism. Many in the Eisenhower administration were especially concerned about the effect of American participation on Nasser, whom they still hoped to woo, and whose growing leadership position among the Arabs they realized would be threatened by this pact. The pact, based in Baghdad, bypassed the Arab League and did seem a slap in the face to Nasser, who responded angrily against Nuri al-Said, the British, and the United States, despite American lack of formal adherence. The United States in any event was a member in every way but name, attending the meetings of the pact, participating in its subcommittees, and supporting it financially and militarily.

The Baghdad Pact had implications not only for great-power rivalries and inter-Arab antagonisms, but also for the Arab–Israeli conflict. Both Egypt and Israel had reason to be fearful of the other, and both also had reason to resent the Western powers and their patronage of Iraq. Indeed, there had been a basic contradiction all along between the avowed intention of the Tripartite Agreement to limit the amount of arms in the area and maintain an arms balance between the Arabs and the Israelis, and the almost simultaneous efforts to induce the Arabs to join Western defense arrangements to contain communism.

American support for the Baghdad Pact was a tactical mistake in the light of subsequent events. It polarized the Arab world between Iraq and Egypt, led to destabilization in many countries in the region, and was indirectly responsible for bringing the Soviet Union into the heart of the Middle East, since it was one reason that Nasser, unsuccessful in getting arms from the United States, turned to Czechoslovakia ɪr arms in September 1955. In one stroke, the Soviets were able to leap over the "northern tier" and emerge for the first time as an important and powerful influence in the area. The Cold War was thus extended into the Middle East, despite policies of containment or new looks.

THE EGYPTIAN-SOVIET ARMS DEAL, 1955

The Egyptian-Soviet arms deal of 1955 was also precipitated by a worsening situation on the border between Egypt and Israel. Except for the border with Lebanon, which was for the most part quiet, raids into Israel by individuals and unorganized groups of Arab refugees from Jordan, Syria, and the Gaza Strip were frequent after the cessation of hostilities in 1949. These incursions reflected, among other things, the artificiality or uncertainty of the armistice lines, which although considered temporary had often divided Arab villages or cut off villagers from their fields or wells. Thus, Arabs crossed over into Israel to reclaim possessions, harvest their crops, steal, smuggle, and sometimes to kill Jews. Mixed Armistice Commissions (MACs), consisting of an equal number of Arab and Israeli delegates, had been set up by the Rhodes agreements. Under the supervision of the UN Truce Supervisory Organization (UNTSO), they were intended to help resolve border disputes peacefully, but they were ineffective in preventing Arab raids.

Although at first most of the incidents were relatively minor and both Israel and the Arab governments took measures to prevent them, violence escalated on all the borders, and a cycle of raids and reprisals began. While both sides argued about the facts and the rights and wrongs of events, raids, counterraids, shootings back and forth, commando attacks, foraging expeditions and day-to-day incidents continued. The MACs were kept busy sorting out claims and counterclaims, censuring and making recommendations, while being powerless to stop the activity.

The Israeli response to what it considered acts of provocation and murder was retaliation, often massive, by regular army units. The first major retaliatory raid took place in October 1953 against the Jordanian village of Qibya, and it destroyed fifty houses and killed more than sixty Jordanians, including women and children. Israel was condemned for this attack in the United Nations. Nevertheless, another large attack against the Jordanian village of Nahhalin occurred in early 1954 to avenge the Arab ambush of an Israeli bus and murder of eleven Israelis at Scorpion's Pass in the eastern Negev. A third major raid against Jordan prior to the Suez war took place in early October 1956, when Israel killed more than twenty-five Arabs at Qalqilye.

It should be noted that the Jordanian government actually tried to prevent this kind of terrorist activity because it was particularly susceptible to Israeli retaliation. Moreover, given the large percentage of the Jordanian population that was Palestinian, there was fear that Palestinian guerrilla groups, given too much leeway, would turn against the Hashemite king. Despite Jordan's annexation of the West Bank of the Jordan

River and extension of citizenship to Palestinian refugees, many Palestinians regarded the Jordanians as "bedouin," and the Jordanians were skeptical about Palestinian loyalty to the royal family. Many Arabs believe that Palestinian guerrilla activities from Jordan were also checked because the Englishman John Bagot Glubb continued to command the Arab Legion.

On the Syrian border there were several crises arising in the DMZ, many of which were the result of conflicting views about the legal status of the DMZ. (See Map 5–1.) The Israelis claimed that the armistice arrangements allowed them complete sovereignty and freedom of movement in the DMZ. Israel, therefore, took over Arab land, extended Israeli cultivation and began to drain Lake Huleh over Arab objections. The Syrians, and the United Nations, argued that the question of sovereignty had not been settled by the armistice agreement, that neither party had a free hand, and that it was the responsibility of the Mixed Armistice Commission to interpret the provisions of the agreement. A particular source of tension involved fishing rights in Lake Tiberius (the Sea of Galilee). Syrian gun positions overlooking the lake fired on Israeli fishing boats and killed Israeli fisherman, while Israel employed armed patrol boats not only to protect the fishermen but also to prevent Arab use of the lake. In December 1955, Israel attacked the Syrian gun positions and nearby Syrian settlements and was censured in the Security Council, partly because of the scale of the attack, and partly because Israel had chosen to bypass the UN peacekeeping machinery. It should be noted, however, that when Israel took a case to the UN, the Soviet Union vetoed resolutions introduced on Israel's behalf.

On the Egyptian border, Arab infiltrators mined roads, blew up pipelines and bridges, murdered Israeli civilians, and carried out deep penetration raids into Israeli territory. The Israelis did not retaliate on a large scale until February 1955, when they launched a massive attack against an Egyptian military post in Gaza that killed thirty-eight and wounded thirty-one. According to Nasser, it was the Gaza raid that impelled him to set up commando training camps for the refugees. These *fedayeen* (those who sacrifice themselves), equipped and encouraged by the Egyptian government, were sent across the borders, beginning in August 1955, to spy, commit acts of sabotage, and to murder Israelis. The fedayeen raids became an extension of other anti-Israel policies like the Arab economic boycott, and Nasser's closing of the Suez Canal and Gulf of Aqaba to Israeli or Israeli-bound shipping. Between September and November of 1955, Israel drove Egyptian units from the demilitarized zone at al-Auja and took over complete control. The Gaza raid in particular, however, had already convinced Nasser that Egyptian arms were not sufficient to retaliate in kind and provided a catalyst for him to seek arms wherever he could acquire them.

Israel was convinced that Egypt sought arms to attack her, but Nasser said he needed arms both to defend Egypt and to offset those that Iraq was receiving through the Baghdad Pact. Appeals to the Western powers, however, fell on deaf ears. In November 1954, President Eisenhower had offered Nasser $13 million in economic aid and $27 million in military aid in return for Egyptian concessions in the British withdrawal arrangements. The American Ambassador to Egypt, Henry A. Byroade, persuaded especially by Nasser's argument after Israel's Gaza raid that Egypt had to secure arms in order to deal with Israel as an equal, recommended that Eisenhower make good on his pledge. But American military aid never materialized, for several reasons. One was Eisenhower's sensitivity to British objections, but others were Nasser's rejection of Western-inspired collective security pacts and his support of "liberation" movements in various countries. Nasser believed that the Arab world had to become self-reliant and completely emancipated from foreign control and influence; that the defense of the Arab countries had to rest upon the Arabs themselves, not their

MAP 5-1

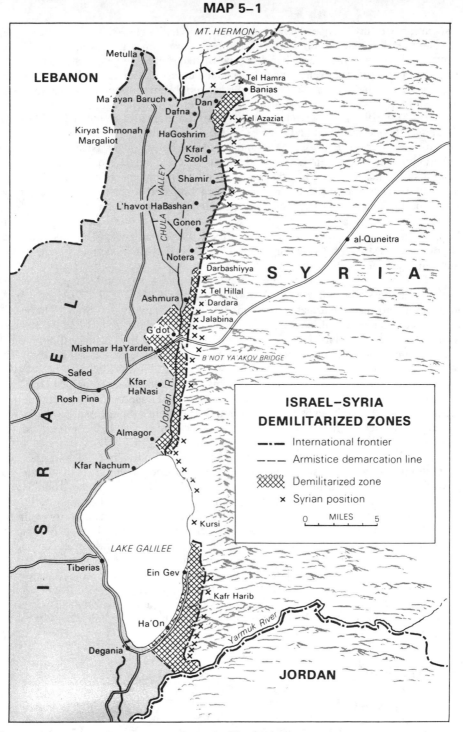

Israel-Syria demilitarized zones.

Source: Howard M. Sachar, A History of Israel: From the Rise of Zionism to our Time,
Vol. I, p. 448. Map by Jean Paul Tremblay. Copyright © 1976 by Howard M. Sachar.
Reprinted by permission of Alfred A. Knopf Inc.

association with any European power; and that it was legitimate to encourage the masses in countries still under foreign control to topple the regimes in power. When Nasser requested arms from the West, therefore, the British sent some tanks, but no ammunition; the French refused even to consider the idea unless Nasser stopped supporting the Algerian rebels; and the United States would not supply arms except in token amounts— for cash in dollars—without the strings of a collective security pact attached.

In April 1955, Nasser attended the first conference of nonaligned nations at Bandung, Indonesia. Israel had been excluded and resolutions were passed endorsing the Arab position on Palestine. At Bandung, Nasser met India's Nehru, Indonesia's Sukarno, China's Chou-en Lai and others, and he embraced the idea of "positive neutralism." This concept seemed to mean avoiding entanglements with the West while remaining free to accept aid from any source prepared to offer it without strings attached. In September 1955, Nasser announced his arms purchase agreement with Czechoslovakia, to be paid for primarily by Egyptian cotton. The weapons were Russian and worth approximately $400 million. Tanks, artillery, MIG jets and other aircraft, two destroyers, two submarines, minesweepers, rifles and guns were part of the arms package Egypt acquired.

From the Soviet point of view, a foothold in the Arab world was a convenient way to embarrass and challenge the West and to outflank NATO. The Russians wanted to effect a shift in the international balance of power. Initially, the Soviet Union had been an early supporter of Israel. The socialist ideology of the Yishuv had led Russian leaders to believe that Israel would commit itself to Soviet goals. (Interestingly, those who opposed a Jewish state in U.S. policy-making circles held the same view.) The Soviet Union supported the UN partition resolution, which was also seen as a way to get the British out of Palestine, and Soviet arms, via Czechoslovakia, helped Israel win its war of independence. The Soviet Union was the first country to extend full de jure recognition to the new Jewish state. Although the United States had been the first country to recognize Israel, it had done so only de facto and did not extend full recognition until early 1949.

Israel, however, sought to remain neutral in the postwar Cold War that was shaping up. Moreover, Israel's reliance on American economic aid, both private and governmental, and its denunciation of North Korea at the time of the Korean War, helped sour its relationship with the Soviet Union. One also cannot dismiss traditional Russian anti-Semitism and the fear within Russia of an important minority with ties abroad. In 1952, through trials of "economic criminals," and in 1953, with charges against a "conspiracy" of doctors, most of whom were Jewish, the Soviets embarked upon an anti-Jewish and anti-Israel campaign. The die was cast when Israel, in response to attempts of the West to establish the MEC, requested consideration for admission into NATO, and when that failed, Israel explored the possibility of a bilateral defense treaty with the United States. As Soviet relations with Israel worsened, Nasser's situation and outlook provided the Soviets with an opportunity to undercut the West and undermine the Baghdad Pact.

THE SUEZ CRISIS

Background

Nasser's enthusiastic reception at the Bandung conference and the arms deal with the Soviet bloc propelled him into the role of a leader of Arab unity and symbol of resistance to "colonialism, imperialism, and Zionism." Syria made its own arms deal with the Soviet bloc in 1956, and in Jordan, where some leaders had discussed joining the Baghdad Pact, there were intense pan-Arab pressures emanating from Egypt and Radio Cairo. Iraq was isolated; obstacles to a combined effort against Israel seemed to have been removed.

Partly in an effort to recoup influence after the Egyptian-Soviet arms deal, and partly out of a continuing desire to maintain good relations with the Arab states, the United States in 1955 indicated its willingness to help Egypt build the Aswan High Dam. Nasser considered this project essential to his plans to combat the effects of poverty and a soaring population and to develop Egypt economically. Nasser did not immediately agree to a World Bank plan to lend Egypt money contingent upon American and British participation, however, perhaps because he was approaching the Soviet Union for economic as well as military aid. He suggested to the Western powers that the Russians might come through with better terms. As the United States expected, however, no grant from the Soviets materialized. Nasser sought to reopen negotiations with the United States—but by then, lobbying efforts by American cotton interests in the South, by Zionists, and by supporters of Nationalist China were beginning to influence American policymakers. American opinion about Nasser was changing, and Secretary of State Dulles was beginning to detest him. Dulles and others had little patience with Arab nationalism and were increasingly frustrated, disappointed, and angry at Nasser's "neutralism" and unwillingness to follow the American game plan for the region. Dulles was infuriated by Nasser's barrage of radio broadcasts against the Baghdad Pact, but the last straw for Dulles was Nasser's recognition of Communist China in May 1956. In a meeting on July 19, 1956, with the Egyptian ambassador to the United States, Dulles abruptly withdrew the loan offer and rebuffed the ambassador. (See Document 5–1.) Official U. S. statements questioned Egypt's ability to assure the success of the project or ever repay any debt that would be incurred, since the country's economy was being mortgaged to pay for Soviet arms.

On the heels of the American renege on the High Dam, an angry Nasser in an emotional speech on July 26 declared that in order to help pay for the costs of building the Aswan Dam, Egypt would nationalize the Suez Canal. (See Document 5–2.) In this dramatic gesture, Nasser also struck at the remaining large symbol of Western imperialism operating on Egyptian soil. He thus set in motion the events that would lead to war in October 1956, when Britain, France, and Israel operated in concert to try to topple him.

The British Role

Suez, as one book on the situation is titled, was "The Lion's Last Roar." Britain had been loathe to give up her hold on Egypt and the Suez Canal Zone, and Nasser's abrupt nationalization of the canal infuriated British Prime Minister Anthony Eden and others who were reluctant to abdicate Britain's imperial interests. The Suez Canal was still seen as the gateway to the Far East and of strategic importance to British oil interests in the Persian Gulf. Not only was there concern that the Egyptians would not be able to run the canal themselves, but Eden also believed that Nasser was an upstart whose ambitions had to be checked. The spectre of Munich was never far from Eden's mind, and he was determined not to be another Neville Chamberlain. The British were also concerned about what they considered Nasser's destabilizing activities in other areas of the Middle East like Jordan, where the British had maintained influence and a military presence in the form of the Arab Legion. (See Documents 5–3(a) and 5–3(b).) In March 1956, in a gesture of support for the ideas of pan-Arabism emanating from Cairo, King Hussein of Jordan abruptly dismissed Glubb, the British commander of the

Arab Legion and the most visible symbol of British and Western influence in Jordan. By the fall of 1956, Eden was convinced that the time had come to deal decisively with Nasser.

The French Role

The French had their own reasons for wanting to get rid of Nasser. France had continued to hold on to former colonies longer than Britain and was attempting to deal with a volatile situation in North Africa. Morocco, Tunisia, and Algeria would eventually become independent, but in the mid-1950s, the French had a serious rebellion on their hands in Algeria. Nasser actively supported the Algerian rebels through anti-French Radio Cairo broadcasts and through the shipment of arms. There was also sympathy for Israel in France at this time. There had been scientific cooperation between the two countries after World War II, and support for Israel existed in both the military and political establishments. French and Israeli socialists shared common ideals, and many Jews had fought in the French Resistance. France was the first Western power to supply up-to-date arms to Israel, beginning in 1954. Like Britain's Anthony Eden, Prime Minister Guy Mollet of France also saw the removal of Nasser as the best way to protect and uphold French interests in the Middle East.

The Israeli Role

Israel was prepared to go to war against Nasser for several reasons. Israel believed an imbalance of arms unfavorable to the Jewish state had arisen because of arms shipments to Iraq as a member of the Baghdad Pact and to Egypt after the Soviet arms deal. Additionally, border raids were becoming more severe and more destructive of life and property, and there was a desire to deal decisively with the fedayeen problem. The Arab economic boycott and continued closing of the Suez Canal and the Gulf of Aqaba to Israeli shipping impeded Israel's economic growth. The strategic thinking of Israeli "hawks," especially those who agreed with Ben-Gurion's policy against the Arabs, was also part of Israel's decision to go to war.

After a very shaky and unpromising start, Israel had begun to make progress economically, but this would not have been possible without outside assistance, which was forthcoming especially from the United States in the form of grants, loans, technical assistance, and support for Export-Import Bank appropriations. American aid totalled about 35 percent of all imports into Israel by 1953. Charitable contributions, funds from the various Israel appeal campaigns all over the world, and the sale of Israel bonds also became important sources of external funding. German reparations for the first several years of Israel's existence were also substantial. With this money, Israel was able to absorb new immigrants, especially from the Arab countries, improve the living standard, and build up her defenses, spending about 7.2 percent of her gross national product (GNP) annually on military expenditures. The Israel Defense Forces (IDF) was shaped into an effective and vigorous army, especially under the leadership of Moshe Dayan, who was appointed chief-of-staff in 1953.

Modern arms, however, were difficult to obtain. By 1955, with Egypt (and shortly Syria) being supplied by the Communist bloc, and Iraq by Western powers, the Israelis felt at a distinct disadvantage. The United States had not invited Israel to join MEC (later MEDO, or Middle East Defense Organization) and had rebuffed Israeli suggestions that Israel be considered for admission into NATO, or that the United States and Israel establish a bilateral mutual defense treaty. The United States would

Moshe Dayan and General E. L. M. Burns [U.N.] studying map of Sinai, December 6, 1956 (*Photo courtesy of Israel National Archives*).

not match the Czech weapons that Egypt was receiving; indeed, Secretary of State John Foster Dulles told the Senate Foreign Relations Committee that Israel would be better off depending for its security on measures other than the acquisition of arms, especially since Israel, with its much smaller size and population, could not possibly win an arms race against Soviet-supplied Arabs.

France approved the sale of twelve Ouragon jet fighters to Israel in December 1954, as Paris became increasingly concerned about and angered at Nasser's support of the Algerian rebels. When David Ben-Gurion returned to the Defense Ministry in February 1955, after twenty-two months of retirement at his desert home in Sde Boker, he accepted the contention of Shimon Peres, the Ministry's Director General, that the French connection should be pursued. By the fall of 1955, after Soviet weapons began flowing in great quantities into Egypt, arrangements were made for fourteen additional Ouragon fighters and twelve Mystere-4 jet fighter-bombers to be sent to Israel. These arrived in the spring of 1956. By this time, as the United States became increasingly disenchanted with Nasser, there was American encouragement for the French arms shipments to Israel, and the United States even requested Canada to provide Israel with American-licensed jets. From then on, until 1967, the French were the major suppliers of Israel's military needs.

The British, meanwhile, were evacuating troops from the Suez Canal Zone in accordance with the treaty negotiated in 1954. The departure of the British troops removed an important potential buffer between Israel and Egypt. Nasser's growing reputation in the Arab world led also to a joint military command between Egypt and Syria in 1955, to which Jordan adhered in 1956. The Israelis interpreted this alliance as an Arab preparation for war. Verbal attacks against Israel, as well as the continued closing of the Suez Canal to Israeli shipping and blockade of the Gulf of Aqaba, did nothing to dispel Israeli fears, nor did the unceasing and punishing Arab raids into Israeli territory.

The Suez Crisis

127

Fedayeen incursions into Israel had increased in intensity and destructiveness, especially after the Gaza raid, when Nasser used them deliberately as a weapon against Israel. In 1955 alone, over twenty-five Israeli civilians were killed or wounded by the fedayeen. The policy of retaliation Israel adopted, however, did not seem to provide any satisfactory solution, at least to Israeli moderates like Moshe Sharett, who had become Prime Minister in November 1953. These moderates believed that repeated censure in the United Nations, no matter how one-sided it seemed to Israel, and American disapproval were counterproductive and only encouraged the cycle of violence. They noted that retaliation did not necessarily discourage fedayeen raids, and they argued further that Israel's policies were creating a situation in which it would be impossible for the Arabs even to consider making peace. They were overruled, however, by the "activists," led by David Ben-Gurion, Golda Meir, and Moshe Dayan.

These Israeli leaders argued that the best defense was a good offense, that Israel within its unacceptable and insecure borders could not afford to dismiss lightly or ignore Arab threats or intimidation, and that murderous raids and constant harassment were just another form of Arab warfare against Israel. They insisted that retaliation was never on a one-to-one basis but after an accumulation of incidents.

Ben-Gurion replaced Sharett as Israeli Prime Minister in November 1955, temporarily retaining the Defense portfolio as well. His detractors insist that his was an activist, aggressive policy, designed to prove Israel's superiority and to persuade the Arab states that they were no match, and that he was determined to undertake a preemptive war against Nasser. They point not only to the often out-of-proportion retaliatory raids launched by Israel, but also to the Lavon affair (see below), and to the eventual taking over of the al-Auja DMZ as a launching pad for invasion.

Ben-Gurion did seem to believe that the Arabs would only understand the use of force, that Israel must operate from a position of strength, and that only an appreciation of Israel's military superiority would convince the Arabs to accept the reality of the Jewish state. He also believed that it was not in the interest of Israel, or the West, or the United States, to favor the Arabs at Israel's expense. Therefore, in 1954, when the United States indicated it might be sympathetic to Egypt's military and economic needs as the British prepared to withdraw, and when the possibility still existed of attracting Egypt into some kind of defense arrangement, Israel used agents in Egypt to sabotage American and British installations in the hope that Egypt would be blamed and a wedge created between Egypt and the United States.

This was the so-called Lavon affair, associated with the then Defense Minister, Pinhas Lavon, who always insisted that the operation had taken place without his authorization, and that Dayan and Chief of Army Intelligence Benjamin Gibli gave the orders behind his back. (It was when Sharett upheld the version of Dayan and Shimon Peres, Director General of the Foreign Ministry, that Lavon resigned and Ben-Gurion returned to office as Defense Minister.) In any event, with Ben-Gurion on the scene, it was almost a certainty that Israel, if possible, would try to seize the advantage. By July 1956, the same month that Nasser nationalized the Suez Canal, Ben-Gurion instructed his general staff to draw up contingency plans for war and to concentrate initially on opening up the Strait of Tiran at the entrance of the Gulf of Aqaba. Thus, the stage was set for the collusion that later occurred with Britain and France and that led to the 1956 Suez-Sinai war.

British, French, and Israeli Collusion

By 1956, primarily as a result of the nationalization of the Suez Canal, Britain, France, and Israel felt that cooperation among the three countries was feasible and even necessary. The British, as the principal shareholders and primary users of the Suez Canal, had been furious at Nasser's action. Prime Minister Anthony Eden and others in Great Britain, intent upon bringing down Nasser, compared him to Hitler and were determined that Suez would not be another Munich. The French, realizing that Nasser was not about to accommodate them by desisting from his efforts to aid the Algerian rebels, to whom he was sending the obsolete weapons that he no longer needed, were more inclined than ever to aid Israel militarily. As the British and the French began to hold discussions about possible military action against Egypt, they hatched a plan that soon provided a role for Israel. Israel was favorable to the idea, since it had already begun preparations for a possible attack on Egypt to secure passage through the Strait of Tiran. A larger military operation would remove Soviet arms from Egypt, destroy the fedayeen threat, and, with any luck, get rid of the arch-enemy, Gamal Abdul Nasser. It is interesting to speculate what Israel believed the political outcome would be in Egypt had Nasser been defeated.

There were attempts to defuse the crisis through diplomacy and negotiations. A conference of the "user states" was held in London in August 1956. Eighteen of the participants drew up guidelines to present to Nasser, including the formation of an international body to administer the Suez Canal, but no agreement was reached between the two sides. At a second London conference, the United States introduced a new proposal to create a Canal Users' Association, which Egypt also rejected. Egypt, meanwhile, was able to run the canal efficiently and effectively, despite the resignation and departure of almost all the former foreign canal personnel. Egypt also permitted continued free shipping through the canal, except for Israeli ships.

In early October, the UN Security Council debated the issue and, indeed, had Britain and France seriously wished to find a compromise, diplomacy might have paid off. But the resolution eventually drafted was unacceptable to one or another of the parties concerned. Clearly, the canal had become a symbolic issue for both the Egyptians and the Europeans. Egypt, insisting on its "sovereign rights," and supported by the Soviet Union, steadfastly refused to accept the idea of an international authority to run the canal—and Britain and France, unwilling to recognize Egypt's sovereignty over the canal, were determined to undertake the war they had been planning, and into which they now brought in the Israelis.

By September 1, 1956, Israel's military attaché in Paris had informed Dayan that there was an Anglo-French plan against the canal, and that the French were considering inviting Israel to participate. Six days later, an initial meeting took place between Israeli and French military representatives, while Shimon Peres, now Israel's Defense Minister, had talks in Paris with his counterpart. At the end of September, an Israeli mission consisting of Foreign Minister Golda Meir, Defense Minister Peres, and Chief-of-Staff Dayan met with a French mission that included the foreign and defense ministers. Then, on October 21, Prime Minister Ben-Gurion, Peres, and Dayan flew to France for joint talks with the British and French missions. Despite Ben-Gurion's desire to take advantage of the opportunity to strike at Nasser, he hesitated, largely because he distrusted the British and insisted on first obtaining written evidence of the British and French role. Moreover, the plan was conceived so that Israel's first moves would not necessarily be interpreted as an invasion and its forces could be withdrawn if the British and the French did not fulfill their part of the agreement.

The timing coincided with the upcoming presidential election in the United States, when it was believed that the American administration would be preoccupied. The Russians were also distracted in Eastern Europe by restiveness in Poland and Hungary that would soon erupt into revolution in Hungary. In order to draw attention away from their mobilization and retain an element of surprise, the Israelis created the impression that they intended to retaliate against Jordan for a fedayeen raid that had occurred on October 10. In that same month, Jordan had joined the Syrian-Egyptian military pact. Israel did attack an Arab League police fort at Qalqilye on October 11, and as the situation on that border heated up, the impression was that Israel was mobilizing to undertake a military offensive against Jordan.

Instead, on October 29, 1956, Israel made a paratroop drop deep into central Sinai and completely surprised the Egyptians who, at first, may have believed that the Israelis were simply making a retaliatory raid. This was a calculated effect, to give Israel the opportunity to halt the operation if the British and French did not follow through. (See Document 5–4.) The Egyptians responded, however, and a full-scale war erupted in the Sinai. The British reminded Egypt of the British right to intervene if Egypt were attacked by a third power. They announced that a combined British and French force would land to secure uninterrupted navigation of the Suez Canal. Through clever use of the reserve clause in the 1954 treaty, the British and French on October 30 delivered an ultimatum calling for a halt to hostilities and a warning to Egypt to withdraw 10 miles from the canal. For Egypt, of course, that would mean a retreat from the canal, and Egypt refused. Nasser replied to the ultimatum on November 1, 1956. (See Document 5–5.)

Meanwhile, British and French planes attacked Egyptian air bases. An allied landing, originally scheduled for November 1, which might have quickly secured the desired results, almost never took place at all and was largely ineffective when it did. The allied task force did not even set sail until November 1, but as it made its way slowly across the Mediterranean, threats from the Russians and diplomatic pressure from the United States in the United Nations grew. So did political limitations internally, especially in Britain, and there was a great deal of hesitation about proceeding further on the part of the political leadership. Britain and France vetoed efforts by the

Israeli tanks moving through Gaza, October 29, 1956 (*Photo courtesy of Israel National Archives*).

UN Security Council for a cease-fire, and the Anglo-French force eventually arrived at Port Said on November 5 and attempted, albeit with some confusion, to secure the area. The French wanted to proceed until concrete military results were achieved, but before more operations could be undertaken, the British agreed to a cease-fire on the night of November 6/7. The French reluctantly followed. Israel, which meanwhile had conquered the entire Sinai all the way to the Suez Canal and had taken control of the Egyptian positions at Sharm al-Sheikh overlooking the Strait of Tiran, also agreed to the cease-fire.

Outcome

Britain and France were completely discredited by the war, and their prestige and influence plummeted throughout the Arab world. In some respects this situation tended to thrust the United States even more definitively into the role formerly played by its allies in the region. American policymakers, however, had no greater love for Nasser than before, and the United States was anyway associated in the popular mind with Western interests and with Israel. Therefore, the United States became more and more closely identified with Israel, as the Soviet Union took advantage of the situation to reinforce its relations with the Arabs and particularly to consolidate its position in Egypt. Soviet arms were quickly replaced, and Soviet aid also arrived for the building of the Aswan High Dam, which became a Russian showpiece in the Middle East.

Israel, by 1957, was forced by international and especially American pressure to withdraw from the Gaza Strip and the Sinai in return for what the Israelis believed were American and United Nations guarantees of freedom of passage through the Gulf of Aqaba. In addition, the United Nations agreed to station an emergency force (UNEF) in Egyptian territory at Sharm al-Sheikh and between Israel and Egypt in Gaza. This removed the fedayeen problem from the Egyptian border. Although navigating the Gulf of Aqaba was a primarily symbolic issue for Israel, the Israeli town of Eilat became an important port on the gulf, and shipping through the Strait of Tiran allowed Israel to receive oil from Iran (under the table). The gulf provided a window on Africa and Asia, which became markets for Israeli goods, influence, and expertise. Israel developed

Egyptian tanks captured by Israel in Sinai, November 1956 (*Photo courtesy of Israel National Archives*).

The Suez Crisis

good relations with many African and Asian countries that lasted until the Arab oil embargo of 1973.

Although defeated militarily, Gamal Abdul Nasser and the Egyptians were the big winners politically. Nasser emerged as the hero of the hour and as the symbol of pan-Arabism and its valiant stand against imperialism, colonialism, and Zionism. It was a role he appeared to relish. In the next decade, Arab nationalism would be an important factor in the domestic politics of most Arab countries, and the idea of Arab unity under Nasser became a compelling goal. The state of Israel, however, was a constant irritant and continued to block the fulfillment of pan-Arabism. The Suez war only deepened the Arab desire for revenge. In the absence of peace, the Middle East remained a powderkeg.

SUGGESTIONS FOR FURTHER READING

CHILDERS, ERSKINE, *The Road to Suez: A Study in Western–Arab Relations,* London, Macgibbon & Kee, 1962.

COOPER, CHESTER L., *The Lion's Last Roar, 1956,* New York, Harper & Row, 1978.

DAYAN, MOSHE, *Diary of the Sinai Campaign,* New York, Harper & Row, 1966.

EDEN, ANTHONY, *Full Circle,* London, Cassell, 1960.

FINER, HERMAN, *Dulles Over Suez,* Chicago, Quadrangle, 1964.

GOLDSCHMIDT, ARTHUR, JR., *Modern Egypt: The Formation of a Nation-State,* Boulder, Colo., Westview Press, 1988.

HEIKAL, MOHAMED, *Nasser: The Cairo Documents,* New York, Doubleday, 1973.

———, *Cutting the Lion's Tail: Suez Through Egyptian Eyes,* New York, William Morrow & Company, Arbor House Imprint, 1987.

LOVE, KENNETT, *Suez: The Twice-Fought War,* New York, McGraw-Hill, 1969.

NEFF, DONALD, *Warriors at Suez,* New York, The Linden Press, Simon & Schuster, 1981.

NUTTING, ANTHONY, *No End of a Lesson: The Story of Suez,* London, Constable, 1967.

STOCK, E., *Israel on the Road to Sinai, 1949–56,* Ithaca, N.Y., Cornell University Press, 1967.

THOMAS, HUGH, *Suez,* New York and Evanston, Ill., Harper & Row, 1966.

DOCUMENT 5-1

**American Statement on withdrawal of offer of financial aid to Egypt
to help build the Aswan High Dam**

<table>
<tr><td>JULY 19, 1956</td><td>DEPARTMENT OF STATE
FOR THE PRESS</td><td>NO. 401</td></tr>
</table>

ASWAN HIGH DAM

At the request of the Government of Egypt, the United States joined in December 1955 with the United Kingdom and with the World Bank in an offer to assist Egypt in the construction of a High Dam on the Nile at Aswan. This project is one of great magnitude. It would require an estimated 12 to 16 years to complete at a total cost estimated at some $1,300,000,000, of which over $900,000,000 represents local currency requirements. It involves not merely the rights and interests of Egypt but of other states whose waters are contributory, including Sudan, Ethiopia and Uganda.

The December offer contemplated an extension by the United States and United Kingdom of grant aid to help finance certain early phases of the work, the effects of which would be confined solely to Egypt, with the understanding that accomplishment of the project as a whole would require a satisfactory resolution of the question of Nile water rights. Another important consideration bearing upon the feasibility of the undertaking and thus the practicability of American aid was Egyptian readiness and ability to concentrate its economic resources upon this vast construction program.

Developments within the succeeding seven months have not been favorable to the success of the project, and the United States Government has concluded that it is not feasible in present circumstances to participate in the project. Agreement by the riparian states has not been achieved, and the ability of Egypt to devote adequate resources to assure the project's success has become more uncertain than at the time the offer was made.

This decision in no way reflects or involves any alteration in the friendly relations of the Government and people of the United States toward the Government and people of Egypt.

The United States remains deeply interested in the welfare of the Egyptian people and in the development of the Nile. It is prepared to consider at an appropriate time and at the request of the riparian states what steps might be taken toward a more effective utilization of the water resources of the Nile for the benefit of the peoples of the region. Furthermore, the United States remains ready to assist Egypt in its effort to improve the economic condition of its people and is prepared, through its appropriate agencies, to discuss these matters within the context of funds appropriated by the Congress.

State—FD, Wash, D.C.

Source: Dwight David Eisenhower Library.

DOCUMENT 5-2

**Speech by President Nasser justifying nationalization
of the Suez Canal Company, 28 July 1956**

The uproar which we anticipated has been taking place in London and Paris. This tremendous uproar is not supported by reason or logic. It is backed only by imperialist methods, by the habits of blood-sucking and of usurping rights, and by interference in the affairs of other countries. An unjustified uproar arose in London, and yesterday Britain submitted a protest to Egypt. I wonder what was the basis of this protest by Britain to Egypt? The Suez Canal Company is an Egyptian company, subject to Egyptian sovereignty. When we nationalized the Suez Canal Company, we only nationalized an Egyptian limited company, and by doing so we exercised a right which stems from the very core of Egyptian sovereignty. What right has Britain to interfere in our internal affairs? What right has Britain to interfere in our affairs and our questions? When we nationalized the Suez Canal Company, we only performed an act stemming from the very heart of our sovereignty. The Suez Canal Company is a limited company, awarded a concession by the Egyptian Government in 1865 to carry out its tasks. Today we withdraw the concession in order to do the job ourselves.

Although we have withdrawn this concession, we shall compensate shareholders of the company, despite the fact that they usurped our rights. Britain usurped 44 per cent of the shares free of charge. Today we shall pay her for her 44 per cent of the shares. We do not treat her as she treated us. We are not usurping the 44 per cent as she did. We do not tell Britain that we shall usurp her right as she usurped ours, but we tell her that we shall compensate her and forget the past.

The Suez Canal would have been restored to us in 12 years. What would have happened in 12 years' time? Would an uproar have been raised? What has happened now has disclosed hidden intentions and has unmasked Britain. If the canal was to fall to us in 12 years, why should it not be restored to us now? Why should it cause an uproar? We understand by this that they had no intention of fulfilling this pledge 12 years from now. What difference is it if the canal is restored to us now or in 12 years' time? Why should Britain say this will affect shipping in the canal? Would it have affected shipping 12 years hence?

• • •

Shipping in the Suez Canal has been normal for the past 48 hours from the time of nationalization until now. Shipping continued and is normal. We nationalized the company. We have not interfered with shipping, and we are facilitating shipping matters. However, I emphatically warn the imperialist countries that their tricks, provocations and interference will be the reason for any hindrance to shipping. I place full responsibility on Britain and France for any curtailment of shipping in the Suez Canal when I state that Egypt will maintain freedom of shipping in the Suez Canal, and that since Egypt nationalized the Suez Canal Company shipping has been normal. Even before that we maintained freedom of shipping in the canal. Who has protected the canal? The canal has been under Egyptian protection because it is part of Egypt and we are the ones who should ensure freedom of shipping. We protect it today, we protected it a month ago, and we protected it for years because it is our territory and a part of our territory. Today we shall continue to protect the canal. But, because of the tricks they are playing, I hold Britain and France responsible for any consequences which may affect shipping.

• • •

Compatriots, we shall maintain our independence and sovereignty. The Suez Canal Company has become our property, and the Egyptian flag flies over it. We shall hold it with our blood and strength, and we shall meet aggression with aggression and evil with evil. We shall proceed towards achieving dignity and prestige for Egypt and building a sound national economy and true freedom. Peace by with you.

SWB, Part IV, Daily Series, no. 6, 30 July 1956

Source: T. G. Fraser, *The Middle East, 1914–1979,* (New York: St. Martin's Press, 1980), pp. 88–89.

DOCUMENT 5–3

Anthony Eden's Views
of Gamal Abdul Nasser
(a) In His Memoirs
(b) In a Letter to Eisenhower, Sept. 6, 1956.

(a) It is important to reduce the stature of the megalomaniacal dictator at an early stage. A check to Hitler when he moved to reoccupy the Rhineland would not have destroyed him, but it would have made him pause. The world would then have had time to assess the truth, and the Germans occasion to question themselves. This process would have been altogether salutary. "Though your enemy be an ant," runs the Turkish proverb, "imagine that he is an elephant." Nowadays it is considered immoral to recognize an enemy. Some say that Nasser is no Hitler or Mussolini. Allowing for a difference in scale, I am not so sure. He has followed Hitler's pattern, even to concentration camps and the propagation of *Mein Kampf* among his officers. He has understood and used the Goebbels pattern of propaganda in all its lying ruthlessness. Egypt's strategic position increases the threat to others from any aggressive militant dictatorship there.

If any dictatorial government has it in mind to pursue an aggressive policy, it will do well to label itself "Socialist" from the start. Hitler was the first to understand the value of this camouflage. Despite the world's experience of German National Socialism, there is still a tendency to regard even a Government like Nasser's as Socialist and therefore as having a left-wing colouring. I have observed with amazement how national leaders in other countries, who hold left-wing views, have thought that they had more affinity with, for example, Colonel Nasser in Egypt than with Nuri es-Said in Iraq. The administration of Iraq under Nuri was infinitely more progressive and mindful of its people's welfare than the Egyptian. Three-quarters of Iraq's revenues from oil were devoted to public works, irrigation, electrification and improved living conditions. Only Kuwait, in a much smaller area, has attempted anything comparable. The poverty of the Egyptians further deepened when Colonel Nasser forced out General Neguib: arms before bread.

Source: Anthony Eden, *Full Circle: The Memoirs of Anthony Eden* (Boston: Houghton Mifflin, 1960), p. 481.

(b) . . . the seizure of the Suez Canal is, we are convinced, the opening gambit in a planned campaign designed by Nasser to expel all Western influence and interests from Arab countries. . . .

In short we are convinced that if Nasser is allowed to defy the eighteen nations it will be a matter of months before revolution breaks out in the oil-bearing countries and the West is wholly deprived of Middle Eastern oil. In this belief we are fortified by the advice of friendly leaders in the Middle East. . . .

You may feel that even if we are right it would be better to wait until Nasser has unmistakably unveiled his intentions. But this was the argument which prevailed in 1936 and which we both rejected in 1948. Admittedly there are risks in the use of force against Egypt now. It is however, clear that military intervention designed to reverse Nasser's revolutions in the whole continent would be a much more costly and difficult undertaking. I am very troubled, as it is, that if we do not reach a conclusion either way about the canal very soon one or other of these Eastern lands may be toppled at any moment by Nasser's revolutionary movements.

Source: Eden, *Full Circle*, pp. 519–521.

DOCUMENT 5-4

Speech to the Security Council by Abba Eban, Israel, on his country's offensive in Sinai, 30 October 1956

33   At this morning's meeting I defined the objective of the security measures which the Israel defence forces have felt bound to take in the Sinai Peninsula in the exercise of our country's inherent right of self-defence. The object of the operations is to eliminate the Egyptian *fedayeen*[1] bases from which armed Egyptian units, under the special care and authority of Mr. Nasser, invade Israel territory for purposes of murder, sabotage and the creation of permanent insecurity to peaceful life.

34   World opinion is naturally asking itself what these *fedayeen* units are, what their activities imply for Israel's security, whether their actions in the past and their plans for the future are really full of peril for Israel, and whether this peril is so acute that Israel may reasonably regard elimination of the danger as a primary condition of its security and indeed of its existence.

35   The Government of Israel is the representative of a people endowed with a mature understanding of international facts. We are not unaware of the limitations of our strength. We fully understand how certain measures might at first sight evoke a lack of comprehension even in friendly minds. Being a democracy, we work under the natural restraints of a public opinion which compels us to weigh drastic choices with care and without undue precipitation. It is therefore a Government which governs its actions by its single exclusive aim of securing life, security and opportunities of self-development for the people whom it represents, whilst also safeguarding the honour and trust of millions linked to it by the strongest ties of fraternity.

36   In recent months and days the Government of Israel has had to face a tormenting question: Do its obligations under the United Nations Charter require us to resign ourselves to the existence of uninterrupted activity to the south and north and east of our country, of armed bands practising open warfare against us and working from their bases in the Sinai Peninsula and elsewhere for the maintenance of carefully regulated invasions of our homes, or lands and our very lives, or, on the other hand, are we acting in accordance with an inherent right of self-defence when having found no other remedy for over two years, we cross the frontier against those who have no scruple or hesitation in crossing the frontier against us?

UNO SCOR, Eleventh Year, 749th meeting

Source: Fraser, *The Middle East,* pp. 90–91.

DOCUMENT 5-5

President Nasser's response to the Anglo-French ultimatum, 1 November 1956

Today, we face these plots as one, one heart, one man. These plots began with the conspiracy of Britain, France and Israel. Israel suddenly on Monday 29 October began an offensive, for no other reason except Britain's rancour. Our armed forces rose and did their duty with rare gallantry. Our air force did its duty with eternal courage, in the history of the homeland. When Israel attacked, Britain announced that she would not seize the opportunity. But when it appeared that Egypt was able to dominate the battle, an Anglo-French ultimatum was presented.

This ultimatum asked for a halt to the fighting—while the Israeli forces were inside Egyptian territory—the aggressor Israeli forces. It asked Egypt and Israel to withdraw 10 km (sic) from the Suez Canal. It then asked Egypt and also Israel to agree to the occupation of

Port Said, Ismailia and Suez by the Anglo-French forces, for the protection of shipping in the Canal. This happened at a time when navigation was in progress and was not threatened. This happened while the Egyptian forces were concentrating to face the aggressor Israeli forces, and the Egyptian forces were repelling the Israeli forces.

In her ultimatum Britain said that if a reply was not received within 12 hours she would act to execute the ultimatum. Do we agree to the occupation by Britain and France of part of Egyptian territory? Do we willingly agree to such occupation? Or do we fight for the freedom of our homeland, for the safety of our territory, for honour and for dignity? After this ultimatum Egypt decided upon her attitude. It was this: It is impossible for her to permit, it is impossible for her to accept, and it is impossible for her to agree to the occupation of Port Said, Ismailia and Suez by foreign forces—Anglo-French—and declared that this was a violation of her freedom—the freedom, sovereignty and dignity of the Egyptian people.

SWB, Part IV, Daily Series, no. 88, 3 Nov. 1956

Source: Fraser, *The Middle East,* pp. 91–92.

THE TURNING POINT: JUNE 1967

CHAPTER 6

CHRONOLOGY

March 5, 1957	Congress approves Eisenhower Doctrine	**Jan. 1966**	King Feisal of Saudi Arabia first proposes Islamic summit
Feb. 1, 1958	Egypt and Syria unite to form United Arab Republic (UAR)	**Feb. 25, 1966**	Salah Jadid takes power in Syria
July 14, 1958	Monarchy overthrown in Iraq	**April 1966**	Clashes between Syria and Israel
July 1958	Civil war in Lebanon; U.S. Marines called in July 15	**Nov. 4, 1966**	Egypt and Syria sign defense pact
July 17, 1958	British troops to Jordan	**Nov. 13, 1966**	as-Samu raid by Israel against Jordan
Oct. 1958	Moscow announces financing for first stage of Aswan High Dam	**Spring 1967**	Syrian–Israeli clashes
Sept. 29, 1961	Syria withdraws from UAR	**May 22, 1967**	Nasser asks for withdrawal of UNEF troops; Gulf of Aqaba closed to Israeli shipping
Sept. 26, 1962	Civil war breaks out in Yemen	**May 30, 1967**	Egypt and Jordan sign defense pact. Arabs and Israel mobilize for war
Sept. 1962	United States announces first direct sale of American weapons (Hawk missiles) to Israel	**June 5, 1967**	Israel attacks Egypt; Six-Day War begins
Late 1962 to Dec. 1967	Egypt involved in civil war in Yemen	**June 10, 1967**	Cease-fire; Israel in possession of East Jerusalem, West Bank, Gaza Strip, Sinai, and the Golan Heights
Jan. 1964	First Arab summit; Arab governments broach idea of a Palestine Liberation Organization under Ahmad Shukairi	**Aug./Sept. 1967**	Khartoum Conference
May 1964	Founding conference of PLO	**Nov. 22, 1967**	UN Security Council passes Resolution 242
Jan. 1, 1965	al-Fatah undertakes first guerrilla raid against Israel		

The decade following the Suez-Sinai war was the longest period in the Arab–Israeli conflict without a major confrontation or war. The years between 1956 and 1967 saw a consolidation of previous gains in Israel and impressive growth economically, militarily, politically, and culturally. In the Arab world, Egyptian President Nasser became the symbol of pan-Arabism, which reached its zenith in the late 1950s. On the other hand, an Arab "Cold War" developed. Some Arab countries, like Syria, followed Nasser's lead in embracing radical social and economic change and rejecting foreign commitments (which, nevertheless, usually meant the acceptance of aid from the Soviet Union). Other Arab states, including those still led by conservative monarchs like Jordan and Saudi Arabia, approached change in a more evolutionary way and were linked financially and ideologically to the West. The almost total discrediting of Britain and France after the Suez misadventure left the United States and the Soviet Union as the major superpower protagonists in the region.

Increasingly, the ties between the Soviets and their allies and between the United States and its Arab friends and Israel assumed the model of a patron-client relationship. In terms of Cold War politics, Soviet-American rivalry, one aspect of which was supporting the arms race between the Arabs and Israel, was a significant factor in the events leading to the next Arab–Israeli war in 1967.

ISRAEL AFTER 1956

Israel made important strides in both domestic and foreign affairs after 1956. The Israelis were forced to relinquish all territorial gains and to withdraw to the 1949 armistice lines, but the fedayeen threat was mitigated by the presence of the UNEF in the Gaza Strip. Passage of Israeli ships and cargo through the Gulf of Aqaba was assured (or so it was assumed) by the presence of the UNEF at Sharm al-Sheikh overlooking the Strait of Tiran at the entrance to the gulf. The U.S. government also seemed to guarantee Israel's right to use the waterway in an Aide Memoire stating that the United States would be prepared to exercise the right of free and innocent passage and would join other nations to secure the general recognition of such a right. For two years between 1957 and 1959, Israeli cargo on ships licensed elsewhere transited the Suez Canal as well, until Nasser forbade this traffic to continue.

The Aqaba outlet was of greater importance than was the Suez Canal, however, and the Israeli seaport of Eilat soon grew from a sleepy little town to a bustling, busy city. Israel now had a window on Africa and Asia, new markets, and new friends. Trade flourished, as did contacts and friendly relations with scores of nations in the developing world from Ethiopia and Ghana to Burma and Nepal. Useful diplomatic connections were made that helped buttress Israel's position in an increasingly hostile United Nations. And the new outlet enabled Israel to obtain oil from Iran, which maintained a de facto relationship with the Jewish state, rather than from suppliers from as far away as Venezuela.

The industrial, commercial, and agricultural development of the Negev Desert was further encouraged by the completion of a national water carrier in 1964. The United States had unsuccessfully proposed a joint irrigation scheme to Israel and the Arabs in 1953, based on sharing the Jordan River waters. President Eisenhower's envoy Eric Johnston attempted to sell this plan in five trips to the Middle East. In 1955, after temporary agreement had been reached, the Arab League decided to "postpone" a decision, thereby in effect rejecting the plan. According to Arab sources, the postponement was the result of Israel's raid on Gaza and the Arabs' assertion that Israel refused UN supervision. Israelis maintain that the Arabs were again unwilling to cooperate in any venture that would imply recognition of the Jewish state.

Water for irrigation, however, was absolutely crucial for Israel's continuing development, and even during the mandate period irrigation possibilities had been studied and plans outlined, especially by Dr. Walter Lowdermilk, an American soil conservationist. Based on his and subsequent appraisals, the Israel Water Planning Authority developed a blueprint for utilization of the Jordan waters it claimed was within the limits established by the Johnston plan. Water was taken from the Sea of Galilee, into which the Jordan emptied, and used to replenish the water table along the coast and to supply water to the northern Negev. Completion of the national water carrier opened up the possibility of industrial and agricultural growth especially in the northern Negev, which by 1967 was self-sufficient in vegetables, dairy products, and fruit. In this way, the Israelis "made the desert bloom" and also provided incentives for the development of new communities and the opportunity for settlement of new immigrants.

Immigration from the Iron Curtain countries increased in the wake of the Hungarian revolution, as it did from Egypt following the Suez war when Nasser imposed certain restrictions against foreigners and Jews. Others came from North Africa, where the establishment of independent governments posed hard choices for those who were not Arabs or Muslims. The new immigrants contributed certain skills and lent their diversified talents to Israel, as well as providing more manpower. Immigration from non-European countries also inaugurated a slow change in the demographic composition of Israel. This would have significant repercussions politically, socially, culturally, and economically in the years to come, as the Sephardim and Oriental Jews came to outnumber the European Jews, or Ashkenazim, who had been the founders and "veterans" of the young state and who continued to lead it.

Meanwhile, if the Israelis were winning new friends in Africa and Asia, they were also mending fences with old enemies. German reparations were already an important part of the Israeli economy, and economic aid was extended by an agreement in 1960 for German loans. A secret weapons agreement had been made after the Suez war, and German weapons, although not as significant to Israel as those from France, began to flow into Israel as early as 1959. Obsolete American equipment was also trans-shipped via Germany beginning in 1964. Finally, in 1965, formal diplomatic relations were initiated between Bonn and Jerusalem.

Interestingly, the relationship with France, Israel's staunchest ally during and immediately after Suez, slowly began to change. France helped Israel build its nuclear reactor at Dimona, and the Israeli air force was almost entirely French-equipped. Nevertheless, in the mid-1960s, with the Algerian war no longer a consideration, the French sought ways to reestablish ties and influence in the Arab and Islamic countries, which meant a lessening of its ties with Israel. Just how significantly the relationship had changed was illustrated graphically in the events preceding the 1967 war when France under Charles de Gaulle stopped the flow of French arms to Israel. By that time, however, Israel had diversified its sources of weapons, and the United States had begun to sell arms directly to Israel, more or less committing itself to maintaining a balance of arms between Israel and the Arab "radicals" (Egypt, Syria, Iraq), who were being supplied with massive amounts of Soviet equipment. The Kennedy administration had agreed to sell Hawk ground-to-air missiles and tanks to Israel, as well as to give further military assistance to Jordan and Saudi Arabia. By 1967, Israel emerged as a major American client in the region.

The unprecedented growth in Israel leveled off by the mid-1960s as the economy began to be plagued by a growing trade deficit, inflationary pressures caused in part by rapid growth, and the continual rise in military expenditures. The government imposed a policy of "restraint" in 1965, partly in order to curb inflation, but the recession and unemployment that followed led to emigration from the country. For the Israeli government, the crisis that was building up was exacerbated by incessant Syrian attacks on the northern borders, and by guerrilla raids emanating from the Jordanian-controlled West Bank and the Syrian-held Golan Heights. These were inspired by two Palestinian movements, the PLO and al-Fatah, which played an important role in the events leading to the Six-Day War.

THE ARABS AFTER 1956

There were many changes in the Arab world after 1956, owing partly to the rise in Nasser's stature as the leader of pan-Arabism and symbol of resistance to "colonialism, imperialism, and Zionism." The appeal of Arab nationalism, whether promoted by Nasser or by the ideology of the Arab Renaissance (or Baath) party, became almost irresistible throughout the Arab world. The Baath party, formed in Syria in the mid-1950s, combined the idea of Arab unity with that of revolutionary socialism, and its slogan became "Arab freedom, Arab socialism, and Arab unity." Described as being "post-Communistic," it rejected Marxist internationalism and allowed for some private ownership in the economic sphere. The party established branches in Lebanon, Jordan, and Iraq. It eventually seized power in Syria and Iraq, although a bitter rivalry marked the relations of the two groups.

For a few heady years after Suez, however, the idea of Arab unity focused on Nasser. The high point for him personally, and for pan-Arabism, was achieved in 1958 when Syria joined Egypt in creating the United Arab Republic (UAR). Yemen, under a hereditary monarch, became a federated member of the UAR. In that same year, the pro-Western monarchy in Iraq was toppled, and one of the first acts of the new military regime was to withdraw from the Baghdad Pact, known henceforth as Cento and headquartered in Ankara, Turkey. Meanwhile, a civil war had erupted in Lebanon, precipitated in part by the waves rippling out from Egypt. The Christian Lebanese president, Camille Chamoun, concerned about the effect in Lebanon of the coup in Iraq, called in the U.S. Marines on July 15. There was also instability in Jordan, where King Hussein in 1957 had dismissed his parliament, alleging a Communist plot against him inspired by Nasser. On July 17, Hussein requested the landing of British troops to help stabilize the monarchy.

In Syria, the Baath party had assumed increasing power in the mid-1950s and had initiated economic and social changes. Supplied with Soviet arms and equipment but coming under Soviet influence internally as well as externally, and fearful of a Communist takeover within Syria, the Baath party leaders precipitated the union with Egypt in 1958. Baath ideology, however, was inconsistent with the goal of international communism, and it was also incompatible with the kind of authoritarian, one-man rule personified by Nasser. Moreover, Syria's economy, which had been built up after the war largely by a vigorous middle class, and which, despite Arab socialism, remained more free-wheeling than that of Egypt, was sacrificed to Egyptian needs.

The UAR was a complete merger of the two countries rather than a confederation of equals, and Egypt was the dominant partner. In 1961, after Nasser announced drastic nationalization decrees affecting almost 90 percent of industry, manufacturing, and trade, Syria withdrew from the UAR. As the Arabs debated the implications of unity, civilian control was temporarily restored in Syria, only to be replaced by a Baath military coup in 1963, and yet another in 1966, which brought to the fore General Salah Jadid, the most radical leader till then in the Arab world. Jadid was critical of other Arab leaders whom he accused of passivity, and he openly threatened Israel. Committed to the idea of guerrilla warfare, he sponsored the activities of Palestinian groups against Israel. The escalating situation on the Israeli–Syrian border, as we shall see, provided the catalyst for the 1967 hostilities.

Despite the prestige that Nasser continued to enjoy with the masses throughout the Arab world and the role he filled as an all-Arab leader, the internal economic situation in Egypt deteriorated. By the mid-1960s, Egypt was in serious financial straits. The costs of interference elsewhere were very high, and especially in Yemen, where Egypt became embroiled after 1962 in a civil war that drained its manpower and money (to the tune of about $1 million per day). A determined but largely frustrated effort to industrialize exhausted foreign-currency reserves. Egypt was simply unable to keep up with population growth, unemployment, and inflation. Nasser had changed Egypt's economy from a basically free-enterprise system to one in which the state predominated, but nationalization had been undertaken largely for political reasons. Although Egypt did make industrial progress, politics continued to impinge on economic planning. Meager resources and bureaucratic inefficiency also hampered development. Therefore, although Nasser personally, and as the symbol of pan-Arabism, may have wanted to destroy the Jewish state, his actual policy, as opposed to his bombastic rhetoric, was cautious and restrained, at least until 1967. The change then, and the brinksmanship that followed, has much to do with the involvement of the superpowers in the region, to which we now turn.

U.S./SOVIET INVOLVEMENT: THE COLD WAR AND THE ARMS RACE

The U.S. Role

The United States played a prominent role in the United Nations in separating the combatants and ending the hostilities in 1956. As became clear, this was hardly because the American administration was sympathetic to Nasser's plight or to Arab nationalism. The Americans felt deeply embarrassed and compromised by their allies, who had acted without consulting them—and right on the eve of a presidential election at that. The American public expressed concern about upholding the principles of the UN Charter, and President Eisenhower displayed a sense of moral outrage that they had been violated. Although the United States, because of this stand, scored points in the short run with the Arabs, its subsequent actions tended to erode Arab goodwill. American refusal to supply medical help for the victims of allied bombing at Port Said, and the cessation of the CARE program in Egypt, which had provided free lunches to Egyptian schoolchildren, spoke louder than pious platitudes. Indeed, the United States adhered to a Western economic boycott of Egypt, refusing to sell surplus wheat and oil. In this way, the United States exhibited its continued friendship for its European allies and its disdain for Nasser. At the same time, this attitude enabled and encouraged the Soviet Union and its satellites to extend their influence. Economic and technical assistance on an increasingly large scale was evident after 1957, capped in Egypt by the Soviet agreement in October 1958, to help build the Aswan High Dam. The worth of Soviet arms to Egypt would eventually total about $2 billion. This compared to

American economic and technical aid to Israel of about $850 million between 1949 and 1965.

Because Britain and France had been so completely discredited in the region, however, the United States found itself in the position of defending Western interests and resisting the expansion of Soviet influence in those countries that had not followed Nasser's lead. The new instrument of American policy became the Eisenhower Doctrine, approved by Congress in March 1957. By its terms, the President was authorized to extend economic and military assistance, including troops, to any Middle Eastern nation that requested it against the threat of international communism. No Arab country, with the exception of Libya and Lebanon, was eager to embrace the doctrine. Zionism, not communism, was considered the enemy. Moreover, the United States was seen as attempting to weaken Arab unity by insisting that the Arab countries line up on one side or the other in the Cold War. Although the United States continued to maintain an important airbase at Dhahran (until 1961), and the Saudis were considered to be "allies," the Saudi king did not endorse the Eisenhower Doctrine. Nor did King Hussein, even though the United States rushed the Sixth Fleet to the eastern Mediterranean and extended $10 million in financial assistance to Jordan when the king quashed a Nasser-supported Communist plot against the monarchy in 1957.

The one Arab country enthusiastic about the Eisenhower Doctrine was Lebanon, especially under its Christian president, Camille Chamoun. Chamoun despised Nasser and was disturbed about growing Egyptian and Soviet influence especially in neighboring Syria. Closer adherence to the West through formal adherence to the Eisenhower Doctrine, however, seemed to violate the spirit of Lebanon's "national pact," through which a balance of interests had been maintained among Lebanon's many religious and family groups. Chamoun's overt identification with Western interests alienated other Lebanese political leaders and a large part of the Muslim population whose sympathies were with Nasser and Arab nationalism. Chamoun attempted to secure a second term as president in violation of the constitution. Anti-Chamoun and pro-Nasserist groups in Lebanon, supplied with funds, weapons, and propaganda from the newly formed United Arab Republic, saw this as an opportunity to gain power, and this set off a civil war in 1958.

At the same time, in July 1958, the pro-Western monarchy in Iraq was overturned. Fearing that the region was ripe for a Communist takeover, and worried about his own safety, Chamoun asked for American help. Largely because of the situation in Iraq, Eisenhower responded promptly. American troops landed on the beaches of Lebanon, as British troops rushed to the aid of King Hussein to help him stabilize his regime. Chamoun, who had helped precipitate the crisis by hinting that he would not give up the presidency, wisely left office at the end of his term. A more neutral government was installed in Lebanon, and the U.S. Marines departed, indicating, among other things, that the United States would not interfere with the Lebanese political process. The new Lebanese government repudiated the Eisenhower Doctrine, which left the next American administration with the task of reevaluating U.S. foreign policy in the region.

For the most part, the Arab–Israeli conflict continued to be placed within the context of basic American interests in the area, which included uninterrupted communications facilities and access to oil; the maintenance of general stability; and the protection of strategic interests against the threat of Soviet expansionism. In the Kennedy administration, however, a new approach to the Arab–Israeli conflict evolved, which John Badeau, Kennedy's ambassador to Egypt, later called the "icebox" device: deal with those issues on which Middle Easterners and Americans can agree, and put the others in cold storage for the time being. One such issue was the refugee problem, which the United States unsuccessfully took a stab at in the fall of 1961. Kennedy sent Dr. Joseph Johnson, president of the Carnegie Foundation, to consult the Israelis and Arabs about ways to deal with the situation. Johnson's own plan was to offer the refugees, under the active supervision of the UN, the choice of return or compensation for settlement outside Israel. Johnson had no luck on his first or on a subsequent trip the next spring in moving the different countries from their respective positions. The Arabs continued to insist on the right of return of all refugees, the Israelis on recognition and direct negotiation of all outstanding issues, including that of the refugees.

The United States assured Israel that it upheld the principle of the territorial integrity of all countries in the region and would defend Israel against aggression. There seemed in the Kennedy years, however, a somewhat greater appreciation of the dynamics and complexities of the Arab world. American policymakers began to realize that the achievement of American objectives did not require a specific form of political or economic system. Indeed, many believed that America could aid constructive change in Middle Eastern society, to the mutual benefit of the Arabs and the United States, through nonmilitary aid and cultural exchange. Economic and technical aid was therefore offered to Egypt, especially through Public Law 480, which enabled recipient countries to purchase surplus wheat and other commodities with local currency that remained in the country to generate development projects. In the early 1960s, for example, the United States supplied about $150 million a year in wheat surpluses, which was more than half the grain consumed in Egypt.

Meanwhile, quantities of Soviet arms were pouring into Egypt, Syria, and Iraq. Nasser's involvement in the Yemen civil war, as well as his hiring of German technicians to help develop surface-to-surface missiles and jet fighters, were arguments used to persuade the United States to sell Israel weapons directly for the first time. The Kennedy administration agreed to sell Israel Hawk ground-to-air missiles and tanks at the end of September 1962, and shipments of American arms went to Saudi Arabia and Jordan. In this way, the United States attempted to maintain a balance between Israel and the Arabs, and between the "radical" Arab countries supplied by the Soviet Union and those supplied by the United States.

The Johnson administration continued the basic approach of an arms balance and upholding the territorial integrity of all Middle Eastern countries including Israel, but with a different style and far less consistency. The different style arose to some extent because of personal antipathy between Nasser and American President Lyndon Johnson. Nasser took an almost instant dislike to Johnson and mentioned in his letters how he was put off by photographs of Johnson showing reporters the scar from his recent gallbladder operation and with his feet up on his desk. Nasser also feared that the United States might move to oust him, as it had Mossadeq, in Iran and Ngo Dinh Diem in South Vietnam. He suspected, too, that the United States had been involved in removing such leaders as Ahmed Ben Bella, Ahmed Sukarno, and Kwame Nkrumah. Johnson himself was not attuned to the sensibilities of foreign leaders, and he had little patience with Nasser. The conduct of American foreign relations in the Middle East was further complicated after 1964 by difficulties on the domestic scene and by the escalating war in Vietnam.

When the United States expressed its displeasure over Nasser's aid to rebels in the Belgian Congo, Nasser told the United States at the end of 1964 to forget its aid and go drink seawater. With less surplus wheat available to dispose of anyway, American economic aid to Egypt was discontinued shortly thereafter, causing severe repercussions in the Egyptian economy. This seemed to end any hope of a rapprochement between the two countries and to signal that Egypt would not break out of the Soviet orbit. The Soviet Union greatly enhanced its role in the Middle East in the 1960s. Still, the United States believed that, by maintaining Israel's military strength and aiding friendly Arab countries like Jordan and Saudi Arabia, its basic goals of maintaining stability in the region, and diminishing the prospect of an Arab–Israeli war that could lead to superpower confrontation, had been preserved.

The Soviet Role

Like the United States, the Soviet Union had its successes and failures in the Middle East. While the Soviet leaders would like to have seen the victory of communism in the area and were constantly reminded by the Chinese not to forget ideological imperatives, Soviet policy was of necessity based on *realpolitik*. Soviet goals included outflanking NATO, neutralizing the United States in the Middle East, and working to achieve preeminence in an area the Russians considered as almost their own backyard. After loosening their ties with socialist Israel in the 1950s and unequivocally adopting the Arab and Palestinian causes, the Soviets imitated the West in extending economic and military aid to their allies in the region. Under Nikita Khrushchev, between 1955 and 1959, the Soviets established a diplomatic presence in the area, made extensive arms deals, trained local armies, offered economic and technical assistance, and energetically supported anti-Western regimes.

The Soviet leap over the so-called northern tier, however, had brought it right into the tangled web of inter-Arab affairs and created unavoidable dilemmas, similar to those experienced by the United States. As America had discovered, the Soviet Union found it difficult to have its cake and eat it too. The events surrounding the Iraqi coup in 1958, when Abdul Karim Qasim came to power supported by local Communists, illustrated the problem. Moscow was delighted by the revolution in Iraq, but alienated Nasser by its support of Qasim, who had very different ideas about Arab unity and who in fact put down a pro-Nasser movement in Iraq. (This climate had, of course, made it easier for the United States to effect its own rapproachment with Nasser in the late 1950s and early 1960s.) Within two years, however, Qasim had also rejected local Communist support and refused recognition to the Iraq Communist party. This was a bitter disappointment to the Soviets.

Nevertheless, Soviet competition with the United States required continued Russian economic and especially military aid, at a high cost to their own economy, to regimes that were anti-West. Thus, the Russians pledged support to Egypt to help build the second stage of the Aswan High Dam at the same time that the United States was providing Egypt with the bulk of its grain; and the arms flow to Egypt, Syria, and Iraq continued, albeit with a temporary halt in Iraq when Qasim was toppled by a Baath coup in 1963 that purged local Communists. In the meantime, the stakes had also been raised. It was one thing to embarrass the West, but another to challenge it. The Soviets began to realize the danger of local outbreaks that could eventually spark a wider conflagration. Moreover, the Russians found themselves in the position of sometimes seeing arms they had supplied being used in ways over which they had little control, or which involved their own warring clients (Nasser versus competitive regimes in Baghdad or Damascus; Baghdad versus the Kurds, etc.).

In particular, the Soviet Union was ambivalent about Nasser, applauding and supporting his actions when they hurt the West but being less sanguine when they threatened other Soviet clients. In the mid-1960s the Soviets themselves decided that their ultimate ideological objectives might be reached by a continuation of aid and a policy of encouraging local Communists to work with the various governments in return for being left alone. This approach may or may not have encouraged the radicalization of the regimes in Egypt, Syria, and Iraq. However, as it became more apparent that circumstances for the achievement of both ideological and Cold War objectives were increasingly favorable, particularly in Syria after 1966, the Russians found themselves in the position of wanting and needing to preserve and extend their gains. The closer involvement in Middle East affairs, however, brought them right into the arena of the Arab–Israeli conflict, a fact illustrated dramatically in the events that precipitated the Six-Day War.

SYRIA, THE PALESTINIANS, AND THE WAR OF 1967

In order to understand the events immediately preceding the outbreak of war in June 1967, it is necessary to examine somewhat more closely the situation in Syria and among the Palestinian groups that had emerged by this time.

In the mid-1960s, as noted above, there were Baath military coups in Syria, first by General Amin al-Hafez (1963–1966), and then by General Salah Jadid (1966–1970), the first Alawite (a minority Muslim sect considered heretical by the Sunni mainstream) to become the Syrian strongman. The Baathists, whose political ideology combined leftist social and economic ideas with pan-Arabism, instituted radical domestic policies and were more openly hostile to the West and to Israel than any previous regime. In the mid-1960s, for example, after Israel had begun to pump water from the Sea of Galilee, Syria tried to prevent the water from reaching Israel by constructing canals to divert the headwaters of the Jordan River arising in her territory. Israeli artillery and planes made this too hazardous to continue, and Nasser refused to help Syria because of the anticipated Israeli reaction. The Syrians abandoned the project, but there was increasing tension on the Syrian-Israeli border (see Map 5–1). Along the DMZ in the north, Syrian gun posts on the Golan Heights fired on Israeli settlements and farmers below, and Israel retaliated. There were also disputes in the central and southern sectors over cultivation rights, with both sides arguing that the other was violating the DMZ provisions.

Under Salah Jadid, Syria established a much closer relationship with the Soviet Union and Maoist China and identified itself with "liberation" movements everywhere from Vietnam to Latin America. Jadid supported Syrian Communists and even appointed two Communist ministers, thus gratifying Syria's Soviet sponsors and providing justification for their continuing protection of the regime which, it was hoped, would turn Syria into the Arab world's first Communist state. However, the government did not enjoy widespread domestic support. Although the Baath dealt a blow to "feudalism" on the land and improved the lot of the peasant farmers and small villagers, the majority Sunnis, drawing strength from the merchant and middle classes, resented Alawi preeminence. Moreover, economically, the long tradition of laissez-faire and free enterprise was hard for them to relinquish. The one issue that united all classes and sects, however, was hostility to Israel, which tended to push Jadid toward ever greater militancy. His admiration of guerrilla-type warfare led him to active sponsorship of Palestinian groups that had been organized over the years, especially the Palestine Liberation Organization (PLO) and al-Fatah.

The PLO was a product of the first Arab summit meeting held at the Arab League headquarters in Cairo in January 1964 to discuss Israel's planned diversion of the

Unit of Palestinian soldiers during a December 1966 rally in Rafah, Gaza Strip (*Photo courtesy of United Press International*).

Galilee waters. At that meeting, Palestinians were called upon to assume the role of liberating their "homeland." At a later meeting in May 1964, King Hussein convened a Palestine National Council of about 400 Palestinians in Jerusalem. This meeting established the Palestine Liberation Organization and provided for the formation of a Palestine Liberation Army (PLA). Ahmad Shukairi, a former influential lawyer from Acre, and spokesman in the service, respectively, of Syria, Saudi Arabia, and Egypt, was elected as chairman of the PLO. Troops for the PLA were recruited from among Palestinians scattered throughout the Arab world. At this point, the PLO was primarily an instrument of the Arab governments, especially Egypt, and was dependent on budgetary support and direction from outside its own ranks. The PLO leadership appeared as disinterested in alleviating the appalling conditions of the many thousands of Palestinians who remained in crowded refugee camps as did the Arab states themselves.

It was not the PLO, however, but al-Fatah, which emerged as the primary Palestinian organization before the war of 1967. *Fatah,* meaning "conquest," was an acronym whose letters in reverse stand for *Harakat al-Tahrir al-Falastini,* or "Movement for the Liberation of Palestine." It had been founded in the late 1950s by a group of Palestinian students in Cairo, including Yasser Arafat, a member of the family of Haj Amin al-Husseini, from whom he evidently inherited some of his Palestinian patriotism and anti-Zionist zeal. Being connected to one of the notable families of Palestine gave Arafat a motive to claim the family's prestige and preeminence as well as providing credibility and a built-in following for his cause. Members of al-Fatah and other Palestinians undoubtedly participated in fedayeen raids before the Suez-Sinai war. After that, with UN Emergency Forces (UNEF) on the borders between Egypt and Israel, al-Fatah tended to languish, and Arafat, trained as an engineer, moved to Kuwait, where he became a successful contractor. In the 1960s, al-Fatah began to gravitate into the orbit of Syria, which saw it as a useful adjunct for its own agenda against Israel. In January 1965, Fatah members carried out their first significant raid against Israel from Syrian territory. After Jadid took power in 1966, he substantially increased weapons and support for Fatah. While the Syrian army fired down on Israeli farmers from the Golan Heights, Fatah guerrillas struck at Israeli patrols and conducted numerous raids, particularly in the Almagor area.

Toward the end of 1966, in a departure from previous policy, PLO leader Shukairi signed an agreement with the Syrian government providing for full coordination between the PLO and al-Fatah. He did this despite Egypt's reservations about the latter organization and Nasser's unwillingness to allow guerrilla bases in Egypt and Gaza. The reasons for Shukairi's rapprochement with Fatah included his fear that the growing popularity of Fatah's exploits would leave him exposed as ineffective. Additionally, the relationship between the PLO and King Hussein had been worsening, and this made an agreement with Fatah an attractive front against the Jordanians. Shukairi had established a headquarters in the Old City of Jerusalem, imposed taxes on the Palestinian refugees, and set up training camps. King Hussein believed that the PLO was building up a state within a state (which would indeed be the case fifteen years later), and he therefore arrested many PLO members and shut down PLO operations.

Hussein's action, which was also a blow against Egyptian and Syrian sponsorship of the Palestinian organizations, intensified the split between the "radicals" and the "reactionaries" in the Arab Cold War. Nasser had labeled Feisal—the Saudi king who had been promoting the idea of an Islamic pact against Nasserism, and who was the chief supporter of the royalists in Yemen—the "Pope of Islam." He cast aspersions against King Hussein, who received his military equipment and financial aid from the United States, as the "dwarf from Amman" and the "Hashemite harlot." The Jordanians and Saudis countered by attacking Nasser, accusing him of cowardice, fear of Israel, and unwillingness to live up to his promises to the other Arabs when they were challenged by Israel. The situation on the borders between Syria and Israel and between Jordan and Israel, exacerbated by Palestinian guerrilla activity, brought many of these inter-Arab tensions to the surface, as well as contributing to the outbreak of full-scale war between Israel and the Arabs in 1967.

Prelude to War

As noted above, al-Fatah's first raids into Israel were from Syrian territory. However, although based in Syria, Palestinians most often launched attacks from Jordanian territory, since the longer border was easier and safer to cross. As in the past, the Israeli government adopted the policy of retaliation by regular army units and held to account the country from which the raid emanated, even though both the Jordanian and Lebanese governments made serious attempts to prevent such incursions from their territory.

Meanwhile, raids from Syria had also continued, and these led in mid-August 1966 to a major clash between Israel and Syria. Both sides eventually agreed to UN requests for a cease-fire, but subsequent guerrilla operations against Israel resulted in Security Council debates in which Western nations called upon Syria to prevent Fatah operations from her territory and the Eastern bloc chastised Israel for her aggressive intentions against Syria.

Nevertheless, the Russians were concerned that the general instability of the Salah Jadid regime in Syria and the volatility of the border situation might lead to massive Israeli retaliation against their client. Their fear that Jadid might be overthrown and/or that a wider conflagration involving the superpowers might be sparked brought the Soviets more directly into the picture in 1966–1967. They called on the Syrian leader to contain the guerrillas and to restrain his bellicose rhetoric against Israel. Moreover, the Soviets encouraged a joint defense pact between Egypt and Syria, signed in early November 1966, either because they hoped it would restrain the Syrians and hold them in check, or because they believed Egyptian adherence would provide a deterrent to Israeli retaliation.

Shortly thereafter, on November 13, 1966, Israel undertook a major military assault against as-Samu and neighboring Jordanian towns, killing eighteen, including three civilians. Fifty-four were wounded, and a clinic, school, and over a hundred houses were destroyed. The Israeli position was that this raid was in retaliation for several guerrilla attacks launched from Jordan over the previous six months, some of which had resulted in death or injury to Israelis. The as-Samu raid, however, was condemned by the world community both within and outside the United Nations. The United States supported the Security Council resolution condemning Israel, not just because of the scale of the attack, but also because it undercut and embarrassed King Hussein. The as-Samu incursion compromised the king in the eyes of the Palestinians and provided the Arab "radicals" and their patron, the Soviet Union, with a further excuse to try to undermine his regime.

There was wide speculation that Israel had struck at Jordan rather than Syria, which unlike Jordan had actively aided and abetted the Palestinian groups, because Israel did not want to provoke Egypt in light of the recently signed Egypt–Syria defense pact. There is no indication, however, that Egypt would have responded to an attack on Syria, if, as we shall see, the events of April 1967 are any proof. Indeed, the escalation that led finally to war in October 1967 appears to have been the result primarily of Russian meddling.

The Road to War

In 1958, Gamal Abdul Nasser was the leading figure in the Arab world. By 1961, however, Syria had seceded from the UAR, and Qasim's regime in Iraq was forging its own destiny, which would continue to diverge from that of Egypt with successive military coups. Internally, as noted above, Egypt's economy was in poor shape. Moreover, Nasser's friends from the Bandung conference and in the third world, leaders like Nehru, Sukarno, Ben Bella, and others, were no longer in power.

Nasser had determined after 1956 that he would not become involved in a major confrontation with Israel unless he could win; that is, unless he were fully prepared militarily and the international circumstances were right. He recognized Israel's growing economic and military strength and the international support Israel enjoyed in the West and among many of the developing nations. Because of Arab unpreparedness and Israel's policy of retaliation, Nasser did not lend support for Syrian efforts to halt Israel's water-diversion scheme. Nor did he react, despite Jordanian taunts, to Israel's attack against as-Samu, except to insist to King Hussein that responsibility for repulsing Israeli reprisal raids rested with the individual countries. Nasser retreated to this position again in April 1967, when, after several months of violent incidents in the north, an air battle erupted between Israel and Syria in which Israel violated Syrian airspace, shot down six MIGs, and buzzed Damascus. Nasser remained aloof.

To the Russians, however, it seemed absolutely crucial to prod the Egyptians into living up to the commitment implied in the joint defense pact. The unstable Jadid regime in Syria had raised the stakes in the north without much apparent success and had embarked on a course that promised the counterproductive effect of massive Israeli retaliation. The achievement of Soviet objectives in Syria seemed to be in jeopardy. Only by the device of Nasser restraining Jadid and/or causing Israel to pause before retaliating for Syrian raids, because of the possibility of Egyptian action in the south, could some Soviet control be exerted over this situation. In early May 1967, therefore, the Russians passed on to the Egyptians information about heavy Israeli troop concentrations on the Syrian border and an Israeli contingency plan for an attack on Syria.

The Soviets, and probably Nasser himself, knew that information about massive Israeli troop concentrations was false. Indeed, the UN Truce Supervision Organization (UNTSO), U.S. intelligence, and Egyptian observers on the spot failed to detect any Israeli moves. Nasser, however, decided to become involved and to take some action for several reasons. He was convinced that the United States was trying to get at him indirectly by urging Israel to hit Syria, but he believed the Russians would now stand behind him whatever action he took. Nasser had a false estimation of Egyptian strength based on the great amounts of military hardware he had amassed. His poor economic situation called for some outlet for the frustration that had been building among the Egyptian people. And he certainly hoped that assuming an active role against Israel would quiet his critics and restore his position of leadership in the Arab world.

Thus, on May 14, 1967, Cairo announced that Egyptian armed forces were in a state of maximum alert, and combat units crossed over the Suez into Sinai. On May 16, Egypt requested the UNEF to be concentrated in the Gaza Strip, and on May 18 the Egyptian foreign minister asked United Nations Secretary General U Thant to recall all troops of the UNEF stationed in the Gaza Strip and on UAR soil. This was a step Nasser had every legal right to take, but instead of procrastinating in order to defuse the growing crisis, U Thant complied almost immediately. Egyptian troops and tanks began to rumble across the Sinai and to take over UN positions. Syria also began to mobilize, as did Jordan and Iraq. On May 22, with Egyptian troops at Sharm al-Sheikh, Nasser announced the closing of the Gulf of Aqaba to Israeli vessels or any vessels carrying goods to Israel. Prime Minister Levi Eshkol replied the next day that Israel would consider any interference with freedom of shipping as an act of aggression against Israel. Bellicose speeches continued to emanate from Cairo, however, and during the next week, Nasser on several occasions stated that Palestine must be liberated and Israel destroyed. (See Document 6–1.)

As the crisis escalated, the Security Council met in emergency session, but its discussions were fruitless and hampered by the Soviet veto. Israeli Foreign Minister Abba Eban flew to Paris, London, and the U.S., as the Western countries groped for some way to defuse the situation. Although President Johnson publicly denounced Nasser's closing of the waterway and promised that the United States would try to get other maritime nations to join in testing the blockade, the American Aide Memoire of 1957 was obviously a worthless scrap of paper. Privately, Johnson warned Israel against a preemptive strike, and Israeli moderates hesitated to act unilaterally. Nasser appeared to have Israel in a bind; the prolonged general mobilization in Israel was beginning to have a dire psychological as well as economic effect. To the Arabs, what had perhaps started as some limited action began to take on the possibility of a potentially successful military operation, as Nasser, believing he had the support of the Russians, went to the brink. On May 30, 1967, King Hussein of Jordan flew to Egypt to sign a defense pact with Egypt. He agreed to allow Iraqi troops to enter Jordanian territory in the event of hostilities. PLO leader Shukairi, although no friend of Hussein, was present at the signing ceremony and flew back to Jordan with the king.

The situation was extremely difficult for Israel. (See Document 6–2.) There were Arab armies poised on all its borders; mobilization was taking a toll economically, as normal life came to a standstill; and politically, there was a crisis situation, as Eshkol's government seemed incapable of making a decision about what course of action to take. All armies have contingency plans, and Israel as early as 1964 had worked out such a plan for an attack against Egypt if necessary. Israel had on several occasions threatened reprisals against Syria and undoubtedly had various alternatives on the drawing board. Given Israel's borders, the idea of the preemptive strike (or what some Israel military leaders like Yigal Allon called the "preemptive counterstrike") had come to be accepted, since Israel within its present borders was not in a position to absorb a first blow and survive. Because of Israel's policies of massive retaliation and offensive warfare as the best defense, some historians and writers see all the Arab–Israeli wars as the result of Israeli aggressiveness and expansionism, which they attribute to an inherent dynamic and master plan of Zionism. In their view, while Nasser may have shown antipathy to Israel, and with good reason, he was not a warmonger—in contrast to Ben-Gurion and a coterie of younger Israeli "hawks" who had been planning another strike against Nasser for a decade.

Other historians argue that despite the existence of military contingency plans, there is no evidence that Israel would have launched a full-scale war against Egypt had Nasser not taken the provocative actions he did. They contend, on the contrary, that the failure of Israel to retaliate for the closing of the Gulf of Aqaba, retaliation that was expected both among the Arabs and the superpowers, and the hesitation and indecisiveness evident in Israel as diplomatic solutions were floated, fed Nasser's megalomania and encouraged King Hussein of Jordan to put aside past differences and climb on the bandwagon. They maintain that no matter how pragmatic Nasser could be, the defeat of 1948, and the drubbing of 1956, had only nourished Arab hatred of Israel and the desire for revenge. In any event, the Egyptian–Jordanian defense pact seems to have galvanized the Israelis, who put together a government of national unity (which included Menachem Begin, the leader of the opposition for all the years since statehood), in which Moshe Dayan was named Minister of Defense.

With Dayan in the cabinet, and with the Israeli belief that the existence of the entire nation was indeed in jeopardy, it was almost a certainty that Israel would strike the first blow. According to apologists for Israel, this is precisely what Nasser wanted. Were he to initiate hostilities, the issue would not be about shipping in the Gulf of Aqaba but about the continued existence of the Jewish state, which the United States was pledged to uphold. In this view, Nasser believed that Israel, in striking a first blow, would be diplomatically isolated, especially from the United States, and that the Americans would hesitate to intervene on Israel's side. Wiser leaders than Eshkol and Nasser, however, could have averted conflict.

The Six-Day War broke out on the morning of June 5, 1967, as Israel planes destroyed most of Egypt's air force on the ground. Details of the war itself have been recounted in countless books and will not be repeated here, but the importance of air power, and the cohesiveness of Israel's citizen army, should be mentioned as significant factors in Israel's success. The outcome was even more dramatic since the Arabs seemed to be superior in almost every weapons category. (See Tables 6–1 and 6–2.) After the initial Israeli air strike, Israeli ground troops defeated the Egyptian army, seizing the Gaza Strip and the entire Sinai Peninsula. In a still-disputed incident on June 8, the Israelis attacked an American intelligence-gathering ship, the USS *Liberty*, sailing off the Egyptian coast. Thirty-four sailors were killed and 164 wounded. Some writers insist that this was a deliberate and premeditated attack; Israel continues to maintain that the attack on the *Liberty* was a case of mistaken identity and an accident. Israel apologized and later paid $3 million in reparations for the families of the victims to the U.S. government which accepted Israel's explanation and apology.

Israel asked King Hussein to stay out of the war and assured him it would not attack him first. Hussein, however, was badly misled by the Egyptians, who intimated that they were being successful against Israel on the southern front. Jordanian guns began to fire from across the borders in Jerusalem while Jordanian troops seized the UN headquarters in no-man's land. This was all the excuse the Israelis needed to take the Old City of Jerusalem and the entire West Bank. Israel then turned toward Syria, which had been attacking Israel's northern settlements by air and with artillery. Although the United Nations called for a cease-fire, the Israelis did not stop until they had captured the Golan Heights in some of the fiercest fighting of the war. By June 10, 1967, six days later, the war was over. (See Table 6–3.)

TABLE 6–1   Approximate Land and Air Force Strengths 1967 War

	Israel	Arabs	Egypt	Jordan	Syria	Iraq
Mobilized Operational Manpower[1]	250,000	328,000	210,000	55,000	63,000	—
Brigades	25	42	22	10	12	—
Artillery Pieces	200	960	575	263	315	—
Tanks	1,000[2]	2,330	1,300[5]	288[7]	750	—
APCs	1,500[3]	1,845	1,050	210	585	—
SAMs	50	160	160	0	0	0
AA Guns	550	2,000+	950	143	1,000	—
Combat Aircraft	286[4]	682	431[6]	18	127[8]	106[9]

[1]On the Arab side includes only forces available for commitment.
[2]200 M48s, 250 Centurions, 150 AMX-13s, 400 Shermans and Super-Shermans.
[3]M3 Halftracks.
[4]Includes 92 Mirages, 24 Super-Mystères, 82 Mystères, 55 Ouragans, 24 light bombers.
[5]Includes 400+ T-34s, 450+ T-54/55s, 100+ Su-100s, 100+ JS-3s.
[6]Includes 55 Su-6s, 163 MiG-21s, 40 MiG-19s, 100 MiG15/17s, 30 Tu-16s, 43 Il-28s; only 350 pilots.
[7]Includes about 200 M48s, about 90 Centurions.
[8]Includes 40 MiG-21/19s, 68 MiG-15/17s, 15 Tu-16s, 4 Il-28s.
[9]About 45 committed.

TABLE 6–2   Estimated Naval Strengths 1967 War

	Israel	Egypt	Syria
Manpower	4,000	13,000	1,000
Patrol and Torpedo Boats	9	44	17
Guided Missile Boats	0	18[1]	4[2]
Destroyers and Frigates	3	7	0
Submarines	3	12	0
Amphibious Craft	0	5	0
Small Craft	?	?	?
Vessel Totals	15+	86+	21+

[1]Includes 8 *Komar* class and 10 *Osa* class.
[2]*Komar* class, just received; not ready for combat.

Source: Trevor N. Dupuy, *Elusive Victory: The Arab–Israeli Wars, 1947–1974* (New York: Harper & Row, 1978), p. 337. Reprinted by permission of Hero Books.

TABLE 6–3 Losses, 1967 War

	Killed	Wounded	Captured /Missing	Total Casualties	Tanks Lost	Aircraft Lost
Israel	983	4,517	15	5,515	394[1]	40
(vs. Egypt)	303	1,450	11	1,764	122	—
(vs. Jordan)	553	2,442	0	2,995	112	—
(vs. Syria)	127	625	4	756	160	—
Arabs	4,296	6,121	7,550	17,967	965[2]	444
(Egypt)	3,000	5,000	4,980	12,980	700	356[3]
(Jordan)[4]	696	421	2,000[5]	3,117	179	18
(Syria)	600	700	570	1,870	86	55
(Iraq)	—	—	—	—	—	15

[1] At least half of these were repaired and returned to full operational status.

[2] About 150 captured T-54/55s were modified by the Israelis and put into their postwar inventory, thus largely offsetting unrepairable losses during the war.

[3] Of these, 322 were lost the first day.

[4] Recent figures, official except for estimate of missing; 20% factor added to killed and wounded to allow for these losses among missing.

[5] Of these, 530 were prisoners of war.

Source: Dupuy, *Elusive Victory*, p. 333. Reprinted by permission of Hero Books.

Results

The results of Israel's stunning and spectacular victory have been far-reaching and of crucial importance in the years since 1967. A new map of the Middle East came into being, with Israel three times larger than it was in 1949. (See Map 6–1.) Israel's occupation of the Sinai Peninsula, the Golan Heights, the West Bank, the Gaza Strip, and East Jerusalem brought new opportunities and new problems. Certainly the conquest of all this territory provided Israel with "strategic depth," presumably more defensible borders, and some breathing room. However, we shall see that the continued occupation of the territories and Jewish settlements on the West Bank and in Gaza have not brought Israel any closer to the peace it desired. On the contrary, with 1.3 million Palestinians under Israeli control in Gaza and on the West Bank, the Palestinian problem became Israel's problem. If Palestinian nationalism was nascent or held in check before 1967 when the Palestinians lived under Arab governments, it grew into an authentic manifestation of the desire of Palestinian Arabs for self-determination as the years passed. Many Palestinian groups representing Palestinian interests came into being. They differed on strategy and tactics and the order in which their various enemies—reactionary Arab regimes, and Israel—should be overcome, but the significant growth of Palestinian national aspirations and the world recognition that was gained for a variety of reasons, especially by a reorganized PLO led after 1968 by Yasser Arafat, are undeniable.

For Israel, a new image of strength and power replaced the previous one of the threatened underdog, the gallant little country surrounded by enemies who wished to exterminate it. Israel's victory had a profound effect on Jews everywhere, engendering self-confidence, pride, and assertiveness. In the Soviet Union, where Jewish religious and national identity had been submerged since the Bolshevik Revolution, a new

MAP 6–1

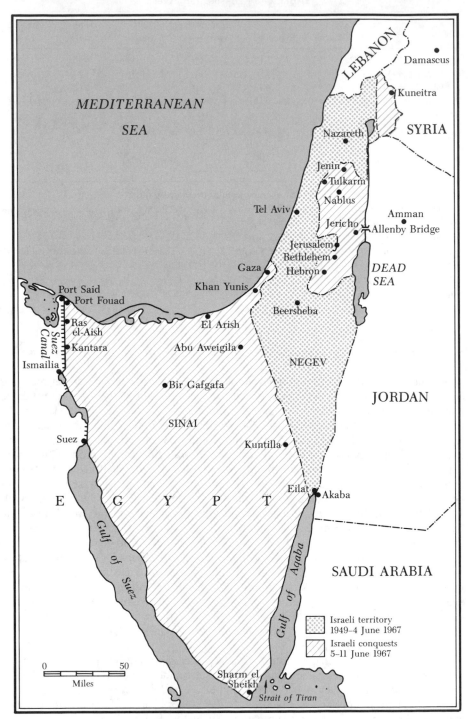

Israeli conquests, 1967.

Source: Martin Gilbert *Atlas of The Arab-Israeli Conflict* (New York: Macmillan, 1974), p. 70.

Israeli soldier on watch at Suez Canal, January 23, 1968 (*Photo courtesy of Britain/Israel Public Affairs Centre*).

Jewish self-consciousness began to emerge that would have significant repercussions. Israelis themselves were euphoric that their army and people had been able to stand up to the combined Arab armies and win a war without help from any other nation even though, in their initial disbelief and humiliation, Nasser and Hussein had fabricated a story that the United States had participated and been responsible for Israel's victory. The image of the Israel Defense Forces as one of the best armies in the world was heady stuff, and, as we shall see, an exaggerated sense of power resulted, as well as an arrogance toward the enemy that led later to serious miscalculations on Israel's part. The results of the Six-Day War on Egypt and Syria will be examined in the next chapter.

The Soviet Union and several East-bloc countries severed diplomatic ties with Israel in the aftermath of the war, which hurt the Soviets more than Israel in the region, since the Russians lost their leverage with both sides. Egypt, Syria, Iraq, Sudan, Algeria, and Yemen severed diplomatic ties with the United States, and American relations with the Arabs in general deteriorated as a result of the war. Nevertheless, the United States still retained important ties with Saudi Arabia and Jordan, while at the same time becoming the guarantor of Israel's survival. France under Charles de Gaulle, anxious to recoup in the Arab world, declined to supply Israel's military needs any longer, and Britain was beginning to withdraw from her installations east of Suez. The United States and Israel were thrown closer together, therefore, although this was a situation that both nations might have wished to avoid. A strong Israel was increasingly seen in the United States as a strategic ally, and the identification of interests became tighter on both sides.

The diplomatic solution to the 1967 hostilities was UN Resolution 242, a master-piece of diplomatic ambiguity that became the key document in all attempts to arrive at a peaceful solution to the conflict (See Document 6–3). While insisting on the inadmissibility of the acquisition of territory by conquest, a rather new and startling international principle, UN Resolution 242 proposed (in so many words) the idea of peace in return for territory—without specifying which should come first. In the first article of Resolution 242, which the Security Council passed in November 1967, Israel was called upon to return occupied territories (but not "the" territories). A second article recognized the right of all states in the region to live in peace within secure and recognized borders. Other important points included freedom of passage through international waterways and a just solution to the "refugee" problem. Resolution 242 was accepted by Israel, Egypt, and Jordan (but not by Syria) and was a notable milestone in its implicit acknowledgement by these Arab states of Israel's existence and its expectation of a negotiated settlement. There was no machinery to implement the resolution, however, except through the good offices of a special UN mediator, Dr. Gunnar Jarring, whose task was to try to facilitate talks among the parties. The Israelis held the view that explicit recognition through direct negotiations should come before withdrawal, and that they were not required to withdraw from all the occupied territory. The Arabs insisted on Israel's withdrawal from all the occupied territory, including East Jerusalem, which the Israelis annexed shortly after the conclusion of hostilities. Nor did the resolution address the escalating arms race. Even more significant in both the short and long run was the absence of any specific reference to the Palestinians, except for the provision that there should be a just solution to the refugee problem. The Eshkol government continued to reiterate its desire for direct peace negotiations (See Document 6–4) but in late August–early September 1967, even before passage of Resolution 242, an Arab summit in Khartoum, the Sudan, proclaimed that there would be "no peace, no recognition, and no negotiations" with Israel. (See Document 6–5.) These were three "no's" that Israel took seriously and that continued to influence Israeli policymakers.

RECAPITULATION

The long-range causes of the 1967 war were the continued inability of the Arabs to recognize and accept the political sovereignty of the Jews in Israel; the antagonism and desire for revenge that had been fueled by defeats and humiliation in the previous wars, as well as by Israel's excessive retaliations; Arab fear of Israeli aggressiveness and expansionism; and Israeli "hawkishness" and the determination to maintain military superiority. The inability to find a solution for the plight of the Palestinian refugees, because of intransigence on both sides, provided the *raison d'etre* and rallying point for the Arab crusade against Israel. The short-term and more proximate causes were the arms buildup on both sides in the previous decade; superpower interference and especially Soviet meddling; the volatile situation in Syria; Nasser's brinksmanship; the defense pacts that linked together Egypt, Syria, and Jordan; and the failure of the international community through diplomacy to prevent war. All sides thus must share the blame for the outbreak of hostilities and for the consequences that followed.

SUGGESTIONS FOR FURTHER READING

Abu-Lughod, Ibrahim, ed., *The Arab-Israeli Confrontation of 1967: An Arab Perspective*, Evanston, Ill., Northwestern University Press, 1970.

Confino, Michael, and Shamir, Shimon, eds., *The U.S.S.R. and the Middle East*, Jerusalem, Israel Universities Press, 1973.

Dupuy, T. N., *Elusive Victory, The Arab-Israeli Wars, 1947–74*, New York, Harper & Row, 1978.

O'BALLANCE, EDGAR, *The Third Arab-Israeli War*, London, Faber and Faber, 1972.

HEIKAL, MOHAMED, *The Sphinx and the Commissar: The Rise and Fall of Soviet Influence in the Middle East*, New York, Harper & Row, 1978.

KERR, MALCOLM, *The Arab Cold War: Gamal Abdul Nasser and His Rivals, 1958–1970* (3rd ed.), London, Oxford and New York, Oxford University Press, 1971.

LAQUEUR, WALTER, *The Road to Jerusalem: The Origins of the Arab-Israeli Conflict, 1967*, New York, Macmillan, 1968.

TILLMAN, SETH P., *The United States and the Middle East*, Bloomington, Indiana University Press, 1982.

QUANDT, WM. B., JABBER, F., AND LESCH, A. M., *The Politics of Palestinian Nationalism*, Berkeley, University of California Press, 1973.

SAFRAN, NADAV, *Israel: The Embattled Ally*, Cambridge, Harvard University Press, 1978.

SEALE, PATRICK, *The Struggle for Syria: A Study of Post-War Arab Politics, 1945–1958*, 2nd ed., New Haven, Conn., Yale University Press, 1987.

DOCUMENT 6–1

Nasser's Speech to Egyptian National Assembly Members, May 29, 1967

Israel used to boast a great deal, and the Western powers, headed by the United States and Britain, used to ignore and even despise us and consider us of no value. But now that the time has come—and I have already said in the past that we will decide the time and place and not allow them to decide—we must be ready for triumph and not for a recurrence of the 1948 comedies. We shall triumph, God willing.

Preparations have already been made. We are now ready to confront Israel. They have claimed many things about the 1956 Suez war, but no one believed them after the secrets of the 1956 collusion were uncovered—that mean collusion in which Israel took part. Now we are ready for the confrontation. We are now ready to deal with the entire Palestine question.

The issue now at hand is not the Gulf of Aqabah, the Straits of Tiran, or the withdrawal of the UNEF, but the rights of the Palestine people. It is the aggression which took place in Palestine in 1948 with the collaboration of Britain and the United States. It is the expulsion of the Arabs from Palestine, the usurpation of their rights, and the plunder of their property. It is the disavowal of all the UN resolutions in favour of the Palestinian people.

The issue today is far more serious than they say. They want to confine the issue to the Straits of Tiran, the UNEF and the right of passage. We demand the full rights of the Palestinian people. We say this out of our belief that Arab rights cannot be squandered because the Arabs throughout the Arab world are demanding these Arab rights.

We are not afraid of the United States and its threats, of Britain and her threats, or of the entire Western world and its partiality to Israel. The United States and Britain are partial to Israel and give no consideration to the Arabs, to the entire Arab nation. Why? Because we have made them believe that we cannot distinguish between friend and foe. We must make them know that we know who our foes are and who our friends are and treat them accordingly.

If the United States and Britain are partial to Israel, we must say that our enemy is not only Israel but also the United States and Britain and treat them as such. If the Western Powers disavow our rights and ridicule and despise us, we Arabs must teach them to respect us and take us seriously. Otherwise all our talk about Palestine, the Palestine people, and Palestinian rights will be null and void and of no consequence. We must treat enemies as enemies and friends as friends.

Source: Walter Laqueur and Barry Rubin, eds., *The Israel–Arab Reader: A Documentary History of The Middle East Conflict*, 4th ed. (New York Penguin Books, 1984), pp. 187–188.

**Speech by Abba Eban, Israeli Foreign Minister, to the Security Council on
Israel's reasons for going to war, 6 June 1967**

I thank you, Mr. President, for giving me this opportunity to address the Council. I have just come from Jerusalem to tell the Security Council that Israel, by its independent action and sacrifice, has passed from serious danger to successful resistance.

Two days ago, Israel's condition caused much concern across the humane and friendly world. Israel had reached a sombre hour. Let me try to evoke the point at which our fortunes stood.

An army, greater than any force ever assembled in history in Sinai, had massed against Israel's southern frontier. Egypt had dismissed the United Nations forces which symbolized the international interest in the maintenance of peace in our region. Nasser had provocatively brought five infantry divisions and two armoured divisions up to our very gates; 80,000 men and 900 tanks were poised to move.

A special striking force, comprising an armoured division with at least 200 tanks, was concentrated against Elath at the Negev's southern tip. Here was a clear design to cut the southern Negev off from the main body of our State. For Egypt had openly proclaimed that Elath did not form part of Israel and had predicted that Israel itself would soon expire. The proclamation was empty; the prediction now lies in ruins. While the main brunt of the hostile threat was focused on the southern front, an alarming plan of encirclement was under way. With Egypt's initiative and guidance, Israel was already being strangled in its maritime approaches to the whole eastern half of the world. For sixteen years, Israel had been illicitly denied passage in the Suez Canal, despite this Security Council's resolution of 1 September 1951. And now the creative enterprise of patient years which had opened an international route across the Strait of Tiran and the Gulf of Aqaba had been suddenly and arbitrarily choked. Israel was and is breathing with only a single lung.

Jordan had been intimidated, against its better interest, into joining a defence pact. It is not a defence pact at all: it is an aggressive pact, of which I saw the consequences with my own eyes yesterday in the shells falling upon institutions of health and culture in the City of Jerusalem. Every house and street in Jerusalem now came into the range of fire as a result of Jordan's adherence to this pact; so also did the crowded, and pathetically narrow coastal strip in which so much of Israel's life and population is concentrated.

Iraqi troops reinforced Jordanian units in areas immediately facing vital and vulnerable Israeli communication centres. Expeditionary forces from Algeria and Kuwait had reached Egyptian territory. Nearly all the Egyptian forces which had been attempting the conquest of the Yemen had been transferred to the coming assault upon Israel. Syrian units, including artillery, overlooked Israeli villages in the Jordan Valley. Terrorist groups came regularly into our territory to kill, plunder and set off explosives, the most recent occasion was five days ago.

In short, there was peril for Israel wherever it looked. Its manpower had been hastily mobilized. Its economy and commerce were beating with feeble pulses. Its streets were dark and empty. There was an apocalyptic air of approaching peril. And Israel faced this danger alone.

We were buoyed up by an unforgettable surge of public sympathy across the world. The friendly Governments expressed the rather ominous hope that Israel would manage to live, but the dominant theme of our condition was danger and solitude.

Now there could be doubt what was intended for us. I heard President Nasser's speech on 26 May. He said:

'We intend to open a general assault against Israel. This will be total war. Our basic aim is the destruction of Israel.'

On 2 June, the Egyptian Commander-in-Chief in Sinai, General Murtagi, published his order of the day, calling on his troops to wage a war of destruction against Israel. Here, then, was a systematic, overt, proclaimed design at politicide, the murder of a State.

The policy, the arms, the men had all been brought together, and the State thus threatened with collective assault was itself the last sanctuary of a people which had seen six million of its sons exterminated by a more powerful dictator two decades before.

UNO SCOR, S/PV, 1348

Source: T. G. Fraser, *The Middle East, 1914–1979* (New York: St. Martin's Press, 1980), pp. 107–109.

DOCUMENT 6–3

U.N. Security Council Resolution 242—Nov. 22, 1967

The Security Council
Expressing its continuing concern with the grave situation in the Middle East.

Emphasizing the inadmissibility of the acquisition of territory by war and the need to work for a just and lasting peace in which every State in the area can live in security,
Emphasizing further that all Member States in their acceptance of the Charter of the United Nations have undertaken a commitment to act in accordance with Article 2 of the Charter,

1. *Affirms* that the fulfillment of Charter principles requires the establishment of a just and lasting peace in the Middle East which should include the application of both the following principles:
    (i) Withdrawal of Israeli armed forces from territories occupied in the recent conflict;
    (ii) Termination of all claims or states of belligerency and respect for and acknowledge-ment of the sovereignty, territorial integrity and political independence of every State in the area and their right to live in peace within secure and recognized boundaries free from threats or acts of force;

2. *Affirms further the necessity*
    (a) For guaranteeing freedom of navigation through international waterways in the area;
    (b) For achieving a just settlement of the refugee problem;
    (c) For guaranteeing the territorial inviolability and political independence of every State in the area, through measures including the establishment of demilitarized zones;

3. *Requests* the Secretary-General to designate a Special Representative to proceed to the Middle East to establish and maintain contacts with the States concerned in order to promote agreement and assist efforts to achieve a peaceful and accepted settlement in accordance with the provisions and principles in this resolution;

4. *Requests* the Secretary-General to report to the Security Council on the progress of the efforts of the Special Representative as soon as possible.

Source: Congressional Quarterly, The Middle East, 7th ed., Washington, D.C., p. 301.

DOCUMENT 6–4

Principles Guiding Israel's Policy in the Aftermath of the
June 1967 War as Outlined by Prime Minister Eshkol.
Jerusalem, 9 August, 1967 [Excerpts]

(a)   The Government of Israel will endeavour to achieve peace with the neighbouring Arab countries. We shall never permit a return to a situation of constant threat to Israel's security, of blockade and of aggression.

(b)   The Government of Israel is prepared for direct negotiations with all the Arab States together, or with any Arab State separately.

(c)   The State of Israel strives for economic cooperation and regional planning with all States in the Middle East.

(d)   Israel will cooperate fully in the solution of the refugees problem . . . within the framework of an international and regional plan.

(e)   The Government endeavours to maintain fair and equitable relations with the population in the new areas, while maintaining order and security.

After our military victory, we confront a fateful dilemma; immigration or stagnation . . . By the end of the century, we must have five million Jews in Israel. We must work hard so that Israel may be able to maintain decent human, cultural, technical and economic standards. This is the test of Israel's existence as a Jewish State in the Middle East.

Source: Yehuda Lukacs, *Documents on the Israeli–Palestinian Conflict, 1967–1983* (Cambridge: Cambridge University Press, 1984), p. 79.

DOCUMENT 6–5

Resolutions of the Khartoum Conference, 1 September 1967

1   The conference has affirmed the unity of Arab ranks, the unity of joint action and the need for coordination and for the elimination of all differences. The Kings, Presidents and representatives of the other Arab Heads of State at the conference have affirmed their countries' stand by and implementation of the Arab Solidarity Charter which was signed at the third Arab summit conference at Casablanca.

2   The conference has agreed on the need to consolidate all efforts to eliminate the effects of the aggression on the basis that the occupied lands are Arab lands and that the burden of regaining these lands falls on the Arab States.

3   The Arab Heads of State have agreed to unite their political efforts at the international and diplomatic level to eliminate the effects of the aggression and to ensure the withdrawal of the aggressive Israeli forces from the Arab lands which have been occupied since the aggression of 5 June. This will be done within the framework of the main principles by which the Arab States abide, namely, no peace with Israel, no recognition of Israel, no negotiations with it, and insistence on the rights of the Palestinian people in their own country.

4   The conference of Arab Ministers of Finance, Economy and Oil recommended that suspension of oil pumping be used as a weapon in the battle. However, after thoroughly studying the matter, the summit conference has come to the conclusion that the pumping of oil can itself be used as a positive weapon, since oil is an Arab resource which can be used to strengthen the economy of the Arab States directly affected by the aggression, so that these States will be able to stand firm in the battle. The conference has, therefore, decided to resume the pumping of oil, since oil is a positive Arab resource that can be used in the service

of Arab goals. It can contribute to the efforts to enable those Arab States which were exposed to the aggression and thereby lost economic resources to stand firm and eliminate the effects of the aggression.

Source: Fraser, *The Middle East,* pp. 115–116.

HOLY DAYS AND HOLY WAR: OCTOBER 1973

CHAPTER 7

CHRONOLOGY

Dec. 1967 through 1968	First Jarring mission	**Early May 1971**	U.S. Secretary of State William Rogers visits Cairo
Dec. 24, 1967	Shukairi resigns as PLO chairman	**May 27, 1971**	Soviet–Egyptian Treaty of Friendship
March 21, 1968	Battle of Karameh	**Nov. 28, 1971**	Black September assassinates Jordanian Prime Minister Wasfi Tell
July 10– 17, 1968	Palestine National Council (PNC) meeting; PLO Covenant revised	**March 15, 1972**	King Hussein proposes federal-type solution for West Bank
July 23, 1968	First PLO airplane hijacking	**May 1972**	Nixon visits Moscow
Jan. 20, 1969	Nixon administration begins	**July 18, 1972**	Sadat expels Russian advisors
Feb. 1969	Yasser Arafat recognized as head of PLO at Fifth PNC meeting	**Sept. 5, 1972**	Israeli athletes murdered at Munich Olympics by Black September terrorists
March 1969	Nasser announces "liberation phase" of War of Attrition along Suez Canal	**June 1973**	U.S./Soviet summit meeting
March 15, 1969	Bar-Lev Line completed by Israel	**Oct. 6, 1973**	Egypt and Syria attack Israel, Yom Kippur, or Ramadan, War begins
June 25, 1970	Rogers Plan announced	**Oct. 17, 1973**	OAPEC imposes oil embargo
Aug. 7, 1970	Cease-fire along Suez Canal	**Oct. 22, 1973**	Cease-fire; UN Security Council Resolution 338 calls for direct negotiations based on Resolution 242
Sept. 16– 25, 1970	Showdown between King Hussein and Palestinians	**Dec. 21, 1973**	Geneva conference
Sept. 28, 1970	Nasser dies; Anwar al-Sadat becomes Egyptian president	**Oct. 28, 1974**	Arab summit at Rabat recognizes PLO as sole, legitimate representative of Palestinian people
Nov. 13, 1970	Hafez al-Assad assumes power in Syria; becomes president March 13, 1971		

PRELUDE

The military defeat of 1967 was a terrible blow for Egypt and for Egyptian President Gamal Abdul Nasser. Although Nasser attempted to resign from office, popular opinion forced his reconsideration. Still a charismatic figure and the leading spokesman in the Arab world, he never again exercised the actual power that he had exhibited before the debacle of the Six-Day War of 1967. Moreover, his health, already bad, steadily deteriorated, and in September 1970, after trying to mediate a civil war in Jordan between King Hussein and the Palestinian resistance movements, Nasser died of a heart attack. He was succeeded by Anwar al-Sadat.

On the positive side, the events of 1967 enabled Egypt to extricate itself from Yemen and to settle differences with the Saudis. The Arab oil-producing nations gave both Egypt and Jordan a yearly subsidy to help compensate for the loss of revenue caused by the closing of the Suez Canal and a decline in tourism because of Israel's capture of the Sinai Peninsula, East Jerusalem, and other important sites. Moreover, the Soviets were quick to resupply the Egyptians, although the marriage between the two countries was always one of convenience. Russian advisors arrived, along with Russian equipment, and many areas of Egypt were declared off-limits to the Egyptians themselves. The Soviet Union began to establish an impressive navy and naval support facilities in the eastern Mediterranean.

The absence of a negotiated settlement, however, made another round in the Arab–Israeli conflict almost a certainty, especially when the damage done to Arab honor, pride, and self-respect is added. The Arab summit meeting in Khartoum in late August–early September 1967 had declared that with regard to Israel there would be no peace, no recognition, and no negotiations, and that action should be taken to safeguard the right of the Palestinian people to their homeland. Some historians explain away these statements as necessary to appease the Arab masses. They point to Egypt's and Jordan's acceptance of UN Security Council Resolution 242 as proof of the willingness of Nasser and King Hussein to work for a political and diplomatic solution. Nevertheless, Nasser's public resolve was that what had been taken by force would be recovered by force.

Indeed, as early as 1968, once the new Russian military equipment was in place, the Egyptians began to harass the Israelis dug in on the other side of the Suez Canal, and these operations soon developed into what would come to be known as the War of Attrition between 1969 and 1970. The War of Attrition certainly had the object, if possible, not only of forcing a political solution but of recovering territory by force if necessary. Both Israel and the Arab states continued to be on a war footing, military expenditures increased, and the inventory of weapons became ever more destructive. The Arab–Israeli conflict remained as a powderkeg of superpower rivalry, both diplomatically and militarily, although a certain thaw between the United States and the Soviet Union and a period of détente did have some important implications for the actors in the Middle East. Nevertheless, it has been said with some truth that the superpowers supplied their various clients in order to test new weapons under battlefield conditions, and détente or not, arms shipments to both Israel and the Arabs continued unabated.

Nevertheless, as we shall see, Nasser on occasion exhibited flexibility as did Israeli leaders. Moshe Dayan had declared that he was simply waiting for a telephone call from King Hussein, and the Israelis indicated that everything was negotiable in return for peace. Israel considered the occupied territories its trump card for peace, especially with Jordan, but the telephone call never came. Hussein and the Israelis, in fact, had many secret meetings, but the king evidently feared the kind of public dealings that had resulted in the assassination of his grandfather, King Abdullah, before his very eyes. Hussein was also constrained by the Arab interpretation of UN Resolution 242 and consensus against direct and separate negotiations, and by the Palestinian dimension of the situation as it developed. As time passed, the fluid situation immediately after the 1967 war hardened into a new reality, as did the official positions of all the governments concerned.

As we saw in the previous chapter, the Israelis were jubilant after their astonishing victory. In less than a week, they had increased their territory by 28,000 square miles, and had achieved, they believed, strategic depth and defensible borders. The Western (or Wailing) Wall of the Second Temple was again under Jewish control, and the barriers separating the two halves of Jerusalem were torn down. Israel annexed the Old City and East Jerusalem at the end of June 1967, and declared that the city would never again be divided. Developed and undeveloped oil fields in the Sinai Peninsula came into Israeli hands, and Israelis could now visit Mount Sinai where Moses had received the Ten Commandments. There was a sense of having "arrived" as a truly independent member of the family of nations. Most Israelis believed that their incredible victory could lead to a negotiated settlement with the Arabs.

However, while waiting for the telephone to ring, they missed opportunities to deal with a situation in the occupied territories whose evolution was foreseen by very few in the heady weeks and months after June 1967. Unable to recognize the sense of Palestinian separateness and emancipation from the Arab governments that was encouraged by Israel's continued occupation of the West Bank and the Gaza Strip, the Israelis failed to foster an indigenous leadership that would be acceptable to the Palestinians. By working through traditional elites and leaders and expelling nationalist leaders, they were partially responsible for the growing influence and success of the PLO not only in the occupied territories but on the world stage.

THE PALESTINIANS AND THE PLO AFTER 1967

Among the most notable features of the Arab–Israeli conflict after 1967 was a growing sense of Palestinian identity and nationalism. With it came increased activity on the part of the Palestinian guerrilla organizations. The approximately 500,000 Palestinians in Sinai and the Gaza Strip, as well as the approximately 800,000 Palestinians on the West Bank under Israeli occupation, could now envisage an alternate future that they might be able to help shape themselves should there be a settlement and Israeli withdrawal from the conquered territories. Prior to the 1967 war, the prospects of the Palestinians had not been bright. The Egyptians had severely restricted the movement of Palestinians in Gaza, and King Hussein had done his best to efface the separate identity of those Palestinians in the West Bank. Most Palestinians could look forward only to the possibility of remaining under Egyptian, Jordanian, or Syrian control. Continued Israeli occupation, however, simply encouraged the development of Palestinian nationalism and the emergence of new leaders not associated with the Arab governments and Arab armies that had so dismally failed the Palestinians in 1967.

For a decade after 1949, primarily because Arab Palestine as envisaged by the partition resolution did not come into being, the plight of the displaced Palestinian Arabs was considered by all parties concerned as a humanitarian issue to be considered within the context of the relationship between Israel and the existing Arab states. Arab leaders certainly did not see the Palestinians as a separate political/national group, nor did most of the refugees define themselves in such terms. Egypt kept a tight rein on the Gaza Strip, and Jordan annexed the Old City of Jerusalem and the West Bank of the Jordan River. No manifestations of Palestinian nationalism were allowed. The Jordanian king was the only ruler in the Arab world to extend citizenship to Palestinians who desired to become Jordanian citizens, but this was less out of altruism than a desire to legitimize the annexation of Arab Palestine and to utilize the talents of many of the Palestinian Arabs in a kingdom that had consisted until then largely of bedouin and peasant farmers.

The Palestinians themselves, up to June 1967, for the most part tended to rely on the Arab governments, and to believe that Arab unity was the key to the liberation of Palestine from the Jews. There were, as we have seen, fedayeen attacks against Israel from across the various borders and, indeed, unorganized guerrilla groups undertook raids in order to encourage a renewal of the conflict between the Arab states and Israel. It was precisely to avoid being drawn into hostilities at a time and place not of their own choosing that the Arab governments had attempted to control the guerrillas through the formation of the Palestine Liberation Organization (PLO) and the Palestine Liberation Army (PLA) in 1964. Popular armed struggle was not part of their plan, and the PLA had been the instrument of the sponsoring Arab governments, to be used only as a conventional army. Moreover, Ahmad Shukairi's chief activity had been to pontificate about how the Arabs were going to push the Jews into the sea. Needless to say, among the Palestinians, the old PLO under Shukairi was entirely discredited in 1967, along with the Arab governments that had sponsored it—and a new type of guerrilla organization appeared, one not tied to any Arab government but committed to the tactic of armed struggle.

The PLO Covenant and Armed Struggle

Israel's control of the Gaza Strip and the West Bank, its destruction of commando bases and houses of those suspected of harboring or aiding fedayeen, and its expulsion of suspected troublemakers presented problems for the Palestinian movements, of course. Nevertheless, because of highly publicized attacks from across the borders, and particularly because of their success in March 1968, at Karameh, Palestinian resistance achieved enormous popularity among the masses and became an important factor in the Arab–Israeli equation. Karameh was a Palestinian camp and guerrilla base in Jordan where Palestinian fighters aided by elements of the Jordanian army fiercely resisted an Israeli assault and inflicted heavy casualties (twenty-six killed and seventy wounded) on the enemy.

In July 1968, at a meeting of the Palestine National Council (PNC) in Cairo, the original PLO covenant drafted when the PLO was formed in 1964 was amended. Both old and new articles negated Israel's right to exist and included the principle of armed struggle in the liberation of Palestine (see Document 7–1). In Article 10 of the new document, the fedayeen were named as the nucleus of the armed struggle. As we shall see, this statement had implications for Jordan as well as Israel. In resolutions adopted in the same period, the PNC suggested that Israel be replaced by a "democratic, secular" state. As Palestinians themselves admitted, this was a euphemism for propaganda purposes to dismantle Israel and was intended to replace the admittedly ineffective slogan of "driving the Jews into the sea." Israel insisted that the covenant be disavowed or changed before it would even consider dealing with the PLO, a proposition the PLO has to date rejected. Ahmad Shukairi had resigned as chairman of the old PLO in December 1967, but the PLO continued to serve as an umbrella organization

CHART 7-1
STRUCTURE OF THE PLO

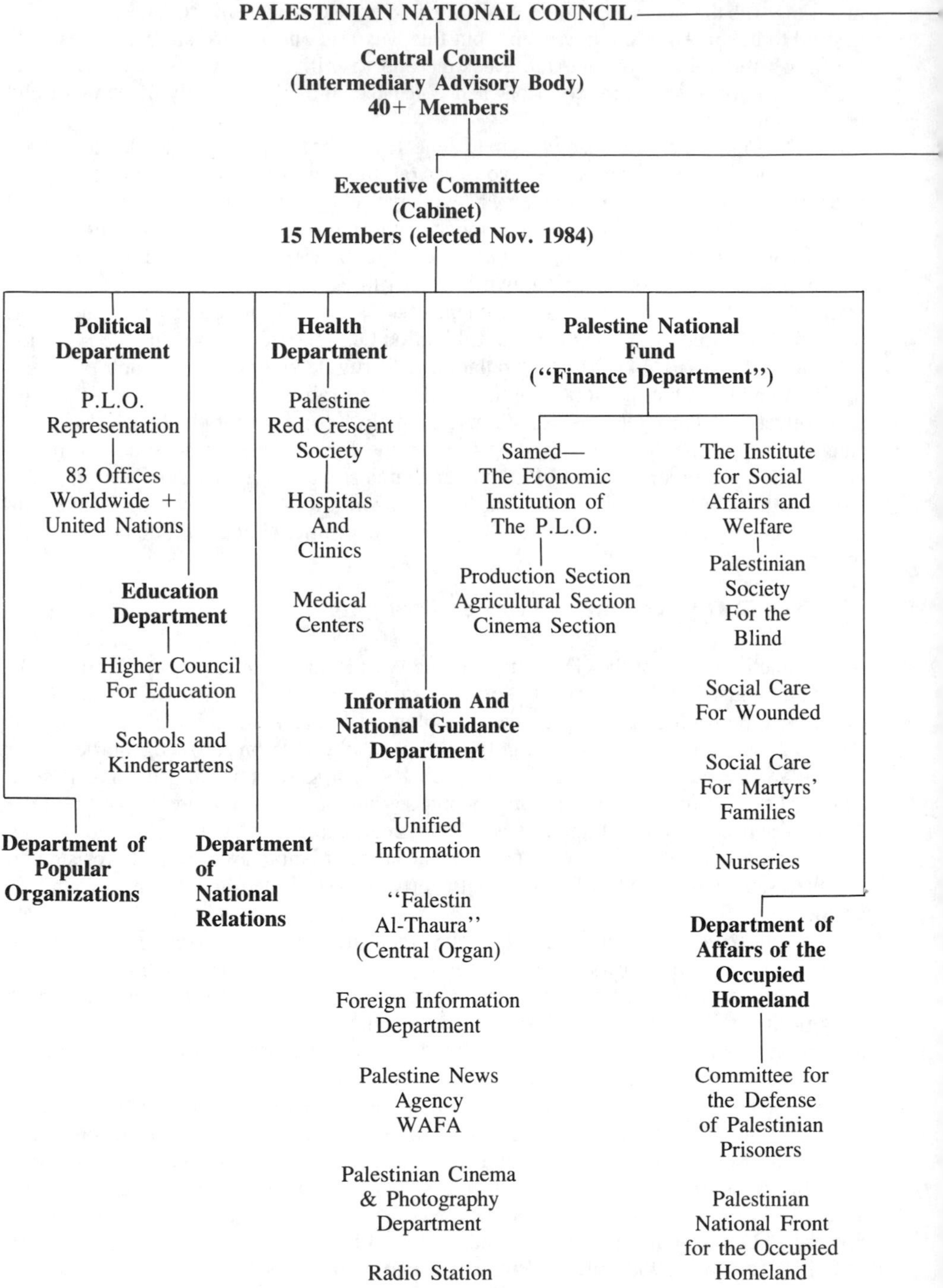

PALESTINIAN NATIONAL COUNCIL

Central Council
(Intermediary Advisory Body)
40+ Members

Executive Committee
(Cabinet)
15 Members (elected Nov. 1984)

Political Department

P.L.O. Representation

83 Offices Worldwide + United Nations

Education Department

Higher Council For Education

Schools and Kindergartens

Department of Popular Organizations

Department of National Relations

Health Department

Palestine Red Crescent Society

Hospitals And Clinics

Medical Centers

Information And National Guidance Department

Unified Information

"Falestin Al-Thaura" (Central Organ)

Foreign Information Department

Palestine News Agency WAFA

Palestinian Cinema & Photography Department

Radio Station

Palestine National Fund ("Finance Department")

Samed— The Economic Institution of The P.L.O.

Production Section
Agricultural Section
Cinema Section

The Institute for Social Affairs and Welfare

Palestinian Society For the Blind

Social Care For Wounded

Social Care For Martyrs' Families

Nurseries

Department of Affairs of the Occupied Homeland

Committee for the Defense of Palestinian Prisoners

Palestinian National Front for the Occupied Homeland

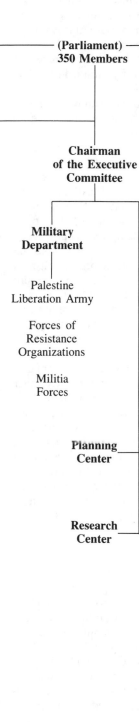

(Parliament)
350 Members

| | **Palestinian Communities Outside Palestine** | **Independent Organizations** |

| **Chairman of the Executive Committee** | **Palestinian Mass Unions + Syndicates** | **Palestinian Resistance Organizations** |

Military Department

Palestine Liberation Army

Forces of Resistance Organizations

Militia Forces

Planning Center

Research Center

The General Union of Palestinian Writers and Journalists

The General Union of Palestinian Workers G.U.P.W.

The General Union of Palestinian Women G.U.P.W.

The General Union of Palestinian Students G.U.P.S.

The General Union of Palestinian Teachers

The General Union of Palestinian Engineers

The General Union of Palestinian Lawyers

The General Union of Palestinian Doctors

The General Union of Palestinian Painters and Artists

The General Union of Palestinian Peasants

Palestine National Liberation Movement "Fatah"

Popular Front for The Liberation of Palestine—P.F.L.P.

Democratic Front for the Liberation of Palestine—D.F.L.P.

Saiqa

Arab Liberation Front—A.L.F.

Popular Front—General Command

Palestine Liberation Front—P.L.F.

Palestine Popular Struggle Front

Palestine Communist Party

for the various guerrilla groups. (See Description of PLO Groups—Document 7–2.) Within two years after the war, al-Fatah had emerged as the most important group within the PLO, and in 1969 the PNC elected its leader, Yasser Arafat (Abu Ammar), chairman of the executive committee, a position he has retained ever since. Although the PLO has a centralized structure on paper (see Chart 7–1) and the PNC meets at regular intervals, all important decisions continue to be made by Arafat himself in consultation with his closest associates in al-Fatah.

Fatah became the largest and most popular Palestinian organization for several reasons. One was its desire and ability, for the most part, to avoid too close an identification with any one Arab country, thus enabling it to stay clear of inter-Arab quarrels. With diverse sources of support, it was not required to follow a particular political line. Indeed, Fatah's very lack of a specific ideology and doctrinal vagueness also enabled it to attract followers, unlike some of the smaller groups that often put ideology ahead of the national struggle. Fatah also had an appeal to Muslim activists, who equated the religious cause with the national cause, and who desired in the name of Islam to liberate Palestine from the Jews. Not surprisingly, all the PLO factions reject the West, which they equate with Zionism and imperialism, and all have been willing to accept aid and support from the Soviet Union. Some, however, like the Popular Front for the Liberation of Palestine (PFLP), led by Dr. George Habash, a Greek Orthodox Christian born in Lydda (now Lod Israel), and the Democratic Front for the Liberation of Palestine (DFLP) led by Nayef Hawatmeh, a Jordanian Christian, became overtly Marxist-Leninist in ideology. These groups believed that there must be fundamental social and economic changes in the Arab world itself, and especially that there must be revolutionary change in the conservative Arab states like Jordan and Saudi Arabia even before the liberation of Palestine.

The PFLP, DFLP, and other splinter groups like the PFLP-General Command, led by Ahmed Jebril, began the tactic of hijacking airplanes in 1968 and initiated other terrorist attacks against civilians outside the Middle East in order to draw attention to the Palestinian cause. Terrorism was condemned by the world community, which seemed powerless or unwilling to do much about it, but it served the Palestinian cause by encouraging the passage of resolutions in the UN General Assembly and other forums that recognize as legitimate the aspirations of the Palestinian people and their right to self-determination. Although there was always diversity and fragmentation over questions of ideology and tactics within the PLO, Yasser Arafat was unable, and perhaps unwilling, to eliminate his more extreme rivals. While using the extremists as a convenient excuse to retain freedom of action, Arafat became their hostage as well, at least until recent years.

The PLO and the Arab States

As for the Arab states, Egypt prevented the Palestinians from operating within or from its territory. Syria and Iraq, however, sponsored their own commando units. These had to follow the political ideology and goals of the host government and were kept on a short leash. The fragmented government of Lebanon was much more vulnerable both to PLO activities within its borders and to punitive reprisals by Israel for terrorist actions against Israel that emanated from Lebanon. In Jordan, the PLO became a serious threat to political stability. It prevented King Hussein from considering any negotiated settlement with Israel that did not include the PLO, it invited Israeli retaliation for its activities, and both indirectly and directly it undermined the monarchy

Gamal Abdul Nasser in his last official act on September 27, 1970, mediating between PLO chief Yasser Arafat and King Hussein of Jordan (*Photo courtesy of United Press International*).

through the PLO Covenant's avowed intention to liberate all of mandatory Palestine and the leftists' death threats against the U.S.-supported king.

The PLO became so much like a state within a state in Jordan that eventually there was a showdown with Hussein. This occurred after Palestinians hijacked three airplanes to Amman (Jordan's capital) in September 1970, and subsequently blew them up on the ground, making the king appear impotent. After bloody confrontations between the Jordanian army and Palestinian commandos in September 1970, and again in July 1971, Hussein reasserted his control, expelling the PLO leadership and fighters from Jordanian territory. One consequence of this action was the spawning of another terrorist group, called Black September, an arm of al-Fatah. Its first act was the murder of the Jordanian Prime Minister, Wasfi Tell, in Cairo on November 28, 1971. The next year, at the 1972 Olympic Games in Munich, Black September was responsible for the deaths of eleven Israeli athletes. Another result of the showdown in Jordan was the removal of the PLO to Lebanon, where their military and political activities were a significant factor in the Lebanese civil war that began in 1975 and in the unravelling of that fractured country.

For many reasons—some of which were adroit public relations efforts, terrorist exploits, sympathy for and popularity of "liberation movements" all over the world, and perceived Israeli intransigence—the Palestinian cause was soon being described as the "crux" of the issue in the Arab–Israeli dispute. Not only in the United Nations but in the capitals of the world, as well as in the deliberations of regional and international conferences, the right of the Palestinian people to self-determination was recognized. Israeli Prime Minister Golda Meir in the late 1960's remarked that there was no such thing as a Palestinian people as a distinct national group within the Arab nation. This statement may have been technically correct when it was uttered, but Palestinian nationalism certainly became a reality. This was especially true after 1967 for several reasons: the absence of a negotiated settlement between the Arab states and Israel; the failure of the Palestinians to achieve repatriation or resettlement (except in Jordan) within the Arab world; the circumstances of continued occupation, first by the Arabs, and then by Israel; and finally the success of their self-generated resistance, given the opportunity to seize the initiative after 1967. This situation fostered and nurtured the feeling of a separate identity among the Palestinian people, and what was originally a refugee problem has indeed become the problem of Palestinian nationalism.

Whether Palestinian nationalism or the inability of the Arabs to accept the reality and legitimacy of Israel's existence is the "crux" of the conflict is a moot question. In any event, the Palestinian question added urgency to the Arab–Israeli dispute after 1967 and made the search for a settlement even more complicated than it already was. Supporters of Israel insist that the fundamental problem in the Arab–Israeli conflict has always been and will continue to be the inability of the Arabs to accept the sovereignty of the Jewish state. All Arabs, whether sympathetic or not to the plight of their Palestinian brothers, can unite behind the Palestinian cause so as to force concessions from Israel to relinquish territory in what Israelis see as the first step toward the eventual dismantling of the Jewish nation. Nevertheless, the Palestinian issue has taken on a life of its own. Palestinians in Gaza and the West Bank have lived under Israeli occupation longer than they had been under Arab control; their destiny has diverged from that of their Arab brothers; and the Arab world has acquiesced in the designation of the PLO, rather than any Arab government, as the sole, legitimate representative of the Palestinian people.

DIPLOMACY, THE WAR OF ATTRITION, AND THE ROGERS PLAN

Resolution 242 of 1967 had provided for a United Nations special mediator to help achieve a settlement. Gunnar Jarring of Sweden was appointed and he began his mission in late December 1967. He made little headway in his meetings with the various governments, meetings that lasted throughout 1968; the Israelis wanted direct negotiations with the Arabs, and the Arabs insisted on indirect negotiations and the withdrawal of Israel from all the occupied territories. The diplomatic effort stalled, although bilateral talks between Egypt and the United States took place in the last few months of the Johnson presidency in an attempt to keep the Jarring mission alive. After the Nixon administration took over in January 1969, the United States sought ways both to improve relations with the Arab world (Egypt and Syria had broken off diplomatic relations with the United States after 1967) and to keep Israel militarily at an advantage. Richard Nixon believed these policies would offset Russian influence and prevent another conflict. The United States also opted initially to work through the United Nations and in concert with the Big Four powers—the United States, Britain, France, and the Soviet Union—to try to find ways out of the diplomatic impasse, but with no immediate result.

Meanwhile, the Soviets had resupplied the Egyptians and Syrians with ammunition, tanks, and planes. Egypt launched commando attacks and shelled Israeli positions across the Suez Canal, and in October 1968 an Egyptian missile boat sank an Israeli destroyer off the coast of Sinai. The Israelis responded with retaliatory raids, sometimes penetrating deep into Egyptian territory. As Egyptian artillery barrages increased, however, the Israelis began construction of the Bar-Lev line of fortifications (named for the then Israeli chief-of-staff) along the length of the Suez Canal. The Egyptians bombarded the fortifications repeatedly in an effort to destroy them, and Egyptian commando units continued to cross the Suez Canal to sabotage and harass. In the spring of 1969, Nasser announced that the cease-fire of June 1967 was null and void, and the "War of Attrition" was officially launched. This war was costly to both sides. (Although the Egyptians did not release casualty figures, they lost many men, and the economy was again sacrificed to the exigencies of combat. Israel, with over 200 dead, suffered more casualties than in the Six-Day War). Evidently, Nasser believed that he could inflict such a heavy toll that the Israelis would retreat back into the Sinai, and/or that they would become more amenable to a political solution on Egypt's terms.

Egyptian success, however, led Israel to commit its air power, and in mid-1969, Israel began to bomb Egyptian gun emplacements on the west bank of the Suez Canal and to undertake deep-penetration raids into Egyptian territory. The situation began to escalate, and another full-scale war became more likely. In January 1970, Nasser made a secret trip to Moscow to request more sophisticated weapons, including planes capable of offensive strikes against Israel. The Russians believed advanced aircraft would increase the likelihood of war and would encourage the United States to step up arms deliveries to Israel. Although the Soviets would not supply the planes, it did agree to participate more actively in the air defense of Egypt and to send Egypt surface-to-air missiles (SAMs) along with Russian crews to man them. By the end of June 1970, Soviet pilots were flying patrols all along the Canal Zone, Soviet military advisors and technicians were supervising Egypt's armed forces, and the Soviets were dramatically increasing their presence in the eastern Mediterranean, building up a naval fleet and an infrastructure to handle and repair Soviet ships. To America, the eastern Mediterranean began to look more and more like a Soviet lake.

The United States, watching these developments and concerned about Britain's intention to pull out of bases and installations east of Suez by 1971, attempted to improve relations with the Arab world and thereby prevent further Soviet encroachment. The United States continued to support Israel militarily and diplomatically (casting its veto in the Security Council when there were anti-Israel resolutions, for example). However, Secretary of State William Rogers, in a December 1969 statement, proclaimed that U.S. policy henceforth would be more "evenhanded." In June 1970, the Rogers Plan was announced. It enunciated the principle of Israeli withdrawal from the occupied territories in return for recognition, provided for a ninety-day cease-fire at the Suez Canal, and called for a renewal of the Jarring mission. Nasser announced Egypt's intention to accept the proposal after a frustrating and prolonged visit (for medical treatment) to Moscow in late June and July. Israel also accepted, albeit with misgivings about Nasser's intentions.

The cease-fire along the canal came into effect in August 1970. Unfortunately for the negotiating process, however, its provisions were violated almost immediately by Egypt, which used the occasion of the military standstill to move the Soviet SAM missiles into the Canal Zone. With the missiles in forward positions, Egypt increased its ability to cross the canal, since the missiles would cover the Israel side on the east bank and neutralize the Israeli air force. Egypt and Jordan accepted the renewed Jarring mission, but Israel refused until Egypt stopped the movement of the missiles. The talks resumed in December, after the United States promised to give Israel increased economic and military aid. Gunnar Jarring made an attempt in the next few months to bring the two sides together, but nothing came of his efforts.

Some observers draw attention to missed opportunities in the months that followed and lay the blame on Israel, insisting that the Arab states had modified their position by 1970. Anwar Sadat, who had succeeded Nasser as Egyptian president in September 1970, and Hafez al-Assad, the Syrian leader, were much more pragmatic men than their predecessors, these critics argue, and Sadat was much more concerned with Egypt than with pan-Arab interests. Even King Hussein, they note, was inclined to be more flexible after his successful showdown with the Palestinians.

Critics further point out that Israel, under the leadership of Golda Meir, who had become prime minister in March 1969, distrusted the Arabs, felt secure in its military superiority, and preferred the status quo unless or until it could secure a peace on its own terms, namely: prior recognition by the Arabs of Israel's right to exist, direct peace negotiations, and the retention of territory deemed necessary to its security and survival. With Meir's tacit encouragement, and the more vocal assertiveness of Defense Minister Moshe Dayan, who was responsible for the administration of the conquered territories, Israel had begun a policy of "creeping annexation" (or "creating facts," in Dayan's terms). Jewish settlements began to appear in militarily strategic places in the Jordan Valley, the Golan Heights, the Gaza Strip, and in the Sinai Peninsula.

This picture of Israeli intransigence is countered by other observers who point to public statements by Israeli leaders indicating flexibility and a desire to compromise, and they emphasize Israel's stated position that, in the context of face-to-face peace talks, every issue would be open to negotiation. They cite the fact that within Israel itself, debate existed from the very beginning on the question of the territories. At one extreme were supporters of the Land of Israel movement, who believed in the retention of the West Bank of the Jordan River on religious-historical grounds. Judea and Samaria, as they called the area, had been part of biblical and historical Israel. Dayan and others wanted to integrate the conquered territories on pragmatic grounds of security. Plans were proposed for the partial retention of territory, the most well-known being that proposed by Yigal Allon, the deputy prime minister, who wanted to retain a string of security outposts along the Jordan River and relinquish the rest. Other Israelis were vehement about the need to return the territories; they envisioned many of the practical and moral problems that confronted Israel as an occupier over the ensuing years. With so much difference of opinion internally, Meir's inclination in terms of any policy decision was to procrastinate. Therefore, in the absence of peace negotiations, the Israeli occupation continued as new realities in the territories emerged.

DÉTENTE AND THE ROLE OF THE SUPERPOWERS

Diplomatic efforts always have to be seen in context, of course, and between 1968 and 1973 not only was an actual, if unofficial, war going on between Egypt and Israel, but the Palestinians were also creating their own "facts" through guerrilla warfare, airplane hijackings, and other terrorist acts (the massacre of tourists at Israel's Lod airport, the murder of Israeli athletes at Munich, etc.). Another factor in this period was the new era of détente between the United States and the Soviet Union, which brings us again to the role of the superpowers in the Middle East.

Détente, or the relaxation of tensions between the United States and the U.S.S.R., had the effect, with regard to superpower involvement in the Middle East, of putting the Arab–Israeli conflict on the back burner. When President Richard Nixon first visited Moscow in May 1972, he and Soviet Premier Leonid Brezhnev agreed to

Notorious Palestinian terrorist and airplane hijacker Leila Khaled (*Photo courtesy of United Press International*).

try to achieve a "military relaxation" in the Middle East, to be followed by a freezing of the situation. Neither superpower wanted to be dragged into a war in behalf of one of its clients, and there was a certain degree of cooperation in attempting to dampen the fires in the Middle East. This had the temporary effect, in terms of Soviet military aid to Egypt, of the Russians holding up or refusing advanced offensive weapons requested by the Egyptians, as we have seen. Such weapons would have enabled the Egyptians to continue the War of Attrition and perhaps even to launch a military offensive to recover lost territory.

To the Israelis, the situation the way it stood was quite satisfactory. They believed that they had secure and defensible borders, and that they were in a strong enough position to be able to force the Arabs eventually to make peace on their terms. They also felt confident in American support for their military requirements. No war was a plus, and no peace could be lived with. For the Arabs, and especially for the Palestinians, no war and no peace was intolerable. This was especially true of the Palestinians. Ignored as they were by Resolution 242, the lack of any movement, either diplomatic or military, diminished any prospects the Palestinians entertained of achieving self-determination. PLO groups did everything possible to hold the attention of the world, including the continuation of spectacular airline hijackings and terrorist activities.

EGYPT PREPARES FOR WAR

The existing situation was particularly problematic for Egypt, however. The war in Yemen had been exceedingly costly, as had the price of Egypt's defeat in 1967. The Egyptian economy was suffering greatly because of the loss of tourism and Suez Canal revenues, and because offshore and Sinai oil fields were in the hands of the Israelis. Egyptian socialism had taken on a Marxist tinge, with individual initiative stifled and the populace increasingly dependent on the state to satisfy all economic needs. No substantial outside economic aid alleviated the burden, and by the early 1970s, the Egyptian treasury was empty and the country almost bankrupt. Anwar Sadat was not able to get the arms he wanted from the Soviet Union, and the Egyptian army was restive. The Egyptian people had followed the charismatic Nasser almost sheepishly, but they were becoming more painfully aware after his death how he had mortgaged the social and economic development of Egypt to his political and military objectives. Sadat, lacking Nasser's charisma, faced mounting internal unrest and unease.

Sadat wrote in his autobiography that he believed that the key to Egypt's political, military, and economic wellbeing was to redress the situation ensuing from the 1967 debacle—that the basic task was to wipe out the disgrace and humiliation of 1967 in order to regain self-confidence at home and the respect of the world community. If diplomacy failed, then Egypt should resort to war. Indeed, he embarked on a two-pronged approach, declaring 1971 to be the "year of decision" and also sending out diplomatic feelers. Sadat had extended the Rogers Plan in November, but in February 1971, after the second ninety-day cease-fire had expired, he said he would extend it again for one month only while Israel and the world had the chance to consider a new "initiative" that he proposed. If Israel were to withdraw to the Mitla and Gidi passes in the Sinai Peninsula, Sadat offered to reopen the Suez Canal, extend the Rogers Plan six months, officially declare a cease-fire, restore diplomatic relations with the United States, and sign a peace agreement with Israel contingent upon the fulfillment of the provisions of Resolution 242.

The political leadership of Egypt, which Sadat had inherited from Nasser, and which included several pro-Soviet ministers, was totally against this proposal. Since Egypt continued to insist that Resolution 242 committed Israel to withdraw completely from all occupied territory, Israel was loathe to accept a proposal such as Sadat's in advance of direct peace negotiations. Moshe Dayan had floated his own proposal for a mutual interim withdrawal, but the basic positions of Israel and Egypt were incompatible in the long run, and nothing came of his idea either. Gunnar Jarring was a persistent but not forceful mediator, and one wonders what would have happened had he been prepared to exert some pressure when opportunities such as those described here arose.

Meanwhile, in early March 1971, Sadat made the first of what would be four trips to Moscow. He wanted to secure replacement ammunition for the vast quantities lost in the War of Attrition. He also wanted to acquire deterrent weapons. The Soviets agreed to send missile-equipped aircraft and to train Egyptian crews but only on the condition that the planes be used with prior Soviet permission, a condition Sadat angrily rejected. Shortly after his return to Cairo, having received no response to his "initiative," Sadat allowed the cease-fire to expire. The Soviets did send Egypt SAM missile batteries in April 1971, but they did not send any aircraft and they replaced only part of the ammunition Sadat requested. Therefore, Sadat was not able to resume the War of Attrition, let alone embark on any decisive offensive. When the "year of decision" came and went without any military action, most observers decided that Arab rhetoric was at work again, and that Egyptian threats were hollow.

The United States had taken the opportunity of Nasser's death to initiate contacts with Egypt and had noted Sadat's relative diplomatic flexibility compared with Nasser's. William Rogers visited Egypt in early May 1971, the first visit by an American Secretary of State in many years. Rogers tried unsuccessfully to get Egypt and Israel to work for an interim agreement. Sadat's "initiative," and flirtation with the United States, spurred the pro-Soviet cabal in Egypt to step up its activity against him. Sadat acted first, however, dismissing several key figures in the government in mid-May 1971. This action was followed shortly by a visit to Egypt by Soviet President Nikolai Podgorny, who pressed Egypt to sign a Treaty of Friendship and Cooperation. Previously, Nasser had wanted a more formal alliance, which the Soviets had rejected; now the Soviets were eager to keep Egypt more firmly tethered through such a treaty. Sadat signed the agreement in late May 1971. Although the United States was deeply suspicious of this move, and indeed tended to view it as a confirmation of the worst fears about Sadat's intentions, the Egyptian president saw the treaty as the only way to allay Soviet fears and to get the arms he wanted.

The Soviets subsequently sent Egypt arms, but not the ones the Egyptians had requested. Sadat made three more trips to Moscow, in October 1971, and in February and April of 1972. Convinced that the Russians would always constrain him, he became angry and disillusioned. Moreover, in July 1972, after Richard Nixon's visit to Moscow, and in the spirit of détente, the United States and the Soviet Union issued a joint communique that hardly mentioned the Middle East and did not refer at all to Resolution 242. Sadat determined that the superpowers had agreed to freeze the situation, which would perpetuate Egypt's military disadvantage.

Yet Sadat had always meant what he said about retaining a military option. He was determined to recover the lost territory either by diplomacy or by force. He reasoned that even a limited war would help him achieve his aims by at least forcing the international community to turn its attention once again to the Middle East. Clearly, his first priority was Egypt; Palestinian goals had little to do with Egyptian military planning. Sadat first removed the 15,000 or so Soviet military technicians and military personnel in Egypt in order to have the freedom of action to go to war. Accordingly, he dismissed the Russian advisors in July 1972. This move was completely misinterpreted in the West and in Israel. In the United States and in Israel, it was widely assumed that Sadat was making some gesture of conciliation toward the West, and that he could not go to war without active Soviet involvement. Yet that is precisely what he intended to do.

Sadat and the Egyptians were disenchanted with the Russians. The Soviet advisors had been resented for their high-handedness, patronizing attitude, and tendency to look down upon the Egyptians. Sadat also saw the United States as the only power capable of bringing about a solution, because only the United States could exert pressure on the Israelis. He wanted and needed direct U.S. involvement for political and diplomatic reasons at the same time that he needed the Soviet Union for arms and military supplies. There was little interaction with the United States after the Rogers visit in May 1971, largely because of Sadat's treaty with the Russians. Rogers had left office in 1972 and was replaced as Secretary of State by Henry Kissinger, who had previously been Nixon's national security advisor. Kissinger would eventually be a key player, but 1972 was not only a year of détente but also an American presidential election year, when U.S. foreign policy initiatives are usually on hold. In early February of 1973, following Nixon's reelection victory, Hafez Ismail, Sadat's representative, met in Washington with Kissinger who, in effect, told him that, although the United States could exert pressure on Israel, it could not impose its will, and that the Egyptians would have to offer something in exchange for Israeli withdrawal from the occupied territories.

Despite the strained relationship between Egypt and the Soviet Union, therefore, the official ties remained. The Soviets were also more amenable to Egyptian arms requirements by the spring of 1973. Earlier, in January, the United States had decided to ship arms to Saudi Arabia and Kuwait, and after Golda Meir's visit to Washington in March, had agreed to sell Israel Phantom F-4E fighter-bombers and other military hardware. The Soviets responded by shipping Egypt SCUD surface-to-surface missiles as a deterrent. The shipment of the SCUDs seems to have been a turning point in Sadat's decision to go to war. Moreover, by 1973 the Egyptian military and intelligence services had been completely overhauled and a sophisticated battle plan had been conceived.

Part of the Egyptian plan was for a two-front attack against Israel, which meant that the Syrians would have to play a role. President Assad, who had assumed power in Syria in 1970–1971, was more than amenable. He believed not only in the cause but also in the use of conventional force to achieve it, unlike his mercurial predecessor, Salah Jadid, who had relied so heavily on guerrilla operations. Syria wanted to regain the Golan Heights and its strategic advantage—and, if possible, to carry the war into Israel. It will be recalled that Syria did not accept Resolution 242 and continued to reject, even implicitly, Israel's right to exist. Sadat also had general discussions with King Feisal of Saudi Arabia about the possible use of oil as a weapon in any future hostilities, and this tactic was generally approved by May 1973. Feelers were put out to

Golda Meir, Israeli Prime Minister during the October 1973 War (*Photo courtesy of Associated Press/Wide World Photos*).

King Hussein, who was not made privy to all the details of the impending operation but who was glad once again to be on the side of the Arab consensus. Egypt had severed diplomatic relations with Jordan after Hussein, in March 1972, had proposed a federal-type plan for the west and east banks of the Jordan that implied the recognition of Israel.

While talks were going on among the Arabs, the United States and the Soviet Union were discussing détente at the second summit meeting that took place in June 1973. Almost simultaneously with discussions about détente, however, came massive infusions of Soviet weapons into Egypt (including the SCUD missiles), and into Syria, where the Soviets supplied a surface-to-air missile system and FROG surface-to-surface missiles. The Soviets acted in a pragmatic manner throughout; having built up an impressive war machine, they were not simply going to abandon Egypt.

Many analysts have noted that Israel did not believe, even at this late date, and in the face of clear evidence and public declarations by Sadat, that Egypt would go to war. The Israeli intelligence services had all the information they needed, but they failed to evaluate it properly. Their thinking was colored by the notion that Israel had defensible borders, was militarily superior, and that the Arabs would not strike a first blow. Even when war was imminent, on the morning of October 6, the total mobilization (including the reserves) requested by Chief-of-Staff David Elazar was opposed by Defense Minister Dayan as superfluous. (A later meeting in the Prime Minister's office resulted in a compromise call-up of 100,000 Israeli troops.) Even when it became clear that hostilities were about to commence, the Israeli military was constrained from making a preemptive attack by the government's own assessment, and by the warning of Secretary of State Henry Kissinger, that to do so would be to forfeit the goodwill and assistance of the United States.

THE 1973 WAR AND ITS AFTERMATH

On October 6, 1973, Egypt and Syria attacked Israel in what the Israelis call the Yom Kippur War. This is because the conflict broke out on the Jewish Day of Atonement. To the Arabs, it was the Ramadan war since Muslims were in the midst of the holy month of Ramadan. The Egyptian code name for the war was "Operation Badr," referring to the site of the Prophet Muhammad's first victory over the pagan Arabs in Arabia. Again, we shall leave the details of the military operations to the military historians, although weapons never before used in combat were employed and there were many noteworthy operations, from the Egyptian crossing of the Suez Canal, to the recrossing of the canal by the Israelis, to the furious and deadly tank battles on the Golan Heights that were the largest since World War II.

The October 1973 war destroyed many myths. It proved, for example, that the Arabs could cooperate and that they could keep their intentions a secret. It demonstrated that they were capable of sophisticated intelligence gathering and analysis, and of a brilliant operational plan to cross the Suez Canal and demolish the Bar-Lev line. It showed that Arab soldiers could fight bravely and well when properly trained and motivated, and that they could handle the most technologically advanced weapons. It proved that Israel was not invincible. Israel turned the tide, but only with difficulty, and not without having come perilously close to running out of ammunition until an American airlift began to arrive on October 14. Indeed, although Secretary of State Kissinger had been kept informed of Israeli losses of planes, tanks, and ammunition in the first week of the war, he withheld American aid in the hope that Israel would accept a cease-fire in place. This, he believed, would preserve the sense of Arab victory and honor and perhaps break the diplomatic stalemate of the Arab–Israeli conflict.

However, by October 11, it was clear that a massive Soviet airlift was underway to both Egypt and Syria. Kissinger (having been given pretty much a free hand by President Nixon, who was mired in the Watergate scandal) decided, in the face of this Soviet challenge, that the military balance had to be restored in Israel's favor in order for the United States to retain influence and leverage in the region. With a massive infusion of material from the United States, Israel captured Mt. Hermon, and advanced to within 40 kilometers of Damascus in the north. In the south, the Israeli army recrossed the Suez Canal and commanded the approaches to Cairo. A Soviet–American cease-fire proposal was approved by the United Nations on October 22, but violations by both sides resulted in the continuation of hostilities and in the surrounding and trapping of the Egyptian Third Army in the western Sinai. After Soviet threats to intercede, and an American military alert—just short of a nuclear alert—a second cease-fire was accepted by both parties on October 24, with Israel the obvious military victor.

But it was a war that Israel had come very close to losing, and it had lasting effects in that country. Israel suffered over 2,500 dead and 3,000 wounded (see Table 7–1) and the direct monetary costs were about $4 billion. The war was an emotional and psychological shock that exposed some serious problems. One was Israel's over-

TABLE 7–1 Estimated Losses, October War, 1973

	Israel	Arab Total	Egypt	Syria	Jordan	Iraq	Other Arabs
Personnel							
Killed	2,838*	8,528	5,000	3,100	28	218	100
Wounded	8,800*	19,549	12,000	6,000	49	600	300
Prisoners							
or							
Missing	508	8,551	8,031	500		20	?
Tanks**	840	2,554	1,100	1,200	54	200	?
APCs	400	850+	450	400		?	?
Artillery							
Pieces	?	550+	300	250		?	?
SAM Batteries							
Aircraft		47	44	3			?
Helicopters	103	392	223	118		21	30
Naval Vessels	6	55	42	13		?	?
	1	15	10	5			

Source: Trevor N. Dupuy, *Elusive Victory: The Arab-Israeli Wars, 1947–1974* (New York: Harper & Row, 1978), p. 609. Reprinted with permission of Hero Books

*About 10% has been added to officially reported Israeli casualties to represent approximately the wounded who died of their injuries, and the fact that official Israeli figures apparently do not include those wounded not evacuated from aid stations and field hospitals.

**Tanks destroyed or put out of action for one or more days. For instance, the Israelis seem to have repaired and returned to operation about 400 of the tank losses shown here. They also recovered about 300 repairable Arab tanks.

confidence that had prevented accurate intelligence assessments. Others were a lack of appreciation for Arab abilities; a static defense line that proved to be a liability; and a generally erroneous concept of defensible borders that were not as defensible as had been thought.

Israel became more and more dependent on the United States, not only for military but also for economic aid, since the war cost Israel about one-third of its yearly budget for 1973. The Arab oil embargo and the resulting skyrocketing price of energy, which was another feature of this war, also hurt Israel. The war weakened the Labor government, which had led Israel since 1948 and virtually ended the political careers of Golda Meir and Moshe Dayan. In a few short years, the Likud coalition headed by Menachem Begin would be voted into office. This occurred in 1977, and it reflected the polarity that had developed in Israel after the 1973 war on a number of issues, including the disposition of the occupied territories. The disengagement agreements between Egypt and Israel that heralded some movement toward the exchange of territory in the Sinai in return for recognition tended to encourage Israeli hardliners to dig in their heels on the issue of the West Bank. The Labor government itself, in the face of political challenges and new developments concerning King Hussein and the PLO, gave the go-ahead to civilian, as opposed to military/security, settlements on the West Bank. This issue and other matters affecting and complicating negotiations will be discussed in the following chapter.

The Arabs lost the October War militarily, but they won an important psychological victory, and, even more crucial, they won the war diplomatically. The war did indeed jolt the attention of the world back to the Arab–Israeli conflict and it provided the impetus for Kissinger and for American diplomacy to mediate the dispute. UN Security Council Resolution 338 secured the cease-fire, but it was a cease-fire worked out by Kissinger in Moscow. (See Document 7–3.) Resolution 338 was extremely important because it called for direct negotiations "between the parties concerned under appropriate auspices" on the basis of Resolution 242, which was passed in 1967. After one meeting of a peace conference convened in Geneva in December 1973, however, a comprehensive approach was scuttled in favor of Kissinger's "step-by-step" diplomacy. The United States became the primary superpower player in the region, a role capped by the part it played in an eventual peace treaty between Egypt and Israel in 1979.

Conversely, the Russians lost ground in the Middle East. They had had no diplomatic relations with Israel since 1967 and had lost their influence and base in Egypt. Syria, therefore, became the keystone of the Soviets' Middle East policy, and they continued to press for comprehensive negotiations as a way of playing a role in the region.

As for the Palestinians, some observers believe that the October War and its aftermath forced the mainline groups to scale down their demands. They say that, although never publicly declared, statements in 1974 suggest that the PLO was willing to forego a "secular, democratic state" in all of Palestine and to settle for a state in any territory evacuated by Israel. On the other hand, recognition of the PLO as the "sole, legitimate representative of the Palestinian people" at a meeting of the Arab League at Rabat in 1974, added a new dimension to the situation. (See Documents 7–4 and 7–5.) This decision undermined the role of King Hussein and his ability to speak for the Palestinians as envisaged by the UN resolutions. Moreover, continuing PLO terrorism and attempts to sabotage the Kissinger shuttle missions and the diplomatic process altogether worked against any moderation of the PLO position.

THE ARAB EMBARGO AND THE OIL WEAPON

The Arab oil embargo was probably one of the most significant features of the 1973 hostilities. On October 17, OAPEC, the Organization of Arab Oil-Producing Countries, including Saudi Arabia, a traditional friend of the United States, imposed a total embargo on oil exports to America. The oil cartel also placed embargoes of varying degrees on other countries, depending upon the extent of their support for Israel, and announced monthly production cuts. Two months later, on December 23, 1973, the Organization of Petroleum Exporting Countries (OPEC), of which the Arab oil states were members, announced a fourfold increase in the posted price of oil to $11.65 per barrel.

Until this time, OPEC, which had been formed in 1960, had achieved only moderate success in its goal of bringing about higher oil prices and profits and a greater share in oil production. During the 1960s, however, OPEC members began increasingly to cooperate, and in 1971, inspired by the success of Libya's Muammar al-Qaddafi, who had come to power in 1969 and who had gotten higher oil prices and more revenue from higher taxes on profits, they won important pricing concessions from the oil companies. By 1973, several OPEC countries (Algeria, Libya, Iraq, Iran) had nationalized their oil and taken over full production. It was the October 1973 War, however, that enabled the Arab countries in OPEC for the first time to utilize oil as a weapon.

The effect of the oil embargo on the economies of the European countries—and their subsequent change of attitude toward Israel in the United Nations—was even more dramatic than the Arabs had hoped for. In 1973, the Arab states produced 37 percent of the oil consumed by the non-Communist world, and the participation in the embargo by Saudi Arabia, which produced over 7.5 million barrels per day (approximately 40 percent of Arab production and the third largest producer in the world), ensured the success of the embargo. American production, on the other hand, had decreased during the three previous years. The nations totally boycotted, in addition to the United States, included the Netherlands (the Dutch port of Rotterdam was the largest refinery and transshipment center in Europe), Canada, Portugal, Rhodesia, and South Africa. Britain, France, and Spain were exempted. According to a 1974 Department of Energy report, the embargo, which lasted five months, until March 1974, cost the United States 500,000 jobs and a $10 billion to $20 billion loss in its gross national product.

Politically, the impact was equally effective. On November 6, 1973, the European Economic Community (EEC) meeting in Brussels called on Israel and Egypt to return to the October 22 cease-fire lines (before Israel had completed the encirclement of the Egyptian Third Army). More significantly, the EEC urged Israel to end its occupation of the territory seized in 1967 and stated that the "legitimate rights" of the Palestinians must be taken into account in any settlement. In December, Japan also urged Israel to withdraw totally from occupied Arab territory. The Arabs rewarded these movements toward their position by exempting Japan and Europe from cuts in oil supplies. The embargo against the United States ended only after America had strenuously exerted itself in mediation efforts that resulted in a disengagement agreement between Israel and Egypt in 1974 and the resumption of U.S.–Egyptian diplomatic relations.

Some mention should be made at this point of the use and limitations of the so-called oil weapon. There is a widespread perception that the oil-producing nations can use their oil policies to favor those who cooperate with them and to punish those who do not. For entirely opposite reasons, it is in the interests of both the Arab states and Israel to encourage this perception. There is no denying that the OAPEC cartel benefitted from this fear of an oil weapon. For example, France agreed to sell Iraq equipment to help develop a nuclear capability in exchange for oil. Similarly, Saudi Arabia threatened a cutback in oil production if Congress rejected the sale of American AWAC radar aircraft to Saudi Arabia. The Senate Energy Committee concluded in 1980 that oil was not merely an economic commodity but was also "a source of enormous political leverage in the hands of the oil-producing nations."

Not all commentators agree with this assessment, however. Some argue, for example, that Arab oil producers will act in their own economic interests, and that as long as so many OPEC countries are dependent on oil revenues exclusively to fuel their own economies, there is no need to fear the oil weapon. They point out that OPEC decisions to limit production and raise prices were goals that predated the 1973 war. Moreover, efforts by the industrialized nations to conserve energy and to discover and exploit alternate sources of fuel, the oil glut of the 1980s, and the unwillingness of some of the OPEC countries to keep to their agreed quotas and prices also lend weight to the argument that the "oil weapon" can be blunted.

We should also note that price rises and cutbacks hurt friends as well as enemies. The economies of pro-Arab countries, especially in the developing world, were seriously hurt by OPEC actions in the 1970s. The damage caused to poor and highly oil-dependent nations threatened to create an anti-Arab political backlash. Indeed, many African countries that broke relations with Israel in 1973 have now resumed ties.

Nevertheless, at that time, the ramifications of the oil embargo of 1973 were numerous, and for a while it caused a disruption of the world economy and recession that many associated with the October 1973 War. As destructive as the conflict was, however, it did set in motion events that would later lead to a peace treaty between Egypt and Israel. That process will be discussed in the next chapter.

SUGGESTIONS FOR FURTHER READING

BAR-SIMAN-TOV, YAACOV, *The Israeli-Egyptian War of Attrition, 1969–70,* New York, Columbia University Press, 1980.

COBBAN, HELENA, *The Palestinian Liberation Organization: People, Power, and Politics,* Cambridge, England, Cambridge University Press, 1984.

HEIKAL, MOHAMED, *The Road to Ramadan,* New York, Quadrangle, 1975.

HERZOG, CHAIM, *The War of Atonement,* Boston, Little, Brown, 1974.

"The October War and Its Aftermath," *Journal of Palestine Studies,* Institute of Palestine Studies, Beirut and Kuwait University, Vol. III, No. 2, 1974.

SHWADRAN, BENJAMIN, *Middle Eastern Oil Crises Since 1973,* Boulder, Colo., Westview Press, 1986.

"Sunday Times" Insight Team, *The Yom Kippur War,* London, Andre Deutsch, 1975.

The Palestinian National Covenant, 1968
[Excerpts]

This Covenant will be called The Palestinian National Covenant (*al-mithaq al-watani al-filastini*).

Article 1: Palestine is the homeland of the Palestinian Arab people and an integral part of the great Arab homeland, and the people of Palestine is a part of the Arab nation.

Article 2: Palestine with its boundaries that existed at the time of the British mandate is an integral regional unit.

Article 3: The Palestinian Arab people possesses the legal right to its homeland, and when the liberation of its homeland is completed it will exercise self-determination solely according to its own will and choice.

Article 4: The Palestinian personality is an innate, persistent characteristic that does not disappear, and it is transferred from fathers to sons. The Zionist occupation, and the dispersal of the Palestinian Arab people as a result of the disasters which came over it, do not deprive it of its Palestinian personality and affiliation and do not nullify them.

Article 5: The Palestinians are the Arab citizens who were living permanently in Palestine until 1947, whether they were expelled from there or remained. Whoever is born to a Palestinian Arab father after this date, within Palestine or outside it, is a Palestinian.

Article 6: Jews who were living permanently in Palestine until the beginning of the Zionist invasion will be considered Palestinians. [For the dating of the Zionist invasion, considered to have begun in 1917.]

Article 7: The Palestinian affiliation and the material, spiritual and historical tie with Palestine are permanent realities. The upbringing of the Palestinian individual in an Arab and revolutionary fashion, the undertaking of all means of forging consciousness and training the Palestinian, in order to acquaint him profoundly with his homeland, spiritually and materially, and preparing him for the conflict and the armed struggle, as well as for the sacrifice of his property and his life to restore his homeland, until the liberation of all is a national duty.

Article 8: The phase in which the people of Palestine is living is that of national (*watani*) struggle for the liberation of Palestine. Therefore, the contradictions among the Palestinian national forces are of secondary order which must be suspended in the interest of the fundamental contradiction between Zionism and colonialism on the one side and the Palestinian Arab people on the other. On this basis, the Palestinian masses, whether in the homeland or in places of exile (*mahajir*), organizations and individuals, comprise one national front which acts to restore Palestine and liberate it through armed struggle.

Article 9: Armed struggle is the only way to liberate Palestine and is therefore a strategy and not tactics. The Palestinian Arab people affirms its absolute resolution and abiding determination to pursue the armed struggle and to march forward towards the armed popular revolution, to liberate its homeland and return to it [to maintain] its right to a natural life in it, and to exercise its right of self-determination in it and sovereignty over it.

Article 10: Fedayeen action forms the nucleus of the popular Palestinian war of liberation. This demands its promotion, extension and protection, and the mobilization of all the masses and scientific capacities of the Palestinians, their organization and involvement in the armed Palestinian revolution and cohesion in the national (*watani*) struggle among the various groups of the people of Palestine, and between them and the Arab masses, to guarantee the continuation of the revolution, its advancement and victory.

Article 13: Arab unity and the liberation of Palestine are two complementary aims. Each one paves the way for realization of the other. Arab unity leads to the liberation of

Palestine, and the liberation of Palestine leads to Arab unity. Working for both goes hand in hand.

Article 15: The liberation of Palestine, from an Arab viewpoint, is a national (*qawmi*) duty to repulse the Zionist, Imperialist invasion from the great Arab homeland and to purge the Zionist presence from Palestine. Its full responsibility falls upon the Arab nation, peoples and governments, with the Palestinian Arab people at their head.

Article 16: The liberation of Palestine, from a spiritual viewpoint, will prepare an atmosphere of tranquillity and peace for the Holy Land in the shade of which all the Holy Places will be safeguarded, and freedom of worship and visitation to all will be guaranteed, without distinction or discrimination of race, colour, language or religion. For this reason, the people of Palestine looks to the support of all the spiritual forces in the world.

Article 17: The liberation of Palestine, from a human viewpoint, will restore to the Palestinian man his dignity, glory and freedom. For this, the Palestinian Arab people looks to the support of those in the world who believe in the dignity and freedom of man.

Article 19: The partitioning of Palestine in 1947 and the establishment of Israel is fundamentally null and void, whatever time has elapsed, because it was contrary to the wish of the people of Palestine and its natural right to its homeland, and contradicts the principles embodied in the Charter of the UN, the first of which is the right of self-determination.

Article 20: The Balfour Declaration, the Mandate document, and what has been based upon them are considered null and void. The claim of a historical or spiritual tie between Jews and Palestine does not tally with historical realities nor with the constituents of statehood in their true sense. Judaism, in its character as a religion of revelation, is not a nationality with an independent existence. Likewise, the Jews are not one people with an independent personality. They are rather citizens of the states to which they belong.

Article 21: The Palestinian Arab people, in expressing itself through the armed Palestinian revolution, rejects every solution that is a substitute for a complete liberation of Palestine, and rejects all plans that aim at the settlement of the Palestine issue or its internationalization.

Article 22: Zionism is a political movement organically related to world Imperialism and hostile to all movements of liberation and progress in the world. It is a racist and fanatical movement in its formation: aggressive, expansionist and colonialist in its aims; and fascist and Nazi in its means. Israel is the tool of the Zionist movement and a human and geographical base for world Imperialism. It is a concentration and jumping-off point for Imperialism in the heart of the Arab homeland, to strike at the hopes of the Arab nation for liberation, unity and progress.

Article 24: The Palestinian Arab people believes in the principles of justice, freedom, sovereignty, self determination, human dignity and the right of peoples to exercise them.

Article 27: The Palestine Liberation Organization will cooperate with all Arab States, each according to its capacities, and will maintain neutrality in their mutual relations in the light of and on the basis of, the requirements of the battle of liberation and will not interfere in the internal affairs of any Arab State.

Article 28: The Palestinian Arab people insists upon the originality and independence of its national (*wataniyya*) revolution and rejects every manner of interference, guardianship and subordination.

Article 33: This covenant cannot be amended except by a two-thirds majority of all the members of the National Assembly of the Palestine Liberation Organization in a special session called for this purpose.

Source: Yehuda Lukacs, ed., *Documents on the Israeli-Palestinian Conflict, 1967–1983* (Cambridge: Cambridge University Press, 1984), pp. 139–143.

PLO Groups

P.L.O. Mainstream
<u>TUNISIA</u>
Al Fatah

Yasir Arafat: P.L.O. chairman, leader of Al Fatah . . . believed to have been born in 1929 in Cairo or Gaza, though Mr. Arafat says he comes from Jerusalem, the home of his mother's family . . . in early 1950's, a student leader in Cairo among Palestinians and in the Muslim Brotherhood . . . in 1957; moved to Kuwait with coterie of associates who still form the core of P.L.O. decision-makers . . . founded Al Fatah in 1959; became P.L.O. chairman a year later . . . moved to Lebanon in 1970, after Jordan fought and then expelled Palestinian guerrillas . . . moved to Tunis after 1982 Israeli invasion ousted P.L.O. from Lebanon.

Saleh Khalef: Al Fatah's No. 2 leader . . . born in 1933 in Jaffa, now in Israel . . . friend of Mr. Arafat from their Cairo-Kuwait days and founding member of Al Fatah . . . viewed as more radical than Mr. Arafat . . . in early 1970's, was associated with Black September terror group . . . identified by British journalist Allan Hart as mastermind of 1972 seizure of Israeli athletes at Munich Olympics . . . , supports P.L.O. peace initiative but opposes further concessions to U.S. or Israel . . . Nom de guerre: Abu Iyad.

Farouk Kaddouml: Left-wing head of Al Fatah's political section . . . born in Nablus, now in Israeli occupied West Bank, in 1931 . . . has close ties to Soviet Union and East bloc . . . Nom de guerre: Abu Lutf.

Khaled al-Hassan: Senior adviser to Mr. Arafat . . . born in Haifa, now in Israel, in 1928 . . . said to have frequently challenged Mr. Arafat, seeking a collective leadership . . . now sometimes depicted as intellectual of Al Fatah's more conservative wing, and a trouble-shooter for Mr. Arafat.

Bassam Abu Sharif: Born in Jordan in 1947 . . . studied at American University of Beirut . . . for many years, a member of Popular Front for Liberation of Palestine; took part in its hijacking of three airliners to Jordan in 1970 . . . now says he was not a guerrilla fighter . . . face and hands disfigured in 1972 by parcel bomb, thought to have been sent by Israelis, that blew up in his Beirut office . . . switched affiliations in 1987 . . . now a political adviser to Mr. Arafat and a new voice speaking for P.L.O.'s new policies.

P.L.O. Radicals
<u>SYRIA</u>
Popular Front for the Liberation of Palestine

George Habash: Born in Lydda (now Lod, Israel) in 1926 to a Greek Orthodox Christian family . . . studied medicine at American University of Beirut . . . in 1968, helped found Popular Front, now second-biggest group in P.L.O. . . . moved to Beirut, then Damascus . . . one-time advocate of hijackings and other acts of terrorism . . . a Marxist revolutionary implacably opposed to recognizing Israel's right to exist . . . opposed decision to accept United Nations resolutions envisioning Israeli withdrawal from occupied land in exchange for peace, but conditionally supports Arafat peace initiative.

Democratic Front for the Liberation of Palestine

Nayef Hawatmeh: Born in Salt, Jordan, in 1935 to Greek Catholic parents . . . degree in social psychology from Arab University in Beirut . . . helped found Popular Front, but broke away to create Democratic Front, which considers itself more pragmatic . . . in 1974, was first P.L.O. figure to advocate a "mini-state" in occupied territories.

Yasir Abd el-Rabbo: Assistant secretary general of group, member of P.L.O. executive committee . . . born in Jaffa in 1945 . . . educated in Egypt, Jordan and Lebanon . . . has frequently visited Moscow . . . led group that met United States envoy last month.

Palestine Communist Party

Suleyman Najab: Grew up in what are now occupied territories . . . has generally supported Arafat peace initiative.

IRAQ
Arab Liberation Front

Abdul Rahim Ahmed: His movement formed as Iraqi response to Syrian support of other Palestinian groups . . . does not support Arafat peace initiative.

Palestine Liberation Front

Mohammed Abbas: Known as Abul Abbas . . . master minded 1985 hijacking of cruise ship Achille Lauro.

Parties Opposed to P.L.O.
SYRIA
Popular Front for the Liberation of Palestine-General Command

Ahmed Jebril: Broke with Popular Front over its emphasis on class conflict . . . closely aligned with Syria . . . some in group linked to technologically sophisticated acts of terrorism, such as discovery in West Germany of a barometrically triggered bomb, apparently designed to attack an airplane, late last year.

Popular Struggle Front

Samir Gosheh: Broke with Mr. Habash in 1960's . . . leads splinter group committed to Arab nationalism . . . thought to display greater independence from Syria than Mr. Jebril.

Fatah dissidents

Saed Musa: Broke with Mr. Arafat in 1983 in Syrian-sponsored revolt . . . widely known as Abu Musa . . . had been regarded as a military hero because of actions in Lebanon during its civil war and 1982 Israeli invasion.

Saiqa

Considered an integral part of Syrian military machine with only nominal Palestinian identity.

Communist Party

Arabl Awad: Leader of a splinter group from Mr. Najab's Communist Party, with little following.

LIBYA
Fatah Revolutionary Council

Abu Nidal: Believed to have been born in Jaffa in 1937 . . . real name Sabry al-Banna . . . came from rich merchant family, later lived in a refugee camp tent . . . studied engineering at Cairo University . . . left Al Fatah in 1974 . . . has taken responsibility for numerous terrorist attacks . . . expelled from Iraq in 1983 . . . expelled from Syria last year under United States pressure . . . American authorities believe he has moved to Libya.

Source: The New York Times, January 22, 1989, Section E, p. 5.

DOCUMENT 7–3

U.N. Security Council Resolution 338—Oct. 22, 1973

The Security Council

1. Calls upon all parties to the present fighting to cease all firing and terminate all military activity immediately, no later than 12 hours after the moment of the adoption of this decision, in the positions they now occupy;

2. Calls upon the parties concerned to start immediately after the cease-fire the implementation of Security Council Resolution 242 (1967) in all of its parts;

3. Decides that, immediately and concurrently with the cease-fire, negotiations start between the parties concerned under appropriate auspices aimed at establishing a just and durable peace in the Middle East.

Source: The Middle East, 7th ed. (Washington, D.C.: Congressional Quarterly, Inc., 1990), p. 301.

DOCUMENT 7-4

Arab Heads of State Declaration at Rabat, October 28, 1974

Rabat, October 28, 1974

The Conference of the Arab Heads of State:

1. *Affirms* the right of the Palestinian people to return to their homeland and to self-determination.

2. *Affirms* the right of the Palestinian people to establish an independent national authority, under the leadership of the PLO in its capacity as the sole legitimate representative of the Palestine people, over all liberated territory. The Arab States are pledged to uphold this authority, when it is established, in all spheres and at all levels.

3. *Supports* the PLO in the exercise of its national and international responsibilities, within the context of the principle of Arab solidarity.

4. *Invites* the kingdoms of Jordan, Syria and Egypt to formalize their relations in the light of these decisions and in order that they be implemented.

5. *Affirms* the obligation of all Arab States to preserve Palestinian unity and not to interfere in Palestinian internal affairs.

Source: The Middle East, 7th ed., Congressional Quarterly, p. 302.

DOCUMENT 7-5

Israel Knesset Statement, Prime Minister, Yitzhak Rabin, Following the Rabat Conference, 5 November, 1974 [Excerpts]

The meaning of [the Rabat] Resolutions is clear. The Rabat Conference decided to charge the organizations of murderers with the establishment of a Palestinian State, and the Arab countries gave the organizations a free hand to decide on their mode of operations. The Arab countries themselves will refrain, as stated in the Resolution, from intervening in the "internal affairs" of this action.

We are not fully aware of the significance of the fourth Resolution, which refers to "outlining a formula" for the coordination of relations between Jordan, Syria, Egypt and the PLO. It is by no means impossible that it is also intended to bring about closer military relations between them.

The significance of these Resolutions is extremely grave. The aim of the terrorist organizations is well known and clear. The Palestine National Covenant speaks bluntly and openly about the liquidation of the State of Israel by means of armed struggle, and the Arab States committed themselves at Rabat to support this struggle. Any attempt to implement them will be accompanied by at least attempts to carry out terrorist operations on a larger scale with the support of the Arab countries.

The decisions of the Rabat Conference are merely a continuation of the resolutions adopted at Khartoum. Only, further to the "no's" of Khartoum, the roof organization of the terrorists has attained the status conferred upon it by the presidents and kings at Rabat. Throughout this conference not a voice was raised expressing readiness for peace. The recurring theme of this conference was the aspiration to destroy a member-state of the United Nations. The content of this gathering has nothing whatsoever in common with social progress or the advancement of humanity among the Arab nations or in the relations with the peoples in the region and throughout the world.

There is no indication of any deviation from the goal and policy of the terrorist organizations, so let us not delude ourselves on this score. The terrorist organizations had no successes in the administered territories, but the successes they achieved at the U.N. General Assembly and at Rabat are encouraging them to believe that the targets they had so confidently set themselves are now within reach.

The policy laid down in Khartoum and Rabat shall not be executed. We have the power to prevent its implementation. The positions of the government of Israel in the face of these resolutions of the Rabat Conference is unequivocal:

A) The government of Israel categorically rejects the conclusions of the Rabat Conference, which are designed to disrupt any progress towards peace, to encourage the terrorist elements, and to foil any step which might lead to peaceful coexistence with Israel.

B) In accordance with the Knesset's resolutions, the government of Israel will not negotiate with terrorist organizations whose avowed policy is to strive for Israel's destruction and whose method is terrorist violence.

C) We warn the Arab leaders against making the mistake of thinking that threats or even the active employment of the weapon of violence or of military force will lead to a political solution. This is a dangerous illusion. The aims of the Palestinian National Charter will not be achieved, either by terrorist acts or by limited or total warfare.

Source: Lukacs, *Documents*, pp. 96–97.

CHAPTER 8

THE SEARCH FOR PEACE, 1973–1979

CHRONOLOGY

Nov. 11, 1973	Israel–Egypt cease-fire signed at Kilometer 101	**July 16, 1977**	Egyptian President Anwar Sadat announces willingness to accept Israel after signing of a peace treaty
Dec. 21, 1973	First Geneva Peace Conference convenes		
Jan. 18, 1974	Israeli–Egyptian disengagement accord	**Nov. 9, 1977**	Sadat states he is prepared to speak to Israeli Knesset if necessary to obtain peace
Feb. 28, 1974	United States and Egypt resume full diplomatic relations	**Nov. 19, 1977**	Sadat addresses Israeli Knesset
May 31, 1974	Israeli–Syrian disengagement accord	**Dec. 25, 1977**	Begin and Sadat meet in Ismailia, Egypt
June 12– 17, 1974	President Nixon visits the Middle East	**March 14, 1978**	Israel occupies Lebanese territory in Operation Litani
June 16, 1974	United States and Syria resume diplomatic relations	**June 13, 1978**	Israel completes withdrawal from Lebanon
Oct. 28, 1974	Arab League summit meeting at Rabat recognizes PLO as sole legitimate representative of Palestinians	**Sept. 17, 1978**	Camp David peace accords signed
		Dec. 10, 1978	Nobel Peace Prize awarded jointly to Sadat and Begin
Nov. 13, 1974	PLO leader Yasser Arafat addresses UN General Assembly	**Jan. 16, 1979**	Shah leaves Iran
June 5, 1975	Suez Canal reopens after 8 years	**Feb. 1, 1979**	Ayatollah Khomeini returns to Iran
Sept. 4, 1975	Israel and Egypt sign second disengagement agreement	**March 8– 13, 1979**	Carter visits Middle East
Nov. 8, 1975	Soviets call for reconvening of Geneva Peace Conference	**March 26, 1979**	Egyptian–Israeli peace treaty signed in Washington, D.C.
Nov. 10, 1975	UN General Assembly passes resolution equating Zionism with racism	**April 1, 1979**	Khomeini proclaims Iran an Islamic Republic—"A Government of God"
Dec. 4, 1975	UN Security Council allows PLO to participate in debate on Arab–Israeli question	**March 31, 1979**	Egypt expelled from Arab League, which moves HQ to Tunis. League and PLO break diplomatic relations with Egypt and impose boycotts
July 4, 1976	Israeli commandos raid airport at Entebbe, Uganda, freeing hostages of hijacked jetliner		
Nov. 2, 1976	Jimmy Carter elected President	**April 30, 1979**	First Israeli freighter since independence passes through Suez Canal
March 16, 1977	Carter endorses a Palestinian "homeland" in address at Clinton, Massachusetts	**May 9, 1979**	Egypt expelled from Islamic Conference
May 17, 1977	Menachem Begin and his Likud coalition win Israeli general elections	**May 25, 1979**	Israel begins withdrawal from Sinai Peninsula
May 19, 1977	Begin calls for new Jewish settlements in Israeli-occupied territories	**Nov. 4, 1979**	American hostages seized at U.S. Embassy in Tehran

IMPACT OF THE 1973 WAR

In the last chapter we learned that the most important consequence of the 1973 war for Israel was that it made more urgent the need to explore ways of achieving peace with the Arabs.

For the Arab states, the war of 1973 resulted in a shift in the balance of power in the Middle East in their favor. The Arabs had always been aware that their military, economic, and political potential—measured in terms of their population, strategic location, large territories, and oil revenue resources—were far greater than their actual performance. All they needed was to coordinate their resources and activities. But they never did; national and traditional rivalries, political instability and corruption, and societies unready for the demands of modern warfare all acted to prevent the collective decision-making necessary to act against Israel. The 1973 war changed all that; Egyptian president Anwar Sadat had achieved the cooperation necessary to launch a combined attack. And it was a preemptive attack.

The Arab states continued in their technical state of war with Israel and gave little thought to making peace. At the same time significant changes were taking place in the Middle East. These changes made the need to reach some resolution to the Arab–Israeli conflict more urgent for both sides, and, perhaps just as importantly, for the United States and the U.S.S.R.. One such change was the dramatic increase in the importance of the Persian Gulf region in the 1960s and 1970s, and the effect of this on the geopolitical balance in the Middle East. The oil of this region was, and still is, critically important to the economy of the free world (Europe imports 85 percent and Japan 90 percent of their oil needs from the Persian Gulf States). During the 1960s and 1970s the Soviet Union attempted to extend and augment its influence in the Gulf region. The Russians also established a naval base in Ethiopia where there were 15,000 Cuban troops, sent arms to Yemen and the Southern Yemen Republic, maintained close ties with Syria and Libya, and invaded Afghanistan to support the pro-Soviet central government there.

A second change that threatened the stability of the region even further was the rise of Islamic fundamentalism in the 1970s and 1980s. Although the rise of religious "fanaticism" is usually dated from the Iranian revolution of 1979, fundamentalist Muslim groups like the Muslim Brotherhood had existed in the Middle East since the 1920s. The charismatic religious preacher Ayatollah Ruhollah Khomeini gained control of Iran in 1979. Subsequent events such as the seizure of over fifty hostages at the American Embassy in Tehran in the fall of 1979, and the Iran–Iraq war, which began in September 1980, added to the instability and volatility of the entire Middle East. One result of the changes taking place was that some Arab states, especially Egypt, began to regard the Arab–Israeli conflict as less threatening to them than the threat of religious fanaticism and Soviet subversion.

THE PEACE PROCESS, 1973–1979

Anwar Sadat used the 1973 war to try to end the struggle with Israel within the broad context of lessening Egyptian dependence upon the Soviet Union. Buoyed by the psychological "victory" of 1973, and concerned for Egypt's economic well-being after the Nasser era, Sadat was ready to make peace with Israel, and he called upon the rest of the Arab world to unite with him. He wanted Syria, Jordan, and the Palestinians to join Egypt in Geneva to negotiate a peace settlement with Israel. What he had in mind was Arab recognition of Israel as an independent state, and the formal renunciation of the "liberation" of Palestine as an Arab national aim. In return, Israel would surrender all the occupied territories, including the Old City of Jerusalem.

Egypt was in a better position to seek peace with Israel than were any of the other Arab states. Because Egyptians feel a deep identification with their own past and cultural heritage and have always seen themselves as Egyptians as well as Muslims or Arabs, Sadat could consider peace with Israel outside the Arab context. Moreover, although the plight of Palestinians moved him, the establishment of an independent Palestinian homeland did not have any particular urgency for Sadat. Thus, following lengthy negotiations, Anwar Sadat succeeded in signing a bilateral peace accord with Menachem Begin on September 17, 1978, at Camp David, the presidential retreat, in the United States. This was confirmed as a formal peace treaty between Egypt and Israel signed in Washington, D.C., on March 26, 1979. For various reasons, however, this was not the first step toward the hoped-for comprehensive peace settlement between Israel and the Arabs.

The "peace process," which in the first instance led to the Camp David accords, began in Washington, D.C. At the conclusion of the war in October 1973, Secretary of State Henry Kissinger, realizing the United States had greater bargaining power with Israel and Egypt, and concerned about the effects of the Arab oil embargo imposed on October 17, decided to seek an American solution in the Middle East. The war had indicated, he now believed, that peace in the Middle East could not be maintained through Israeli military strength. Peace would necessitate Israel making some territorial concessions. Since Sadat had expelled his Russian advisors, Kissinger saw an opportunity to seize the advantage, with regard to Egypt, owing to the Soviet absence.

KISSINGER'S SHUTTLE DIPLOMACY

Kissinger acted quickly, visiting the Middle East in November 1973, and securing, on November 11, a cease-fire agreement between Israel and Egypt that resulted in a return to the cease-fire lines of October 22 and the relief of the Egyptian Third Army. This accord (signed in a tent 101 kilometers from Cairo) was the first bilateral agreement signed by the two parties since the 1949 armistice at the end of the first Arab–Israeli war. In early December, Kissinger persuaded the Egyptians and the Jordanians (the Syrians refused) to negotiate with the Israelis—even to sit in the same room—through a UN-sponsored peace conference to be convened in Geneva, Switzerland, in accordance with the provisions of UN Resolution 338. Israel agreed to participate on condition that the negotiations were "face to face" and that no member of the PLO would be present. This conference was held on December 21 with Egypt, Jordan, Israel, the United States, and the U.S.S.R. present. It collapsed after one day, although there was an agreement to begin talks on separating Egyptian and Israeli forces along the Suez Canal.

This provided the opportunity for Kissinger to bypass the United Nations and Soviet Union, while appearing to keep within the parameters of UN Resolution 338, which called for all the parties to implement Resolution 242 in its entirety. Although initially believing he could secure a comprehensive peace settlement and supremely confident in his negotiating skills, persuasiveness, and energy, Kissinger soon realized (just like his predecessors in "shuttle diplomacy," Ralph Bunche and Gunnar Jarring) that peace would be achieved only through a "step-by-step" approach.

In January 1974, on another round of shuttle diplomacy, Kissinger persuaded

MAP 8–1

Golan Heights Disengagement, May 1974

Lebanon

Qiryat Shemona

U.N. ZONE

Jordan River

El Quneitra

Syria

GOLAN HEIGHTS (Occupied by Israel)

Israel

Sea of Galilee

Tiberias

Miles

0   10

Jordan

1974 Israel–Syria disengagement accord.

Source: The Middle East, 6th ed. (Washington, D.C.: Congressional Quarterly, Inc., 1986), p. 45.

Egypt and Israel to sign a disengagement accord, whereby Israel withdrew from the western bank of the Suez Canal, to about twenty miles from the east bank of the canal. Egypt agreed to a major reduction of troops east of Suez, the establishment of a UN-patrolled buffer zone, defensive missile emplacements only west of Suez, and the allowing of nonmilitary Israeli shipping through the canal (though not in Israeli vessels). In late February 1974, the United States and Egypt renewed full diplomatic relations after a seven-year hiatus. In May 1974, Kissinger also achieved a disengagement accord between Israel and Syria regarding the Golan Heights. Israel agreed to withdraw from occupied territory in the Heights in return for the establishment of a buffer zone and defensive Arab missile placements. (See Map 8–1.) President Hafez al-Assad of Syria also agreed in a private memorandum to prevent any Palestinian terrorist groups from launching attacks from Syria. In addition, the United States and Syria resumed diplomatic relations.

DIVISIONS WITHIN ISRAEL

Kissinger was very successful in these early stages. American prestige was high, all the Arab states involved regarded Kissinger as a mediator, and President Nixon was well received during a tour of the Middle East in June 1974. But there was a long way to go before any peace treaty could be agreed upon. Kissinger was, in fact, making contradictory and unrealistic promises to both parties. He promised the Israelis that disengagement accords would reduce American demands for concessions and lessen criticism of Israel. He told Egypt the opposite, namely that accords would set the peace process in motion and increase the pressure on Israel for further concessions. Israel was not particularly happy with Kissinger's efforts.

In December 1973, Israel had held elections and was undergoing a political reappraisal following the findings of the official report on the war. The ruling Labor party led by Golda Meir and Moshe Dayan won the election with a significantly reduced plurality in the Knesset: down to 39 percent (51 seats) from 46 percent (56 seats). The main challenge had come from the newly formed Likud party led by Menachem Begin. The Likud was a coalition of the Herut party, the Liberal party, and other parties of the political right, engineered by the hero of the 1973 campaign in Egypt, former general Ariel Sharon. The Likud, which opposed returning any territory to Egypt, won 30 percent of the vote and 39 seats in the Knesset.

Golda Meir resigned in April 1974, and the Labor party elected Yitzhak Rabin, Chief of Staff during the Six-Day War and former Ambassador to the United States, as Prime Minister. Policy-making was further complicated by internal strife within the Labor party. The ambitious Shimon Peres, who became Defense Minister, wanted the top job and sought to undermine Rabin's authority. He and Deputy Prime Minister Yigal Allon frequently disagreed with their nominal leader. In March 1975, Kissinger began a new round of shuttle diplomacy seeking further disengagement accords in the Sinai. Rabin resisted an Israeli pullback from the Sinai Peninsula and insisted upon retaining the important oil fields of Abu Rudeis, the two strategic passes in the area (Mitla and Gidi), and the post-1967 Israeli settlements in the Sinai. Egypt regarded these conditions as unacceptable. Negotiations stalled. President Gerald Ford threatened a total reassessment of American Middle East policy and suspended arms deliveries to Israel. Sadat met with Ford in Salzburg, Austria, on June 2, and on June 5 the Suez Canal was reopened to commercial shipping after having been closed for eight years.

A week later, Rabin met with Ford and Kissinger in Washington and agreed to renew efforts to negotiate another Sinai peace accord. In August 1975, Kissinger once more visited the Middle East, and Rabin reluctantly agreed to a package deal. The package, signed by Israel and Egypt on September 4, 1975, involved Israeli withdrawal from the oil fields and the passes and the stationing of American personnel manning the warning systems in the Sinai. (See Map 8–2.) The United States was committed to the security of both countries and promised large sums of aid to both. Each side agreed to avoid "the threat or use of force or military blockade against each other." Kissinger also assured Israeli leaders that the United States would not pressure them into a treaty with Jordan, or demand that they make major territorial concessions in future negotiations with Syria. Finally, in a commitment that was to become more

MAP 8-2

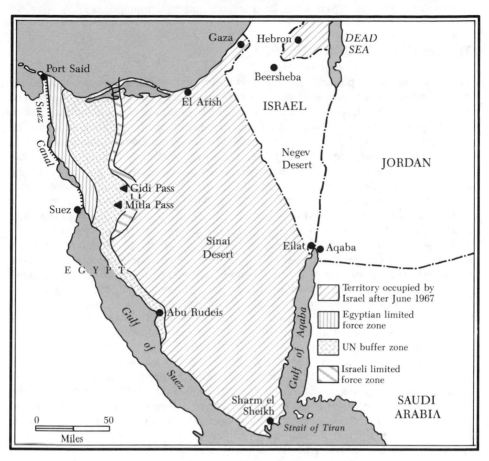

Second Israel-Egypt disengagement accord, 1975.

Source: T. G. Fraser, *The Middle East, 1914–1979* (New York: St. Martin's Press, 1980), p. xviii.

important as the years passed, the United States assured Israel that it would not talk to the PLO unless the PLO specifically recognized Israel's right to exist and accepted UN Resolution 242. Later, the United States added the rider that the PLO must also renounce terrorism. (See Document 8—1.)

Despite all his skill, Kissinger failed to achieve any further progress in his personal diplomacy. There seemed little likelihood at that time that Egypt, much less any other Arab state, would recognize Israel's right to exist or formally end the state of war. The 1973 war had also indicated to the Israelis that the military, economic, and diplomatic balance was shifting in favor of the Arab states, and in any future conflict the task of defending Israel would be correspondingly greater. The UN General Assembly resolution of November 1975, which described Israel as a racist regime in occupied Palestine, and which equated Zionism with racism, underscored not only the effectiveness of oil as an Arab weapon but also Israel's diplomatic isolation in the world community. The United States remained Israel's only major supporter.

THE ARAB STATES AND THE PLO

The momentum of diplomacy and the possibility that the disengagement agreements would lead to a more general settlement were destroyed by several developments. The assassination of Saudi King Faisal in March 1975 (by his nephew), and the outbreak of Lebanon's new civil war in April, had also derailed the peace process during 1975. The whole question of Arab unity has been one of the major problems of Arab diplomacy— and a major issue in Israeli foreign policy. It has been argued by both Israeli and Arab scholars that peace can only come to the Middle East with the agreement of the majority of the Arab world. What is needed is the support of five key states: Egypt, Syria, Iraq, Jordan, Saudi Arabia—as well as the PLO. If these parties agreed on a certain set of principles to form the basis for negotiations with Israel, then the other Arab states would follow. Agreement among the Arab states is necessary for an enduring peace, it was argued, because if any one leader negotiated terms with Israel unacceptable to elements of his nation's population, he could only guarantee domestic security (as well as his own) if the negotiations were part of a larger package involving other Arab states. And, these scholars agreed, only if there were multilateral agreement could there be any guarantee that, should a regime be replaced and its successor reneged on the terms, the agreements would still be honored. Given inter-Arab feuds, however, this kind of multinational unity has been impossible to achieve.

Anger and disagreement certainly followed the disengagement treaties between Israel and Egypt in relation to Syria and Jordan. Egypt's negotiations with Kissinger and indirectly through him with the Israelis (although the negotiations at Kilometer 101 were face to face) increasingly isolated Egypt from the other Arab states. In particular, King Hussein of Jordan and President Assad of Syria felt that Sadat had acted purely in his own interests. Consequently, they developed a new, albeit short-lived, alliance. Hussein had hoped that as a result of the October 1973 war he would recover the West Bank of the Jordan; he wanted it as a part of Jordan and to keep the Palestinians from claiming it as their own. He also wanted to regain the holy places of East Jerusalem. Israel rejected the proposal that Hussein put to Kissinger in January 1974, for Israeli withdrawal from the West Bank, and was unwilling to work out a solution with Hussein that would preempt the Palestinians.

In October 1974, at the Arab summit conference at Rabat (See Document 8–2), the PLO was unanimously recognized by the Arab League nations as "the sole legitimate representative of the Palestinian people" and was authorized to negotiate establishment of an independent national authority "in any liberated Palestinian territory." At that meeting, King Hussein also agreed to honor the PLO's claim to negotiate for the West Bank. A week later, on November 4, Hussein further stated that Jordan would write the West Bank out of the Jordanian constitution, and that it was "totally inconceivable" that Jordan and a Palestinian state could form a federation. Perhaps the real significance of the Rabat summit was that this decision meant that Hussein was forced to acknowledge Palestinian rights to what he had lost physically to the Israelis in 1967. It was a diplomatic triumph for the PLO that repaid the defeat of Black September in 1970. The Rabat decision also weakened the American position. Kissinger agreed with the Israelis in believing it was preferable to negotiate with Hussein than with the PLO.

President Hafez al-Assad, too, felt that Sadat had left Syria out in the cold, especially after the second disengagement agreement in 1975. Assad wanted all the Golan Heights back. He may have thought, briefly in 1974, that the U.S. government would somehow pry the Heights from Israeli hands. Syria could not make war without Egypt, but on the other hand, Egypt could not make peace without Syria. Rather than fall into line with Egypt, Syria chose to support the PLO. It was these circumstances that enabled Yasser Arafat and the PLO to take center stage in the proceedings. As we noted in the previous chapter, the PLO was a loose conglomerate of groups with quite different attitudes toward Israel and the policies they should pursue to achieve their goals. Formally and constitutionally, the PLO remained committed to its covenant as revised in 1968, which called for the dissolution (destruction) of Israel, but in reality the membership was divided over how to achieve this end.

PLO POLICY

PLO policy as stated in the Palestinian National Covenant asserted that "armed struggle is the only way to liberate Palestine," and later Palestinian National Council Resolutions called for the establishment of a secular democratic state to replace Israel. In terms that must have troubled King Hussein as much as Israel, the covenant stated that "Palestine, with the boundaries it had during the British Mandate, is an indivisible territorial unit." Leftist Palestinian groups like the Popular Front for the Liberation of Palestine (PFLP), led by George Habash, and the Democratic Front for the Liberation of Palestine (DFLP), led by Nayef Hawatmeh, called for the overthrow of King Hussein as part of the liberation of all Palestine. In fact, prior to 1975, these groups argued that before Palestine could be freed, all reactionary Arab governments would have to be reformed or overthrown.

By 1974, however, the PLO had modified its position on the liberation of Palestine, and, at the twelfth Palestine National Council (PNC) meeting in June–July 1974, it indicated through the term "national authority" a willingness to consider the establishment of a Palestinian Arab state in the West Bank and Gaza. Israel's analysts insisted that the modification in policy was only to substitute a two-stage for a one-stage process in the destruction of Israel, and that a so-called national authority would only be a launching pad for the achievement of that aim.

The approach of claiming to be a national authority within the confines of the West Bank and Gaza was seen by the PLO as a way of combating both Israeli and Jordanian claims to the occupied territories. Elements within the Palestinian cause, like the PFLP and DFLP as well as Habash's former associate, Ahmed Jebril, who formed his own splinter group backed by Syria, opposed this approach. They believed it not only gave Israel an opportunity to reject the claim but that it also weakened Arab revolutionary struggle to regain all of Palestine. Arafat himself and the majority of West Bank Palestinians preferred the option of the limited goal of regaining the West bank and Gaza, but Arafat felt his leadership of the PLO was not secure enough for him to speak out against the factions calling for the liberation of all Palestine. The diverse approaches within the Palestinian cause led to many years of ambiguity and confusion as to what the PLO meant by the term "national authority." The situation was compounded by the fact that the PLO would not accept UN Resolution 242. The United States demanded PLO acceptance of Resolution 242 recognizing Israel as a precondition to negotiations; the PLO objected to Resolution 242 because it referred only to Arab refugees and did not recognize Palestinian rights of self-determination.

In April and May of 1974, in an attempt to derail United States efforts to mediate the Syrian–Israeli disengagement accords signed in Geneva on May 31, groups within the PLO mounted a series of spectacular terrorist missions: one in April in the northern Israeli town of Kiryat Shemona in which the three terrorists (members of the PFLP) and eighteen Israelis—eight of them children—were killed; and another in May in Galilee, in the village of Ma'alot, where DFLP terrorists and twenty of the ninety children they were holding hostage were killed. The Israeli government's response to these acts of terrorism was to harden its resolve against the Palestinians despite the increasingly unrealistic nature of continuing to deny the existence of a Palestinian people. Arafat's unwillingness or inability to control the extremists in his organization not only weakened the credibility of the moderates within the PLO but also seemed to add weight to the argument that the PLO was a terrorist organization that should not be negotiated with. At this point of stalemate the UN General Assembly once again stepped in. It called for a full debate on the "Question of Palestine" and invited the PLO as representative of the Palestinian people to take part in it. This was a far greater triumph for the PLO, and for the more moderate elements in that organization, than any achieved by the extremists and their terrorist acts. And it was a complete rejection of the Israeli position. (See Document 8–3.)

Palestine/Israel had come full circle in the United Nations. In 1947, the General Assembly was a smaller, more Western-oriented body that was sympathetic to the cause of the Jewish survivors of the Holocaust and the Zionist argument for a Jewish homeland; in 1974, in a larger General Assembly, the votes of newly formed third-world states—many of them Muslim—and countries fearful of economic repercussions because of their dependence upon Arab oil, reflected sympathy for the Palesti-

After terrorist attack on Maalot Kibbutz, the nursery, May 1974 (*Photo courtesy of Britain/Israel Public Affairs Centre*).

Shatila camp, Beirut, Lebanon, 1985
(*Photo courtesy of UNRWA*).

nian cause. In 1969, the General Assembly had affirmed for the first time the right of "the people of Palestine" to "self-determination," and had restated and extended that view in 1970 and again in 1973. On November 13, 1974, Arafat himself spoke before the General Assembly, the first representative of a nonmember state to be invited to do so. After setting out the PLO position calling for a democratic, secular state in Palestine—which did not include a recognition or acceptance of Israel—Arafat concluded his speech with this appeal: "I have come bearing an olive branch and a freedom fighter's gun. Do not let the olive branch fall from my hand." (See Document 8–4.)

The majority of Israelis saw only Arafat's gun. (See Document 8–5.) The Israeli government believed a Palestinian state would be merely a platform for renewing warfare against an Israel reduced to its earlier, more vulnerable, size. Strategic considerations precluded even the Israeli doves from disagreeing with their government's

Yasser Arafat, leader of the Palestine Liberation Organization, at U.N. (*Photo courtesy of UPI/Bettmann Newsphotos*).

PLO Policy

policy. Israel repeated the position it held throughout the 1970s that Jordan was Palestine since a majority of the Jordanian population were Palestinians. King Hussein, despite the 1974 Rabat decision, maintained that he had the right to speak for Palestinians on both sides of the Jordan River. In 1974, the majority of the PLO were vehemently against the negotiation process with Israel. On the other hand, a minority of Palestinians saw Arafat's olive branch, and they began to believe that if a Palestinian state were to be established, diplomacy could achieve more than force.

THE WEST BANK AND GAZA

Nevertheless, the situation in the West Bank and Gaza was becoming increasingly more problematic for Israel. When the Israelis captured the West Bank and the Gaza Strip in the Six-Day War, more than a million Arabs came under Israeli control. The military occupation raised some fundamental questions for Israel. One was the so-called demographic time bomb. If Israel were to retain and annex the occupied territories, the higher birthrate of the Arab population might eventually endanger the Jewish character of Israel. Becoming a minority in their own land was unthinkable to Israel's Jews. On the other hand, if Arabs were to be denied their rights, the democratic nature of Israel would be compromised. Other options, such as the annexation of the occupied territories and the expulsion of the Arab population, or returning the areas to their former—Jordanian—status, seemed equally unacceptable to various parties. The option of a Palestinian "entity" alongside Israel was not seriously considered by anybody on either side at that time. Meanwhile the continuing occupation was bound to create conditions of oppression and further moral and practical dilemmas for Israel.

Not surprisingly, Palestinian and Israeli spokespersons disagree over the conditions of the Palestinians under Israeli occupation. Supporters of Israel argue that the material prosperity of the Palestinian Arabs occupying the West Bank increased dramatically under Israeli rule. They point out that under Jordanian control, between 1948 and 1967, the Palestinians had been kept politically and socially divided in an effort to limit the growth of Palestinian, as opposed to Jordanian, nationalism. Israel continued this policy to prevent the growth of a collective Palestinian identity. The West Bank economy and labor force were incorporated into the Israeli economy. Traditional large landowners suffered as a result of this as they were forbidden to grow crops that competed with those grown in Israel; but their workers, who then became unskilled workers in the Israeli economy (primarily in the construction industry), gained in terms of real wages and living conditions.

Israel and the West Bank and Gaza benefitted economically from this arrangement. A very high level of employment existed among the Arabs—approximately 98 percent—and many Jews within Israel experienced upward mobility, leaving the menial and unskilled jobs to be performed now by the Palestinians. At the same time, it must be noted that, as the occupation continued, the cost to Israel of defending the territories increased enormously. This in turn contributed significantly to the high rate of inflation—a record 130 percent in 1981. Furthermore, the dilemma of occupying lands inhabited by a people who did not want to live under Israeli rule caused a breakdown in the sense of national purpose and political consensus in Israel that had not been questioned between 1948 and 1967. Some Israelis even began to call for the expulsion of the Palestinians from the occupied territories.

Of the many options open to it following the 1967 war, Israel soon set out on the path of deliberately establishing Jewish settlements in the Gaza Strip, the Jordan Valley, and in the Golan Heights. These were at first military settlements, and most of them were outside the main centers of Arab population in the so-called Allon Belt, which ran along the Jordan Valley. They were approved, it was argued, for security reasons. This policy was pursued by the ruling Labor party and its coalition partner, the National Religious party, and a new organization that emerged in 1974, Gush Emunim (The Bloc of the Faithful). Gush Emunim and similar groups, evoking religious and historical sentiments, called for the absorption of the West Bank, or, as they termed it, Judea and Samaria, as part of what had been Eretz *Yisrael,* the Biblical term denoting the Promised Land. Within a few years, settlements were established among existing Arab towns, and the government was forced to accept them. Gush Emunim was supported by Defense Minister Shimon Peres, who saw another opportunity to embarrass his personal rival, Prime Minister Yitzhak Rabin. The result was that the number of new settlements increased by half in the two years from mid-1975, and, by 1977, approximately eighty-five settlements had been established in the occupied territories.

The Labor party also sought cooperation with elected Arab local officials. Municipal elections were held in April 1976, but these did not have the results the Israeli government expected. Many of the candidates put forward by the West Bank towns were either pro-PLO or more radical in their opposition to Israeli rule than the government could tolerate, and within a few years most of the mayors had been deported or forced to step down. As the 1977 Israeli elections approached, economic malaise, political problems (including a scandal involving an illegal U.S. bank account held by Mrs. Rabin), and diplomatic isolation caused Israelis to lose confidence in the Labor party, which had ruled the country ever since its creation. In addition to the changing demographics of Israel, the Labor party had also lost support because of its failure to avert the 1973 war.

The victory of Menachem Begin and his right-wing Likud coalition in the Israeli national elections of May 1977 marked a turning point in the history of Israel and the Arab-Israeli conflict. It brought to an end the dominance the Labor party had exercised in setting the national agenda since Israel's foundation. Sephardic Jews, for example, overwhelmingly supported Begin because they were disenchanted by the previous Socialist governments. Ideologically, Begin's election represented a victory for Revisionist Zionism which had always envisaged a Jewish state encompassing both sides of the Jordan River. Begin and his supporters had no intention of relinquishing the West Bank—which they termed "Judea and Samaria"—East Jerusalem or the Gaza Strip that Israel had acquired in 1967. Ultra-nationalists and the ultra-religious agreed with Begin's policy of retaining the territories. Many Begin supporters opposed trading

Deir el-Balah camp, Gaza Strip (*Photo courtesy of UNRWA*).

Khan Younis camp, Gaza Strip (*Photo courtesy of UNRWA*).

"land for peace" because, believing they knew the Arab mentality, they did not trust the Palestinians. These attitudes gave new ideological impetus to the settlement movement. Menachem Begin approved twenty-one more settlements between 1980 and 1981. This brought the number of Jewish settlers in the occupied territories to about 110,000. Jews controlled more than one-third of the land and 90 percent of the water in the region.

JIMMY CARTER AND THE CAMP DAVID ACCORDS

The changes in administration that took place in 1977 in both the United States (Jimmy Carter became President in January) and Israel produced spectacular results. Menachem Begin, given his strong views and many hawkish statements about the inviolability of the territories occupied since 1967, seemed the most unlikely person to agree to any surrender of territory. Nevertheless, he was willing to make a deal for Sinai in exchange for a free hand in the West Bank. He was correct in thinking that Sadat was so determined to regain Egyptian sovereignty over all the Sinai Peninsula that he would agree to overlook the demands of the PLO for an independent Palestine on the West Bank of the Jordan River. Nevertheless, if the Egyptian leader were to sign an agreement, it would have to satisfy (or at least be capable of interpretation that it did) some of the aspirations of the Palestinian Arabs.

Jimmy Carter came to the presidency with strong Fundamentalist Christian convictions and considerable idealism. He sought a comprehensive settlement, and believed that if everyone could sit down around a negotiating table this could be reached. Carter had great faith in his mediating abilities. During 1977, Carter and Sadat sent many signals that they believed that negotiations toward normalization of relations between Egypt and Israel could be fruitful. The chronology of events during the year can be summarized as follows. In March 1977, Carter, at a town meeting in Clinton, Massachusetts, endorsed the idea of a "Palestinian homeland." In April, during a visit to Washington, D.C., Sadat indicated to Carter that he believed relations with Israel could be "normalized." In May, Carter once again called for a Palestinian homeland (probably contributing to Menachem Begin's victory in the Israeli elections!). This proposal was met with such opposition from Israel and the American Jewish community that Carter reconsidered his position. On July 12, he said that the Palestinian "entity" should be tied in with Jordan, and not be "independent." Undeterred, Sadat, speaking to members of Congress on July 13, expressed his willingness to work toward normalization of relations with Israel, and, in a Cairo radio broadcast three days later, stated he would accept Israel as a Middle East nation following the signing of a peace treaty. In late July, Carter criticized Israel's legalization of three formerly unapproved settlements in heavily populated areas of the West Bank, and he stated that the "major stumbling block" to reconvening the Geneva talks was the issue of the participation of "the Palestinian representative." Encouraged by Sadat's statements two weeks earlier and hoping to set something in motion, on July 31 Carter sent Secretary of State Cyrus Vance to the Middle East to find a way to proceed with diplomacy either at Geneva or some other way. Israel is said to have secretly warned Sadat of an assassination plot by Libya against him in July, and that may have been a possible contributing factor to his peace initiative. In any event, in September he bypassed the United States and initiated secret high-level talks between Egyptian and Israeli officials in Morocco to reach informal agreement with Israel before the reconvening of the Geneva Peace Conference.

Surprisingly, Carter then adopted a Soviet suggestion that the United States and the Soviets jointly reconvene the Geneva Peace Conference. On October 1, the United States and the Soviet Union issued a joint statement calling for a comprehensive settlement of the Arab–Israeli dispute, including an eventual Israeli military withdrawal from the 1967 occupied territories and the guarantee of the "legitimate rights of the Palestinian people." The following day, Israel rejected the American–Soviet statement as "unacceptable," but continued discussions with the American administration to reconvene the Geneva Peace Conference without PLO participation. Sadat, who had expelled thousands of Russian advisors in Egypt in 1972 and had been trying to remove all Russian pressure and influence in his country, was aghast. Nevertheless, he requested that the PLO be specifically included in any Geneva peace talks. Israel opposed this suggestion.

Anwar Sadat then took matters into his own hands. In an address to the Egyptian National Assembly he declared he was ready to go to the Israeli Parliament itself to discuss peace. The surprised Begin could do little but agree, and he extended to Sadat (and to any other Arab leader who so wished) an invitation to come to Israel. Sadat, in an extraordinary move, accepted and arrived in Israel on November 19, 1977. In his speech to the Knesset (the Israeli Parliament), Sadat told his audience: "I declare to the whole world that we accept to live with you in permanent peace based on justice." In his speech, however, Sadat, no doubt hoping (unrealistically) to placate other Arab heads of state, made a series of demands he knew the Israelis would not meet: Israeli withdrawal from all territories occupied in 1967, and Israeli recognition of the right of the Palestinians to self-determination. Although little came of the private talks between Sadat and Begin, the visit did, as Sadat hoped it would, break down some of the psychological barriers between Israel and Egypt that stood in the way of reaching a settlement. Begin agreed to meet with Sadat in December at Ismailia, Egypt, and there he rejected the idea of a Palestinian state in the West Bank and Gaza. Begin said he would agree only to limited home rule for the Palestinians. He later spelled out that what he meant by that was "administrative autonomy"—in the form of elected municipalities, with the Israeli army maintaining law and order. Begin vowed he would have nothing to do with the PLO. Begin and Sadat were a long way from agreement.

Sadat's initiative had, at first, seemed to bypass both the United States and the Soviet Union, but President Jimmy Carter quickly climbed on the bandwagon and determined to seize the reins. On January 4, 1978, he unveiled an American plan for joint Arab–Israeli administration of the occupied West Bank and Gaza. (See Document 8–6.) Egypt and Israel, meanwhile, had formed two committees—one political and one military—to discuss the terms of a peace treaty, but in mid-January, Sadat recalled members of the Egyptian political committee who were meeting with the Israelis in Jerusalem, blaming the Israelis for the deadlock. Carter urged him to continue the talks. Sadat responded by visiting Washington in February 1978 with a list of arms he needed before he would sign any agreement with Israel. Plans were submitted and rejected by both sides, and talks dragged on fruitlessly for the next seven months.

In March, Carter and Begin failed to reach agreement on the major points blocking progress in the peace negotiations after two days of meetings in Washington, and Israeli Defense Minister Ezer Weizman went to Cairo to talk directly with Sadat to try to revive the faltering talks. On July 5, Egypt formally announced a plan for peace in which Israel would withdraw from the occupied territories over a five-year period, and the Arabs of the West Bank and Gaza would be able to determine their own future. As Begin had told Carter earlier, on March 4, that his government did not interpret UN Resolution 242 to mean that Israel was specifically obliged to withdraw from the West Bank and Gaza, it was not surprising that four days after the Egyptians announced their proposal, on July 9, the Israeli Cabinet rejected the plan, which called for Israel to relinquish the occupied territories.

Finally, in August 1978 Carter requested that Begin and Sadat meet with him at the presidential retreat in Maryland, Camp David. Several meetings took place; Carter called this "one of the most frustrating experiences of my life," but eventually two accords were agreed upon on September 17, 1978. Begin agreed only after Carter threatened to cut off all aid to Israel, and then promised to increase it.

The Camp David accords consisted of two agreements. The first, a "Framework for Peace in the Middle East," called for negotiations among Egypt, Jordan, Israel, and "representatives of the Palestinian people" to settle the question of the West Bank and the Gaza Strip. A self-governing Arab authority would be set up to replace the Israeli military forces for five years while negotiations were taking place on the "final status

Sadat and Begin meet with Carter at presidential retreat, Camp David (*Photo courtesy of Britain/Israel Public Affairs Centre*).

of the West Bank and Gaza." The second accord, "Framework for the Conclusion of a Peace Treaty Between Egypt and Israel," was a draft proposal for a peace agreement to be negotiated and signed within three months. This provided for a phased Israeli withdrawal from the Sinai over three years, and a full restoration of the area to Egypt. Israeli ships were to be allowed free passage through the Suez Canal. The United Nations would oversee provisions of the accords so as to satisfy both sides. The thorny question of Jerusalem was simply ignored in the Camp David accords, as was the future of the Golan Heights. (See Documents 8–7 and 8–8.)

In reaching these accords both parties made several concessions. Begin agreed to remove all the Israeli settlements from the Sinai as well as to turn over to Egypt the oil fields and Israeli air bases (to be used for civilian purposes). Sadat agreed, in essence, to a separate peace with Israel, without regard for the other Arab states or the Palestinians. Begin, nevertheless, continued to clarify his view that the Israeli position on the final status of the territories was autonomy for the people, not for the land; that is, that the end result could never be an independent Palestinian state. Begin was willing to compromise to achieve peace with Egypt because in his mind the Sinai had always been negotiable. The ideological and national reasons for retaining the West Bank and Gaza did not apply to the Sinai. Begin was also conscious of the growing belief in Israel that the occupied territories, rather than creating secure and defensible borders, were doing the reverse.

The fact that Israel's occupation of the Sinai had enabled Sadat to launch his surprise attack added force to this argument. Prior to 1967, Egypt could not change from a defensive to offensive posture without mobilizing its tanks and moving them across the desert, thereby alerting the Israelis. Israel also gained freedom from Egyptian attack for three years, and neither Jordan nor Syria would go to war without Egypt. Egypt promised "normal commercial sales" of oil to Israel, a promise backed by American guarantees.

Sadat was prepared to come to terms with Israel in 1978–1979 because of his "Egypt first" policy. He wanted to free up resources that had been devoted to waging war in order to reconstruct and widen the Suez Canal, and to free Egypt from the Soviet orbit. Sadat had conceived the 1973 war as a political as well as military operation; he had hoped to provoke superpower intervention to force Israel to give up the Sinai. This had been achieved not only by the military operation against Israel but also by the pressure of OPEC's oil embargo. As a result, Sadat and Kissinger were able to set American–Egyptian relations on a more stable basis. We should remember, also, that Sadat and Kissinger both hoped that Jordan would be drawn into entering peace negotiations with Israel.

Both sides, but especially the Israelis, were fully aware of the importance of future relations with the United States. It was concern for this relationship perhaps more than any other factor that led Begin reluctantly to agree to the concessions to produce the peace settlements. Both sides received massive American economic and military aid as part of separate agreements accompanying the Camp David accords. Israel was to receive $3 billion in military and financial assistance, approximately $800 million of which was to assist the relocation of Israel's two Sinai air bases to the Negev. Egypt was to receive $2 billion in tanks, planes, and antiaircraft weapons. All this was in addition to the existing 1979 foreign aid allocation for the two countries of $1 billion to Egypt and $1.8 billion to Israel.

Predictably, the PLO rejected the accords since they did not specifically call for a fully independent Palestinian state. Even more of a disappointment for Carter was the fact that Jordan and Saudi Arabia, considered Arab moderates and "friends" of the

United States, rejected the Camp David agreements. The more radical Arab states like Syria and Iraq, which immediately emerged as leaders of the "rejectionist front," denounced not only the agreements but also Sadat for what they saw as his treason to the Arab cause.

There was little likelihood, even at the time, that the Camp David peace accords signed between Egypt and Israel would lead to a comprehensive Middle East peace settlement. Even negotiating the peace treaty between Egypt and Israel proved difficult. Disagreements broke out almost immediately among Carter, Begin, and Sadat as to exactly what had been agreed upon at Camp David. Begin was determined to go ahead with new settlements on the West Bank and Gaza, and he claimed that the accords permitted him to do so after a three-month moratorium. Carter said that Begin had agreed that no new settlements would be established during the five-year transition period. For his part, Sadat claimed that the treaty was linked to the issue of the occupied territories, and he stated that a peace treaty between Egypt and Israel could be signed only after a timetable for Palestinian self-rule had been finalized. And throughout the period, from the signing of the accords until the signing of the peace treaty, both Sadat and Begin were under intense domestic political pressure not to make concessions. This led to last-minute difficulties over such issues as the terms of Egyptian oil sales to Israel and the drawing up of a detailed timetable for Israeli withdrawal from the Sinai. It was not until Carter himself visited Cairo and Jerusalem, in early March 1979, that the Israeli and Egyptian cabinets approved the compromise peace treaty put forward by President Carter. The formal signing of the treaty took place at the White House on March 26, 1979.

For the Camp David accords and the Egyptian–Israeli peace treaty to have led to a further and more comprehensive peace settlement in the Middle East, as we noted above, there would have to have been general agreement among the Arab states on the two "Frameworks" cited earlier, and Israeli goodwill concerning the West Bank and Gaza. It is difficult to see how the other major Arab states could have supported the Egyptian–Israeli accords. In the first place, the accords did not mention Jerusalem. The king of Saudi Arabia—a country in which Islam pervades social customs, dominates the political structure, and legitimizes the regime—could not have endorsed an agreement that did not even mention the third holiest city of Islam after Mecca and Medina, namely Jerusalem, a city that houses the Dome of the Rock from which the Koran says Muhammad ascended into heaven. It was also unlikely that Saddam Hussein of Iraq, who claimed to be the champion of Arab nationalism, would have been party to accords that omitted any reference to the recovery of all of Palestine. Syria would certainly not agree to any negotiations that omitted an indication that Israel was willing to withdraw from the Golan heights.

Similarly, King Hussein of Jordan, with his Palestinian subjects, could not have signed an accord that was unacceptable to the majority of his people and his three powerful neighbors. These Arab leaders did not agree to the Camp David accords, therefore, since to have done so would have endangered their own political survival owing to the ideological and spiritual importance of the issues to their people. They felt threatened by internal instability and external threats. Arab leaders do not rely for their legitimacy and continued role on established political institutions such as parties and parliaments to the extent that Western leaders do. They are much more dependent upon popular support and success in carrying out what is perceived as the popular will. Sadat, as we noted above, was free from these constraints to some extent, and, furthermore, Egypt gained specific benefits. He also demonstrated that a single Arab state could act independently of the rest of the Arab "nations"; Pan-Arabism was no longer—if indeed it ever had been—a straightjacket determining Egyptian policy.

Nevertheless, the reaction of the Arab states to the signing of the peace treaty was far more harsh and swift than anticipated by Egypt or by the United States. Nineteen members of the Arab League immediately met in Baghdad, Iraq, and, on March 31, 1979, issued a communiqué outlining political and economic sanctions against Egypt. (See Document 8–9.) By early May, all the Arab countries except Oman and Sudan, close allies of Sadat, had severed diplomatic relations with Egypt. In addition, Egypt was suspended from the twenty-two-member Arab League, expelled from the Islamic Conference, and ousted from a number of Arab financial and economic institutions such as the Federation of Arab Banks and the Organization of Arab Petroleum Exporting Countries (OAPEC).

Some have argued that the Camp David accords hindered the achievement of a comprehensive peace settlement, that the accords radicalized Arab opinion; it was seen by the Arabs as a separate peace "designed to neutralize Egypt from the anti-Zionist struggle." The Arabs saw this as a way of preventing joint Arab action to dislodge Israel from Arab territory, and as weakening the legitimate right of the Palestinians for a national home. Overall, the Camp David agreements increased Arab suspicion of Israel and the United States, and the Arabs refused to be drawn into the process. This hostility, in turn, hardened Israeli attitudes toward the Arabs.

The real achievements of the Camp David accords should not be diminished, however. Millions in Israel, Egypt, and throughout the world were thrilled at the sight of Anwar Sadat, the President of Egypt, stepping from his plane at Ben-Gurion Airport, Israel, to a flourish of trumpets. And millions later watched with gratitude and expectation as the television cameras recorded Sadat and Begin, witnessed by Jimmy Carter, signing a peace treaty on the White House Lawn on March 26, 1979. In the words of Abba Eban, Israel's Foreign Minister from 1966 to 1974, Sadat's main achievement "was to separate our future from our past." In an article published in *Foreign Affairs* in 1979, which strongly defended the Camp David negotiations, Eban, who was then one of the leaders of the opposition Labor party in the Knesset, made the telling point that the past is the enemy of the future in the Middle East. He pointed out that nothing in Arab history prepared the Arabs for a Jewish state in the Middle East. Throughout Arab history, Jews have always appeared as subjects, merchants and craftsmen, scholars and doctors, members of a deviant religion, but never as an autonomous political and territorial entity in their own right. He added that Arab difficulties in coming to terms with Israel, in addition to their immediate grievances, should not be taken lightly.

The history of Israel was also one that made conciliation a difficult course to follow. Because they view so much of their history as self-defense, Israelis tend to overreact to any perceived threat to their security. Just as Israelis should appreciate Arab behavior, Arabs should perhaps understand Israel's reaction. The Camp David agreements simultaneously lessened Arab rejectionism and Israeli suspicion. In this context, the accords could be viewed as a major step forward, and, however viewed, must be regarded as a vast improvement on the methods of violence and terror so often employed by both sides.

The future of the West Bank, Gaza, the Golan Heights, and East Jerusalem remained the major unresolved issues of the Camp David accords. Some 800,000 Arabs inhabited the West Bank and 500,000 more were in Gaza, and they did not regard themselves as part of Israel in any way. (See Document 8–10.) There was a complete separation of language, religion, and culture between the Arabs of the West Bank and the Jews of Israel. Neither of these two worlds sought harmony with the other. Although religious and nationalistic Jews described the region as Judea and Samaria, the inhabitants were Arab in all their loyalties. Israeli "doves" argue that although Israel may be smaller in size if the West Bank and Gaza are returned to Arab sovereignty, a major reason for the Arab world's military, economic, and psychological hostility to Israel would be destroyed, thereby creating a much more secure Israel. Israel would then be freer of the oppressive burdens of its military priorities and diplomatic problems and, if peace resulted, would be able to trade and invest in Arab markets to great economic advantage. Of course the ultimate fate of the West Bank and Gaza is in large part in the hands of the Palestinians themselves, both within and outside the territories. We deal with the post–Camp David period in the next chapter and set out some of the options for the future.

SUGGESTIONS FOR FURTHER READING

CARTER, JIMMY, *Keeping Faith,* New York, Bantam, 1982.

DAYAN, MOSHE, *Breakthrough: A Personal Account of the Egypt-Israel Peace Negotiations,* New York, Alfred A. Knopf, 1981.

QUANDT, WILLIAM, *Camp David: Peacemaking and Politics,* Washington, D.C., Brookings Institution, 1986.

SADAT, ANWAR, *In Search of Identity: An Autobiography,* New York, Harper & Row, 1978.

SACHAR, HOWARD M., *A History of Israel, Vol. II, From the Aftermath of the Yom Kippur War,* New York, Oxford University Press, 1987.

SHOUKRI, GHALI, *Egypt: Portrait of a President. Sadat's Road to Jerusalem,* London, Zed, 1981.

WEIZMAN, EZER, *The Battle for Peace,* New York, Bantam, 1981.

DOCUMENT 8–1

Memorandum of Agreement Between the Governments of Israel and the United States, September 1975

The Geneva Peace Conference

    1.   The Geneva Peace Conference will be reconvened at a time coordinated between the United States and Israel.

    2.   The United States will continue to adhere to its present policy with respect to the Palestine Liberation Organization, whereby it will not recognize or negotiate with the Palestine Liberation Organization so long as the Palestine Liberation Organization does not recognize Israel's right to exist and does not accept Security Council Resolutions 242 and 338. The United States Government will consult fully and seek to concert its position and strategy at the Geneva Peace Conference on this issue with the Government of Israel. Similarly, the United States will consult fully and seek to concert its position and strategy with Israel with regard to the participation of any other additional states. It is understood that the participation at a subsequent phase of the Conference of any possible additional state, group or organization will require the agreement of all the initial participants.

3.   The United States will make every effort to ensure at the Conference that all the substantive negotiations will be on a bilateral basis.

4.   The United States will oppose and, if necessary, vote against any initiative in the Security Council to alter adversely the terms of reference of the Geneva Peace Conference or to change Resolutions 242 and 338 in ways which are incompatible with their original purpose.

5.   The United States will seek to ensure that the role of the co-sponsors will be consistent with what was agreed in the Memorandum of Understanding between the United States Government and the Government of Israel of December 20, 1973.

6.   The United States and Israel will concert action to assure that the Conference will be conducted in a manner consonant with the objectives of this document and with the declared purpose of the Conference, namely the advancement of a negotiated peace between Israel and each one of its neighbors.

Henry A. Kissinger	Yigal Allon
Secretary of State	Deputy Prime Minister &
for the Government of	Minister of Foreign Affairs
the United States	For the Government of Israel

Source: Yehuda Lukacs, ed., Documents on the Israeli-Palestinian Conflict, 1967–1983 (Cambridge: Cambridge University Press, 1984), pp. 23–24.

DOCUMENT 8–2

Resolution of the Rabat Arab summit, 28 October 1974

The Conference of the Arab Heads of State:

1 *Affirms* the right of the Palestinian people to return to their homeland and to self-determination.

2 *Affirms* the right of the Palestinian people to establish an independent national authority, under the leadership of the PLO in its capacity as the sole legitimate representative of the Palestine people, over all liberated territory. The Arab States are pledged to uphold this authority, when it is established, in all spheres and at all levels.

3 *Supports* the PLO in the exercise of its national and international responsibilities, within the context of the principle of Arab solidarity.

4 *Invites* the Kingdom of Jordan, Syria and Egypt to formalize their relations in the light of these decisions and in order that they may be implemented.

5 *Affirms* the obligations of all Arab States to preserve Palestinian unity and not to interfere in Palestinian internal affairs.

Europa Yearbook of the Middle East and North Africa

Source: T. G. Fraser, *The Middle East, 1914–1979* (New York: St. Martin's Press, 1980), p. 136.

DOCUMENT 8–3

General Assembly Resolution 3236(XXIX), 22 November 1974

The General Assembly
Having considered the question of Palestine,

Having heard the statement of the Palestine Liberation Organization, the representative of the Palestinian people,

Having also heard other statements made during the debate,

Deeply concerned that no just solution to the problem of Palestine has yet been achieved and recognizing that the problem of Palestine continues to endanger international peace and security,

Recognizing that the Palestinian people is entitled to self-determination in accordance with the Charter of the United Nations,

Expressing its grave concern that the Palestinian people has been prevented from enjoying its inalienable rights, in particular its right to self-determination,

Guided by the purposes and principles of the Charter,

Recalling its relevant resolutions which affirm the right of the Palestinian people to self-determination,

1   *Reaffirms* the inalienable rights of the Palestinian people in Palestine, including:

(a) The right of self-determination without external interference;

(b) The right to national independence and sovereignty;

2   *Reaffirms also* the inalienable right of the Palestinians to return to their homes and property from which they have been displaced and uprooted, and calls for their return;

3   *Emphasizes* that full respect for and the realization of these inalienable rights of the Palestinian people are indispensable for the solution of the question of Palestine;

4   *Recognizes* that the Palestinian people is a principal party in the establishment of a just and durable peace in the Middle East;

5   *Further recognizes* the right of the Palestinian people to regain its rights by all means in accordance with the purposes and principles of the Charter of the United Nations;

6   *Appeals* to all States and international organizations to extend their support to the Palestinian people in its struggle to restore its rights, in accordance with the Charter;

7   *Requests* the Secretary-General to establish contacts with the Palestine Liberation Organization on all matters concerning with question of Palestine;

8   *Requests* the Secretary-General to report to the General Assembly at its thirtieth session on the implementation of the present resolution;

9   *Decides* to include the item 'Question of Palestine' in the provisional agenda of its thirtieth session.

UNO, doc. BR/74/55(1974)

Source: Fraser, *The Middle East*, pp. 143–144.

DOCUMENT 8–4

Speech by Yasser Arafat, Palestine Liberation Organization, to the General Assembly, 13 November 1974

As a result of the collusion between the mandatory Power and the Zionist movement and with the support of some countries, this General Assembly early in its history approved a recommendation to partition our Palestinian homeland. This took place in an atmosphere poisoned with questionable actions and strong pressure. The General Assembly partitioned what it had no right to divide—an indivisible homeland. When we rejected that decision, our position corresponded to that of the natural mother who refused to permit King Solomon to cut her son in two when the unnatural mother claimed the child for herself and agreed to his dismemberment. Furthermore, even though the partition resolution granted the colonialist settlers 54 per cent of the land of Palestine, their dissatisfaction with the decision prompted them to wage a war of terror against the civilian Arab population. They occupied 81 per cent of the total area of Palestine, uprooting a million Arabs. Thus, they occupied 524 Arab towns and villages, of which they destroyed 385, completely obliterating them in the process. Having done so, they built their own settlements and colonies on the ruins of our farms and our groves. The roots of the Palestine question lie here. Its causes do not stem from any conflict between two religions or two nationalisms. Neither is it a border conflict between neighbouring states. It is the cause of people deprived of its homeland, dispersed and uprooted, and living mostly in exile and in refugee camps. . . .

It pains our people greatly to witness the propagation of the myth that its homeland was a desert until it was made to bloom by the toil of foreign settlers, that it was a land without a people, and that the colonialist entity caused no harm to any human being. No: such lies must be exposed from this rostrum, for the world must know that Palestine was the cradle of the most ancient cultures and civilizations. Its Arab people were engaged in farming and building, spreading culture throughout the land for thousands of years, setting an example in the practice of freedom of worship, acting as faithful guardians of the holy places of all religions. As a son of Jerusalem, I treasure for myself and my people beautiful memories and vivid images of the religious brotherhood that was the hallmark of our Holy City before it succumbed (to) catastrophe. Our people continued to pursue this enlightened policy until the establishment of the State of Israel and their dispersion. This did not deter our people from pursuing their humanitarian role on Palestinian soil. Nor will they permit their land to become a launching pad for aggression or a racist camp predicated on the destruction of civilization, cultures, progress and peace. Our people cannot but maintain the heritage of their ancestors in resisting the invaders, in assuming the privileged task of defending their native land, their Arab nationhood, their culture and civilization, and in safeguarding the cradle of monotheistic religion.

The Palestinian people produced thousands of physicians, lawyers, teachers and scientists who actively participated in the development of the Arab countries bordering on their usurped homeland. They utilized their income to assist the young and aged amongst their people who remained in the refugee camps. They educated their younger sisters and brothers, supported their parents and cared for their children. All along, the Palestinian dreamt of return. Neither the Palestinian's allegiance to Palestine nor his determination to return waned; nothing could persuade him to relinquish his Palestinian identity or to foresake his homeland. The passage of time did not make him forget, as some hoped he would. When our people lost faith in the international community which persisted in ignoring its rights and when it became obvious that the Palestinians would not recuperate one inch of Palestine through exclusively political means, our people had no choice but to resort to armed struggle. Into that struggle it poured its material and human resources. We bravely faced the most vicious acts of Israeli terrorism which were aimed at diverting our struggle and arresting it.

In the past ten years of our struggle, thousands of martyrs and twice as many wounded, maimed and imprisoned were offered in sacrifice, all in an effort to resist the imminent threat of liquidation, to regain our right to self-determination and our undisputed right to return to our homeland. With the utmost dignity and the most admirable revolutionary spirit, our Palestinian people has not lost its spirit in Israeli prisons and concentration camps or when faced with all forms of harassment and intimidation. It struggles for sheer existence and it continues to strive to preserve the Arab character of its land. Thus it resists oppression, tyranny and terrorism in their ugliest forms. . . .

The Palestine Liberation Organization has earned its legitimacy because of the sacrifice inherent in its pioneering role, and also because of its dedicated leadership of the struggle. It has also been granted this legitimacy of the Palestinian masses, which in harmony with it have chosen it to lead the struggle according to its directives. The Palestine Liberation Organization has also gained its legitimacy by representing every faction, union or group as well as every Palestinian talent, either in the National Council or in people's institutions. This legitimacy was further strengthened by the support of the entire Arab nation, and it was consecrated during the last Arab Summit Conference, which reiterated the right of the

Palestine Liberation Organization, in its capacity as the sole representative of the Palestinian people, to establish an independent national State on all liberated Palestinian territory. . . .

In my formal capacity as Chairman of the Palestine Liberation Organization and leader of the Palestinian revolution I proclaim before you that when we speak of our common hopes for the Palestine of tomorrow we include in our perspective all Jews now living in Palestine who choose to live with us there in peace and without discrimination.

In my formal capacity as Chairman of the Palestine Liberation Organization and leader of the Palestinian revolution I call upon Jews to turn away one by one from the illusory promises made to them by Zionist ideology and Israeli leadership. They are offering Jews perpetual bloodshed, endless war and continuous thraldom.

We invite them to emerge from their moral isolation into a more open realm of free choice, far from their present leadership's efforts to implant in them a Masada complex.

We offer them the most generous solution, that we might live together in a framework of just peace in our democratic Palestine.

In my formal capacity as Chairman of the Palestine Liberation Organization, I announce here that we do not wish one drop of either Arab or Jewish (sic) to be shed; neither do we delight in the continuation of killing, which would end once a just peace, based on our people's rights, hopes and aspirations had been finally established.

In my formal capacity as Chairman of the Palestine Liberation Organization and leader of the Palestinian revolution I appeal to you to accompany our people in its struggle to attain its right to self-determination. This right is consecrated in the United Nations Charter and has been repeatedly confirmed in resolutions adopted by this august body since the drafting of the Charter. I appeal to you, further, to aid our people's return to its homeland from an involuntary exile imposed upon it by force of arms, by tyranny, by oppression, so that we may regain our property, our land, and thereafter live in our national homeland, free and sovereign, enjoying all the privileges of nationhood. Only then can we pour all our resources into the mainstream of human civilization. Only then can Palestinian creativity be concentrated on the service of humanity. Only then will our Jerusalem resume its historic role as a peaceful shrine for all religions.

I appeal to you to enable our people to establish national independent sovereignty over its own land.

Today I have come bearing an olive branch and a freedom-fighter's gun. Do not let the olive branch fall from my hand. I repeat: do not let the olive branch fall from my hand.

War flares up in Palestine, and yet it is in Palestine that peace will be born.

> UNO, GAOR, 29th Session, Two
> Thousand Two Hundred and Eighty-
> Second Meeting, A/PV. 2282/Corr. 1

Source: Fraser, *The Middle East,* pp. 136—140.

DOCUMENT 8–5

Speech by Yosef Tekoah, Israel, to the General Assembly, 13 November 1974

On 14 October 1974 the General Assembly turned its back on the UN Charter, on law and humanity, and virtually capitulated to a murder organization which aims at the destruction of a State Member of the UN. On 14 October the UN hung out a sign reading 'Murderers of children are welcome here.'

Today these murderers have come to the General Assembly, certain that it would do their bidding. Today this rostrum was defiled by their chieftain, who proclaimed that the shedding of Jewish blood would end only when the murderers' demands had been accepted and their objectives achieved.

On 14 October the UN and Governments which made the invitation to the Palestine Liberation Organization (PLO) possible became the object of worldwide criticism. Editorials and caricatures in the press and demonstrations on all continents expressed revulsion at the spectacle of the UN tearing asunder its own principles and precepts and paying homage to bloodshed and bestiality.

Today bloodshed and bestiality have come here to collect the spoils of the UN surrender. This surrender must be absolute they told the world this morning. The victim of bloodshed and bestiality should not even defend himself.

The United Nations is entrusted with the responsibility to guide mankind away from war, away from violence and oppression, toward peace, toward international understanding and the vindication of the rights of peoples and individuals. What remains of that responsibility now that the UN has prostrated itself before the PLO, which stands for premeditated, deliberate murder of innocent civilians, denies to the Jewish people its right to live, and seeks to destroy the Jewish State by armed force? . . .

Are the Arabs of Palestine suffering starvation as are, according to UN statistics, almost 500 million people in Asia, Africa and Latin America? Has the UN left the Palestinian refugees without assistance as it has tens of millions of refugees all over the world, including Jewish refugees in Israel from Arab lands? Are the Palestinian refugees the only ones who cannot be reintegrated as others have been? Have the Palestinian Arabs no State of their own? What is Jordan if not a Palestinian Arab State?

The real reason for the special consideration accorded to questions concerning the Arabs of Palestine has been one and one only—the continuous exploitation of these questions as a weapon of Arab belligerency against Israel. As King Hussein said of the Arab leaders: 'They have used the Palestine people for selfish political purposes.' This is also the real motivation of the present debate,

In fact, no nation has enjoyed greater fulfilment of its political rights, no nation has been endowed with territory, sovereignty and independence more abundantly than the Arabs. . . .

Now, as a result of centuries of acquisition of territory by war, the Arab nation is represented in the UN by twenty sovereign States. Among them is also the Palestinian Arab State of Jordan.

Geographically and ethnically Jordan is Palestine. Historically both the West and East Banks of the Jordan river are parts of the Land of Israel or Palestine. Both were parts of Palestine under the British Mandate until Jordan and then Israel became independent. The population of Jordan is composed of two elements—the sedentary population and nomads. Both are, of course, Palestinian. The nomad Bedouins constitute a minority of Jordan's population. Moreover, the majority of the sedentary inhabitants, even on the East Bank, are of Palestinian West Bank origin. Without the Palestinians, Jordan is a State without a people.

That is why when on 29 April 1950 King Abdullah inaugurated the commemorative session of the Jordanian Parliament he declared: 'I open the session of the Parliament with both banks of the Jordan united by the will of the people, one homeland and one hope.'

On 23 August 1959, the Prime Minister of Jordan stated: 'We are the Government of Palestine, the army of Palestine and the refugees of Palestine.'

Indeed, the vast majority of Palestinian refugees never left Palestine, but moved, as a result of the 1948 and 1967 wars, from one part of the country to another. At the same time, an approximately equal number of Jewish refugees fled from Arab countries to Israel.

It is, therefore, false to allege that the Palestinian people has been deprived of a State of its own or that it has been uprooted from its national homeland. Most Palestinians continue to live in Palestine. Most Palestinians continue to live in a Palestinian State. The vast majority of Palestinian Arabs are citizens of that Palestinian State.

The choice before the General Assembly is clear. On the one hand there is the Charter of the UN; on the other there is the PLO, whose sinister objectives, defined in its Covenant, and savage outrages are a desecration of the Charter.

On the one hand, there is Israel's readiness and desire to reach a peaceful settlement with the Palestinian Arab State of Jordan in which the Palestinian national identity would find full expression. On the other hand there is the PLO's denial of Israel's right to independence and of the Jewish people's right to self-determination.

The choice is between understanding and continued conflict in the Middle East, between suppression of terror and its encouragement, between satisfying the needs of the Palestinians through the peacemaking process already under way or undermining that process by trying to introduce into it a murder organization which aims at the elimination of one of the negotiating states.

The question is: should there be peace between Israel and its eastern neighbour or should an attempt be made to establish a Palestine Liberation Organization base to the east of Israel from which the terrorist campaign against the Jewish State's existence could be pursued?

On 14 October the General Assembly opted for the PLO, it opted for terrorism, it opted for savagery. Can there be any hope that it might now undo the harm it has already done, by that action, to the cause of peace in the Middle East and to humanity in general? Israel has also made its choice.

The United Nations, whose duty it is to combat terrorism and barbarity may agree to consort with them. Israel will not.

The murderers of athletes in the Olympic Games of Munich, the butchers of children in Ma'alot, the assassins of diplomats in Khartoum do not belong in the international community. They have no place in international diplomatic efforts. Israel shall see to it that they have no place in them.

Israel will pursue the PLO murderers until justice is meted out to them. It will continue to take action against their organization and against their bases until a definitive end is put to their atrocities. The blood of Jewish children will not be shed with inpunity.

Israel will not permit the establishment of PLO authority in any part of Palestine. The PLO will not be forced on the Palestinian Arabs. It will not be tolerated by the Jews of Israel.

UNO, GAOR, 29th Session, Two
Thousand Two Hundred and Eighty-
Second Meeting, A/PV. 2282/Corr. 1

Source: Fraser, *The Middle East,* pp. 140–143.

DOCUMENT 8–6

President Carter, Statement on Recognition of Palestinians, Aswan, Egypt, 4 January, 1978

It is an honor and a pleasure for us to be in this great country, led by such a strong and courageous man.

Mr. President, your bold initiative in seeking peace has aroused the admiration of the entire world. One of my most valued possessions is the warm, personal relationship which binds me and President Sadat together and which exemplifies the friendship and the common purpose of the people of Egypt and the people of the United States of America.

The Egyptian-Israeli peace initiative must succeed, while still guarding the sacred and historic principles held by the nations who have suffered so much in this region. There is no good reason why accommodation cannot be reached.

In my own private discussions with both Arab and Israeli leaders, I have been deeply impressed by the unanimous desire for peace. My presence here today is a direct result of the courageous initiative which President Sadat undertook in his recent trip to Jerusalem.

The negotiating process will continue in the near future. We fully support this effort and we intend to play an active role in the work of the Political Committee of Cairo, which will soon reconvene in Jerusalem.

We believe that there are certain principles, fundamentally, which must be observed before a just and a comprehensive peace can be achieved.

* First, true peace must be based on normal relations among the parties to the peace. Peace means more than just an end to belligerency.

* Second, there must be withdrawal by Israel from territories occupied in 1967 and agreement on secure and recognized borders for all parties in the context of normal and peaceful relations in accordance with U.N. Resolutions 242 and 338.

* Third, there must be a resolution of the Palestinian problem in all its aspects. The problem must recognize the legitimate rights of the Palestinian people and enable the Palestinians to participate in the determination of their own future.

Source: Lukacs, *Documents*, pp. 34–35.

DOCUMENT 8–7

Framework for Peace in the Middle East Agreed at Camp David and Signed at the White House, Sept. 17, 1978.
[Excerpts]

Preamble.

The search for peace in the Middle East must be guided by the following:

The agreed basis for a peaceful settlement of the conflict between Israel and its neighbors is United Nations Security Council Resolution 242, in all its parts. . . .

To achieve a relationship of peace, in the spirit of Article 2 of the United Nations Charter, future negotiations between Israel and any neighbor prepared to negotiate peace and security with it, are necessary for the purpose of carrying out all the provisions and principles of Resolutions 242 and 338.

Peace requires respect for the sovereignty, territorial integrity and political independence of every state in the area and their right to live in peace within secure and recognized boundaries free from threats or acts of force. Progress toward that goal can accelerate movement toward a new era of reconciliation in the Middle East marked by cooperation in promoting economic development, in maintaining stability, and in assuring security.

Security is enhanced by a relationship of peace and by cooperation between nations which enjoy normal relations. In addition, under the terms of peace treaties, the parties can, on the basis of reciprocity, agree to special security arrangements such as demilitarized zones, limited armaments areas, early warning stations, the presence of international forces, liaison, agreed measures for monitoring, and other arrangements that they agree are useful.

Framework:

Taking these factors into account, the parties are determined to reach a just, comprehensive, and durable settlement of the Middle East conflict through the conclusion of peace treaties based on Security Council Resolutions 242 and 338 in all their parts. Their purpose is to achieve peace and good neighborly relations. They recognize that, for peace to endure, it must involve all those who have been most deeply affected by the conflict. They therefore agree that this framework is intended by them to constitute a basis for peace not only between

Egypt and Israel, but also between Israel and each of its other neighbors which is prepared to negotiate peace with Israel on this basis. With that objective in mind, they have agreed to proceed as follows:

A. West Bank and Gaza.

1. Egypt, Israel, Jordan and the representatives of the Palestinian people should participate in negotiations on the resolution of the Palestinian problem in all its aspects. To achieve that objective, negotiations relating to the West Bank and Gaza should proceed in three stages:

a) Egypt and Israel agree that, in order to ensure a peaceful and orderly transfer of authority, and taking into account the security concerns of all the parties, there should be transitional arrangements for the West Bank and Gaza for a period not exceeding five years. In order to provide full autonomy to the inhabitants, under these arrangements the Israeli Military Government and its civilian administration will be withdrawn as soon as a self-governing authority has been freely elected by the inhabitants of these areas to replace the existing military government. To negotiate the details of a transitional arrangement, the Government of Jordan will be invited to join the negotiations on the basis of this framework. These new arrangements should give due consideration both to the principle of self-government by the inhabitants of these territories and to the legitimate security concerns of the parties involved.

b) Egypt, Israel, and Jordan will agree on the modalities for establishing the elected self-governing authority in the West Bank and Gaza. The delegations of Egypt and Jordan may include Palestinians from the West Bank and Gaza or other Palestinians as mutually agreed. The parties will negotiate an agreement which will define the powers and responsibilities of the self-governing authority to be exercised in the West Bank and Gaza. A withdrawal of Israeli armed forces will take place and there will be a redeployment of the remaining Israeli forces into specified security locations. The agreement will also include arrangements for assuring internal and external security and public order. A strong local police force will be established, which may include Jordanian citizens. In addition, Israeli and Jordanian forces will participate in joint patrols and in the manning of control posts to assure the security of the borders.

c) When the self-governing authority (administrative council) in the West Bank and Gaza is established and inaugurated, the transitional period of five years will begin. As soon as possible, but not later than the third year after the beginning of the transitional period, negotiations will take place to determine the final status of the West Bank and Gaza and its relationship with its neighbors, and to conclude a peace treaty between Israel and Jordan by the end of the transitional period. These negotiations will be conducted among Egypt, Israel, Jordan, and the elected representatives of the inhabitants of the West Bank and Gaza. . . . The negotiations will resolve, among other matters, the location of the boundaries and the nature of the security arrangements. The solution from the negotiations must also recognize the legitimate rights of the Palestinian people and their just requirements. In this way, the Palestinians will participate in the determinations of their own future through:

1) The negotiations among Egypt, Israel, Jordan and the representatives of the inhabitants of the West Bank and Gaza to agree on the final status of the West Bank and Gaza and other outstanding issues by the end of the transitional period.

2) Submitting their agreement to a vote by the elected representatives of the inhabitants of the West Bank and Gaza.

3) Providing for the elected representatives of the inhabitants of the West Bank and Gaza to decide how they shall govern themselves consistent with the provisions of their agreement.

4) Participating as stated above in the work of the committee negotiating the peace treaty between Israel and Jordan. . . .

4. Egypt and Israel will work with each other and with other interested parties to establish agreed procedures for a prompt, just and permanent implementation of the resolution of the refugee problem.

B. Egypt–Israel.

1. Egypt and Israel undertake not to resort to the threat or the use of force to settle disputes. Any disputes shall be settled by peaceful means in accordance with the provisions of Article 33 of the charter of the United Nations.

2. In order to achieve peace between them, the parties agree to negotiate in good faith with a goal of concluding within three months from the signing of this framework a peace treaty between them, while inviting the other parties to the conflict to proceed simultaneously to negotiate and conclude similar peace treaties with a view to achieving a comprehensive peace in the area. The framework for the conclusion of a peace treaty between Egypt and Israel will govern the peace negotiations between them. The parties will agree on the modalities and the timetable for the implementation of their obligations under the treaty.

C. Associated Principles.

1. Egypt and Israel state that the principles and provisions described below should apply to peace treaties between Israel and each of its neighbors—Egypt, Jordan, Syria and Lebanon.

2. Signatories shall establish among themselves relationships normal to states at peace with one another. To this end, they should undertake to abide by all the provisions of the charter of the United Nations. Steps to be taken in this respect include:

a) Full recognition,
b) Abolishing economic boycotts
c) Guaranteeing that under their jurisdiction the citizens of the other parties shall enjoy the protection of the due process of law.

For the Government of the Arab Republic of Egypt: Al-Sadat

For the Government of Israel: M. Begin

Witnessed by: Jimmy Carter, President of the United States of America.

Source: The Middle East, 7th ed. (Washington, D.C.: Congressional Quarterly, Inc., 1990), pp. 302–303.

DOCUMENT 8–8

Framework for the Conclusion of a Peace Treaty Between Egypt and Israel Signed at the White House on Sept. 17, 1978.

In order to achieve peace between them, Israel and Egypt agree to negotiate in good faith with a goal of concluding within three months of the signing of this framework a peace treaty between them.

It is agreed that:

The site of the negotiations will be under a United Nations flag at a location or locations to be mutually agreed.

All of the principles of U.N. Resolution 242 will apply in this resolution of the dispute between Israel and Egypt.

Unless otherwise mutually agreed, terms of the peace treaty will be implemented between two and three years after the peace treaty is signed.

The following matters are agreed between the parties:

A)   The full exercise of Egyptian sovereignty up to the internationally recognized border between Egypt and mandated Palestine,

B)   The withdrawal of Israeli armed forces from the Sinai,

C)   The use of airfields left by the Israelis near El Arish, Rafah, Ras en Naqb, and Sharm el Sheikh for civilian purposes only, including possible commercial use by all nations,

D)   The right of free passage by ships of Israel through the Gulf of Suez and the Suez Canal on the basis of the Constantinople Convention of 1888 applying to all nations, the Strait of Tiran and the Gulf of Aqaba are international waterways to be open to all nations for unimpeded and nonsuspendable freedom of navigation and overflight,

E)   The construction of a highway between the Sinai and Jordan near Eilat with guaranteed free and peaceful passage by Egypt and Jordan,

F)   The stationing of forces listed below.

* * * *

After a peace treaty is signed, and after the interim withdrawal is complete, normal relations will be established between Egypt and Israel, including: Full recognition, including diplomatic, economic and cultural relations, termination of economic boycotts and barriers to the free movement of goods and people, and mutual protection of citizens by the due process of law.

Interim withdrawal:

Between three months and nine months after the signing of the peace treaty, all Israeli forces will withdraw east of a line extending from a point east of El Arish to Ras Muhammad, the exact location of this line to be determined by mutual agreement.

For the Government of the Arab Republic of Egypt: A. Sadat

For the Government of Israel: M. Begin

Witnessed by: Jimmy Carter, President of the United States of America.

Source: The Middle East, 7th ed., Congressional Quarterly, pp. 303–304.

DOCUMENT 8–9

Arab League Summit Communiqué
(March 31, 1979)*

As the Government of the Arab Republic of Egypt has ignored the Arab summit conferences' resolutions, especially those of the sixth and seventh conferences held in Algiers and Rabat; as it has at the same time ignored the ninth Arab summit conference resolutions—especially the call made by the Arab kings, presidents and princes to avoid signing the peace treaty with the Zionist enemy—and signed the peace treaty on 26 March 1979;

It has thus deviated from the Arab ranks and has chosen, in collusion with the United States, to stand by the side of the Zionist enemy in one trench; has behaved unilaterally in the Arab-Zionist struggle affairs; has violated the Arab nation's rights; has exposed the nation's destiny, its struggle and aims to dangers and challenges; has relinquished its pan-Arab duty of liberating the occupied Arab territories, particularly Jerusalem, and of restoring the Palestinian Arab people's inalienable national rights, including their right to repatriation, self-determination and establishment of the independent Palestinian state on their national soil.

. . . The Arab League Council, on the level of Arab foreign ministers, has decided the following:

1. A. To withdraw the ambassadors of the Arab states from Egypt immediately.

B. To recommend the severance of political and diplomatic relations with the Egyptian Government. The Arab governments will adopt the necessary measures to apply this recommendation within a maximum period of one month from the date of issuance of this decision, in accordance with the constitutional measures in force in each country.

2. To consider the suspension of the Egyptian Government's membership in the Arab League as operative from the date of the Egyptian Government's signing of the peace treaty with the Zionist enemy. This means depriving it of all rights resulting from this membership.

3. To make the city of Tunis, capital of the Tunisian Republic, the temporary headquarters of the Arab League. . . .

Source: Walter Laqueur and Barry Rubin, eds., *The Israel-Arab Reader: A Documentary History of the Middle East Conflict,* 4th ed. (New York: Penguin Books, 1984), pp. 616–617.

*Excerpts. The communiqué was issued in Baghdad, Iraq.

DOCUMENT 8–10

West Bank Palestinians: Reactions to Camp David
(August 30, 1981)*

The Palestinian masses in the occupied West Bank and Gaza Strip continue to reject the declaration made by Sadat and Begin . . . that they had agreed to resume talks concerning so-called "autonomy" for the inhabitants of the West Bank and the Gaza Strip. A large number of Palestinian figures and personalities have commented . . . that the autonomy plan does not concern them in any respect, and that they consider the autonomy plan to be a conspiracy directed against the hopes and aspirations of the Palestinian people who are striving to attain their legitimate rights—which have been established by the international community, as represented by the UN. . . .

Dr. Amin al-Khatib, head of the Federation of Charity Associations in Jerusalem, said: "I do not believe that any plan for a solution to the Palestine problem which does not include the establishment of an independent Palestinian state in the territory of Palestine will be successful, no matter how skillfully its sponsors choose names for it and think up methods of attempting to convince us to accept it. We are quite confident that a people such as the Palestinian people, who have gone through great hardships and have become seasoned concerning all different types of plans and half-solutions, will not be able to accept or be content with any solution other than a Palestinian state. . . .

"We have the following to say to Sadat: 'The Palestinian people, inside the occupied territories, do not wish to have you speak or negotiate in their behalf. Give both yourself and us some peace and do not bother us with this whirlpool which is called "autonomy."'

Zalikhah Shihabi, the head of the Jerusalem Women's Federation, said: "Everything concerning autonomy—whether it be the autonomy talks, resumption of such talks, their cessation, or the breaking off of such talks altogether—does not concern us. The reason for this is that we know that it is merely a waste of time, and the objective of those who are calling for autonomy is to decrease the resentment of world public opinion against them, to attempt to outflank and encircle the PLO, and to flee from the truth which is shining as brightly as the sun. This truth is that the PLO is the only body authorized to discuss all matters which concern the Palestine question. All of us here agree that there should be an independent Palestinian state. Anything other than that will only meet with rejection and indifference on the part of the Palestinian people."

Mustafa 'Abd al-Nabi al-Natshah, deputy mayor of Hebron: "Autonomy is a continuation of military occupation, only with a mask over it. Autonomy, which is tantamount to local rule, does not contain any of the elements of establishing an independent state. It is a deception utilized in order to impose permanent occupation and would confer permanent legitimacy upon the military occupation. This is something which we totally reject."

Source: Laqueur and Rubin, eds., *The Israel-Arab Reader*, pp. 624–626.

*Excerpts from an article in the Algerian newspaper *Al-Sha'b*.

9 | LEBANON AND INTIFADA

CHRONOLOGY

Sept. 22, 1980	Outbreak of Iran–Iraq War	**June 10, 1985**	Israeli withdrawal of Lebanon completed
June 7, 1981	Israel bombs Iraqi nuclear reactor at Osirak	**Oct. 1, 1985**	Israel attacks PLO H.Q. in Tunis in response to PLO attack on Israelis in Cyprus
Oct. 6, 1981	Anwar Sadat assassinated		
Oct. 13, 1981	Hosni Mubarak becomes President of Egypt	**Oct. 21, 1985**	Israeli Prime Minister Peres in UN speech calls for Middle East conference and peace with Jordan
Nov. 30, 1981	U.S.–Israel strategic pact signed; U.S. suspends pact December 18		
		Oct. 20, 1986	Unity Coalition partner Yitzhak Shamir takes over as Israeli Prime Minister
Dec. 14, 1981	Israel annexes the Golan Heights		
April 25, 1982	Israel returns last portion of Sinai to Egypt	**Dec. 9, 1987**	Intifada breaks out
June 6, 1982	Israel invades Lebanon in "Operation Peace for Galilee"	**July 31, 1988**	King Hussein renounces claims to West Bank
		Sept. 29, 1988	Taba is given to Egypt by international arbitration panel
Aug. 21– Sept. 1, 1982	PLO withdraws from Beirut; Multinational peacekeeping force arrives	**Nov. 1, 1988**	Israel general elections; coalition government formed Dec. 17 with Shamir as Prime Minister
Sept. 1, 1982	Reagan peace plan		
Sept. 9, 1982	Fez peace plan	**Nov. 15, 1988**	Palestine National Council, in Algiers, proclaims Palestinian state
Sept. 18, 1982	Sabra and Shatila massacres		
Sept. 20, 1982	Amin Gemayel becomes President of Lebanon after his brother, Bashir, is killed on September 17	**Dec. 13, 1988**	Arafat addresses United Nations in Geneva; says PNC accepts Resolutions 242 and 338, and rejects terrorism
Aug. 28, 1983	Menachem Begin resigns	**Dec. 14, 1988**	Arafat, at press conference, explicitly recognizes Israel's right to exist, accepts U.N. Resolutions 242 and 338, and renounces terrorism; United States opens dialogue with PLO
Sept. 12, 1983	Yitzhak Shamir forms government in Israel		
Oct. 23, 1983	241 U.S. Marines killed in truck-bomb attack in Beirut		
		April 6, 1989	Shamir announces election plan for the occupied territories
Nov. 29, 1983	U.S.–Israel memo of strategic cooperation	**May 22, 1989**	Secretary of State Baker's speech; Egypt re-admitted to Arab League
Dec. 20, 1983	PLO leaders depart Tripoli to establish headquarters in Tunis		
Dec. 22, 1983	PLO and Egypt resume diplomatic relations	**Jan.–Feb. 1990**	Christian militias battle in Beirut
Jan. 19, 1984	Islamic Conference re-admits Egypt	**March 15, 1990**	Shamir government falls on no-confidence vote
Feb. 21, 1984	U.S. peacekeeping force departs Lebanon	**May 1990**	Violence escalates in Intifada
		June 8, 1990	Shamir forms new Likud government
Sept. 25, 1984	Jordan resumes diplomatic relations with Egypt	**Aug. 2–4, 1990**	Iraq invades and annexes Kuwait
Jan. 20, 1985	Israel begins initial withdrawal from Lebanon	**Aug. 4– , 1990**	UN and U.S. respond to Iraq's actions
Feb. 22, 1985	Jordanian–PLO peace plan		

As the Egypt–Israel peace treaty formally went into effect, the two countries moved to "normalize" relations, and Israel began its withdrawal from the Sinai. The other Arab states rejected Israel's offer of negotiations, and most of the Arab nations boycotted Egypt. Despite Arab diplomatic and economic sanctions against Egypt, President Anwar Sadat said he would pursue the idea of Palestinian autonomy on the West Bank. Israeli Prime Minister Menachem Begin also publicly upheld the idea of autonomy, although he talked about autonomy for the people, not the land, and he authorized new Jewish settlements in the territories despite Egyptian and American objections.

During the Camp David meetings, Israel, for the first time, had agreed that a solution to the Arab–Israeli conflict must acknowledge the "legitimate rights of the Palestinian people and their just demands." Begin had agreed to negotiate with Palestinian representatives over the future of the occupied territories and had specified a limited five-year period of autonomy. As new Jewish settlements continued, however, it became increasingly clear that, if there were ever any negotiations on the "final status" of the territories, the Begin government intended to establish Israel's claim to sovereignty over the land, regardless of any interim arrangements. The Palestinians feared that an interim period of internal autonomy might become a permanent state of affairs and perpetuate the Israeli occupation in a different guise. They were also unwilling to recognize the existence of the state of Israel through participation in a negotiating process. These factors prevented both the Palestinians in the territories and the PLO from cooperating in any attempt to implement the autonomy provisions of the Camp David accords.

Although the Carter administration wished to continue the momentum of Camp David, the United States was distracted throughout 1979 and 1980 by a number of critical developments in the Persian Gulf region. In Iran, 1979 marked the collapse of the Shah's government and the return of the Ayatollah Ruhollah Khomeini from exile. In November 1979, Iranian militants stormed the American Embassy in Tehran and took over fifty hostages. This episode, which lasted for 444 days, preoccupied the American government, led to an abortive rescue attempt in April 1980, and probably caused the defeat of Jimmy Carter and the election of Ronald Reagan as president of the United States in November 1980. (The hostages were released Inauguration Day, January 20, 1981.) In addition, war had broken out in September 1980 between Iran and Iraq, and this raised concerns about the continued flow of oil and the future stability of the Persian Gulf region. Additional uncertainty was created in October 1981, when Anwar Sadat was assassinated by a Muslim fundamentalist opposed to the Egyptian leader's domestic policies and to the peace treaty with Israel. Sadat's successor was Hosni Mubarak, former commander of the Egyptian air force, a vice-president since 1975, and reputedly Sadat's closest advisor. Although Mubarak pledged to uphold the peace treaty with Israel, any further movement toward a comprehensive settlement stalled, as the Reagan administration settled in, and as Mubarak attempted to deal with internal economic and political problems. Meanwhile, in Israel, Menachem Begin's mandate was extended in the elections of 1981, and attention turned to the situation on Israel's northern border.

LEBANON

The border with Lebanon had generally been quiet after the cease-fire in 1949. A Mixed Armistice Commission (MAC) had been set up after the first Arab–Israeli war, but as observers liked to point out, the most serious problems the MAC had to deal with involved sheep straying over the frontiers. Although opposed to Israel, Lebanon was notable for its virtual nonparticipation in the 1956, 1967, and 1973 wars. A number of developments in the 1970s, however, brought Lebanon into the forefront of international politics and the Arab–Israeli conflict. A brief background discussion may be necessary to understand how this happened.

As noted earlier in this text, the modern country of Lebanon resulted from the decision after World War I to create French and British mandates out of former Ottoman territory in the Levant area. France was awarded the mandate for Syria and Lebanon, and the boundaries of both countries were drawn in such a way as to facilitate French economic and political control, particularly through a kind of deliberate "balkanization" of the territory and "divide-and-rule" policies between Christians and Muslims. In Lebanon, the French also perpetuated and enshrined the power-sharing formulas among the various religious groups, which had begun in the Ottoman period and which recognized the predominantly Christian character of the Lebanon. In general, the French favored, worked through, and recognized the preeminence of the Maronite Christians, namely Catholics who had accepted the authority of the Pope at Rome since the Middle Ages. Many Maronites considered themselves descendants of the ancient Phoenicians and identified with French (and Western) values and ideologies.

In the mid-nineteenth century, the Ottomans had bowed to European pressures to create an autonomous sanjak in Mount Lebanon with a Christian governor, and after the establishment of the mandate, the French worked through a Maronite president. Lebanese political institutions, however, were clearly subordinate to the will of the French High Commissioner. Since the French did little to encourage national unity, the major sectarian and ethnic groups of Lebanon—Maronite Christians, Greek Orthodox, Greek Catholics, Sunni and Shiite Muslims, the Druze, and a host of others—continued, in almost tribal fashion, to follow the dictates of their feudal or godfather-type lords (the so-called zaims) or their individual or confessional leaders.

Lebanon contains a baffling number of mutually exclusive ethnic and religious groups, and by continuing to recognize these divisions in the population, and indeed by encouraging them, the French tried to ensure their own ongoing prominent presence. The Mandate of Greater Lebanon was divided geographically and ethnically as follows. To the east was the Bekaa Valley and the anti-Lebanon mountain area, populated largely by a mixed Muslim population that continued to desire close ties with neighboring Syria. These portions were added to Mount Lebanon, traditional home of Maronite Christians, Druze, and Shiites. Large numbers of Sunni Muslims also lived in the coastal areas, along with Maronites, Druze, and Shiites who had migrated in the nineteenth century, especially to Beirut. The south was inhabited largely by Shiite Muslims, the poorest and until recently the most quiescent group among the many definable groups in the population.

In addition to the differences among the various sectarian groups, there was tension on a larger scale between the Maronites, especially those who saw Lebanon as a Christian and Western outpost in the Middle East, and those Lebanese, especially Muslims, who espoused the cause of pan-Arab unity, who often looked to Syria, and who identified more with the Arab world and its causes.

Lebanon had fallen under control of the pro-German Vichy government of France between 1940 and 1941. The Free French who "liberated" the country granted the Lebanese their independence in 1941, although elections were not held until 1943. The leaders of the major sectarian communities made an unwritten agreement, the so-called National Pact of 1943, to make government possible by a power-sharing formula that provided for a Maronite president, a Sunni prime minister, and a Shiite speaker of the parliament. It was further agreed that in the parliament there would be six Christians for every five Muslims, reflecting the claim, based on the 1932 census, that the Christians were still the numerically superior group in the population.

This internal political "balance" was also reflected in Lebanon's foreign policy. Although Lebanon had joined the Arab League and had declared war on Israel in 1948, its participation in the Arab–Israeli conflict was minimal. Lebanon did not join the Baghdad Pact in 1955 but did not fault the then pro-British government in Iraq for doing so. In 1957, Lebanon was the only Arab country to endorse the Eisenhower Doctrine against communism, but that obvious tilt to the West, as well as too great an assertion of Christian hegemony on the part of the government of President Camille Chamoun, helped create the conditions for a brief civil war in 1958. (At that time, the pan-Arab appeal of Egyptian president Nasser was very strong throughout the region.) That episode encouraged Lebanon to try to restore its previous, if fragile, internal balance and to resume walking the tightrope in its external affairs.

Unfortunately, by the 1970s, a number of changes had occurred that made it impossible to maintain the precarious internal and external balancing act. For one thing, despite the lack of an official census since 1932, it was quite clear that the Muslim population now exceeded that of the Christian, and Muslim demands for greater political parity became more insistent. The Maronite political leaders consistently ignored these demands. Second, greater economic disparities began to be evident throughout the population. Most observers tend to focus on religious differences among the Lebanese, to the exclusion of major and complex nonreligious variables such as locality and economic factors. Class and economic status have created cleavages even within the different confessional groupings. Although Lebanon was lauded as the "Switzerland of the Middle East," there were sections of glittering Beirut that had no electricity or sewage facilities. Southern Lebanon in general was an economically depressed area usually ignored by the central government. There was never a complete correlation between political power and economic status. Nevertheless, in general, the Christian community was wealthier than the Muslim community and had greater economic opportunity. In part, this was because of the economic and educational advantages Christians had enjoyed as a result of their special relationship with the European powers dating back to the nineteenth century. It was also due to a patronage system that reserved certain jobs and positions for Christians.

In the 1970s, as the result of the Arab oil embargo and increased oil revenues in the Arab world, Lebanon both benefited and suffered. The gross national product grew, but burgeoning inflation caused the economic disparities and discord between the rich and the poor to increase.

Perhaps most importantly for the Arab–Israeli conflict, however, the Palestinian dimension began to intrude into Lebanese politics and into Lebanon's role as a confrontation state.

The Palestinian Factor

Emancipation of the PLO from control by the Arab governments after 1967 and added attention to the Palestinian cause increasingly affected Lebanon's internal situation. With Israel in control of the Golan Heights and the West Bank, PLO guerrilla raids against Israel, launched across Israel's northern border, became more frequent. Israeli retaliation often followed, and in one such series of incidents in 1968, the Israelis undertook a daring commando attack on Beirut International airport and destroyed thirteen civilian aircraft. PLO raids were greatly resented by the Maronites in particular, who attempted, both through the Arab League and internally, to curb and restrain PLO activity against Israel from Lebanon. In 1969, the so-called Cairo agreement limited PLO guerrillas to certain portions of southern Lebanon, soon called *Fatahland*. However, following the showdown with Jordan's King Hussein in 1970–1971, and their expulsion from Jordan, the PLO leaders and many PLO fighters moved to Lebanon, established bases in that country, and began to organize the Palestinian refugees in the camps. They also began to dominate the Shiite areas of southern Lebanon. Israeli retaliatory strikes against refugee camps and into southern Lebanon began to affect the Shiites in the south, who also came to resent the Palestinian presence. Many of them began to migrate to the north, where they would eventually organize politically and become a significant new political factor in Lebanese politics.

With Lebanon being drawn increasingly into the Palestinian–Israeli situation, tension grew between those attempting to maintain Lebanese "sovereignty" (that is, the present governmental arrangements, the Western connection, and opposition to the presence of the PLO), and those especially among the Muslims who supported the Arab and Palestinian cause against Israel and the activities of the PLO. Thus, the Palestinian issue exacerbated already tense economic and political differences. These differences exploded again into civil war in 1975.

Civil War and Its Consequences

In April 1975, civil war broke out in Lebanon between the Maronite militias and those of the Lebanese National Movement (LNM). The LNM represented the Druze and various factions such as the Syrian Socialist Nationalist party, the Lebanese Communist party, and others, mainly Muslims, who were dissatisfied with the prevailing system. Although holding aloof initially, the PLO soon joined the Muslim belligerents. In this critical situation, the Lebanese army fragmented, and many individual soldiers joined one or another of the competing militias. When it became apparent by March 1976 that the Christian militias were on the defensive, the Syrian army intervened to restore the *status quo ante*. Evidently, Syrian president Hafez al Assad was afraid of a radical government in Lebanon, in part because it would strengthen the PLO, which would then be capable of operating independently of Syria. Moreover, the Syrians worried that anarchy in Lebanon could lead to an Israeli invasion of Lebanon that could threaten Syria. Syria thus intervened to rescue and to fight for the existing government against the PLO and the Muslim militias. By October 1976, a cease-fire had been worked out by the Arab League, which sanctioned the presence of an Arab Deterrent Force (soon limited to Syrian troops) in Lebanon. The Syrian presence in the form of approximately 40,000 troops continues today.

The Maronite leaders had no particular love for the Syrians, however; nor were Syrian sympathies necessarily with the Christians. In 1976, a group of Christian leaders had formed the Lebanese Front, a political coalition, whose military arm was the Lebanese Forces. The Lebanese Forces brought together four Christian militias, but the dominant role in both the Lebanese Front and Lebanese Forces was played by the Phalange, a Maronite party founded in the 1930s and led by Pierre Gemayel. Syria did attempt to mediate among the various parties and militias but did not try to disarm them; thus the level of violence remained high. Nor did the Syrians prevent the PLO from continuing to build up its power south of the so-called red line (generally taken to be the Litani River), where the Israelis said they would not tolerate the presence of Syrian troops. Israel, meanwhile, had been in contact with Pierre Gemayel to discuss matters of common concern. Although both sides had reservations about too close an alliance, by 1978 Israel was supporting the Lebanese Front with arms and training. Israel also helped organize and arm a predominantly Christian militia in southern Lebanon, led by Major Saad Haddad, a Greek Catholic.

PLO attacks against Israel from Lebanon had increased during the period of Secretary of State Henry Kissinger's shuttle diplomacy and the disengagement agreements of 1974 and 1975, when it appeared that the United States and the belligerent countries were ignoring the Palestinian cause. Palestinian attacks also increased after Anwar Sadat's trip to Jerusalem in November 1977, and as Israel and Egypt began to negotiate. Lebanon was the usual PLO base, and a PLO operation in which terrorists commandeered a bus on the coastal highway south of Haifa and in which over thirty people were killed led to a major Israeli invasion of Lebanon (Operation Litani) in March 1978. Although the Israelis withdrew three months later, they established a security zone under Major Haddad's control. In addition, UN troops (UNIFIL, or United Nations Interim Forces in Lebanon) were sent to southern Lebanon. Neither UNIFIL nor Major Haddad, however, was able to prevent the PLO, which was in virtual control of many villages and camps, from developing into a conventional army replete with a growing arsenal that included long-range weapons and rockets.

The Israeli government, especially after the Likud victory in 1977, began to look for ways to crush the PLO and, perhaps at the same time, to deal with the problem of the West Bank. Some Israeli strategists argued that if the PLO were cut off at the head in Lebanon, PLO influence in the occupied territories might also wane, and perhaps Palestinian leaders would emerge who were willing to strike a deal with Israel. PLO funds, patronage, and physical threats—as well as the assassination of those who cooperated with Israeli authorities—had prevented moderate Palestinians from emerging as an alternative to the PLO. Israeli policies in the territories, which included the expulsion or deportation of leaders and others who supported the PLO or publicly espoused the idea of national self-determination, also deprived the Israelis of the opportunity to deal with acknowledged leaders and opinion-makers.

Israel invaded Lebanon on June 6, 1982. The pretext was provided by the nearly fatal shooting on June 3 of Shlomo Argov, Israel's Ambassador to London. His attackers were not, as claimed, PLO at all, but members of the Abu Nidal group, an anti-Arafat Palestinian faction operating independently of the PLO. Abu Nidal's Fatah Revolutionary Council targeted anyone identified with Israel or the West and is said to have been responsible for the death or wounding of 900 people in twenty countries since breaking away from Arafat in 1974.

In the years prior to 1982, Israel had responded to PLO rocket attacks against its northern border with air strikes on Palestinian refugee camps, which often killed innocent civilians, most notably in Beirut in the summer of 1981. An American mediator, Philip Habib, secured a cease-fire in 1981 that held into early 1982. There were no PLO incursions and no Israeli strikes. In April 1982, however, a number of incidents occurred that heightened tensions on the border. At this same time, Israel was completing its withdrawal from the Sinai in accordance with the provisions of the peace treaty with Egypt. Reasonably sure of noninterference from Egypt, Israel began seriously to consider an invasion of Lebanon. It is also possible that the unpleasant and even at times violent confrontation of the Israeli army with Jewish settlers, who were forced to evacuate their homes when Egypt regained the Sinai, also impelled Prime Minister Begin (who had been handily reelected in 1981) to exhibit a show of strength against the PLO in Lebanon. Israel also realized that the Arab world was divided over the Iraq–Iran war. Acting from a position of strength, Israel bombed Iraq's nuclear reactor in 1981 and annexed the Israeli-held portions of the Golan Heights in December 1981.

The official explanation for the 1982 invasion of Lebanon, termed "Operation Peace for Galilee," was that Israel was going to eliminate the PLO in southern Lebanon and create a secure area up to twenty-five miles (or forty kilometers) north of its border. However, in a plan conceived by Defense Minister Ariel Sharon, a hero of the 1973 war, and Israel's leading hawk, Israeli forces continued to advance, reaching the outskirts of Beirut within four days. On the way, Israel destroyed Syria's surface-to-air missiles in the Bekaa Valley, shot down Syrian fighter planes, and outflanked Syrian ground forces. Confronted with this situation, President Assad of Syria accepted a cease-fire on June 11. During the ensuing siege of Beirut, the PLO withstood Israel's military and political pressures. The Israelis repeatedly bombarded the city, causing many civilian casualties. The idea was to destroy the PLO and to restore the "legitimate" government, preferably in the person of Bashir Gemayel, Pierre Gemayel's son, who now headed the Lebanese forces. He believed in Christian hegemony in Lebanon and was vehemently opposed to the PLO and to the Syrian presence. For some time previously, he had had contacts with the Israelis, and a personal relationship had developed between him and Ariel Sharon. The Israelis had come to view Bashir as a powerful and potentially successful political leader, and as a real ally.

After shelling Beirut for two months, the Israelis entered the city in August, finally compelling the PLO to leave. A multinational peacekeeping force (representing the United States, Italy, and France) arrived to supervise the evacuation and dispersal of the PLO leadership and PLO fighters to eight different countries. In mid-1983, with Syria still entrenched in Lebanon, President Assad fomented a split in al-Fatah and expelled Yasser Arafat from Syria. Assad continues to support the anti-Arafat faction in al-Fatah, and to provide hospitality in Damascus for Arafat rivals like George Habash of the PFLP, and Nayef Hawatmeh of the DFLP.

Although the PLO leadership had left Lebanon, Bashir Gemayel soon backed away from too close an association or public assertion of friendship with Israel, which undoubtedly helped assure his election as Lebanese President on August 23, 1982. On September 10, the multinational peacekeeping force began to withdraw, but on September 14, Bashir was assassinated at his headquarters, an act attributed to either the Syrians or Palestinians. The Israelis immediately moved into West Beirut to "keep the peace," but between September 15 and September 18, in an area controlled by the Israelis, Christian Phalangists, avenging the death of their leader, were permitted by the Israelis to enter the refugee camps of Sabra and Shatila. A fearful massacre of hundreds of Palestinians ensued, for which the Israelis later accepted indirect responsibility, and Ariel Sharon was forced to resign as Israeli defense minister. As a result of this tragedy, President Ronald Reagan agreed to the return and expansion of the multinational peacekeeping force. Amin Gemayel, Bashir's brother, became President. He was less charismatic than his brother but more amenable to pluralism in Lebanon. Seeking to mend fences, he did little but serve as a point around which the multitudinous factions swirled.

The bitter internecine rivalries of the different factions, religious groups, and even families in Lebanon reemerged following the departure of the PLO. Indeed, new groups and militias appeared on the scene. (See Map 9–1.) One of the most important of these was Amal. Organized in the mid-1970s by the Imam Musa al-Sadr (who mysteriously disappeared on a trip to Libya in 1978), Amal sought greater recognition and political representation for the Shiite Muslims who had largely been ignored by the Lebanese government. Galvanized by the Iranian revolution, other Shiite groups

MAP 9–1

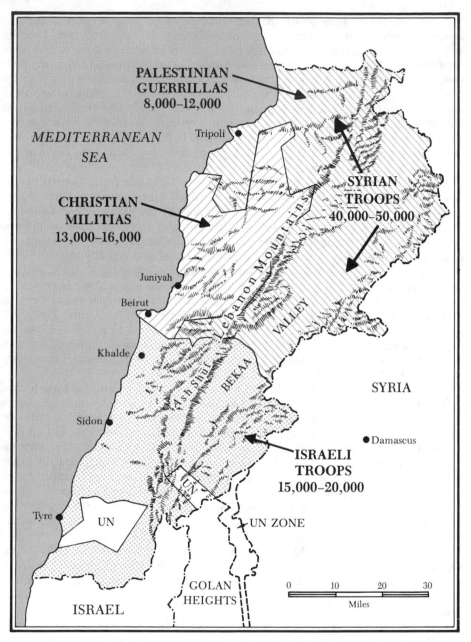

Major factional military dispositions in Lebanon, May, 1983.

formed, including Hizbullah, an umbrella organization of several Shiite fundamentalist groups taking their cues from Iran. (It should be noted that President Assad of Syria is a Shiite Muslim of the Alawi sect, and that Syria backed Iran, a non-Arab country, in the Iraq–Iran war.) The Shiites became increasingly aware of the strength of their numbers, and they have now become the largest Muslim group in Lebanon. They also became more radicalized, particularly in the south and in the southern suburbs of Beirut where many had migrated, first because of their enmity toward the PLO and then because of Israel's prolonged occupation after the 1982 invasion.

Not only were internal divisions at the time as sharp as ever, but Syrian and now Israeli troops were in Lebanon. The Israelis had been encouraging an accord between themselves and Lebanon in return for their withdrawal, which, in effect, would have made Lebanon the second Arab country to recognize the Jewish state. The American government, and especially Secretary of State George Shultz, supported this idea. Shultz, indeed, brokered such an agreement in May 1983. It called for an end to the state of war between Israel and Lebanon and withdrawal of Israeli troops, if those of Syria also left. President Assad, who had not been consulted, and who vehemently opposed the pact, refused to budge. Two weeks before the initialing of the agreement, on April 18, 1983, a pro-Iranian group called Islamic Jihad bombed the American embassy in Beirut, killing over sixty people, including many CIA operatives. This attack was a portent of much worse to come. (See Map 9–2.)

The United States, in fact, in closely identifying itself with the "legitimate government" of Lebanon—that is, with Christian predominance—was also backing the *status quo* and simply ignoring what the Lebanese themselves had been fighting about since 1975. The Western, and especially American, presence began to be greatly resented by almost all the Lebanese, for their own particular reasons. In October 1983, a terrorist driving a car filled with explosives blew up the U.S. Marine barracks killing 247 men. (The French contingent's compound was also bombed.) By March 1984, the United States had left Lebanon, and shortly thereafter, Amin Gemayel cancelled the accord with Israel and moved to mend fences with Syria, which continued to occupy the country militarily and to play a role in Lebanese affairs. Western hostages were seized by Lebanese factions, some Westerners were killed, the politicians continued their bickering, the militias became little governments unto themselves, violence and anarchy reigned, and Lebanon slid into economic and political chaos.

The Israeli invasion, then, not only set in motion a train of events that further complicated and worsened the situation in Lebanon, but also failed to achieve its objectives. Many in the PLO returned to Lebanon, including Yasser Arafat. In a showdown with Syrian-supported PLO rebels, however, he was forced to leave Tripoli and to seek refuge in Tunis. Despite President Assad's continuing attempts to undercut Arafat's influence, the PLO leader survived to play a significant role in the further shaping of Israel–Palestinian relations.

Israel Withdraws

Israel found it much harder to get out of Lebanon than it had expected. The Shiites and southern Lebanese, who had originally welcomed Israeli troops as a means of dislodging the PLO, became unhappy at the disregard for their property and traditional economic patterns and at policies that seemed designed to incorporate them into the Israeli economy. Suicide car-bombings and sniper attacks against Israeli soldiers escalated, some organized locally, some controlled from Damascus. This led, in turn, to "iron fist" retaliation, in which Israeli squads invaded villages and assassinated

MAP 9–2

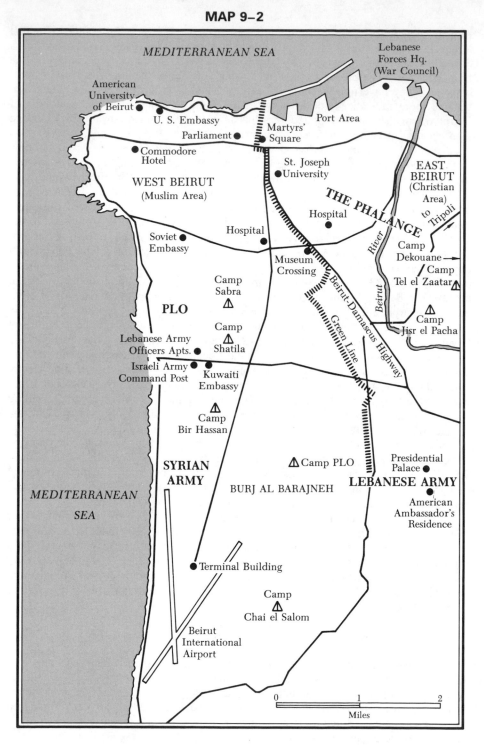

Beirut showing militias before Israeli withdrawal.

suspected leaders of the resistance. Over 500 Israeli troops were killed in Lebanon. These casualties led to enormous internal dissension in Israel and (along with the shock of the death of his wife) to the resignation of Prime Minister Begin in August 1983. Casualties among the occupying troops continued until the withdrawal was completed in June 1985. The Lebanon adventure exposed weaknesses and divisions within the Israeli armed forces and shocked some of the more moderate Israeli leaders. Begin was succeeded by the even more extreme Yitzhak Shamir, a man who had opposed the Camp David accords.

Furthermore, the Israelis achieved few of their goals by going into Lebanon. The Lebanese government remained weak and divided, and the civil war continued. The Maronites and the Phalange were unable to reestablish their former control over the country, and, in any event, did not seek closer ties with Israel. Israeli and American political influence in Lebanon was commensurately reduced. The Syrian presence was, in fact, strengthened, and it continues to this day, backed up by modern Soviet weapons, thus preventing Israel from using Lebanon as a springboard from which to attack Syria. Although PLO leaders were dispersed, and Yasser Arafat correspondingly weakened, even challenged, by Assad-backed factions and other splinter groups, by the late 1980s Arafat had asserted his control over the PLO more strongly than ever. The Palestinians suffered considerable military and civilian casualties during the Israeli invasion, but they also demonstrated a greater capacity for fighting than the Israelis had anticipated. This raised morale and pride among Palestinians everywhere, leading not to greater cooperation in the West Bank and Gaza, as Ariel Sharon had expected, but to an increased determination to resist Israeli rule. Deprived of bases in southern Lebanon, from this time on, the PLO encouraged attacks on Israelis from within the occupied territories. Finally, the large number of casualties among Lebanese and Palestinian civilians, and the widespread destruction that resulted from the Israeli invasion, not only brought worldwide condemnation of Israel but also an upsurge of sympathy and support for the Palestinian cause from all quarters of the globe.

In the Israeli elections of July 1984, the outcome was so close between the Likud and the Labor coalition that the two groups had to form a "National Unity" government in which both parties shared power and took turns in governing. Thus, Shimon Peres was Prime Minister until October 1986 with Likud's Yitzhak Shamir as Foreign Minister, and then the roles were reversed. It was an uneasy alliance of power between two men whose policies were diametrically opposed. Peres remained committed to his earlier policy of reaching an agreement with Jordan's King Hussein concerning the West Bank, thereby excluding the PLO. The Peres solution involved giving up some territory to Jordan in return for peace and recognition of Israel, although the status of the land to be given up, and the area itself, remained unclear. The Likud's Ariel Sharon (Minister of Commerce and Industry) wanted straight-out Israeli annexation of the occupied land. The ongoing rivalry between Peres and Labor hard-liner Yitzhak Rabin, who was now defense minister and also opposed to negotiations with King Hussein, further blocked any consensus among Israeli politicians on the future of the West Bank.

Israeli occupation of Lebanon continued, and Begin authorized a program for the creation of new settlements in the West Bank. But increasingly, domestic problems were of greater concern to Israel's leaders. Under Begin, Israel's foreign debt had risen from $11 billion to $21.5 billion; the annual inflation rate from 48 percent to over 150 percent. The basic problem was military expenditure: one-third of the budget went to defense. The Lebanon adventure cost a million dollars a day; the promotion of West Bank settlements nearly as much again. Only massive American aid kept Israel afloat. U.S. aid went from $250 million a year after the 1967 war to $1.5 billion after 1973, and to over $3 billion in 1990. (See Table 9–1.)

TABLE 9–1 United States Assistance to the Middle East, 1946–1988
(U.S. fiscal year — millions of dollars)

	1987	1988	Total Loans and Grants 1946–1988		1987	1988	Total Loans and Grants 1946–1988
ALGERIA				**LIBYA**			
Economic	$—	$—	$ 203.6	Economic	—	—	212.5
Loans	—	—	11.6	Loans	—	—	7.0
Grants	—	—	192.0	Grants	—	—	205.5
Other	—	53.7	1,098.3	Military	—	—	17.6
EGYPT				Grants	—	—	17.6
Economic	1,015.3	873.4	14,847.3	**OMAN**			
Loans	191.7	153.0	5,969.7	Economic	$ 14.9	$ 13.0	$ 121.3
Grants	823.6	720.4	8,877.6	Loans	9.9	8.0	77.3
Military	1,301.8	1,301.5	12,105.1	Grants	5.0	5.0	44.0
Loans	—	—	5,981.2	Military	—	0.2	167.8
Grants	1,301.8	1,301.5	6,123.9	Loans	—	—	167.1
Other	—	0.3	471.3	Grants	—	0.2	0.7
IRAN				Other	—	—	—
Economic	—	—	761.8	**SAUDI**			
Loans	—	—	297.6	**ARABIA**			
Grants	—	—	464.2	Economic	—	—	31.8
Military	—	—	1,404.8	Loans	—	—	4.3
Loans	—	—	496.4	Grants	—	—	27.5
Grants	—	—	908.4	Military	—	—	292.4
Other	—	—	128.7	Loans	—	—	254.2
IRAQ				Grants	—	—	38.2
Economic	—	—	45.5	Other	—	—	47.3
Loans	—	—	14.4	**SUDAN**			
Grants	—	—	31.1	Economic	96.6	63.2	1,379.7
Military	—	—	50.0	Loans	74.6	40.0	385.3
Grants	—	—	50.0	Grants	22.0	23.2	994.4
Other	—	—	100.5	Military	6.0	0.9	372.6
ISRAEL				Loans	—	—	156.3
Economic	1,200.0	1,200.0	15,025.6	Grants	6.0	0.9	216.3
Loans	—	—	2,009.9	Other	—	—	41.7
Grants	1,200.0	1,200.0	13,015.7	**SYRIA**			
Military	1,800.0	1,800.0	25,826.8	Economic	—	—	353.3
Loans	—	—	11,204.2	Loans	—	—	274.3
Grants	1,800.0	1,800.0	14,622.6	Grants	—	—	79.0
Other	—	—	897.4	**TUNISIA**			
JORDAN				Economic	51.7	42.0	1,134.3
Economic	111.1	23.7	1,798.8	Loans	31.6	27.0	521.8
Loans	2.0	5.2	329.0	Grants	20.1	15.0	612.5
Grants	109.1	18.5	1,469.8	Military	34.1	28.4	695.6
Military	41.9	28.3	1,510.9	Loans	—	—	487.4
Loans	—	—	877.7	Grants	34.1	28.4	209.2
Grants	41.9	28.3	633.2	Other	—	—	138.3
Other	5.7	28.2	426.5	**TURKEY**			
KUWAIT				Economic	103.1	32.4	4,326.8
Other	—	—	50.0	Loans	2.4	—	2,035.0
LEBANON				Grants	100.7	32.4	2,291.8
Economic	22.5	11.9	348.7	Military	493.5	493.5	9,894.6
Loans	—	—	33.1	Loans	177.9	178.0	4,137.9
Grants	22.5	11.9	315.6	Grants	315.6	315.3	5,756.7
Military	0.5	0.4	265.9	Other	—	—	491.6
Loans	—	—	243.7	**YEMEN**			
Grants	0.5	0.4	22.2	**ARAB**			
Other	—	—	83.2				

(*continued*)

TABLE 9–1 *(Continued)*

	1987	1988	Total Loans and Grants 1946–1988		1987	1988	Total Loans and Grants 1946–1988
REPUBLIC				YEMEN,			
Economic	45.5	33.7	384.7	PEOPLE'S			
Loans	18.6	10.0	62.1	DEMO-			
Grants	26.9	23.7	322.6	CRATIC			
Military	2.3	2.0	41.3	REPUBLIC			
Loans	—	—	14.0	OF			
Grants	2.3	2.0	17.3	Economic	—	—	4.5
Other	—	—	0.6	Grants	—	—	4.5

The cumulative figures for 1946–1988 are on a net basis, reflecting total obligations where funds obligated were not actually spent.

Economic aid totals include official development assistance, Food for Peace programs, Peace Corps, and miscellaneous programs.

Military aid includes the Foreign Assistance Act credit sales and grant programs, transfers from excess stocks, and other grants and loans.

Other includes Export-Import Bank loans often made to the private sector within a country, Agriculture Department short-term credits, OPIC direct loans, and private trade agreements under PL-480, Title I.

Source: The Middle East, 7th ed. (Washington, D.C.: Congressional Quarterly, Inc., 1990), p. 77.

Despite these very high levels of assistance, the United States gained surprisingly little influence over Israeli conduct in the Middle East. President Reagan took advantage of the crisis in Lebanon to produce a peace plan in September 1982. (See Document 9–1.) This was essentially a return to the Jordanian option already implicit in the Camp David accords. It opposed an independent Palestinian state in the West Bank and Gaza, but also was against Israeli annexation of these areas. Rather, it suggested "self-government by the Palestinians of the West Bank and Gaza in association with Jordan." And, in an accompanying note to Begin, Reagan assured the Israeli Prime Minister that the United States opposed even the dismantling of existing Israeli settlements in the occupied areas. For the Palestinians this was a very small sop. The Israelis rejected the initiative out of hand. In September 1982, at an Arab summit held in Fez, Morocco, Arab leaders responded with their own—the Fez—plan. (See Document 9–2.) The main provisions of the Fez plan called for the complete withdrawal by Israel from all territories occupied in 1967, including East Jerusalem, the dismantling of Israeli settlements in the occupied territories, and a Palestinian state under PLO leadership.

In an effort to return to the arena as a major player, on September 15, the Soviets came up with their own—the Brezhnev—peace plan, which essentially mirrored the Fez plan, although it did make specific reference to the future security of Israel, something the Fez plan failed to mention.

The Israeli also rejected these initiatives. One reason the Reagan initiative withered was the crisis in Lebanon and the return of U.S. troops as a result of the assassination of Bashir Gemayel in mid-September 1982. Nevertheless, American–Israeli relations remained very close into the second Reagan administration. The Reagan administration remained committed to essentially the Jordanian solution, and supported the Israeli determination not to negotiate with the PLO. The Americans hoped that if negotiations took place between Israel and Jordan without the PLO they could pressure Israel to make concessions. If successful, this would strengthen the American position that the United States was acting as an honest broker in the conflict. At the same time, the administration encouraged Israel to talk with selected non-PLO Palestinians from the West Bank and Gaza. Some observers thought that a real chance for peace would come only when the other superpower, the Soviet Union, was also involved, but for most of the Reagan period, the President's staunch anti-Communist stance precluded this possibility. Mikhail Gorbachev's recent policy of lessening tensions with the West and the subsequent "thaw" in U.S./U.S.S.R. relations holds the promise of participation by both superpowers in a settlement of the conflict.

Communal Conflict Continues

Lebanon remained fractured and rent by bloody strife. During 1985–1986, Amal attacked Palestinian camps to prevent the return of the PLO, causing heavy civilian casualties. Amal's military actions against the Israelis and the Palestinians was backed by President Hafez al-Assad of Syria. Assad was angry with Yasser Arafat because of his apparent willingness to negotiate with King Hussein of Jordan as a potential partner in negotiations with Israel.

At the end of 1985, an accord was signed in Lebanon under Syrian auspices by the leaders of the Shiites, the Druze, and the Christian leader of the Lebanese Forces. This agreement, which would have reduced the powers of the president and reapportioned parliamentary seats more equitably between Christians and Muslims, was rejected by the Maronite Christian leaders, thus perpetuating the cycle of casual violence, bombings, and revenge killings that had ruined Lebanon over the previous ten years. The failure in 1988 to select a new president after the expiration of Amin Gemayel's term of office resulted in a divided government with Muslims following Prime Minister Salim al-Hoss, and the Christians following the commander of the Lebanese Armed Forces, General Michel Aoun, a Maronite Christian trained in France and the United States.

Aoun, backed by Iraq, which became a player on the Lebanese scene after the cease-fire in the Iran–Iraq war in 1987, vowed to drive the Syrians from Lebanon. This resulted in, among other things, the near-total destruction of the already badly bombarded city of Beirut. On October 24, 1989, the Lebanese Parliament endorsed an Arab peace plan worked out at Taif, Saudi Arabia, to reduce Christian power and to give greater weight to the Muslims. Aoun did not accept this plan, which would have reduced the power of the president, by tradition a Christian. He also condemned the plan because it did not set a date for a speedy Syrian withdrawal. On November 5, 1989, against the wishes of Aoun, the Lebanese deputies elected Rene Moawad, a moderate Maronite, president, but he was assassinated in a bomb blast after only seventeen days in office. Two days later, on November 24, the Lebanese legislators elected Elias Hrawi president. In early February 1990, particularly fierce and senseless violence broke out between the rival Maronite militias of Aoun and warlord Samir Geagea, over control of East Beirut. Geagea, a former medical student at the American University in Beirut, has been chairman of the militia known as the Lebanese Forces since 1986. The Lebanese Forces, founded by Bashir Gemayel, were associated with the Phalange. Geagea has had a long association with violence; he reportedly led the assassination of President Sulayman Franjiyah's son, Tony, in 1979, General Aoun commanded about 15,000 Lebanese Army regulars while Mr. Geagea commanded 1,000 fighters of the Lebanese Forces militia. In the fighting in the first half of 1990, over 450 Lebanese were killed and more than 2,000 wounded. Christians in Lebanon, it seemed, had as much to fear from other Christian militias as they did from Muslim forces.

The PLO

The Palestinians took some time to recover from the setbacks of 1982. The PLO split badly in mutual recriminations after the siege of Beirut. Arafat's opponents within the PLO blamed him for the defeat of the Palestinians and their withdrawal in 1982, and attacked him for his preference for diplomacy rather than the military option for achieving a Palestinian homeland. In November 1983, Amal and rebel Fatah units backed by Syria drove Arafat from Tripoli in northern Lebanon to new PLO head-quarters in Tunis. The PLO lost its official status in Lebanon in May 1987 when the Lebanese Parliament scrapped the so-called Cairo agreement. While the weak Lebanese government sought to establish its own authority, and rival Christian factions fought their own war for control of the country's Christian enclave, the PLO rebuilt its forces in Lebanon. By April 1990, just eight years after Israel had driven the PLO guerrillas out of Lebanon, the organization had rebuilt its military strength. At that time, the PLO had 11,000 trained forces, compared with the 8,000 who were forced out in 1982. Arafat came under pressure from the hardline members of the PLO—Ahmed Jebril of the PFLPGC, and the DFLP—to abandon efforts to negotiate with Israel. The radicals within the PLO asserted that concessions to Israel had achieved nothing, and that a return to force was necessary to realize Palestinian goals. In the meantime, the PLO was seeking formal recognition in any redistribution of political power in Lebanon.

The widespread dispersal of the PLO made united action even more difficult, and despite the fact that he had almost total support within the PLO's governing body, the Palestine National Council (See Document 9–3.), Arafat had to cope with Syrian hostility and President Assad's admittedly unsuccessful attempts to set up a puppet Palestinian organization. In February 1985, King Hussein and Yasser Arafat announced a joint policy. They called for a UN-sponsored international conference with the PLO representing the Palestinians within a joint Palestinian–PLO delegation to oversee the following settlement: Israel to withdraw from all the occupied territories, including East Jerusalem, and the establishment of a Palestinian state on the West Bank within the context of a Jordan–Palestine confederation. Although they sought different, even competing, goals, Hussein and Arafat viewed this plan as setting in motion the first steps toward meeting their immediate needs. Hussein needed the legitimizing support of the PLO if he were to regain the West Bank, and Arafat needed U.S. and international support for PLO participation in negotiations with Israel. Also, the settlement policy that enabled Israel to take even more control over the West Bank and Gaza would be stopped.

Both Israel and the United States opposed an international conference. Both political parties in Israel rejected any negotiations with the PLO over the West Bank. Shimon Peres proposed discussion between Israel and Jordan including some non-PLO Palestinians, but the Likud dismissed the proposals out of hand. The United States insisted that PLO acceptance of UN Resolution 242 was a precondition for a conference in which the PLO might take part. The United States also opposed an international meeting because it did not want the Soviets to be a party to negotiations at that point. Arafat claimed that by calling for such a conference he had implicitly abandoned the 1968 PLO covenant, with its call for the destruction of Israel. In reality, Arafat did not have the support within the PLO at that time to give the assurances the United States demanded prior to opening negotiations, although he did indicate that he would openly do so as part of the settlement.

Many observers believe that American policy at this point, by its negative re-

MAP 9–3

The West Bank, 1984.

Source: *Atlantic Monthly*, June, 1984, p. 59.

sponse to the Hussein–Arafat initiative, encouraged the extremists within both Israel and the PLO. The extremists within Israel, especially followers of the American-born ultra-nationalist rabbi and leader of the Kach party, Meir Kahane, not only increased their demands for more Jewish settlements and the annexation of the West Bank (See Map 9–3.) but also advocated the forceful removal of the Palestinian Arabs. (See Document 9–4.) "Rejectionist Front" elements of the PLO, claiming that moderation would achieve nothing, felt justified in renewing their terrorist activities. On September 25, 1985, three Israeli citizens in Cyprus were assassinated by a PLO extremist group. Israeli retaliated by bombing the PLO headquarters in Tunis on October 1. The cycle of violence escalated. Between June and December 1985 there were a series of dramatic terrorist acts of violence that captured world attention. Among the more highly publicized of these episodes were the hijacking of a TWA airliner in the Middle East, the shooting up of the airport passenger lounges in Rome and Vienna, and the hijacking, on October 7, 1985 of the cruise ship *Achille Lauro* by the Palestine National Front headed by Abul Abbas. Extremist voices on both sides prevailed over the advocates of moderation. Israel claimed that PLO terrorism indicated that Arafat could not curb the violent tendencies of the PLO or claim to speak for the Palestinian people. Rejectionist PLO elements and the Saudis refused to give Arafat the green light to continue his diplomatic approach through Jordan. Hussein abandoned the Hussein–Arafat plan and instead began his own discussions with Israel for an international conference. In this situation of stalemate, Yitzhak Shamir and the Likud party took over the government of Israel at the end of 1986.

INTIFADA

Violence in the West Bank and Gaza increased throughout 1986–1987. By the mid-1980s an entire generation of Palestinian youth had grown up under Israeli occupation. They had lived with curtailed civil rights, with their lowly economic status (although perhaps better under the Israelis than previously under Jordanian rule) hostage to Israel's economy, and in political limbo. They had little faith in the Arab governments who tended to view them as a nuisance and who for over twenty years had done little for them. They were disillusioned with the PLO, which, although a potent symbol of their nationalist feelings, had not succeeded either militarily or diplomatically in securing Palestinian self-determination. Moreover, the Arab summit held in Amman in November, 1987, preoccupied with the Iran–Iraq situation, failed to raise the issue of the Palestinians' future. Palestinian rage and frustration began to boil over in incidents against the Israel Defense Forces and Jewish settlers, as Israeli settlers became more militant against Arab resistance to the increasing number of settlements, expropriations, and land sales, often forced, taking place. Shamir did little to control the violence.

The Palestinian resistance was unorganized, but in December 1987, following a series of accidental deaths and reprisals in the Gaza, Palestinian frustration exploded into what soon became a full-fledged uprising despite Israel's all-out efforts to contain the situation. This uprising, or "shaking-off"—termed the Intifada—spread to the West Bank, and by November 1988, despite the fact that over 150 Palestinians had been killed and many more arrested; leaders deported; over 11,500 casualties (almost two-thirds of whom were under 15 years of age); universities, colleges, and schools closed; houses demolished; and curfews applied—Israel had failed to stop the rock-throwing and harassment that had characterized the Intifada throughout the year.

Young boys and girls participate in Intifada, Nablus, April 16, 1988 (*Photo courtesy of Britain/Israel Public Affairs Centre*).

During the first six weeks of the Intifada, thirty-eight Palestinians were shot and killed by the Israel Defense Forces. Israel's response was deemed by the world to be too harsh, and the Jewish state was widely criticized, even by Jews in the United States. Thirty thousand Israeli demonstrators marched in Tel Aviv, also, to protest the severity of the government's reaction. Israel's Fall 1988 election, which produced another National Unity coalition of the Likud and Labor parties, indicated that opinion within Israel remained divided. While there was no popular mandate for convening an international conference over the future of the territories, or trading land for peace with security (the Labor position), neither was there a clear mandate in support of annexation or a massive Jewish settlement drive in, or retention of, all the territories (the Likud position). During the year, the Peace Now movement, consisting of leftist groups and many of Israel's most senior and respected military leaders, called for an end to the military occupation of the conquered territories, while right-wing extremists, fundamentalists, and utra-nationalists alike insisted upon a continued Israeli presence.

It took the PLO some time to take control of the Intifada. Although at first the uprising appeared to be spontaneous and the result of individual grievances, Arafat claimed credit for its continuation. The PLO leader skillfully marshalled his forces. Between June and August 1988, he began, through aides, publicly to float ideas outlining what Palestinians would accept in the way of a solution: a Palestinian state in the West Bank and Gaza based on the 1947 UN Partition Plan, and "lasting peace and security" with Israel. King Hussein of Jordan and President Mubarak of Egypt still preferred the land-for-peace solution favored by Shimon Peres, but with Yitzhak Shamir as Prime Minister there seemed little likelihood of that eventuality. President Hafez al-Assad of Syria wanted neither the Jordanian solution nor an independent Palestinian state; he still dreamed of regaining the Golan Heights and of achieving a "Greater Syria."

In the spring of 1988, U.S. Secretary of State George Shultz, doubtless hoping to achieve a lasting monument for the Reagan administration, placed finding a solution to the Palestinian–Israeli conflict on the front burner, and he launched himself into "shuttle diplomacy," without much visible success.

On July 31, 1988, no doubt despairing of success in setting up an international conference, perhaps seeing in the Intifada a threat to his own kingdom, and realizing that, indeed, the Palestinians, especially the younger generation, would never accept him as their spokesman, King Hussein of Jordan renounced his claim to the West Bank, which in effect reversed the annexation decision made in 1950. (See Document 9–4.) "The independent Palestinian state will be established on the occupied Palestinian land after its liberation, God willing," Hussein stated. Although Jordan continued administration of the daily affairs of the West Bank, the PLO gradually took some responsibility for funding these activities. The Jordanian monarch distanced himself even further from the PLO. On August 7, 1988, he stated that Jordan would not be part of a Jordanian–Palestinian delegation in any peace process.

In the second half of 1988, the harsh Israeli response to the Intifada enabled the PLO to take the diplomatic initiative. Publicizing the Palestinian case on the world stage, the PLO achieved dramatic results. As the PLO increasingly assumed the appearance of a government in exile, the Israeli position hardened. On August 10, 1988, Prime Minister Shamir said that Israel would crush any attempt by the PLO to establish a government in exile. He continued the deportation of Palestinian resistance leaders, a policy adopted the previous January. On August 26, the UN Security Council called on Israel, yet again, to stop the deportations, and to allow the return of those already deported (approximately three dozen). The standoff continued.

The Islamic resistance movement, HAMAS, and the Unified National Leadership of the Uprising successfully organized a series of general strikes throughout the West Bank and Gaza. On September 16, *Jerusalem Post* diplomatic correspondent Benny Morris became the thirty-eighth Israeli to be jailed (he received a twenty-one-day sentence) for refusing to serve his reserve duty in the territories. In mid-September 1988, Arafat, in an address to the Socialist deputies of the European Parliament in Strasbourg, France, called for an international conference—to include Israel and the PLO—based on Resolution 242, recognizing the rights of the Palestinians. Secretary of State Shultz responded, on September 16, with the announcement that the United States would oppose any declaration of an independent Palestinian state, or government in exile, involving the occupied territories.

In another turnabout, in mid-October, Arafat, to satisfy American and Israeli objections, modified his position on an independent Palestinian state, stating that the PLO would accept a federation with Jordan. A week later, on October 22, 1988, he met with King Hussein and President Mubarak, at Aqaba, to work out the possibilities. Israel seemed unable to convince the United Nations that its methods in containing the Intifada were those of restraint; on November 3, the UN General Assembly, by a vote of 130–2 (Israel and the United States voted no) condemned Israeli oppression in the occupied territories and the violations of Palestinian human rights.

Despite the vows of PLO hardliners to derail the PLO chairman's peace initiatives, by the end of the year Arafat appeared to be firmly in control of a more unified PLO. Nevertheless, the PLO was unable, or unwilling, to define its goals or its relationship to Israel in a way that was unambiguous to the Israelis. The first year of the Intifada culminated in the Arab League summit meeting held in Algiers in mid-November 1988. There, at the nineteenth meeting of the Palestine National Council (PNC), considered by the PLO to be its "parliament in exile," the PNC, on November

15, 1988, proclaimed—by a vote of 253 to 46 with 10 abstentions—the establishment of an independent Palestinian state.

The PLO Declaration of Independence attracted immediate worldwide attention. (See Document 9–6.) Within three days, at least twenty-seven nations, mostly Arab and Muslim, extended recognition to the government in exile. On November 18, 1988, the Soviet Union recognized the proclamation of the Palestinian state, and, after initial hesitation, on November 21, Egypt recognized the Palestinian state. Israel denounced the declaration, dismissing it as irrelevant, and the United States rejected the declaration stating that unilateral PLO actions did not satisfy U.S. conditions for determining the future of the occupied territories. It was ambiguous and did not go far enough to warrant opening a dialogue with the PLO. By mid-1990, more states recognized the PLO declaration than recognized Israel. As with so many of the public documents crucial to the arguments of each side, almost all aspects of the Palestinian Declaration of Independence are in dispute between Israel and Israeli supporters on the one hand, and the PLO and Palestinian supporters on the other. Pro-Palestinians pointed to the declaration's reference to the UN partition resolution—Resolution 181—and "resolutions of the United Nations organizations since 1947," as evidence that the PLO implicitly recognized Israel, and accepted Resolutions 242 and 338. They also asserted that the PNC had voted specifically to accept Resolutions 242 and 338 on November 14, the day before the declaration was issued. (See Document 9–5.)

Pro-Israelis, in addition to pointing out that there is no authorized English translation of the declaration and no public record of votes taken, searched in vain for clear and unambiguous statements recognizing Israel and accepting Resolutions 242 and 338. Palestinian supporters argued that the declaration, by stating that UN Resolution 181 "provides the conditions of international legitimacy that ensures the right of the Palestinian people to sovereignty," defines the area of the Palestinian state to be the West Bank and the Gaza. Israeli supporters replied that the references to the area the Palestinian state is to occupy remain undefined and vague. Palestinians pointed to the affirmation of Palestine as a peace-loving state as evidence of a rejection of terrorism. Israelis dismissed this as deception, and pointed to the statements of hard-line PLO leaders who contradicted the so-called official policy and called for a continuation of the Intifada.

The weeks following the PNC declaration provided opportunities for both sides to amplify and clarify their positions and seek international support for them. We should not forget, however, that these diplomatic activities had little impact on events taking place on the ground in Israel, the occupied territories, and southern Lebanon.

On October 19, 1988, a PLO member of the Hizbullah suicided in a car bomb killing seven Israeli soldiers in the Israeli "security zone" in southern Lebanon. Israel responded with a commando air-raid on the PFLP–General Command headquarters just south of Beirut, claiming to kill twenty PLO militia—bringing the number of air attacks on Lebanon in 1988 to twenty-three. The Intifada continued unabated.

Nevertheless, most commentators agree that the final weeks of 1988 opened a new chapter in the Arab–Israeli conflict. A group of American Jews met with PLO representative Khalid al-Hassan in Stockholm on November 22, and later, on December 6–7, with Arafat himself and the Swedish Foreign Minister. They issued a joint statement—quickly dubbed the Stockholm Declaration—stating that the PNC recognized Israel as a state in the region, and condemned and rejected terrorism in all its forms, including state terrorism—the PLO's euphemism for Israel's actions. When Arafat was denied a transit visa by the United States to speak to the UN General

Bus crash, Jerusalem–Tel Aviv highway. Palestinian activist forced bus off road causing injury and death, July 6, 1989 (*Photo courtesy of Britain/Israel Public Affairs Centre*).

Assembly, the General Assembly took the unprecedented step of reconvening in Geneva. There, on December 13, 1988, Arafat detailed the proposals agreed to at Algiers. He also outlined his own three-point peace plan, which included the establishment of a UN committee to organize a peace conference, an international conference held under UN auspices with representatives from Israel, Palestine, and their neighbors, and Israeli withdrawal from the West Bank and Gaza to be replaced by a temporary UN peacekeeping force. Still, Secretary of State George Shultz was not satisfied.

Shamir accused Arafat of a "monumental act of deception." "We are not ready, and will never be ready to talk to the PLO," he fumed. Frantic discussions took place to ensure a positive response from the United States. In addition to Arafat himself, those involved included diplomats from the United States, Egypt, Saudi Arabia, and the Swedish Foreign Minister. The following day, on December 14, Arafat was more explicit. During a press conference in Geneva, Arafat repeated the PLO's acceptance of UN Resolutions 242 and 338 and fully renounced—not just condemned—terrorism. "Enough is enough. Enough is enough. Enough is enough," he repeated. (See Document 9–7.) Hours later, George Shultz announced that the United States would open a dialogue with the PLO.

Israel was crippled by the fact that no government had been formed since the recent elections. Acting Prime Minister Shamir, however, stood by the statement he had made shortly before, that the PLO were "our most extreme enemies. They will never change their position, their philosophy, which is the destruction of Israel," he stated. Arafat lent credence to Shamir's view in early January 1989. American officials claimed that a tape recording of a radio broadcast in which Arafat was speaking about the Intifada revealed that he threatened to kill any Arabs who opposed the uprising.

After his government was in place and under U.S. pressure, Shamir presented his own four-point plan as a response to Arafat's November 1988 diplomatic bombshell. (See Document 9–8.)

Rejecting the notion of direct Israeli negotiations with the PLO, Shamir proposed that elections be held in the territories under Israeli supervision to determine who should negotiate with Israel for the Palestinians over the future of the occupied territories.

Shamir's plan was similar to the formula for Palestinian autonomy agreed to at Camp David. President George Bush, who became President on January 20, 1989, supported the proposal, and King Hussein, after a meeting with Secretary of State James Baker, expressed his qualified support. Shamir stated unequivocally that the result would be, at best, Palestinian autonomy. This was seen by the Palestinians as totally out of touch with the new realities created by the Intifada and the Rabat decision. They believed they should be free to choose their own representatives, whether PLO or not, and that the outcome of any negotiations should not preclude Palestinian self-determination and an independent Palestinian state.

Shamir was under pressure from all sides: on the one hand, the PLO—and the United States to some extent—wanted further Israeli concessions; while on the other, conservatives within his own Likud party saw Shamir as already having gone too far. On May 9, 1989, following a meeting with French President Mitterand, Arafat declared that the provisions of the PLO charter calling for the destruction of Israel were *caduc,* "null and void." Israeli spokesmen replied with the observation that Arafat could say what he liked, but that the PNC had not issued such a statement. In any event, they added, this could be reversed at any time.

In a further effort to get Israel to accept PLO involvement even indirectly in the election process and peace talks, and to consider some form of territorial compromise, on May 22, 1989, Secretary Baker announced a new American peace plan. Echoing the cry of the Eisenhower administration, Baker called on Israel to "lay aside once and for all the unrealistic vision of a greater Israel," and to "reach out to Palestinians as neighbors who deserve political rights." (See Document 9–9.) Baker's program for peace included Israeli and Egyptian representatives drawing up a list of Palestinians who might take part in Israeli–Palestinian discussions on how to put the Shamir plan into effect. Already under pressure from right-wing elements at home, Shamir immediately rejected Baker's plan.

Nevertheless, variations of the Shamir and Baker plans remained the focus of diplomatic activity for the remainder of 1989. Israel finally agreed to a modified version of the Baker plan, and Egyptian President Hosni Mubarak convinced Arafat to let him act for the PLO in arranging a preliminary dialogue between Israel and the Palestinians. In November, the U.S. State Department began plans to arrange a trilateral meeting among the U.S. Secretary of State and the Foreign Ministers of both Israel and Egypt to discuss the formation of a Palestinian delegation to meet with the Israelis. The PLO, while accepting the Baker plan in principle, insisted that it should have the right to choose its own delegation in any negotiations with the Israelis. It rejected—as it had for the previous fifteen years—the notion that Egypt—or Jordan with whom Mubarak consulted closely—could speak for the Palestinians. The PLO had been there before.

In November 1989, the Israeli defense ministry revealed that up to that time, the Intifada had cost the Israel Defense Forces (IDF) $500 million. By mid-1990, according to International Red Cross figures, over 800 Palestinians had been killed by Israeli security forces, more than 200 of whom were children under the age of sixteen. Some

16,000 Palestinians were in prison, approximately 1,100 being held under administrative detention. Over 300 Arab homes in the West Bank and in Gaza had been demolished or sealed up. The IDF estimated that an additional 255 Palestinians suspected of collaborating with the Israeli authorities had been killed by Arabs. According to The Associated Press, 47 Israelis had died.

THE CONTINUING CONFLICT

Seemingly basing its actions on the principle that the occupied territories were an integral part of Israel, throughout 1986–87, as we have seen, the Israeli government continued its policy of establishing settlements, expropriating property, and encouraging Israeli citizens to move to the occupied territories. By the end of 1987, over 55% of the West Bank and 30% of the Gaza Strip had been expropriated by Israel. (See Map 9–4.) Under the "iron fist" policy Israel adopted toward the more than 835,000 Palestinian inhabitants, the level of despair and hopelessness, violence and tension in the territories intensified. After December 1987, the question of the future of the Palestinian Arabs acquired special urgency when the Intifada became the center of world attention. The Intifada reordered the political and diplomatic priorities of the Arab-Israeli conflict, bringing the issue of the future of the Palestinian Arabs to the forefront of the conflict.

The Intifada resulted in tragedy for both sides, with young unarmed Palestinian youths in conflict with and confronting Israeli soldiers their own age. Both demonstrating Palestinians and defending Israelis used tactics that put children at risk. The Palestinian organizers of the Intifada were reluctant to weaken the central community-based character of their resistance by making the tactical changes that would help keep children out of harm's way. The Israeli army similarly hesitated to yield its prerogatives as an occupation force, and was often unable to enforce the military discipline that was intended to minimize casualties against a civilian population that had become experienced practitioners of violence without guns. The outcome was that Palestinian children were shot and beaten by Israeli soldiers. The death rate of rock-throwing Palestinians in the first year of the Intifada was six times the annual per capita death rate of American soldiers in Vietnam. The likelihood of either side forgetting the often justified resentment at past wrongs, and understanding the legitimate grievances and interests of the other diminished under the invective and abuse each side employed against each other, and the denial by both that the other side existed. The answer to this tragedy, and to the causes that led to the uprising, is not to be found on the streets; it has to be solved at the conference table.

In March 1990, following the defection of Shamir's coalition partner, Labor's Shimon Peres, who advocated adoption of the Baker plan, and opposition from factions within his own party led by hard-liner Ariel Sharon, the Knesset passed a vote of no-confidence against Shamir. For the first time in Israel's history, a government fell through a vote of no-confidence. Shamir's fall was caused by his refusal to accept U.S. Secretary of State Baker's compromise plan hammered out in February to continue the peace process. Baker's 5 point formula called for Israel to accept meetings with Palestinians not active in PLO although known to have links with the organization. The PLO, in turn, would not insist on direct participation, and would drop its demand for prior Israeli agreement to an independent Palestinian state. Under pressure from Likud "hawks," Shamir rejected even this scheme to initiate "talks about talks." (See Document 9–10.)

MAP 9–4

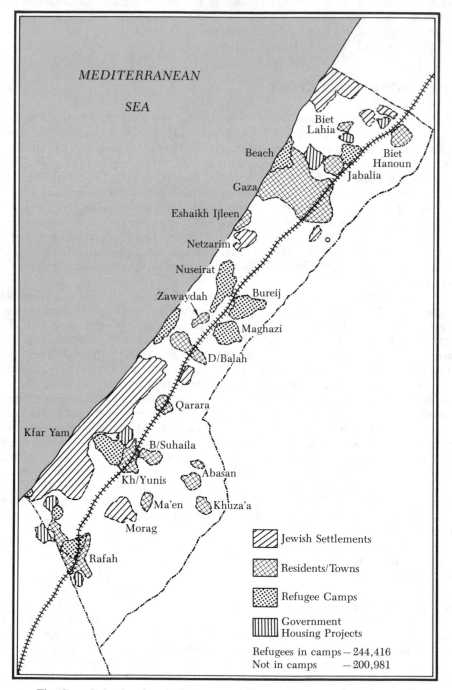

The Gaza Strip showing Arab towns, refugee camps and Jewish settlements, 1988.

Source: UNRWA

Israel's political stalemate continued through May 1990. Peres failed in his attempt to form a "peace coalition" government, so Shamir once more sought to form a Likud-led government. Encouraged by Peres's failure, Shamir repeated his view that there was no need to hold a dialogue with the Palestinians in the near future. And, in a rebuff to Egyptian President Hosni Mubarak, he stated that once talks began they did not have to take place in Cairo. Egypt had played a pivotal role in convincing the PLO to support a Palestinian-Israeli dialogue, to be held in Cairo.

Israel's prolonged unwillingness or inability to form a government created a dangerous political vacuum in the Middle East. The "peace process" came to a complete halt. Israel was faced with the issue of creating a government capable of working for a West Bank and Gaza settlement or risking a major break with Washington. Under the impact of the Intifada, relations between the Bush administration and Israel had become strained. By mid-1990, the United States was demanding that Israel stop the beatings and killings (especially of children), harsh detentions, humiliating and inhumane surveillance and curfews (routinely since May 1989, the entire Gaza Strip population has been subjected to dawn to dusk curfew), and open the universities that had been closed for over two years.

At a time when Israeli military leaders were predicting that the Intifada was dying or "in retreat," a further outbreak of violence occurred on May 20, 1990, when seven Palestinians were killed in Rishon Lezion south of Tel Aviv in an unprovoked attack by a reportedly "deranged" former Israeli soldier. Palestinian rage and frustration boiled over into the most violent rioting since the Intifada had begun, and the following day another 7 Palestinians were killed and over 600 wounded when the Israeli army attempted to quell the disturbances. A blanket curfew was imposed throughout the Gaza Strip and the major population centers of the West Bank. It took Israeli troops three days to restore order; 17 protesters were killed and over 1000 wounded. Israeli and Palestinian leaders quickly blamed each other for the renewed outbreak of violence. PLO leader Arafat called on Palestinians to step up protests "in every village, every city and every camp." U.S. State Department officials condemned the "tragic violence," and, expressing concern at the number of casualties inflicted by the Israeli army, called for a renewal of the stalled peace process. Even more disturbing to Israeli officials was the open rebellion by the 650,000 Israeli Arabs, the majority of whom joined the general strike called by the heads of the regional Arab councils. The strikes turned violent in many centers, especially cities like Nazareth, Haifa, and other towns with large Arab populations. Within days, a radical element within the PLO, the Palestine Liberation Front led by Abul Abbas, attempted a sea-launched reprisal raid against Israeli civilians. Israeli naval forces intercepted the raiders, killing four. A beleaguered Acting Prime Minister Shamir immediately went on the diplomatic offensive, claiming that the abortive attack proved that the PLO had not kept Arafat's December 1988 pledge to renounce terrorism, and calling on the United States to halt its dialogue with the PLO. Arafat disclaimed any responsibility for the thwarted attack, and distanced himself from the Libyan backed PLF, but he did not condemn the operation. In late June, the U.S. indeed broke off its dialogue with the PLO.

Following the rioting in May 1990, Egyptian President Mubarak told President Bush that if the peace process remained stalled more violence would erupt from the Palestinians. The Palestinians had endured extreme economic hardship and deprivation for nearly a quarter of a century without armed revolt, Mubarak told Bush. But, he warned, they would not continue to do so. To the United States, the solution to the Palestinian problem was a central factor in the Middle East situation and could only be resolved within the framework of a comprehensive settlement. Israel claimed that the core of the conflict was not the issue of the Palestine Arabs, nor the territories occupied as a result of the 1967 war; it was the fact that the Arab world had not recognized Israel's right to exist. In this context, it is important to keep in mind that in the unfolding Arab-Israeli conflict a crucial theme in the Palestinian Arabs' struggle for personal identity and national autonomy has been that the Arab world generally has treated them as political pawns for political purposes. Individual Arab states played a dominant, and not particularly constructive, role in the Palestinian question from the mid-1930s through the mid-1980s.

Soviet Jewish Immigration to Israel

A potentially explosive issue in the Arab-Israeli conflict to emerge in 1990 was the question of Jewish immigration from the Soviet Union. Once again, as has occurred so often in the past century, major changes in Europe stand to alter dramatically the fate of the Zionist enterprise, and with it the delicate balance of power and people in the Middle East. In the first four months of 1990, over 33,000 Soviet Jews arrived in Israel. The number predicted to arrive in Israel over the next five years varies between 500,000 (by the Israelis) to over a million (by the Palestinian Arabs). Israelis see the arrivals as the beginning of a great and long-awaited historic wave of aliyah, completing the Soviet aliyah that began in the 1970s and that brought over 200,000 Soviet Jews to Israel. To them, the questions arising from the immigration center around the economic, educational and social status of the immigrants and their impact on Israel's employment and housing situations. Israeli economic planners are concerned about finding suitable work for the predominantly professional arrivals in a population of about four million already severely burdened by unemployment, a long running recession, and a chronic housing shortage.

To Israelis, Soviet Jewish immigration represents a renewal of Israel's purpose. Palestinians and other Arabs regard the Soviet influx as a disaster equal to that of the Israeli War of Independence and the 1967 War. While claiming not to oppose Soviet immigration to Israel proper, they believe that the Soviet Jews will be settled in the West Bank and a concerted effort will be made to force the Palestinian Arabs across the Jordan River into Jordan. Shamir's policy of supporting Israeli settlers in the West Bank—and in the Old City of Jerusalem—and the sheer value (estimated at around $35 billion) of Jewish West Bank settlements, lends weight to Arab fears. The Palestinian Arabs are not alone among those who believe that Jewish immigration from the Soviet Union is a major threat to the future of a Palestine homeland. In May 1990, the White House put on hold the $400 million voted by Congress for housing loan guarantees for Soviet Jewish immigrants until Israel gives assurances that the funds will not be used to settle the immigrants in the occupied territories. During the Bush-Gorbachev Summit held in the United States in June 1990, President Gorbachev speculated that the Soviet Union might delay granting exit visas to Jews if they were to be settled in the territories. Shamir, who had forged a coalition with the minority hard-line parties of the Knesset and had formed a Likud-led government by June 8, promptly authorized two more Jewish settlements in the occupied territories, asserting that Israeli citizens had the right to live where they pleased.

The End of the Cold War

Other issues surfaced during 1990. The broad-ranging implications of the rapidly accelerating Soviet-American detente and democratic revolution sweeping Eastern Europe were not lost on either side in the Arab-Israeli conflict. The superpower rivalry of the Cold War had enabled the Arab states, by aligning themselves with the Soviet Union, to arm themselves and maintain their opposition to Israel. Israel, also, benefited enormously by drawing upon United States fears of Soviet expansion in the region.

The perceived collapse of Soviet power has forced Arab states, rather than turn to the United States, to fall back on Arab solidarity for strength and sustenance. The Arab states, especially Syria and Iraq, fear the consequences of American policy no longer held in check by the Soviet Union. They especially fear a U.S. backed expansionist Israel. Jordan, in particular, believes that a right-wing led Israeli government, backed by American capital and political support, will settle hundreds of thousands of Russian immigrants in the West Bank driving the Palestinians living there into Jordan, destabilizing, even overthrowing, that already economically shaky regime.

Israelis view the effects of these changes in Cold War and world power realities in two ways. Some argue that withdrawal of Soviet support for the Arab states makes war less likely because it means the Arabs are less able to make war, or to fight it to a successful conclusion. They believe that it has led to an almost unprecedented improvement in Israel's strategic situation. Others argue that if the Arab states successfully bury the hatchet of inter-Arab rivalry and face the world and Israel in a united front, they could form a formidable military threat against Israel. The Israelis consider Iraq, in particular, to be a major threat, especially since the end of the Iran-Iraq War.

Iraq's Invasion and Annexation of Kuwait

On August 2, 1990, Iraqi troops suddenly and unexpectedly invaded Kuwait. The Middle East, and indeed most of the world, was thrown into confusion. Kuwait's ruling family, the al-Sabah, fled, and two day later, Iraq's president, Saddam Hussein, formally annexed the Gulf kingdom. The Iraqi leader, deprived of port facilities in the Gulf, and with massive debts as the result of his punishing eight-year war with Iran, had genuine grievances against the policies of the Sabah family in helping keep oil prices low. In addition, Iraq claimed historical territorial rights over Kuwait. But the outright seizure of Kuwait provoked one of the worst global crises in recent memory. Many thousands of foreign nationals were trapped, and there was widespread fear that the Iraqi leader planned to invade Saudi Arabia. The industrial countries, and especially the United States, recoiled at the thought of Saddam Hussein in control of over 40% of the world's oil reserves.

The international response was immediate and overwhelming. On August 6, the Security Council unanimously adopted a comprehensive trade embargo against Iraq, and President Bush called for collective action to enforce it. Within weeks, a massive multi-national naval task-force was in place in the Gulf, effectively blockading Iraq. Over 50,000 American air and ground forces were airlifted to Saudi Arabia. The world watched anxiously as the storm clouds of war gathered over the Middle East.

Saddam Hussein's action was a clear indication that the Cold War was over in the region. Soviet support for UN sanctions and acquiescence in the stationing of extensive U.S. forces in Saudi Arabia illustrated a growing agreement between the U.S. and the U.S.S.R. on a variety of issues, including the danger of potentially explosive regional conflicts. Saddam Hussein seriously miscalculated the extent of coincidence of Soviet–United States interests in opposing his seizure of Kuwait.

Another myth was shattered by Iraq's action, that of pan-Arab unity. The other ruling families in the Gulf felt threatened and supported the West and Japan in condemning Saddam Hussein and imposing UN sanctions. They were joined by the traditional Arab enemies of Iraq, especially Egypt. King Hussein of Jordan, torn between his traditional ties with the West and U.S. on the one hand, and his economic dependence on Iraq on the other, trod the impossibly fine line of mediator, advocating an Arab-imposed rather than an American-imposed solution. His situation was made all the more difficult by the spontaneous support Palestinians in Jordan—over 60% of his population—gave Saddam Hussein. The PLO, caught in a dilemma, further damaged its relationship with the United States when Arafat called for Arab solidarity against the West and did not condemn Saddam Hussein. He did offer to mediate the conflict, however.

Israel's response to the Gulf crisis was mixed. Saddam Hussein's actions appeared to confirm Israel's claim that a solution to the Arab–Israeli conflict was not confined to the question of the future of the Palestinians, but was one that involved all the Arab states. The crisis also distracted world attention from Israel's handling of the Intifada and focused it on the capriciousness and fragility of Arab leadership. At the same time, Iraq's military adventurism seriously alarmed Israel. Although Israel was confident that it could withstand an Iraqi attack, the risk of an immediate war—with the possibility of chemical weapons being used—was dramatically heightened. Israel's anxiety was increased by the realization that, as with the end of the Cold War, its claim to be the most important ally of the United States in the region was undermined. Indeed, Israel, at the request of the U.S., played a very low-key role in the Gulf crisis, while President Bush pledged new arms to Saudi Arabia, praised Syria's stand against Iraq, and gave considerable prominence to Egypt's contribution, even suggesting that Congress forgive Egypt's $7 billion debt. Furthermore, there were signs that in the new post-Cold War era the United States would regard Israel's failure to resolve the future of the occupied territories as a liability. The events of the Gulf crisis, therefore, only increased the tension on all sides.

SUGGESTIONS FOR FURTHER READING

AJAMI, FOUAD, *The Vanishing Imam, Musa al-Sadr and the Shi'a of Lebanon*, Ithaca, N.Y., Cornell University Press, 1986.

FRIEDMAN, THOMAS, *From Beirut to Jerusalem*, New York, Farrar, Straus & Giroux, 1989.

HART, ALAN, *Arafat: A Political Biography*, Bloomington, Indiana University Press, 1984.

HELLER, MARK, *A Palestinian State: The Implications for Israel*, Cambridge, Mass., Harvard University Press, 1988.

LESCH, ANN MOSELY, AND TESSLER, MARK, *Israel, Egypt and the Palestinians from Camp David to Intifada*, Bloomington, Indiana University Press, 1989.

PERETZ, DON, *The Intifada*, Boulder, Colo., Westview Press, 1989.

RABINOVICH, ITAMAR, *The War for Lebanon, 1970–1983*, Ithaca, N.Y., Cornell University Press, 1984.

SCHIFF, ZE'EV, AND YA'ARI, EHUD, *Israel's Lebanon War*, New York, Simon & Schuster, 1984.

———, *Intifada: The Palestinian Uprising—Israel's Third Front*, New York, Simon & Schuster, 1990.

DOCUMENT 9–1

The Reagan
Peace Initiative

Following the Israeli invasion of Lebanon in June 1982, on September 1, 1982, President Ronald Reagan presented the following proposal:

First, as outlined in the Camp David accords, there must be a period of time during which the Palestinian inhabitants of the West Bank and Gaza will have full autonomy over their own affairs. Due consideration must be given to the principle of self-government by the inhabitants of the territories and to the legitimate security concerns of the parties involved.

The purpose of the 5-year period of transition, which would begin after free elections for a self-governing Palestinian authority, is to prove to the Palestinians that they can run their own affairs and that such Palestinian autonomy poses no threat to Israel's security.

The United States will not support the use of any additional land for the purpose of settlements during the transition period. Indeed, the immediate adoption of a settlement freeze by Israel, more than any other action, could create the confidence needed for wider participation in these talks. Further settlement activity is in no way necessary for the security of Israel and only diminishes the confidence of the Arabs that a final outcome can be freely and fairly negotiated.

I want to make the American position well understood: The purpose of this transition period is the peaceful and orderly transfer of authority from Israel to the Palestinian inhabitants of the West Bank and Gaza. At the same time, such a transfer must not interfere with Israel's security requirements.

Beyond the transition period, as we look to the future of the West Bank and Gaza, it is clear to me that peace cannot be achieved by the formation of an independent Palestinian state in those territories. Nor is it achievable on the basis of Israeli sovereignty or permanent control over the West Bank and Gaza.

So the United States will not support the establishment of an independent Palestinian state in the West Bank and we will not support annexation or permanent control by Israel.

There is, however, another way to peace. The final status of these lands must, of course, be reached through the give-and-take of negotiations. But it is the firm view of the United States that self-government by the Palestinians of the West Bank and Gaza in association with Jordan offers the best chance for a durable, just and lasting peace.

We base our approach squarely on the principle that the Arab-Israeli conflict should be resolved through negotiations involving an exchange of territory for peace. This exchange is enshrined in U.N. Security Council Resolution 242, which is, in turn, incorporated in all its parts in the Camp David agreements. U.N. Resolution 242 remains wholly valid as the foundation stone of America's Middle East peace effort.

It is the United States' position that—in return for peace—the withdrawal provision of Resolution 242 applies to all fronts, including the West Bank and Gaza.

When the border is negotiated between Jordan and Israel, our view on the extent to which Israel should be asked to give up territory will be heavily affected by the extent of true peace and normalization and the security arrangements offered in return.

Finally, we remain convinced that Jerusalem must remain undivided, but its final status should be decided through negotiations.

In the course of the negotiations to come, the United States will support positions that seem to us fair and reasonable compromises and likely to promote a sound agreement. We will also put forward our own detailed proposals when we believe they can be helpful. And, make no mistake, the United States will oppose any proposal—from any party and at any point in the negotiating process—that threatens the security of Israel. American's commitment to the security of Israel is ironclad. And, I might add, so is mine.

Source: The Middle East, 7th ed. (Washington, D.C.: Congressional Quarterly, Inc., 1990), p. 306.

DOCUMENT 9–2

Fez Summit
Peace Proposal

An Arab summit was held in Fez, Morocco, in September 1982 in response to the Israeli invasion of Lebanon and President Reagan's September initiative. The following eight-point plan came from that summit.

1. The withdrawal of Israel from all Arab territories occupied in 1967 including Arab Al Qods (East Jerusalem).
2. The dismantling of settlements established by Israel on the Arab territories after 1967.
3. The guarantee of freedom of worship and practice of religious rites for all religions in the holy shrine.
4. The reaffirmation of the Palestinian people's right to self-determination and the exercise of its imprescriptible and inalienable national rights under the leadership of the Palestine Liberation Organization (PLO), its sole and legitimate representative, and the indemnification of all those who do not desire to return.
5. Placing the West Bank and Gaza Strip under the control of the United Nations for a transitory period not exceeding a few months.
6. The establishment of an independent Palestinian state with Al Qods as its capital.
7. The Security Council guarantees peace among all states of the region including the independent Palestinian state.
8. The Security Council guarantees the respect of these principles.

Source: Middle East, Congressional Quarterly, 7th ed., p. 306.

DOCUMENT 9–3

Palestinian National Council Political Resolutions,
Algiers, 22 February, 1983 [Excerpts]

On the Arab Front

3. Jordan

(i) Affirmation of the special and distinctive relations linking the Palestinian and Jordanian peoples. Affirmation of the need to work to develop this harmony and the national interest of the two peoples and the Arab nation to attain the firm national rights of the Palestinian people, including the right of return, self-determination and the establishment of an independent Palestinian State.

(ii) Adherence to the resolutions of the PNC concerning relations with Jordan, starting with the PLO as the sole legitimate representative of the Palestinian people, *inside* and *outside* the occupied territories.

The PNC sees future relations with Jordan developing on the basis of a confederation between two independent states.

7. Egypt

The PNC affirms its rejection of the Camp David accords and related plans for autonomy and civil administration. From its deep-rooted belief in the role of Egypt and its great people in the Arab struggle, the council affirms its stand alongside the struggle of the Egyptian people and their national forces to end the policy of Camp David, so that Egypt can return to its position of struggle at the heart of the Arab nation. The council calls on the executive committee to develop the PLO's relations with the Egyptian popular democratic national forces struggling against the normalization of relations with the Zionist enemy in various forms. It regards this (struggle) as expressing the basic interests of the Arab nation and supporting the struggle of our Palestinian people for their national rights. The council calls on the executive committee to define relations with the Egyptian regime on the basis of the latter's abandoning the Camp David policy.

On the International Front

1. The Brezhnev Plan

The PNC expresses its esteem and support for the proposals contained in the plan of President Brezhnev published on September 16, 1980 and which affirm the inalienable national rights of our Palestinian people, including those of return, self-determination and the establishment of an independent Palestinian State under the leadership of the PLO, the sole legitimate representative of the Palestinian people. The council also expresses its esteem for the stand of the socialist bloc countries on the just cause of our people as affirmed by the Prague declaration on the Middle East situation, published on January 3, 1983.

2. The Reagan Plan

The Reagan plan, in form and content, does not fulfill the inalienable national rights of the Palestinian people because it denies the right of return, self-determination, the establishment of an independent Palestinian State and that the PLO is sole legitimate representative of the Palestinian people and it contradicts international law. For these reasons, the PNC declares its refusal to consider the plan as a proper basis for a lasting and just solution to the Palestinian cause and the Zionist-Arab conflict.

Source: Yehuda Lukacs, *Documents on the Israeli–Palestine Conflict, 1967–1983* (Cambridge, England: Cambridge University Press, 1984), pp. 208–210.

DOCUMENT 9–4

Hussein's Renunciation of Claim to West Bank

In a July 31, 1988, speech King Hussein of Jordan renounced his nation's claims to the West Bank and severed all legal and administrative links with it.

In the name of God, the compassionate, the merciful and peace be upon his faithful Arab messenger

Brother citizens. . . . [W]e have initiated, after seeking God's assistance, and in light of a thorough and extensive study, a series of measures with the aim of enhancing the Palestinian national orientation, and highlighting the Palestinian identity. Our objective is the benefit of the Palestinian cause and the Arab Palestinian people.

Our decision, as you know, comes after thirty-eight years of the unity of the two banks, and fourteen years after the Rabat Summit Resolution, designating the Palestine Liberation Organization (PLO) as the sole legitimate representative of the Palestinian people. It also comes six years after the Fez [Morocco] Summit Resolution of an independent Palestinian state in the occupied West Bank and the Gaza Strip. . . .

The considerations leading to the search to identify the relationship between the West Bank and the Hashemite Kingdom of Jordan, against the background of the PLO's call for the establishment of an independent Palestinian state, are twofold:

    I. The principle of Arab unity, this being a national objective to which all the Arab peoples aspire, and which they all seek to realize.

    II. The political reality of the scope of benefit to the Palestinian struggle that accrues from maintaining the legal relationship between the two banks of the kingdom. . . .

. . . We respect the wish of the PLO, the sole legitimate representative of the Palestinian people, to secede from us in an independent Palestinian state. We say this in all understanding. Nevertheless, Jordan will remain the proud bearer of the message of the great Arab revolt; faithful to its principles; believing in the common Arab destiny; and committed to joint Arab action.

Regarding the political factor, it has been our belief, since the Israeli aggression of June 1967, that our first priority should be to liberate the land and holy places from Israeli occupation.

Accordingly, as is well known, we have concentrated all our efforts during the twenty-one years since the occupation towards this goal. We had never imagined that the preservation of the legal and administrative links between the two banks could constitute an obstacle to the liberation of the occupied Palestinian land. . . .

Lately, it has transpired that there is a general Palestinian and Arab orientation towards highlighting the Palestinian identity in a complete manner. . . . It is also viewed that these [Jordanian-West Bank] links hamper the Palestinian struggle to gain international support for the Palestinian cause, as the national cause of a people struggling against foreign occupation. . . .

. . . [T]here is a general conviction that the struggle to liberate the occupied Palestinian land could be enhanced by dismantling the legal and administrative links between the two banks, we have to fulfill our duty, and do what is required of us. At the Rabat Summit of 1974 we responded to the Arab leaders' appeal to us to continue our interaction with the occupied West Bank through the Jordanian institutions, to support the steadfastness of our brothers there. Today we respond to the wish of the Palestine Liberation Organization, the sole legitimate representative of the Palestinian people, and to the Arab orientation to affirm the Palestinian identity in all its aspects. . . .

Brother citizens. . . . We cannot continue in this state of suspension, which can neither serve Jordan nor the Palestinian cause. We had to leave the labyrinth of fears and doubts, towards clearer horizons where mutual trust, understanding, and cooperation can prevail, to the benefit of the Palestinian cause and Arab unity. This unity will remain a goal which all the Arab peoples cherish and seek to realize.

At the same time, it has to be understood in all clarity, and without any ambiguity or equivocation, that our measures regarding the West Bank, concern only the occupied Palestinian land and its people. They naturally do not relate in any way to the Jordanian citizens of Palestinian origin in the Hashemite Kingdom of Jordan. They all have the full rights of citizenship and all its obligations, the same as any other citizen irrespective of his origin. They are an integral part of the Jordanian state. They belong to it, they live on its land, and they participate in its life and all its activities. Jordan is not Palestine; and the independent Palestinian state will be established on the occupied Palestinian land after its liberation, God willing. There the Palestinian identity will be embodied, and there the Palestinian struggle shall come to fruition, as confirmed by the glorious uprising of the Palestinian people under occupation.

National unity is precious in any country; but in Jordan it is more than that. It is the basis of our stability, and the springboard of our development and prosperity. It is the foundation of our national security and the source of our faith in the future. It is the living embodiment of the principles of the great Arab revolt, which we inherited, and whose banner we proudly bear. It is a living example of constructive plurality, and a sound nucleus for wider Arab unity.

. . . Citizens, Palestinian brothers in the occupied Palestinian lands, to dispel any doubts that may arise out of our measures, we assure you that these measures do not mean the abandonment of our national duty, either towards the Arab-Israeli conflict, or towards the Palestinian cause. . . . Jordan will continue its support for the steadfastness of the Palestinian people, and their courageous uprising in the occupied Palestinian land, within its capabilities.

I have to mention, that when we decided to cancel the Jordanian Development Plan in the occupied territories, we contacted, at the same time, various friendly governments and international institutions, which had expressed their wish to contribute to the plan, urging them to continue financing development projects in the occupied Palestinian lands, through the relevant Palestinian quarters.

. . . No one outside Palestine has had, nor can have, an attachment to Palestine, or its cause, firmer than that of Jordan or of my family. Moreover, Jordan is a confrontation state, whose borders with Israel are longer than those of any other Arab state, longer even than the combined borders of the West Bank and Gaza with Israel.

In addition, Jordan will not give up its commitment to take part in the peace process. We have contributed to the peace process until it reached the stage of a consensus to convene an international peace conference on the Middle East. The purpose of the conference would be to achieve a just and comprehensive peace settlement to the Arab-Israeli conflict, and the settlement of the Palestinian problem in all its aspects. . . .

Jordan, dear brothers, is a principal party to the Arab-Israeli conflict, and to the peace process. It shoulders its national responsibilities on that basis.

I thank you and salute you, and reiterate my heartfelt wishes to you, praying God the almighty to grant us assistance and guidance, and to grant our Palestinian brothers victory and success.

May God's peace, mercy, and blessings be upon you.

Source: Middle East, Congressional Quarterly, 7th ed., p. 309.

DOCUMENT 9–5

The Palestine National Council affirms the necessity of holding an effective international conference concerning the Middle East issue and its essence, the Palestinian cause, under the auspices of the United Nations and with the participation of the permanent member states of the U.N. Security Council and all the parties to the struggle in the region, including the P.L.O., the sole legitimate representative of the Palestine people, on an equal footing, and by considering that the international conference will be held on the basis of U.N. Security Council Resolutions 242 and 338 and the assurance of the legitimate national rights of the Palestinian people and, first and foremost, their right to self-determination in application of the principles and provisions of the U.N. charter concerning the right of peoples to self-determination and the inadmissibility of seizing the lands of others by force or military invasion, and in accordance with the resolutions of the U.N. regarding the Palestinian and Arab territories that it has occupied since 1967, including Arab Jerusalem.

From an unofficial U.S. translation of resolution, adopted by the Palestine National Council on Nov. 14, 1988.

DOCUMENT 9–6

**Palestine National Council,
"Palestinian Declaration of Independence,"
Algiers, 15 November 1988**

Below is the official translation of the Declaration of Independence as carried by WAFA from Algiers, 17 November 1988.

In the name of God, the Compassionate, the Merciful.

Palestine, the land of the three monotheistic faiths, is where the Palestinian Arab people was born, on which it grew, developed, and excelled. The Palestinian people was never separated from or diminished in its integral bonds with Palestine. Thus the Palestinian Arab people ensured for itself an everlasting union between itself, its land, and its history. . . .

Despite the historical injustice inflicted on the Palestinian Arab people resulting in their dispersion and depriving them of their right to self-determination, following upon UN General Assembly Resolution 181 (1947), which partitioned Palestine into two states, one Arab, one Jewish, yet it is this resolution that still provides those conditions of international legitimacy that ensure the right of the Palestinian Arab people to sovereignty and national independence.

By stages, the occupation of Palestine and parts of other Arab territories by Israeli forces, the willed dispossession and expulsion from their ancestral homes of the majority of Palestine's civilian inhabitants was achieved by organized terror; those Palestinians who remained, as a vestige subjugated in its homeland, were persecuted and forced to endure the destruction of their national life.

Thus were principles of international legitimacy violated. Thus were the Charter of the United Nations and its resolutions disfigured, for they had recognized the Palestinian Arab people's national rights, including the Right of Return, the Right to Independence, the Right to Sovereignty over territory and homeland.

In Palestine and on its perimeters, in exile distant and near, the Palestinian Arab people never faltered and never abandoned its conviction in its rights of return and independence. Occupation, massacres, and dispersion achieved no gain in the unabated Palestinian consciousness of self and political identity, as Palestinians went forward with their destiny, undeterred and unbowed. And from out of the long years of trial in evermounting struggle, the Palestinian political identity emerged further consolidated and confirmed. And the collective Palestinian national will forged itself in a political embodiment, the Palestine Liberation Organization, its sole, legitimate representative, recognized by the world community as a whole, as well as by related regional and international institutions. Standing on the very rock of conviction in the Palestinian people's inalienable rights, and on the ground of Arab national consensus, and of international legitimacy, the PLO led the campaigns of its great people, molded into unity and powerful resolve, one and indivisible in the triumphs, even as it suffered massacres and confinement within and without its home. And so Palestinian resistance was clarified and raised into the forefront of Arab and world awareness, as the struggle of the Palestinian Arab people achieved unique prominence among the world's liberation movements in the modern era.

The massive national uprising, the *intifadah,* now intensifying in cumulative scope and power on occupied Palestinian territories, as well as the unflinching resistance of the refugee camps outside the homeland, have elevated consciousness of the Palestinian truth and right into still higher realms of comprehension and actuality. Now at last the curtain has been dropped around a whole epoch of prevarication and negation. The Intifadah has set siege to the mind of official Israel, which has for too long relied exclusively upon myth and terror to deny Palestinian existence altogether. Because of the Intifadah and its revolutionary irreversible impulse, the history of Palestine has therefore arrived at a decisive juncture.

Whereas the Palestinian people reaffirms most definitely its inalienable rights in the land of its patrimony:

Now by virtue of natural, historical, and legal rights and the sacrifices of successive generations who gave of themselves in defense of the freedom and independence of their homeland;

In pursuance of resolutions adopted by Arab summit conferences and relying on the authority bestowed by international legitimacy as embodied in the resolutions of the United Nations Organization since 1947;

And in exercise by the Palestinian Arab people of its rights to self-determination, political independence, and sovereignty over its territory;

The Palestine National Council, in the name of God, and in the name of the Palestinian Arab people, hereby proclaims the establishment of the State of Palestine on our Palestinian territory with its capital Jerusalem (Al-Quds Ash-Sharif).

The State of Palestine is the state of Palestinians wherever they may be. The state is for them to enjoy in it their collective national and cultural identity, theirs to pursue in it a complete equality of rights. In it will be safeguarded their political and religious convictions and their human dignity by means of a parliamentary democratic system of governance, itself based on freedom of expression and the freedom to form parties. The rights of minorities will duly be respected by the majority, as minorities must abide by decisions of the majority. Governance will be based on principles of social justice, equality and nondiscrimination in public rights on grounds of race, religion, color, or sex under the aegis of a constitution which ensures the role of law and on independent judiciary. Thus shall these principles allow no departure from Palestine's age-old spiritual and civilizational heritage of tolerance and re-ligious co-existence.

The State of Palestine is an Arab state, an integral and indivisible part of the Arab nation, at one with that nation in heritage and civilization, with it also in its aspiration for liberation, progress, democracy, and unity. The State of Palestine affirms its obligation to abide by the Charter of the League of Arab States, whereby the coordination of the Arab states with each other shall be strengthened. It calls upon Arab compatriots to consolidate and enhance the emergence in reality of our State, to mobilize potential, and to intensify efforts whose goal is to end Israeli occupation.

The State of Palestine proclaims its commitment to the principles and purposes of the United Nations, and to the Universal Declaration of Human Rights. It proclaims its commit-ment as well to the principles and policies of the Non-Aligned Movement.

It further announces itself to be a peace-loving state, in adherence to the principles of peaceful co-existence. It will join with all states and peoples in order to assure a permanent peace based upon justice and the respect of rights so that humanity's potential for well-being may be assured, an earnest competition for excellence be maintained, and in which confi-dence in the future will eliminate fear for those who are just and for whom justice is the only recourse.

In the context of its struggle for peace in the land of love and peace, the State of Palestine calls upon the United Nations to bear special responsibility for the Palestinian Arab people and its homeland. It calls upon all peace- and freedom-loving peoples and states to assist it in the attainment of its objectives, to provide it with security, to alleviate the tragedy of its people, and to help to terminate Israel's occupation of the Palestinian territories.

The State of Palestine herewith declares that it believes in the settlement of regional and international disputes by peaceful means, in accordance with the UN Charter and resolu-tions. Without prejudice to its natural right to defend its territorial integrity and indepen-dence, it therefore rejects the threat or use of force, violence, and terrorism against its territorial integrity, or political independence, as it also rejects their use against the territorial integrity of other states.

Therefore, on this day unlike all others, 15 November, 1988, as we stand at the threshold of a new dawn, in all honor and modesty we humbly bow to the sacred spirits of our fallen ones, Palestinian and Arab, by the purity of whose sacrifice for the homeland our sky has been illuminated and our land given life. Our hearts are lifted up and irradiated by the light emanating from the much blessed *intifadah,* from those who have endured and have fought the fight of the camps, of dispersion, of exile, from those who have borne the standard of freedom, our children, our aged, our youth, our prisoners, detainees, and wounded, all those whose ties to our sacred soil are confirmed in camp, village, and town. We render special tribute to that brave Palestinian woman, guardian of sustenance and life, keeper of our people's perennial flame. To the souls of our sainted martyrs, to the whole of our Palestinian Arab people, to all free and honorable peoples everywhere, we pledge that our struggle shall be continued until the occupation ends, and the foundation of our sovereignty and indepen-dence shall be fortified accordingly.

Therefore, we call upon our great people to rally to the banner of Palestine, to cherish and defend it, so that it may forever be the symbol of our freedom and dignity in that homeland, which is a homeland for the free, now and always.

In the name of God, the Compassionate, the Merciful.

"Say: 'O God, Master of the Kingdom, Thou givest the Kingdom to whom Thou wilt, and seizest the Kingdom from whom Thou wilt. Thou exaltest whom Thou wilt, and Thou abasest whom Thou wilt; in Thy hand is the good; Thou art powerful over everything.' "
Sadaqa Allahu al-'Azim

Source: Journal of Palestine Studies, No. 70, Winter 1988, pp. 213–216.

DOCUMENT 9–7

Arafat Statement
on Israel, Terrorism

At a December 14, 1988, press conference in Geneva, Palestine Liberation organization leader Yasir Arafat explicitly recognized Israel's right to exist, renounced terrorism, and accepted UN Security Council resolutions 242 and 338. Following is the text of Arafat's statement as recorded by Reuters.

Let me highlight my views before you. Our desire for peace is a strategy and not an interim tactic. We are bent on peace come what may, come what may.

Our statehood provides salvation to the Palestinians and peace to both Palestinians and Israelis.

Self-determination means survival for the Palestinians and our survival does not destroy the survival of the Israelis as their rulers claim.

Yesterday in my speech I made reference to United Nations Resolution 181 as the basis for Palestinian independence. I also made reference to our acceptance of Resolution 242 and 338 as the basis for negotiations with Israel within the framework of the international conference. These three resolutions were endorsed by our Palestine National Council session in Algiers.

In my speech also yesterday, it was clear that we mean our people's rights to freedom and national independence, according to Resolution 181, and the right of all parties concerned in the Middle East conflict to exist in peace and security, and, as I have mentioned, including the state of Palestine, Israel and other neighbors, according to Resolution 242 and 338.

As for terrorism, I renounced it yesterday in no uncertain terms, and yet, I repeat for the record. I repeat for the record that we totally and absolutely renounce all forms of terrorism, including individual, group and state terrorism.

Between Geneva and Algiers, we have made our position crystal clear. Any more talk such as "The Palestinians should give more"—you remember this slogan?—or "It is not enough" or "The Palestinians are engaging in propaganda games, and public-relations exercises" will be damaging and counterproductive.

Enough is enough. Enough is enough. Enough is enough. All remaining matters should be discussed around the table and within the international conference.

Let it be absolutely clear that neither Arafat, nor any [one] for that matter, can stop the intifada, the uprising. The intifada will come to an end only when practical and tangible steps have been taken towards the achievement of our national aims and establishment of our independent Palestinian state.

In this context, I expect the E.E.C. to play a more effective role in promoting peace in our region. They have a political responsibility, they have a moral responsibility, and they can deal with it.

Finally, I declare before you and I ask you to kindly quote me on that: We want peace. We want peace. We are committed to peace. We are committed to peace. We want to live in our Palestinian state, and let live. Thank you.

Source: The Middle East, 7th ed., Congressional Quarterly, p. 311.

DOCUMENT 9-8

Shamir's Four-Point Plan

The official Israeli Foreign Ministry formulation of the prime minister's proposal, approved by the government on May 14, 1989. Twenty ministers voted in favor of the plan and six voted against. Voting against were three Likud members—Ariel Sharon, Itzkhak Modai and David Levy—and Mafdal member Avner Shaki. Two labor members—Ezer Weitzmann and Rafi Edri—also voted against, but for opposite reasons: they said the plan hinges on PLO agreement and that therefore there should be direct Israeli-PLO talks.

1. The Camp David Partners—Reconfirmation of the Commitment to Peace

Ten years ago, the peace treaty between Israel and Egypt was concluded on the basis of the Camp David Accords. When the accords were signed, it was expected that more Arab countries would shortly join the circle of peace. This expectation was not realized.

The strength of Israel-Egyptian relations and the cooperation between the three partners to the accords have a decisive influence on the chances for Middle East peace, and the Israeli-Egyptian treaty is the cornerstone to the building of peace in the region.

Therefore, the prime minister has called on the three countries whose leaders affixed their signature to the Camp David Accords—the US, Egypt, and Israel—to renew, 10 years later, their commitment to the agreements and to peace.

2. The Arab Countries—From a State of War to a Process of Peace

The prime minister urged the US and Egypt to call on the other Arab countries to desist from hostility toward Israel and to replace belligerency and boycott with negotiation and cooperation. Of all the Arab countries, only Egypt has recognized Israel and its right to exist. Many of these states actively participated in wars against Israel by direct involvement or indirect assistance. To this day, the Arab countries are partners in an economic boycott against Israel, refuse to recognize it, and refuse to establish diplomatic relations with it.

The solution to the Arab-Israeli conflict and the building of confidence leading to a permanent settlement require a change in the attitude of the Arab countries toward Israel. Israel, therefore, calls on these states to put an end to this historic anomaly and to join direct bilateral negotiations aimed at normalization and peace.

3. A Solution to the Refugee Problem—An International Effort

The prime minister has called for an international effort, led by the US and with the significant participation of Israel, to solve the problem of the Arab refugees. The refugee problem has been perpetuated by the leaders of the Arab countries, while Israel with its meagre resources is absorbing hundreds of thousands of Jewish refugees from Arab countries. Settling the refugees must not wait for a political process or come in its stead.

The matter must be viewed as a humanitarian problem and action must be taken to ease the human distress of the refugees and to ensure for their families appropriate living quarters and self-respect.

Some 300,000 people live in refugee camps in Judea, Samaria and the Gaza District. In the 1970s, Israel unilaterally undertook the rehabilitation of residents of refugee camps in Gaza and erected 10 neighborhoods in which 11,000 families reside. This operation was carried out in partnership with the residents despite PLO objections.

The time has now come to ensure appropriate infrastructure, living quarters and services for the rest of the residents of the camps who, at the same time, are victims of the conflict, hostages to it, and an element which perpetuates its continued existence.

Good will and an international effort to allocate the necessary resources will ensure a satisfactory solution to this humanitarian effort and will help improve the political climate in the region.

4. Free Elections in Judea, Samaria and Gaza on the Road to Negotiations

In order to bring about a process of political negotiations and in order to locate legitimate representatives of the Palestinian population, the prime minister proposes that free elections be held among the Arabs of Judea, Samaria and Gaza—elections that will be free of the intimidation and terror of the PLO.

These elections will permit the development of an authentic representation that is not self-appointed from the outside. This representation will be comprised of people who will be chosen by the population in free elections and who will express, in advance, their willingness to take part in the following diplomatic process.

The aim of the elections is to bring about the establishment of a delegation that will participate in negotiations on an interim settlement, in which a self-governing administration will be set up. The interim period will serve as an essential test of cooperation and coexistence. It will be followed by negotiations on the final settlement, in which Israel will be prepared to discuss any option which will be presented.

The US administration has expressed its support for the idea, and following the prime minister's return, his proposals will be discussed here and the various questions surrounding the holding of elections will be examined. Contacts necessary for the implementation of the proposals will be maintained.

Source: Israel Government Press Release, May 14, 1989.

DOCUMENT 9–9

Secretary of State Baker's Address
before the American-Israel
Public Affairs Committee (AIPAC),
Washington, D.C., May 22, 1989.

As we approach the peace process, together, we understand Israel's caution especially when assessing Arab attitudes about peace. I don't blame Israel for exercising this caution. Its history and, indeed, its geopolitical situation require it.

At the same time, I think that caution must never become paralysis. Ten years after Camp David, Egypt remains firmly committed to peace, and Arab attitudes are changing. Egypt's readmission into the Arab League on its own terms and with the peace treaty intact, I think, is one sign of change. Evolving Palestinian attitudes are another. Much more needs to be done—to be demonstrated—that such change is real. But I don't think that change can be ignored even now. This is surely a time when, as the Prime Minister said, the right mix of principles and pragmatism is required.

U.S. Views

As we assess these changes, U.S. policies benefit from a longstanding commitment to sound principles, principles which have worked in practice to advance the peace process. Let me mention some of those principles for you.

First, the United States believes that the objective of the peace process is a comprehensive settlement achieved through negotiations based on UN Security Council Resolutions 242 and 338. In our view, these negotiations must involve territory for peace, security and recognition for Israel and all of the states of the region, and Palestinian political rights.

Second, for negotiations to succeed they must allow the parties to deal directly with each other, face to face. A properly structured international conference could be useful at an appropriate time, but only if it did not interfere with or in any way replace or be a substitute for direct talks between the parties.

Third, the issues involved in the negotiations are far too complex, and the emotions are far too deep, to move directly to a final settlement. Accordingly, some transitional period is needed, associated in time and sequence with negotiations on final status. Such a transition will allow the parties to take the measure of each other's performance, to encourage attitudes to change, and to demonstrate that peace and coexistence is desired.

Fourth, in advance of direct negotiations, neither the United States nor any other party, inside or outside, can or will dictate an outcome. That is why the United States does not support annexation or permanent Israeli control of the West Bank and Gaza, nor do we support the creation of an independent Palestinian state.

I would add here, that we do have an idea about the reasonable middle ground to which a settlement should be directed. That is, self-government for Palestinians in the West Bank and Gaza in a manner acceptable to Palestinians, Israel, and Jordan. Such a formula provides ample scope for Palestinians to achieve their full political rights. It also provides ample protection for Israel's security as well.

Prenegotiations

Following these principles, we face a pragmatic issue, the issue of how do we get negotiations underway. Unfortunately, the gap between the parties on key issues such as Palestinian representation and the shape of a final settlement remains very, very wide. Violence has soured the atmosphere, and so a quick move to negotiations is quite unlikely. And in the absence of either a minimum of good will or any movement to close the gap, a high-visibility American initiative, we think, has little basis on which to stand. . . .

Challenges Ahead

We do not think there is a real constructive alternative to the process which I have outlined. Continuation of the status quo will lead to increasing violence and worsening prospects for peace. We think now is the time to move toward a serious negotiating process, to create the atmosphere for a renewed peace process.

Let the **Arab world** take concrete steps toward accommodation with Israel—not in place of the peace process, but as a catalyst for it. And so we would say: end the economic boycott; stop the challenges to Israel's standing in international organizations; repudiate the odious line that Zionism is racism.

For Israel, now is the time to lay aside, once and for all, the unrealistic vision of a greater Israel. Israeli interests in the West Bank and Gaza—security and otherwise—can be accommodated in a settlement based on Resolution 242. Forswear annexation. Stop settlement activity. Allow schools to reopen. Reach out to the Palestinians as neighbors who deserve political rights.

For Palestinians, now is the time to speak with one voice for peace. Renounce the policy of phases in all languages, not just those addressed to the West. Practice constructive diplomacy, not attempts to distort international organizations, such as the World Health Organization. Amend the covenant. Translate the dialogue of violence in the *intifada* into a dialogue of politics and diplomacy. Violence will not work. Reach out to Israelis and convince them of your peaceful intentions. You have the most to gain from doing so, and no one else can or *will* do it for you. Finally, understand that no one is going to "deliver" Israel for you.

For outside parties—in particular, the Soviet Union—now is the time to make "new thinking" a reality as it applies to the Middle East. I must say that Chairman Gorbachev and Foreign Minister Shevardnadze told me in Moscow 10 days ago that Soviet policy is changing. New laws regarding emigration will soon be discussed by the Supreme Soviet. Jewish life in the Soviet Union is also looking better, with students beginning to study their heritage freely. Finally, the Soviet Union agreed with us last week that Prime Minister Shamir's election proposal was worthy of consideration.

These, of course, are all positive signs. But the Soviets must go further to demonstrate convincingly that they are serious about new thinking in the Arab-Israeli conflict. Let Moscow restore diplomatic ties with Israel, for example.

The Soviets should also help promote a serious peace process, not just empty slogans. And it is time for the Soviet Union, we think, to behave responsibly when it comes to arms and stop the supply of sophisticated weapons to countries like Libya.

I said at the beginning of these remarks that the Middle East had approached a turning point. I believe that this region, which is so full of potential, will not remain immune from the changes which are sweeping the rest of the world. These changes begin with the quest for democracy, for individual freedom, and for choice. Long ago, of course, Israel chose this path. And long ago, the American people decided to walk with Israel in its quest for peace and in its quest for security.

The policy I have described today reaffirms and renews that course. For our part, the United States will move ahead steadily and carefully, in a step-by-step approach designed to help the parties make the necessary decisions for peace. Perhaps Judge Learned Hand expressed it best when he said, ". . . we shall have to be content with short steps; . . . but we shall have gone forward, if we bring to our task . . . patience, understanding, sympathy, forbearance, generosity, fortitude and above all an inflexible determination."

Source: United States Department of State • Bureau of Public Affairs, Office of Public Communication • Editorial Division • Washington, D.C. • May 1989.

DOCUMENT 9–10

The Likud Party Platform 1981 [Excerpts]

The Right of the Jewish People to Eretz Israel

A. The right of the Jewish people to Eretz Israel is an eternal one, which cannot be challenged and is a part of Israel's right to security and peace.

B. The state of Israel has a right to, and demands, sovereignty over Judea, Samaria and the Gaza District. Following the interim period stipulated in the Camp David Accords, Israel will press its demand and take action to realize this right.

C. Any program which entails relinquishing part of Western Eretz Israel to foreign rule, as suggested by the Alignment Party, undermines our right to the land; will inevitably lead to the establishment of a "Palestinian" State; harms the security of the civilian population; endangers the existence of the state of Israel; and frustrates all possibilities for peace. A state in which the cities, towns and villages resided in by the majority of the population would be within firing range of the enemy would serve as a perpetual temptation to aggressors who would again try to destroy it.

D. The autonomy arrangements agreed upon at Camp David are the only guarantee that under no circumstances will a "Palestinian" State be established in part of Western Eretz Israel.

Our Central Objective—True Peace and the Prevention of War

A. The Likud will give the struggle for peace top priority and spare no effort to further peace. The peace treaty between Israel and Egypt is a result of the Likud Government's policies and is a historic turning point for the status of Israel in the Middle East.

B. The government will respect the Camp David Accords.

C. The Likud will act to renew negotiations concerning implementation of the full autonomy agreement for the Arab inhabitants of Judea, Samaria and the Gaza District.

D. The autonomy agreed upon at Camp David does not signify a state, or sovereignty, or self-determination. The Arab nation enjoys self-determination thanks to the existence of twenty-one Arab States.

Continuing Protection of Israel Citizens from Harm

The terrorist organization which calls itself "PLO" seeks to destroy the state of Israel. There will be no negotiations with this murderous organization, which aims its weapons, supplied by the Soviet Union, against men, women and children. The government will act to protect the civilian population from the terrorists. This will be done by initiating offensive action and preventive attacks against their bases and within them. This policy pursued by the Likud government has proved itself to be the best method for protecting the civilian population.

Settlements

Wide-scale settlement activities have been conducted over the past four years in Judea and Samaria: 55 towns were established in Judea and Samaria; 55 posts and towns in the Galilee; five towns in the Golan Heights; six in the Gaza District; five in the Arava; ten in the Besor region; eight on the Negev plateau and the slopes of Mount Hebron. Altogether, 144 towns have been established throughout Eretz Yisrael in the past four years.

Settlement in the Land of Israel is a right and an integral part of the nation's security. We have observed the rule, and will continue to do so, that Jewish settlement shall not cause the removal of a man from his land, his village or his town. The Likud will act to strengthen the development of, and consolidate its hold over, existing settlements.

Source: Lukacs, *Documents,* pp. 120–122.

CONCLUSION

PROSPECTS FOR RESOLUTION OF THE CONFLICT

There are several possible outcomes of the Arab–Israeli conflict. The scenarios put forward by commentators usually range from the one extreme of a Greater Israel in which Israel has annexed at least the West Bank and Gaza (in some cases the Jewish state is described as extending from the Litani River in the north to the Jordan River in the east, with southern boundaries at the Gulf of Aqaba and the Sinai), to the other extreme of a Palestinian state in place of Israel.

Annexation is rejected by most Israelis because of the demographic problem but is openly favored by the Kach party, Rabbi Meir Kahane's political party, which also talks about expulsion of the Arabs, and by hawks like Ariel Sharon. Advocates of annexation argue that such decisive action would convince the Palestinians to accept Israeli rule; those who did not could be deported, and this would solve the demographic problem. If Israel did annex the occupied territories, it would then have to decide whether to give the Arabs full political rights as Israeli citizens (transforming them into a huge voting bloc that could undermine the state) or to give them some kind of second-class citizenship similar to that given to Jews in Muslim countries in earlier times. Some Israelis have suggested that Israel absorb the occupied territories and give them a status such as that of the U.S. protectorates of Guam and Puerto Rico. A Palestinian state that would replace Israel is equally unrealistic in view of Israel's viability as a nation and its military superiority. In fact, many Palestinians have given up hope that a Palestinian state will replace Israel, owing to Israel's capacity to protect its borders.

A more realistic range of possible outcomes include the following:

1. Continuation of the *status quo* of Israeli military occupation of the West Bank and Gaza, and a continuation of exploratory talks among the parties, interrupted by limited tensions and conflicts. Whereas for Israel this leaves open a wide range of options, it encourages continued Palestinian violence and the possible formation of a united Arab front against Israel, and it erodes Arab relations with the United States because of its failure to deliver justice and peace. For most Palestinians, and certainly for the PLO, this option does not provide an acceptable solution to their aspirations, and, although it further isolates and eventually weakens Israel, the longer the present situation continues, the greater the risk that some Palestinians and others will acquiesce. It must be added that the Intifada, which has galvanized Palestinians old and young alike, has made this option far less likely.

2. Autonomy, or a version of the Camp David formula, in which Palestinians are given limited self-government for a five-year period within a mini-state similar to a South African Bantustan. Some Israelis see this as progress toward solving the problem in that it involves Palestinians in negotiations, reduces the immediate danger of war, strengthens the "peace process," and ensures continued United States support. Other Israelis believe this option, by reducing Israeli control of the West Bank and Gaza, increases the risk of Palestinian terrorist activity and strengthens the possibility of creating a Palestinian state following the five years of autonomy. For Palestinians, this option involves recognizing Israel as the price of negotiations and autonomy, and involves giving up hopes of immediate statehood. Although the plan has American support and is a further step toward eventual attainment of sovereignty, it is unacceptable to most Palestinians because it does not recognize what Palestinians regard as their legitimate rights to national self-determination.

3. Variations of the "Jordan is Palestine" option. This scenario ranges from a Jordanian–Palestinian federation, or an Israeli–Jordanian–Palestinian confederation, to the straight-out proposition that Jordan is the Palestinian state. (In 1977, the Jerusalem Center for Public affairs identified eleven possible options.) In these options, if the Jordan/Palestine entity extended across both sides of the Jordan River, Israel would have to give up the notion of Greater Israel and relinquish rule in the West Bank and Gaza. If the Jordan/Palestine entity were limited to the east side of the Jordan River, Israel would not have to give up anything.

For Israel, this option would resolve the Palestinian problem and end the situation of Israeli rule over a hostile neighboring population, except perhaps for some border security arrangements. The risk of war would be reduced; Jordan, Israelis hope, would act as a stabilizing factor over Palestinian extremists, and Israel would continue to receive U.S. economic and military aid.

For the Palestinians, such an option would require giving up the claim to the rest of Mandatory Palestine, and might lead to the recognition of Israel. It would, however, end Israeli rule and would create a foundation upon which to build a Palestinian state in the future.

For Jordan, this scenario offers the possibility of unifying both banks of the Jordan River, but in view of King Hussein's decision to relinquish control over the West Bank, this option is not likely. Nor would he risk the "Palestinization" of Jordan.

All the above variations of the "Jordan is Palestine" option to some extent deny the national aspirations of the Palestinians, and for that reason alone they are not likely to produce a final resolution to the conflict.

4. The creation of a Palestinian state alongside Israel, with a concomitant Israeli–Palestinian peace treaty, and appropriate military provisions. This seems a likely eventual outcome to some observers, and their reasoning is as follows.

In considering the prospects for the resolution of the Arab–Israeli conflict, the period from 1967 to 1973 serves as a useful initial focal point. Until that point, the main issue in the conflict as far as Israelis were concerned was the continued existence and security of Israel in the face of seemingly implacable hostility from its neighboring Arab states. The wars of 1967 and 1973 made the continuation of the Jewish state unmistakably clear to friend and foe alike. For Israelis, beginning in the early 1970s the focus came to be more on how the question of the Palestinian Arab "refugees" in the occupied territories was to be resolved. For the Arabs of the former British Mandate and the neighboring Arab states, the question prior to 1967–1973 was essentially what military means could be used to destroy the Jewish state. Since then, the Palestinians have gradually abandoned this approach to resolving the issues confronting them, and they have focused attention on defining and establishing a Palestinian state. This has led most recently to Arafat's public acceptance of Israel as part of the Middle East landscape. These shifts in emphasis by the parties to the conflict, and their implications for the future, can be illustrated by a brief review of some of the proposals and agreements made over the past twenty years that are referred to in the text.

Following the wars of 1967 and 1973, the United Nations Security Council—in Resolutions 242 and 338—contented itself with broad ambiguous resolutions concerning the settlement of the conflict referring only to the existing states. By 1978, there had been a distinct change of attitude in the United Nations. In addition to attempting to resolve issues among the nations of the region, the participants now acknowledged the Palestinian Arabs as a distinct entity, not just refugees. In 1974 the United Nations and the Arab League passed a number of resolutions recognizing the PLO as representative of the Palestinian people, and in an address to the General Assembly on "the Palestine question," Yasser Arafat had stated the PLO goal as "one democratic [Palestinian] state where Christian, Jew and Moslem live in justice, equality and fraternity." The Camp David accords that Israel and Egypt signed in September 1978 included the proposal that "Egypt, Israel, Jordan and the representatives of the Palestinian people should participate in negotiations on the resolution of the Palestinian problem in all its aspects." In his peace proposals of September 1982, President Ronald Reagan stated that "self-government by the Palestinians of the West Bank and Gaza in association with Jordan offers the best chance for a durable, just and lasting peace. We base our approach squarely on the principle that the Arab–Israeli conflict should be resolved through negotiations involving an exchange of territory for peace." Although the Palestinians have repeatedly indicated that they regard the PLO as their representatives during the past decade, Israel has thus far refused to recognize or negotiate with the PLO, as the PLO, in Israel's eyes, failed to recognize both Israel's right to exist and Security Council Resolutions 242 and 338.

In taking this stand, Israel had the support of the United States throughout the 1970s and most of the 1980s. The decision by Jordan to relinquish all claims to the West Bank, and public statements by PLO leader Yasser Arafat in late 1988 and early 1989 recognizing Israel and accepting the United Nations resolutions, were important factors in leading the United States to open a dialogue with the PLO and to urge Israel to negotiate directly with the organization. Despite the still occasional extremist rhetoric and action on both sides, there are signs that Israel is willing to speak directly with Palestinian "representatives," who, presumably, will include PLO members. Indeed, there have been such unofficial contacts over the past few years. The subject of these discussions will initially be limited to one of the plans currently under consideration for elections in the West Bank and Gaza. In the past twenty years, the Palestinians have moved from being pawns to participants in the resolution of the conflict.

Increasingly then, over the past two decades, the focus of the Arab–Israeli conflict has been narrowing in scope. A degree of uneasy stability has been established by the parties themselves, sometimes facilitated and sometimes hindered through the intervention of the superpowers and the United Nations. The conflict has come full circle. The essential questions today are those posed in 1947–1948: How can Palestine be partitioned into a Jewish and an Arab state, where are the boundaries to be drawn, and what is to be the relationship between the two states? In 1948, the Arabs said no to partition and resorted to force; the Israelis accepted partition and established a state. Today, the Arabs say yes and seek to establish a separate state; the Israelis say no and use force to prevent Palestinian self determination.

The key to the solution proposed in the United Nations partition resolution of 1947 is the nature of an economic union of the two entities. The boundaries of the two states, while important, can be resolved with patience, as can the status of Jerusalem. The most likely outcome in Jerusalem is a united Greater Jerusalem with separate Jewish and Arab boroughs. The economic issues to be resolved include the divisibility and use of the available water supplies; joint economic ventures; trade and currency arrangements; the nature of the physical connection between the West Bank and Gaza; Arab free port facilities; the future of the Jewish settlers in the West Bank; passports; the question of compensation and the right of return for Palestinian Arabs; freedom of movement between the two entities and the conditions of employment in and between the two states. Palestinian and Israeli views on many of these issues are already strikingly similar.

All the options outlined above involve to a greater or lesser degree the economic if not military support of at least one of the two superpowers, the United States and the Soviet Union. Superpower rivalry in the Middle East heightened the conflict at various points in the past, but in the post–Cold War era, this is clearly lessening. Nevertheless, there remain significant differences in the approaches of the two superpowers to the resolution of the Arab–Israeli conflict.

Since 1967, the United States has advocated a settlement reached through what it termed the "peace process" carried out with U.S. participation. The peace process consists of direct bilateral negotiations between Israel and existing Arab states, using UN Resolutions 242 and 338 as the basis for a settlement, and proceeding toward a final settlement on a step-by-step basis, separating issues from each other as much as possible. This approach favors Israel in that, although the notion of Israel giving up territory in exchange for peace was implicit, there was always doubt as to how much territory would be given up, and to whom. The United States supported Israel's interpretation of Resolution 242, always a problematic document because it altered the status of the West Bank and Gaza from occupied territory to disputed territory and therefore was subject to negotiation. This approach favors Israel also in that it allows Israel undue influence in setting the agenda, and the choice of Arab participants in negotiations. Until the end of the Reagan administration, for example, the United States accepted Israel's definition of the Palestinians as terrorists, which undermined peace efforts, supported Israel's response to the Intifada, and backed Israeli efforts to exclude the PLO from direct bilateral negotiations. Although the United States has abandoned this position, at the present time Israel still refuses to negotiate directly with the PLO.

During the decade of the 1980s, Israel was upgraded from a client to a strategic ally, furthering American Cold War aims in the Middle East region. Washington opted for the policy of greater reliance on Israel as a means of securing American strategic interests in the region. Israel was given greater access to U.S. military technology, and American aid was increased and converted to outright grants. The United States, anxious to weaken the Soviet-backed regime in Syria and what it regarded as the Soviet-dominated PLO, supported the 1982 Israeli invasion of Lebanon as part of a long-term plan to create Western-oriented states: Lebanon, Israel, Jordan, and Egypt in the west; Saudi Arabia in the east. As a result of these close American–Israeli ties, Israel has been to some extent protected from international pressure to withdraw from the occupied territories and to negotiate a settlement acceptable to the Palestinians and Arab countries. American policy assisted Israel in pursuing a hard-line approach; indeed, Israel rejected even U.S. peace plans that called for any Israeli withdrawal from the territories. In the meantime, Jewish settlements in the West Bank and even in Gaza have become larger, more numerous, and more entrenched.

The Soviet Union, on the other hand, supports the approach favored by the PLO, the Arab states, and many European and African nations—namely an international peace conference that would work out a comprehensive peace settlement (also based on UN Resolutions 242 and 338) and set up an international authority to oversee the settlement. The main point of this settlement would be that the Arab states and the Palestinians recognize the permanence of Israel within its 1967 borders, and that Israel recognize the right of the Palestinians to self-determination. The Soviet Union, preoc-cupied with internal economic problems, hurt by the Afghanistan debacle, humiliated by Syria's inability (using Russian arms) to contain Israel in Lebanon, and frustrated by the failure to protect the Palestinians in Lebanon, did not play a significant role in the Arab–Israeli conflict during most of the 1970s and 1980s. Soviet President Mikhail Gorbachev, however, has now moved to restore Soviet diplomatic relations with Israel, has improved relations with Egypt, and has established diplomatic ties with conser-vative Arab Gulf states. The Soviets once again wish to have a presence in the Middle East and see an opportunity to achieve this by co-sponsoring with the Arabs an international settlement. It is still too early to say just how the end of the Cold War will affect the approaches of the two superpowers to a resolution of the Arab–Israeli conflict.

Rather than concentrating on specific formulas or options for a resolution to the conflict, it may be more useful to isolate the underlying principles at stake upon which considerable agreement is already to be found, even in the hard-line rhetoric of both sides. Gidon Gottlieb, in the Fall 1989 issue of *Foreign Affairs,* delineated several of these principles.

The first and most important of these principles on which there has been wide-spread unanimity since Camp David, is that Israel should end its rule over the more than 1.5 million Palestinian Arabs of the West Bank and Gaza. Implicit in this principle is the notion that Israel will withdraw its forces to specified security locations, and all sides will agree to security arrangements and boundaries.

A second principle that most parties agree must be incorporated in any peace settlement, is that there will be some kind of political and economic linkage among Jordan, the Palestinians, and Israel. The political linkages will involve different kinds of arrangements (probably reached at different points in time) for the rights of the Palestinians, and will separate the concepts of "statehood," "homeland," and "sov-ereignty" held by both Israelis and Palestinians. The economic linkages will be based on the concept of "association through separation," safeguarding resource use for all parties, and creating close economic and trade links among the parties.

Resolution of the conflict in the immediate future, given the tremendous difficulties involved, appears unlikely. For peace to be achieved even in the long term, most commentators admit that major changes in attitude by both sides are necessary. Palestinian Arabs would have to abandon their dreams of Jaffa and Haifa as Palestine; Israelis would have to give up their notions of Judea and Samaria as part of Israel. Israelis would have to accept the PLO as more than just a group of terrorists and recognize that nations—including Israel—also act criminally. They would have to acknowledge—as in the case of the establishment of Israel itself—that the use of force, even the repugnant use of so-called terrorism, does not deny a people the right to statehood. They must accept that the Palestinians are a political community and need a state, not merely "autonomy." There was a time when Israelis themselves believed it was imperative to use violence, and they achieved independence against odds far greater than those the Palestinians face today. Moreover, Israeli doves argue that Israel's military superiority is such that a Palestinian state would not seriously threaten Israel's security, even conceding that Israel would sacrifice so-called strategic depth.

Palestinians, for their part, would have to recognize the futility of using force to achieve their goals; they have lost territory rather than gained it by using force. The PLO has reached no political settlement through the military option; nor is it likely to do so in the future. Palestinians must also face the reality of the declining importance of Palestine in an Arab world absorbed by such past and present crises as the Iran–Iraq war, the ongoing situation in Lebanon, and Iraq's annexation of Kuwait. Because the Arab nations have been unsuccessful in achieving Palestinian goals, the PLO must negotiate directly in settling outstanding issues with Israel; this means recognition of Israel and accepting an independent state in the West Bank and Gaza beside Israel.

Many Israelis appear to believe that the historical record—on both an ideological and practical level—indicates that Palestinian hostility to Israel is irreconcilable and never-ending, and that Palestinian promises of peace are worthless. They point out that the PLO has not revoked those clauses in the Palestine National Covenant calling for the liberation of all of Palestine through armed struggle and the establishment of a single, secular, democratic state. Israelis call to mind PLO and Arab hostility to the Camp David accords and to the Egypt–Israel peace treaty. They point to the continuation of terrorist attacks by the PLO despite Arafat's renunciation of terrorism, and to Arafat's and the Palestinians' support of Iraqi president Saddam Hussein. They are concerned also about the threat of Islamic fundamentalism to Israel's existence. They argue that concessions by Israel would be seen by the Palestinians as a sign of weakness rather than an attempt to come to satisfactory terms. They emphasize that the concessions would include the evacuation of Jewish settlers across the "green line,"—the pre-1967 border between Israel and the West Bank—which is unacceptable to extreme religious and nationalistic groups.

Many Israelis also believe that even if the present PLO leadership honestly meant what it said about living together with Israel, the personal, factional, and class-based rivalries within the Palestinians themselves are such that the resulting conflicts and divisions would prevent any peaceful cooperation with the Jewish state. This, they argue, is the nature of Arab politics.

Some Israeli leaders believe the PLO is so fragmented that it has little true substantive base or authority, and they hope that authentic leadership will emerge from within the inhabitants of the territories. They point to PLO intimidation and torture of those Palestinians in the occupied territories who have cooperated with Israel, and they claim that the PLO has killed at least 150 Palestinians who have not obeyed the Intifada. Yet despite divisions within the PLO, and the hostility of some Arab leaders (notably President Assad of Syria) to Yasser Arafat, local Palestinian leaders show little sign of moving without PLO approval.

Some observers postulate that fear of Israeli military strength, the geographic vulnerability of a Palestinian state to Israeli attack, and the normal political process of state building would weaken the extremists among the Palestinians. At the moment, the extremists believe they have nothing to lose by a continuation of a violent anti-Israeli policy; the Palestinians are landless and powerless, and Israel refuses to consider the option of a Palestinian state. With their own state, however, the Palestinians would have power and international recognition of nationhood, free of Israeli occupation. It is generally accepted that the Palestinian people are a reasonably unified political community. The majority of Palestinians are Sunni Muslims, and class, ethnic, and religious divisions are not likely to challenge the state's leadership to the extent they do in many other Middle Eastern countries. And, as was the case with Israel itself, the new state could call upon a well-educated and experienced body of Palestinians from around the world to help establish and run its businesses, industries, schools, and bureaucracy. Finally, dependence on economic assistance from the Arab nations, from Europe, and from the United States (perhaps even Israel) would further ensure that an Arab Palestinian state would be no serious threat to Israel's existence.

Palestinian spokespersons contend that there have been changes in PLO and Arab attitudes and actions in relation to Israel in the past fifteen years, and that it is Israel who is intransigent in opposition to a peace settlement. They claim that acceptance of UN Resolutions 242 and 338 by Jordan, Egypt, and now Arafat—which call for the right of "every state in the area to live in peace and security within secure and recognized boundaries"—implies the recognition of Israel, and acceptance of these resolutions does not require formal peace treaties or formal recognition of Israel. These Palestinians support their claim of Arab willingness to change by pointing out that it was Anwar Sadat who took the initiative that led to Camp David and the Egypt–Israel peace treaty. They add that this is further evidence of Arab readiness to negotiate directly with Israel.

Palestinians also argue that most movements do not formally revoke their charters or covenants, but they do reinterpret them or allow them to fade away. Since 1974, they assert, Palestine National Council resolutions have spelled out new interpretations of the Palestine National Covenant. Council resolutions no longer call for the liberation of Palestine but refer to a Palestinian state in areas to be evacuated by Israel, and they support peace initiatives that provide for the existence and security of Israel. Leaders point out that these new interpretations have been significant enough to lead to splits within the PLO between the minority of extreme, ideological hardliners who want to continue the armed struggle to eliminate Israel, and the majority who are willing to negotiate for the lesser goal of a Palestinian state beside Israel. They also mention that the charter of the Herut party, which has never been changed, calls for an Israel on both sides of the Jordan River.

Many Palestinian leaders believe that as they have shown more flexibility and preparedness to negotiate with Israel since 1973, the Israeli government's opposition to the Palestinians has hardened. This, they argue, has made it more difficult for the moderates to assert their leadership and to maintain unity within the PLO. They point to the question of Israel's attitude to the relationship between PLO recognition of Israel and peace negotiations as one example. Israel has claimed that recognition must precede negotiations; the PLO has argued that prior recognition is not essential to negotiations taking place. They emphasize that the United States negotiated with China, Korea, and North Vietnam without recognition, and that Israel has repeatedly said it would not negotiate with the PLO even if it did recognize Israel. Without some indication from Israel, or the United States, that benefits would result from such action, unilateral recognition of Israel by the PLO would simply encourage the extremists within the Palestinian movement.

Inevitably, some Palestinians and some Israelis will seek to subvert or undermine any agreement reached. This is not a reason to defer negotiations; instead, it is a reason to make any agreement specific and detailed rather than indulging in "constructive ambiguity." Deferring a settlement only strengthens the arguments of the extremists on both sides. And, of course, any peace settlement will be incremental; there will be no sudden transformations in the resolution of this conflict.

Finally, we must reject the claims made by both sides that in perpetuating the conflict in pursuit of their goals they have some kind of Divine sanction. In truth, the conflict is man-made, and it can be resolved only if men and women accept responsibility for their actions and seek to bring peace to their segment of this earth. In the end there will be no one winner to the Arab–Israeli conflict. For both sides, the choice is not between what is good and what is bad, but the lesser of two evils. In this situation the concern is not about how to overcome hatred, or fear or suspicion, but rather what will happen if they are not overcome.

INDEX

Wallenberg, Raoul, 70
War of Attrition, 163, 170–72
Warsaw Ghetto Revolt, 70
Weizmann, Chaim, 40–42, 45, 54, 70,
    73–74, 94, 102–3
Weizman, Ezer, 202
West Bank, 97, 121, 141, 152–53, 194,
    198–200, 204, 229, 231, 235, 241–
    43, 261–65
See also Occupied Territories
White Paper of 1922 (Churchill White Pa-
    per), 49–51. *See also* Haycraft
    Commission
White Paper of 1930 (Passfield White Pa-
    per), 51–52. *See also* Shaw
    Commission
White Paper of 1939, 54–55, 67
Wilson, Woodrow, 38, 42–43
Wingate, Orde, 53
Wise, Rabbi Stephen, 54, 73
Woodhead Commission and Report,
    54
World War II. *See* Holocaust

World Zionist Organization, 24, 41, 43,
    45–46, 49, 73. *See also* Zionism

Yemen Civil War, 144
Yishuv, 27–28, 45, 54, 67, 74–75, 77,
    93, 98, 124
Yom Kippur War, 177. *See* Arab-Israeli
    Wars
Young Turk Revolution (1908), 18, 28

Zionism:
    and creation of Israel, 98–99, 102
    immigration to Palestine, 19th century,
        17
    during Mandate, 45–46
    since 1948, 104–106, 115, 125, 199
    origins, 6, 19–22
    and Partition of Palestine, 77, 81, 88,
        90–91
    Theodore Herzl and, 23–25
    during World War II, 68, 70–71, 73, 75
Zionist Congress, first, 24
Zionist Organization of America, 90